WEALTH
AND POVERTY IN
EARLY CHURCH AND
SOCIETY

HOLY CROSS STUDIES
IN PATRISTIC THEOLOGY AND HISTORY

WEALTH
AND POVERTY IN
EARLY CHURCH AND
SOCIETY

EDITED BY
SUSAN R. HOLMAN

B
Baker Academic
a division of Baker Publishing Group
Grand Rapids, Michigan

ORTHODOX
PRESS

D

Published by Baker Academic
a division of Baker Publishing Group
P.O. Box 6287, Grand Rapids, MI 49516-6287
www.bakeracademic.com

Printed in the United States of America

Library of Congress Cataloging-in-Publication Data
Wealth and poverty in early church and society / edited by Susan R. Holman.
    p. cm.
  Includes bibliographical references and index.
  ISBN 978-0-8010-3549-4 (pbk.)
    1. Wealth—Religious aspects—Christianity—Congresses. 2. Poverty—Religious aspects—Christianity—Congresses. 3. Church history—Primitive and early church, ca. 30–600—Congresses. I. Holman, Susan R.
  BR115.W4W39 2008
  261.8′3250915—dc22   2008000426

CONTENTS

Foreword

Wealth and Poverty in Early Church and Society

by His Eminence Archbishop Demetrios of America

The insights offered by the prolific Fathers of the patristic age continue to reverberate with striking and contemporary relevance. Such insights are vividly revealed in the arena of wealth and poverty in the period of the early church and society. What were the Fathers of the Church witnessing with regard to the plight of the poor in those first centuries of Christendom? How did they articulate a theology that could address the obligations of the wealthy to respond to the needs of the poor in their time? What impact did they have upon the structural functioning of their environments to address such complex needs? What parallels do the creation of charitable institutions and the formation of social policies to address wealth and poverty in their age share with contemporary models of the twenty-first century in our world?

Questions such as these, and indeed many more, are dealt with in the many essays that comprise the contents of this book, *Wealth and Poverty in Early Church and Society*, a publication made possible by the Holy Cross Orthodox Press and the Pappas Patristic Institute of Holy Cross Greek Orthodox School of Theology. The reader of this book will no doubt be struck by the sense of immediacy that runs as an underlying theme throughout the essays. For the Fathers of the Church, the "problem" of wealth and poverty demanded immediate action. More importantly, they knew that such action required that social, political, and religious actors in society have an informed Christian understanding of the wide-ranging issues pertaining to wealth and poverty. The Fathers used all possible means available to them for an effective, pertinent education: the production of action-oriented literature, passionate preaching based upon the Holy Scriptures, and strong recommendations generated by Christian principles for implementing successful social policies and programs to alleviate dire conditions that were facing their communities in their respective times.

Today, we stand to gain much from returning to that same sense of urgent and sensitive action that the Fathers of the Church considered necessary when facing issues of wealth and poverty. We have witnessed in the very recent past the positive and negative effects of globalization on commerce, the outsourcing of labor and its effects, and the growing dependence upon technology for robust economies in varying regions of the world. All of these issues affect wealth and poverty. More importantly, from a Christian perspective, they affect the manner by which people of wealth interact with people in conditions of poverty. Here, perhaps, the insights offered by the patristic age continue to constitute invaluable and most effective tools for dealing with the issues of wealth and poverty in our contemporary times. While form may have changed much, substance has remained constant in terms of the importance of communicating Christian understandings of wealth and poverty and of the obligations of the wealthy toward the needy. Indeed, we have much to learn from the Fathers of the Church in this domain; and I am pleased to commend the present book of significant essays, offered by the Pappas Patristic Institute, as an important step forward in coping with the burning issue of wealth and poverty in our contemporary world.

† DEMETRIOS
Archbishop of America

PREFACE

This collection of essays represents a cross section of recent research on the dynamics of poverty and wealth in Christianity in late antiquity. The essays range from close textual readings to broad topical overviews, to creative application and contemporary issues, and were originally presented as papers at the conference on "Wealth and Poverty in Early Christianity," sponsored by the Stephen and Catherine Pappas Patristic Institute at Holy Cross Greek Orthodox School of Theology in Brookline, Massachusetts, in October 2005. This was the Institute's second annual conference inviting international scholars, graduate students, and interested clergy together to discuss leading topics relevant to patristic studies. In addition to several papers that could not be included here for various reasons, the conference also included a panel discussion and dialogue between His Eminence Archbishop Demetrios, primate of the Greek Orthodox Church in America, and the Reverend J. Bryan Hehir, SJ, president and treasurer of Catholic Charities in the Archdiocese of Boston, on the contemporary topic of poverty and wealth as it relates to religion and patristic studies. The range of these conversations is a measure of the Institute's commitment to foster international and ecumenical participation in the study of patristic texts and the issues they raise.

Poverty and wealth are never purely academic. Human need and affluence have been treated as moral issues across most cultures throughout history. The Christian responses may have characteristics particular to Christian views on such things as the material world, the divine body, and the incarnation of God in Christ, but, as these essays show, there was a great deal of variety in the how and why of early Christian choices to speak and act on the economic discrepancies that existed—and bothered—writers in antiquity as much as they bother many of us today.

In examining these ancient views, the authors of these essays have asked of their sources certain basic questions: How did New Testament texts and cultural ideals influence the development of social welfare in the subsequent centuries of the "patristic period"? How might modern readers understand the economic strata of the early church, and how did these differences in the community and church distribution between wealthy and poor influence the way they viewed human need and one another? What did these texts have to say about such issues as ownership, divestment, and the moral valence of poverty, and what are some ways they differ on these issues? What were the ideological differences between voluntary and involuntary poverty? What lifestyle did patristic authors expect, recommend, or even demand of the poor and their fellow believers? How did poor monks give alms, and what did they worry about when they did? What went on between rich and poor in healing sanctuaries, where both were sick? If *philanthrōpia* to the poor was so important, how did Christians justify the bejeweled splendor of magnificent churches? How did they understand work and trade? And what might these texts offer today in dialogue with modern efforts to address global poverty and injustice? The essays offer various frameworks for informed and thoughtful discussion of these and similar questions.

The book is divided into five parts that proceed more or less chronologically. Part 1 explores several texts and issues that are particularly relevant to New Testament studies. Steven Friesen begins with a look at how four early Christian texts explained the cause of poverty. Considering in turn passages from Revelation, the Letter of Jacob (or James), Acts, and the *Shepherd of Hermas*, he examines the distinctly different ways these texts explain poverty, with different calls to action, and suggests that patristic studies be more attentive to the reconstruction of submerged perspectives in considering models for the future. Denise Buell continues this challenge, also drawing from the *Shepherd of Hermas*, as well as the *Didache* and the so-called *First Letter of Clement*. Her study examines textual hints for Christian charity within a social setting where both donors and recipients were poor, and challenges the binary rhetoric of donor/recipient by interpreting these texts in light of the fact that most early Christians lived on the economic margins. Görge Hasselhoff homes in on a single passage—James 2:2–7—and looks "back" at the scarce patristic exegesis of this passage, especially considering those sources that might have been available to Bede in the seventh-century West. His conclusions suggest a curious marginalization of this passage that may hint at a long-standing discomfort concerning its comments on rich and poor. Concluding the first section, Edward Moore looks at the gnostic *Hymn of the Pearl* as it too evokes the passage in James. The *Hymn*, Moore argues, understands the promise of wealth as a call to transcendence, and poverty as a lack of a transformative vision of God.

Part 2 brings the reader to four different case studies from Egypt in late antiquity: wealthy lay patrons, monks, church-supported widows, and the sick. Annewies van den Hoek offers a close reading of one of the most frequently cited patristic texts on wealth and poverty: Clement of Alexandria's treatise *Quis dives salvetur?*, one of the earliest exegetical studies on the story of the rich young ruler in Mark 10. Comparing Clement's treatise with later texts from Augustine and Paulinus of Nola, van den Hoek suggests striking theological similarities among these authors' defense of an intellectual detachment from wealth, a detachment that reflects a very cautious attitude toward renunciation. David Brakke unveils the anxieties about money, charity, and economic activity that percolate through Evagrius's advice to those more seemingly intrepid about renunciation: his fellow hermit-monks in the Egyptian desert. In their battle against that crafty demon, Love of Money, monks ought to seek economic sufficiency combined with charity, Evagrius says, rather than fiscal security in this life. While Evagrius's advice suggests that monks came from a range of social classes, his comments on the lower-class monks suggest that Evagrius, like Clement, wrote for upper-class readers. Adam Serfass pushes at the curtain of this literary bias in his essay, a detailed look at Egyptian papyri that provide documentary evidence for how churches sought to meet the everyday needs of the poor, testaments to the cautious redistribution of wealth in several churches, at least as it concerned the control and administration of wine (and clothing) donations for church-supported widows. Finally, I offer a few observations on the rhetoric of rich and poor in a text about an incubation-healing shrine near Alexandria as it operated in the late sixth and early seventh centuries, particularly as views on wealth and poverty may have related to monastic social ideals about humility and moral justice.

John Chrysostom and the fourth-century Cappadocians, particularly Basil of Caesarea, are perhaps the best-known Greek examples of patristic beneficence. Part 3 offers five studies on themes from this period in Antioch and Asia Minor. Rudolf Brändle builds on his 1979 landmark study of John Chrysostom's use of Matt. 25:31–46 with several exciting new insights. Believing that all wealth was rooted in injustice, Chrysostom invited his audience to take on the self-ordained priestly dignity that accompanies the role of stewards for the poor. Arguing that the Matthew text is the integrative force behind the central thought in Chrysostom's theology, Brändle's theological study suggests that John Chrysostom offers a new approach to soteriology that deserves further study. Wendy Mayer then teases out the relationship, in John's time, between private asceticism, wealth, and economic poverty. Her tightly nuanced essay suggests that economic and voluntary poverty were valued differently, and that these differences lie at the heart of understanding the shifting roles of wealth and poverty in society from the fourth century onward. She introduces the idea that beggars who "performed" for their alms were granted higher moral value, perhaps because such performance was regarded as a form of work, thus contributing to rather than threatening the social balance of the community. In the next essay, Francine Cardman builds on this theme of theater with a study of Chrysostom's sermons on Lazarus and the rich man, particularly focusing on the irony of John's use of theater. Even as he railed against the circus and the shows, John used theatrical devices as a deliberate preaching rhetoric. As we read these texts, Cardman suggests, we too must learn how to see the story play out in our own rhetoric and practice. Efthalia Makris Walsh then returns the reader's gaze to widows, with a short summary of Chrysostom's exegesis of Old and New Testament widows and its application to the theology about, and practical issues concerning, the care of widows in his day. Lest we judge too harshly John's use of Hellenistic culture to make his point, Demetrios Constantelos concludes the section with a reminder of how classical Greek texts influenced the development of Christian rhetoric about philanthropy in this period, particularly in the example of Basil of Caesarea.

Part 4 looks at several issues that characterized the tension between wealth and poverty in late antiquity and the early Byzantine period: church finery, monastic gift exchange, and the question of trade, profit, and salvation. Edward Siecienski begins with a turn of the coin, to discuss the dazzling liturgical splendor that characterized that space within which late antique ascetic preachers denounced ostentation and wealth. Their failure to denounce church finery universally and consistently may suggest in part the aesthetic pressures they faced from theological competitors, but it more likely relates also to patristic views of spiritual beauty. Gold and silver came to represent heaven's majesty, but such material substances remained relative in contrast with the souls that were the true body of the church. Daniel Caner asks how early Byzantine monks conceptualized their surplus resources, when they had any. Focusing on *eulogia*, or "blessings," this essay suggests a monastic economy of charitable leftovers that might be compared with Jewish gleanings and that existed within an ascetic environment that was often characterized by extreme scarcity, where leftovers were a blessing indeed. Angeliki Laiou concludes part 4 with an examination of how hagiographical texts from the late patristic and Byzantine periods discuss trade and profit. Her examples suggest that merchants were not vilified, and that neither profit nor trade was considered illegitimate for Christians. The church may have sought to turn economic behavior upside down through its "miraculous economy," but, as these texts show, both the saints and professional merchants were positive forces in the manner in which "charity" used the marketplace.

The two chapters in Part 5 turn to the modern problems of poverty to suggest ways that patristic texts might contribute to modern religious and policy dialogue. Timothy Patitsas offers an unusual, provocative study of modern international responses to need that have (or have not) worked, and what the Christian tradition might offer in building the future. Patitsas considers the work of economist Jane Jacobs as well as leading models for global microlending initiatives, and offers these as conceptual stimuli for envisioning how Basil of Caesarea's fourth-century philanthropic program might be instructive in contemporary development issues. Finally, Brian Matz concludes the volume with his description of a very different project, one emerging from the international academy, that seeks to develop and apply a systematic approach to patristic socioethical texts that directly relate to modern Catholic Social Thought, particularly in modern Europe. These two essays hint at the creative potential for patristic studies in the coming decades. They suggest the immediate relevance of such studies as those in this volume to a broad range of readers, both those working in an academic setting as well as those engaged in social justice and social action that serves the world through the *ecclesia*.

As volume editor and on behalf of the Institute, I am delighted to acknowledge those who made possible both the conference and this book. The Reverend Dr. Emmanuel Clapsis, then dean of Holy Cross Greek Orthodox School of Theology, brought the vision and gift of the late Stephen and Catherine Pappas for a patristic institute to a reality in 2003, inviting eminent scholars in patristic studies to draft the charter and to establish its founding board, with the support of His Eminence Archbishop Demetrios Trakatellis and the Reverend Nicholas Triantafilou, president of Holy Cross. The Reverend Dr. Thomas Fitzgerald, the present dean, carries the vision forward with his continuing support. The Reverend Dr. Robert J. Daly, SJ, founding chairman of the Institute's board, has, with inspiring clarity, guided the practical concerns of the Institute to fulfill its goals by encouraging young scholars in patristic studies through conferences, research opportunities, and publications. My own role would have been far more onerous without the Institute's board as conversation partners, including Drs. François Bovon, Demetrios Katos, James Skedros, and Aristotle Papanikolaou. And the book would not exist in its present form without the generous administrative and collaborative gifts of Dr. Bruce Beck, the institute's director and series editor. Finally, we thank Dr. James Ernest, editor at Baker Academic and a fellow patristic scholar, who made it possible to publish the series with Baker in collaboration with Holy Cross Greek Orthodox Press.

Susan R. Holman

Part One

The New Testament Period

1

Injustice or God's Will?

Early Christian Explanations of Poverty

Steven J. Friesen

Brazilian theologian, churchman, and activist Dom Hélder Câmara was known as an advocate for the poorest of the poor, not only in the slums of Rio de Janeiro, Olinda, and Recife, but throughout the world. Reflecting on his ministry he observed, "When I give food to the poor, they call me a saint. When I ask why the poor have no food, they call me a communist." While the accusation of being a communist may seem somewhat quaint in North America in the early twenty-first century, in Latin America in the late twentieth century the accusation was often fatal. Nevertheless, between his ordination to the Roman Catholic priesthood in 1931 and his death in 1999, Câmara persisted in spite of great opposition, and these experiences allowed him to explore the difference between offering charity and promoting economic equality.[1]

With his life, Câmara raised the question of whether almsgiving is a sufficient Christian response to poverty. Does the Christian gospel also require

---

1. For recent descriptions of Câmara's life, see Daniel S. Schipani and Anton Wessels, eds., *The Promise of Hope: A Tribute to Dom Hélder* (Elkhart, IN: Institute for Mennonite Studies, 2002); David Regan, *Why Are They Poor? Helder Câmara in Pastoral Perspective* (London: Lit, 2002); and John Okwoeze Odey, *Church and State: Profiles in Costly Discipleship; Dietrich Bonhoeffer, Helder Camara, Oscar Romero* (Enugu, Nigeria: Snaap Press, 2001).

an analysis of the forces that create and exploit poverty? This is not an easy question, and I cannot answer it in the next few pages. But we can begin by asking whether the writers of the early church posed such questions. Did they analyze the phenomenon of poverty? Did they ask *why* the poor had no food? And if so, what did they say about it? What did the earliest churches see as the sources of poverty? Did they think the misery came from divine action or human action? And in response to the existence of poverty, did they promote charity or economic equality?

These are not burning issues in patristic studies. One can find many studies that talk about early Christian attitudes toward wealth and poverty (and especially toward wealth), but I was not able to find a single study on early Christian analyses of the causes of poverty. So let us boldly forge ahead where wiser minds have chosen not to go.[2]

I focus on the earliest period—the texts from the first and early second centuries of the Common Era. Most of the Christian texts from this period do not address these questions directly. As far as I can tell, the origins of poverty is not a topic for discussion in Hebrews, 1–2 Peter, 1–3 John, Jude, 1 Clement, the letters of Paul, the letters of Ignatius, the Acts of Paul, Justin Martyr, or Irenaeus. Scattered references are found in the Jesus traditions of the gospels, but these are quite complicated and they will have to wait for a different study.

That leaves four texts around which to organize my investigation: the Revelation of John; the Letter of James, which is more accurately called "the Letter of Jacob"; the Acts of the Apostles; and the *Shepherd of Hermas*. Together, these four proto-Christian texts provide us with four distinct ways of explaining the causes of poverty, and with four calls to action regarding one of the most intractable human problems. They do not demonstrate a linear evolution in the economic thinking and practices of the early assemblies, for the texts come from several communities over the course of several decades. Rather, the texts illustrate four models for study and for action that I hope will facilitate analysis without oversimplifying the issues. Before we examine the texts, however, we need a framework for understanding economic inequality in the early Roman Empire, where these texts were produced.

Economic Inequality in the Early Roman Empire

In their analysis of Roman imperial society, Peter Garnsey and Richard Saller employ the poignant phrase, "the Roman system of inequality."[3] With

---

2. This essay is a revision of material first presented in *Christian Origins: A People's History of Christianity*, ed. Richard Horsley (Minneapolis: Augsburg Fortress, 2005), 240–60. I thank the publisher for permission to republish.

3. Peter Garnsey and Richard Saller, *The Roman Empire: Economy, Society, and Culture* (Berkeley: University of California Press, 1987), 125.

this phrase Garnsey and Saller call our attention to the fact that the Roman Empire maintained its domination of the Mediterranean world through judicial institutions, legislative systems, property ownership, control of labor, and brute force. Like all societies, the empire developed mechanisms for maintaining multifaceted inequality, and like all so-called civilized societies the empire promoted justifications that made the inequity seem normal, or at least inevitable.

As we turn our attention specifically to the economic facets of the Roman system of inequality, there are three fundamental ideas to keep in mind. First, as economic historians point out, the Roman imperial economy was preindustrial. The vast majority of people lived in rural areas or in small towns, with only about 10 to 15 percent of the population in big cities of ten thousand people or more. This means that most of the population worked in agriculture (80 to 90 percent) and that large-scale commercial or manufacturing activity was rare.

Second, there was no middle class in the Roman Empire. Because the economy was primarily agricultural, wealth was based on the ownership of land. Most land was controlled by a small number of wealthy, elite families. These families earned rent and produce from the subsistence farmers or slaves who actually worked the land. With their wealth and status, these families were able to control local and regional governance, which allowed them to profit also from taxation and from governmental policies. These same families also controlled public religion.

Third, poverty was widespread both in rural and urban areas. Interpreters of early Christian literature tend to underestimate the overwhelming poverty that characterized the Roman Empire. And when we do mention the problem of poverty, we tend to use the undefined binary categories of "rich" and "poor" in our descriptions. To promote clarity (and to force people to define their terms), I have developed a poverty scale that provides seven categories for describing economic resources[4] (see table 1.1). The percentages are based on data from urban centers of ten thousand inhabitants or more, but we need to remember that in rural areas poverty was even worse: while superwealthy elites (categories 1–3) made up about 3 percent of an urban population, they were only about 1 percent of the total imperial population. The focus on urban centers is necessary because this type of city is where the audiences for these four texts lived. Another way to understand these figures is to render them as a pyramid chart that visually depicts the inequity involved (see figure 1.1). It is difficult to put monetary values on these categories because prices varied greatly in rural and urban areas; table 1.2 provides some rough guidelines.

---

4. I published detailed arguments for the scale in "Poverty in Pauline Studies: Beyond the So-called New Consensus," *JSNT* 26 (2004): 323–61.

Table 1.1. Poverty Scale for a Large City in the Roman Empire

Percent of Population	Poverty Scale Categories
0.04%	PS 1. Imperial elites: imperial dynasty, Roman senatorial families, a few retainers, local royalty, a few freedpersons.
1%	PS 2. Regional or provincial elites: equestrian families, provincial officials, some retainers, some decurial families, some freedpersons, some retired military officers.
1.76%	PS 3. Municipal elites: most decurial families, wealthy men and women who do not hold office, some freedpersons, some retainers, some veterans, some merchants.
7% (estimated)	PS 4. Moderate surplus resources: some merchants, some traders, some freedpersons, some artisans (especially those who employ others), and military veterans.
22% (estimated)	PS 5. Stable near subsistence level (with reasonable hope of remaining above the minimum level to sustain life): many merchants and traders, regular wage earners, artisans, large shop owners, freedpersons, some farm families.
40%	PS 6. At subsistence level and often below minimum level to sustain life: small farm families, laborers (skilled and unskilled), artisans (especially those employed by others), wage earners, most merchants and traders, small shop/tavern owners.
28%	PS 7. Below subsistence level: some farm families, unattached widows, orphans, beggars, disabled, unskilled day laborers, prisoners.

Poverty is, of course, a more complicated phenomenon than the mere possession of financial resources. In the twenty-first century poverty is affected by many factors, and we should expect no fewer complications in ancient societies. In the early Roman Empire financial resources were probably the single most influential factor in determining one's place in the social economy, but financial resources were not the only factor. Other factors would have included gender, ethnicity, family lineage (common or noble), legal status

Table 1.2. Annual Income Needed by Family of Four

Categories from the poverty scale are found in parentheses.

For wealth in Rome (PS 3)	25,000–150,000 denarii
For modest prosperity in Rome (PS 4)	5,000 denarii
For subsistence in Rome (PS 5–6)	900–1,000 denarii
For subsistence in a city (PS 5–6)	600–700 denarii
For subsistence in the country (PS 5–6)	250–300 denarii

Note: Adapted from Ekkehard W. Stegemann and Wolfgang Stegemann, *The Jesus Movement: A Social History of Its First Century* (Minneapolis: Fortress, 1999), 81–85. The estimates are based on 2,500 calories per day for an adult male, and include nonfood expenses such as housing, clothing, and taxes.

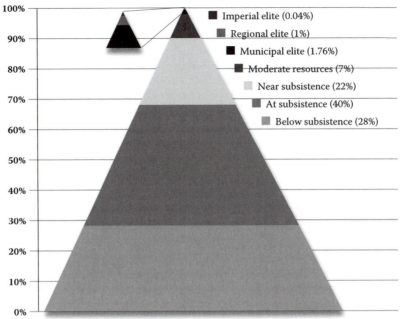

Figure 1.1. Poverty Scale Percentages

(slave, freed, or freeborn), occupation, and education. Patronage relationships were especially important in one's economic survival, for a patron gave one access to restricted resources that were otherwise unavailable. In times of crisis a patron could mean the difference between life and death. But financial resources provide us with one way to open the discussions, and also have the virtue of sometimes being quantifiable in ways that other factors are not.[5]

When we discuss the explanations of economic inequality found in early Christian texts, then, we must fight the tendency to impose the categories of modern industrial economies on the Roman Empire. Most of the recipients of these four texts lived in large urban areas with a preindustrial economy. Unless there is evidence to the contrary, we should assume that most or all of the recipients of a particular text lived near the level of subsistence.

Revelation of John: Apocalyptic Condemnation of Imperialism

The Revelation of John presents a blistering critique of Roman imperialism as the source of injustice and poverty. The text began to circulate in the late

5. For further discussions of these issues, a good starting point is Anthony J. Blasi, Jean Duhaime, and Paul-André Turcotte, eds., *Handbook of Early Christianity: Social Science Approaches* (Walnut Creek, CA: AltaMira, 2002).

first century among urban churches in western Asia Minor (modern Turkey). The author described Roman imperialism as a system of blasphemous arrogance and deception: the powerful imperial elites (mostly PS 1) collaborate with members of the local aristocracies (PS 2–3) in order to deceive the masses into compliance.

Since the text is visionary with spectacular imagery, it makes its case not so much through argumentation as through symbols. The symbols are steeped in the traditions of Israel, but the author seldom quotes them. Instead, John narrates visions that mix elements of biblical traditions with allusions to the sociohistorical settings of the churches. The result is an apocalypse that portrays the Roman Empire as Satan's tool, opposed to the God of Israel, and destined for destruction.

Two texts help us understand the critique better. The first text is the vision of two beasts in Rev. 13. The first half of the vision reveals a beast from the sea that clearly represents Roman imperialism; if we miss this in Rev. 13 the identification is made explicit by an interpreting angel in chapter 17. This seven-headed, ten-horned imperial monstrosity receives satanic authority to blaspheme and to conquer. The details of the vision draw heavily on the book of Daniel to portray Roman rule as the ultimate superpower opposed to God. It conquers the world, defeats the saints, and is worshiped by the whole world.

The second half of the vision in Rev. 13 fills out the description of the Roman system of inequality by introducing a second beast, this one from the land. This beast represents the local aristocracies (mostly PS 2–3), who exercise the authority of the first beast.[6] This second beast deceives and coerces the world into submission. The populace must worship Rome or die, according to John. Significantly, the second beast is said to control the local economy for Rome. Note Rev. 13:16–17: "Also it causes all, both small and great, both rich and poor, both free and slave, to be marked on the right hand or the forehead, so that no one can buy or sell who does not have the mark, that is, the name of the beast or the number of its name." In U.S. popular culture this mark of the beast—666—has become the subject of ongoing prophecy speculation. In the first century, however, no speculation was necessary. The domination of the imperial beast was made possible by the aristocratic beast.

A second text elaborates specifically the economic system of exploitation at the heart of this military domination. In Rev. 18 the author takes the reader through a series of proclamations and laments that portray how international commerce and politics figure into the Roman system of inequality. Four sets of players are mentioned: Babylon the queen (mostly PS 1), the kings

6. See my chapter, "The Beast from the Earth: Revelation 13:11–18 and Social Setting," in *Readings in the Book of Revelation: A Resource for Students*, ed. David Barr (Atlanta: Scholars Press, 2003), 49–64.

of the earth (PS 1–2), merchants and shippers (PS 2–3), and the general population ("the peoples of the earth," mostly PS 4–7). Babylon the queen— another image for Rome—is the central figure in the system, manipulating each of the other figures in different ways. Her relationship with the kings of the earth is called prostitution (*porneia*; Rev. 18:9), for theirs is a game of power and payment. With the merchants and shippers, however, the issue is only payment. When the queen is destroyed, their laments are only for the lost profits (18:16–19). According to the Seer, the general population is also complicit in this system of commercial and political exploitation, but their motives are different. They were drunk on the queen's wine (18:3), deceived by her potions and spells (18:23).

The Seer's call to action is radical: he advocates a total withdrawal from the machinations of empire in the interests of purity until the Lamb intervenes in history. In the words of the angel of Rev. 18:4, "Come out of her, my people, so that you do not take part in her sins, and so that you do not share in her plagues." John's denunciations of injustice are also extreme, with attacks on the entire imperial system (government, economy, religion, and enforcement) and with threats of divine judgment—eternal suffering in the lake of fire.

The Seer's model for understanding economic inequality, then, is that Satan controls this world through the empire. The empire suppresses all opposition to its domination. This hegemony is a form of blasphemy because the emperor claims to be the king of kings, the ruler of history, the lord of the destinies of all peoples. According to this apocalyptic model, the political foundation of exploitation is the system of alliances among kings and rulers. The local aristocracies implement the exploitation and ensure that commerce benefits the wealthy, allowing goods to move around the empire to the places where they will most benefit the oppressors. This system of inequality requires the participation of its victims. They are deceived or awed or intimidated into compliance. John's admonition to the people is that they remove themselves from this system even if it requires martyrdom, for their blood will be avenged by God in the end.

The Letter of Jacob: A Local Prophetic Critique

The second text under consideration is normally called the Letter of James, but I refer to it as the Letter of Jacob. This is a more accurate rendering of the name, and it reminds us of the Jewish facets of this letter.[7]

7. We do not know exactly when this letter was written, but it probably comes from the last half of the first century. Some scholars think the text reflects the ideas and life of Jacob the brother of Jesus, which would make it one of the earliest documents in the New Testament, while other scholars consider it to be a document of the late first century. Those who take a late date tend to consider the author to be an anonymous writer claiming the authority of Jacob.

We do not need to settle the questions of date and authorship of Jacob at this point. For the purpose of charting proto-Christian explanations of poverty, it is enough to recognize that this is a text from the last half of the first century that was intended for wide circulation among believers. The text probably claims the authority of Jacob, brother of Jesus and leader of the Jerusalem assemblies, whether he was actually responsible for the content or not. In general, the content focuses on the theme of proper living in ways that echo the prophetic traditions of Israel: one should trust God completely and act accordingly, keeping one's life pure and taking care of those who suffer.

In terms of the spectrum of models I am building, the Letter of Jacob moves us closer to the middle: Jacob blames poverty on injustice, but its critique had a narrower vision than did Revelation's. Rather than condemning the entire Roman Empire, the Letter of Jacob condemned local economic exploitation. It called the faithful not to withdraw from the imperial system, but rather to resist the wealth-based system of status that characterized dominant society.

We can see this by examining two sections of the letter. The first is 2:1–7, where the author criticizes the dominant social system and the judicial system. With great rhetorical energy, Jacob describes a hypothetical situation in which two men visit the synagogue of his readers. One wears fine clothes and a gold ring, placing him in category 4 or higher on the poverty scale.[8] The other is filthy and desperately poor (a *ptōchos*, PS 7). According to Jacob, if the synagogue operates according to the normal standards of social status by showing honor to the wealthy and disrespect or neglect to the poor, then they are contradicting the faith of their Lord Jesus Christ.

The author's rhetorical purpose in verses 1–4 is to distance fellow synagogue members from this status system based on wealth. The author asserts that in the synagogue all should be treated with compassion. Normal social interaction that showed honor to someone simply because he or she was rich was wrong. If believers participated in the wealth-based status system of their time, they perpetuated inequality and became accomplices in the victimization of the poor.

As the author works to convince his audience to abstain from showing honor based on wealth, he poses a rhetorical question that implies a condemnation of the judicial system as well.

> Listen, my beloved brothers and sisters. Has not God chosen the poor in the world to be rich in faith and to be heirs of the kingdom that he has promised to those who love him? But you have dishonored the poor. Is it not the rich who oppress you? Is it not they who drag you into court? Is it not they who blaspheme the excellent name that was invoked over you? (James 2:5–7)

8. The gold ring could indicate equestrian rank, but this is unlikely; Luke Timothy Johnson, *The Letter of James*, AB 37A (New York: Doubleday, 1995), 221.

The rhetoric of this section asserts that there are two alternatives: the system of the world and the system of God's kingdom. In the synagogues of God's kingdom, the materially poor are rich in faith and so they should not be dishonored by brothers and sisters who are financially better off. The author then seals the argument with a rhetorical question: why do they honor the rich of the world, the very people who use the court system to oppress them? So in the course of discussing the gap between society's system of honor and God's system of honor, Jacob cites a second reason for economic inequality: the courts are not for justice, but rather for injustice.

In a second passage, James 5:1–6, we see the author's most caustic critique of the economic system. Here Jacob criticizes a fundamental feature of the Roman system of inequality: wealthy landowners exploiting the laborers who worked their fields. As noted earlier, land ownership was the primary means by which the elite minority generated and maintained their wealth. Poor laborers, sharecroppers, and slaves did most of the production in exchange for subsistence wages or provisions. Much of the value of their labor was taken by the elite families, who paid them low wages, charged them rent, appropriated their crops, and/or demanded payment of taxes.[9] According to Jacob, this economic practice of the rich was equivalent to murder.

There are two aspects to Jacob's critique of rich landowners, both of which drew on the traditions of the Israelite prophets. First, Jacob condemns the accumulation of capital using the imagery of corrosion (compare Isa. 51, especially verses 8–16): the corrosion on their precious metals would be evidence against them in the final judgment; the corrosion would consume even their very flesh. Second, Jacob accuses the wealthy of squandering the surplus generated by the unpaid labor of the workers (James 5:1–3). Because the rich use that surplus for their own satisfaction, the divine warrior of Israel, the Lord of Hosts (*ho kyrios sabaōth*), will avenge those who oppress the poor (5:4–6, drawing explicitly on Isa. 5, Jer. 12:9, and other biblical texts).

Can we locate Jacob's audiences on the poverty scale? The author assumes that there are no wealthy landowners in the congregations to which he writes, since 5:1–6 speaks of them as outsiders. The author also assumes that a man with the gold ring and fine clothes would be unusual but not out of the question. So the rhetoric of 2:1–6 locates the audiences mostly between the desperate poor man (PS 7) and that man with extravagant clothes (PS 4).[10]

9. Garnsey and Saller, *Roman Empire*, 64–112.

10. The case of the arrogant merchants (PS 4 or maybe 3) is harder to evaluate: does the author speak of them as outsiders or insiders (4:14–16)? They are perhaps insiders because they are told that they should have recognized God's prerogative, but sorting out rhetoric from reality is even harder here than elsewhere. Elsa Tamez (*The Scandalous Message of James: Faith without Works Is Dead*, trans. John Eagleson [New York: Crossroad, 1990], 25) thinks they are members of the synagogue; David Hutchinson Edgar (*Has God Not Chosen the Poor? The Social Setting of the Epistle of James*, JSNTSup 206 [Sheffield: Sheffield Academic Press, 2001], 198–99) thinks they are not. For a good

Thus the author's implied audiences lived near subsistence level (PS 5–6), probably with some destitute (PS 7), and perhaps a few with moderate surplus resources (PS 4), but no one from the wealthy elite (PS 1–3).

To sum up what we know of the Jacobean perspective, then, resources are distributed unequally in society because landowners exploit workers, because the rich manipulate the justice system, and because the rich squander their immoral gains on self-indulgence. The system survives because those who are exploited participate in the system; they reproduce the system of honor for the wealthy few and dishonor for those who are financially disadvantaged.

In terms of its economic analysis, this perspective draws on the conceptual world and public protests of the prophets of Israel. There is a special concern for the poor and disadvantaged, and strident criticism of wealthy elites. The roots of this prophetic critique are in the ancient history of Israel's struggles with its own ruling elites. Jacob relocates this ancient critique to the contemporary oppression of the urban poor by the local aristocracies of the Roman Empire. This relocation results in less discussion of the responsibilities of the emperor and greater focus on the abuses of those who are rich. Jacob denounces injustice and advises the community to share what resources they have until the Lord of Hosts avenges the cries of the exploited workers.

Acts of the Apostles: A Charity Model

Our third text represents yet another form of literature. We have already examined an apocalypse and a general letter, but in Acts we encounter historical writing that has strong theological interests. The author first composed the Gospel of Luke and then followed that gospel with a second volume that we now know as the Acts of the Apostles. Scholars conclude that Acts was written in either the late first century or the early second century.

All history writing is done with certain goals in mind. In the case of Acts, the author used travel narratives and the sequence of events to portray the early decades of the assemblies as a trajectory away from the movement's Jewish roots. The narrative begins in Jerusalem but moves out into Judea, then Samaria, and finally to Rome. Jews tend to oppose the churches in this narrative, whether in the homeland or in the Diaspora. Gentiles tend to be more receptive to the gospel, and they need not adopt the requirements of Torah (circumcision, Sabbath observance, etc.). Thus as the narrative moves from the periphery of the empire to the imperial capital, the author moves the readers toward imperial culture and away from Judaism.

The author of Acts is silent on the issue of economic injustice. He does not look for institutional causes of poverty. Instead, he focuses his economic policy

---

brief treatment of the situation of the audiences, see Richard Bauckham, *James: Wisdom of James, Disciple of Jesus the Sage* (New York: Routledge, 1999), 188–90.

on charity, and restricts economic redistribution among believers to an idealized past in the Jerusalem church. Four observations support this conclusion.[11]

First, the author of Acts does not criticize any facets of the Roman system of inequality and makes no attempt to explain the huge gap between the wealthy imperial elites and everyone else. In contrast to our previous two texts, the author of Acts presents Roman military officers—the enforcers of imperialism—as sympathetic characters, and he portrays Roman governors mostly as disinterested protectors of the fledgling assemblies.

Second, the author of Acts organizes his narrative to avoid the topic of economic inequality. Even though the author was aware of poverty in assemblies and knew of assemblies that implemented economic redistribution in Jerusalem, he portrays systematic economic sharing as a quaint artifact of an idealized past (Acts 2:42–45; 4:32–37). Economic redistribution was limited in time and space to the original Jerusalem assemblies. Since Acts was written after the Roman destruction of Jerusalem, the narrative effectively presented redistribution of goods as restricted to an earlier period of history.

The author's effort to suppress criticism of economic inequality can be seen especially in three important examples in the narrative. One example is the renunciation of private property in the early Jerusalem assemblies (Acts 2:42–45; 4:32–37). The author's summaries of this practice are idealized rather than pragmatic, and he concludes his discussion of the practice with a story that undercuts the utopian ethos: two saints—Ananias and Sapphira—abuse the practice and are struck dead (5:1–11) in an extreme "one strike and you're out" sentencing policy. A second example is the care for widows in the Jerusalem assemblies (6:1–7), which heightens the author's subtle criticism of communal property. The author suggests that the attempt to end inequality was hampered also by ethnic and cultural favoritism. Again, the author does not deal with the root causes but treats it as an administrative problem, solved by the appointment of more administrators.

The third example of the author's attempt to restrict references to economic inequality in the narrative is more drastic: the author suppresses the story of Paul's collection for the destitute in the Jerusalem assemblies. While some argue that the author did not know about Paul's collection, it seems clear that Paul's final trip to Jerusalem in Acts 20–26 reflects an account of Paul's ill-fated attempt to deliver the collection. Even though the author attempts to recast the trip as an effort to end Paul's mission journey in Jerusalem on Pentecost, the original purpose of the journey (delivery of the collection to Jerusalem) shows through the cracks: the use of some of the money to pay a vow (21:24) and a speech that mentions Paul's gift (24:17).[12]

---

11. For an excellent summary of recent interpretation, see Thomas E. Phillips, "Reading Recent Readings of Issues of Wealth and Poverty in Luke and Acts," *CBR* 1 (2003): 231–69.

12. Dieter Georgi suggests that the author of Acts did not know about the collection (*Remembering the Poor: The History of Paul's Collection for Jerusalem* [Nashville: Abingdon, 1992], 122);

Paul's own letters, however, show that Paul himself undertook the collection as a crucial part of his ministry. The collection was a dramatic initiative by Paul, designed to accomplish several goals: to provide for the needy saints in Jerusalem; to build bridges between Jewish and gentile congregations; and to give material expression to his proclamation of the gospel (Rom. 15:25–27; 2 Cor. 9:13). Paul's gospel called for a network of horizontal sharing among the Mediterranean assemblies (2 Cor. 8:13–15), not an exploitative vertical flow of resources, which characterized the imperial system. This collection for Jerusalem entailed a renunciation of the ideals of patronage, where large occasional benefactions would come from a patron whose wealth was built on the daily exploitation of the masses. The collection, rather, would be built with many gifts from many moderately poor saints in order to provide for brothers and sisters who were desperately poor (1 Cor. 16:1–4; 2 Cor. 8:10–12).

In spite of the collection's importance for Paul, the author of Acts suppressed it, and the reason for the suppression is my third observation about the economic model proposed by Acts: the author presents personal gifts and household hospitality (rather than redistribution) as the normal method of economic sharing for the assemblies after the early period.[13] As the narrative moves out of Jerusalem the economic references begin to shift toward the practice of charity. In Acts 8 the Samaritan magician Simon Magus wants to dispense the Holy Spirit and offers a lot of money for the local franchise. Peter rebukes him for trying to commodify the free gift of the Spirit, but there is no hint of communal property or redistribution as the proper alternative. In chapter 9 Peter goes down to the coast and raises Tabitha from the dead, a woman who was known for her assistance to widows. Her deeds are presented as acts of charity, not as assembly policy. In chapter 10 Peter goes up the coast to Caesarea, where he converts Cornelius, the gentile centurion. Cornelius is described as a man whose piety is manifested in the giving of alms (10:4, 31). His household is saved, but the narrative does not record any further economic developments.

Once the narrative moves beyond Judea and Samaria the shift from community property to faith-based initiatives is almost complete.[14] Beyond Palestine, the normal model for assemblies is hospitality and charity. Lydia offers hospitality for Paul and his companions in Philippi (Acts 16), Jason

---

Joseph A. Fitzmyer does see an awareness of the collection (*The Acts of the Apostles*, AB 31 [New York: Doubleday, 1998], 692).

13. Here I reject the idea of K. F. Nickle that the author of Acts left out the collection because it might have been deemed illegal by readers (*The Collection: A Study in Paul's Strategy*, SBT 48 [London: SCM Press, 1966], 148–51); followed by C. K. Barrett, *A Critical and Exegetical Commentary on the Acts of the Apostles* (Edinburgh: T & T Clark, 1994), 1:599. If that was the author's concern, he would have also expunged accounts of the community of goods in the Jerusalem assemblies.

14. There is one exception—the peculiar note in 11:27–30 that a prophecy about a worldwide famine caused the Antioch assembly to send a gift to Jerusalem, with Saul and Barnabas making the delivery. A hint of the collection seems to be behind this story, but the narrative in Acts 11 recounts a gift only from the assemblies of Antioch to alleviate hardship in anticipation of a crisis.

Table 1.3. Economic Profile of Paul's Assemblies Based on the Undisputed Letters

PS	Name	Reference	Location
[4]	[Chloe?][a]	1 Cor. 1:11	Corinth
4	Gaius	Rom. 16:23	Corinth
4–5	Erastus	Rom. 16:23	Corinth
4–5	Philemon	Philem. 4–22	Colossae?
4–5	Phoebe	Rom. 16:1–2	Cenchraea, Rome
4–5	Aquila	Rom. 16:3–5	Rome (or Ephesus?)
4–5	Prisca	Rom. 16:3–5	Rome (or Ephesus?)
5	Chloe's people	1 Cor. 1:11	Ephesus
5–6	Stephanas	1 Cor. 16:17–18	Ephesus
5–6	The household of Stephanas	1 Cor. 16:15–16	Corinth
5–6	(Many) saints in Corinth	1 Cor. 16:1–2	Corinth
5–6	Churches in Galatia	1 Cor. 16:1–2	Galatia
5–7	(Many) brothers (and sisters)	1 Thess. 4:11	Thessalonica
6	(Many) saints in Corinth	2 Cor. 8:12–15	Corinth
6	The assemblies of Macedonia	2 Cor. 8:1–6	Macedonia
6	Paul	2 Cor. 11:1–21	Corinth
6	Paul	1 Thess. 2:1–12	Thessalonica
6	Paul	Phil. 4:12–13	Rome? Ephesus? Caesarea?
6–7	Onesimus	Philem. 10–19	Ephesus? Rome?
6–7	Those who do not have food for the Lord's supper	1 Cor. 11:22	Corinth
7	Paul	Phil. 2:25–30	Rome? Ephesus? Caesarea?

[a] The text does not clearly state that Chloe was a participant in an assembly, but I think that is the most likely inference.

provides housing in Thessalonica (17:7–8), and so on.[15] Thus the unfolding of the narrative suggests that the early period of systematic redistribution in Jerusalem is over; for the long haul, the standard economic practices will be individual charity and household hospitality.

This policy of the author may be related to my fourth observation: the author of Acts portrays the assemblies as much wealthier than the portrait

15. In Corinth Paul stays with Priscilla and Aquila (18:3). In his farewell to the Ephesian elders he plays down sharing by pointing out that he supported himself and his coworkers and coveted no one's silver and gold. Paul presents this practice as a model for others based on the words of Jesus—they must support the weak and give rather than receive (20:33–35, where a dominical word about sharing becomes the legitimation for self-sufficiency). In Jerusalem, Paul alludes to the collection as his alms and offerings for his nation (24:17). When Paul is shipwrecked on Malta, a prominent local family takes him in and gives him gifts when he leaves (28:7–10), and then finally the narrative ends with Paul apparently paying his own keep under house arrest in Rome (28:30–31).

gleaned from Paul's undisputed letters. Table 1.3 constructs an economic profile of Paul's assemblies. It is based on references to economic resources in his undisputed letters.[16] The numbers in the left column come from the poverty scale outlined earlier.[17]

The results can be summarized as follows: In Paul's undisputed letters only two people can certainly be categorized in the "moderate surplus resources" category, and one of them (Chloe) was perhaps not a participant in the assemblies. Five individuals were either above subsistence level or had moderate surplus resources. Beyond that, we have three references to individuals (including Paul) and eight references to groups or assemblies that were near subsistence level or below. According to Paul's undisputed letters, then, the overwhelming majority of saints in Paul's assemblies were poor, very poor, or desperately poor (PS 5–7).

We can contrast this with an economic profile constructed from the references in Acts to Paul's assemblies (see table 1.4).[18] The economic profile based on Acts is radically different from the one based on Paul's letters. According to Acts, it is possible that Paul was the only believer near the subsistence level. Everyone else about whom we are given some economic information in the narrative could be in the top 10 percent of the poverty scale (PS 1–4). The contrast is even clearer if we place the two charts side by side, as in table 1.5. Note that while there are no references in Paul's undisputed letters to any members from the superwealthy elites (PS 1–3), in Acts there are members of the elites at least in Thessalonica, Beroea, and Athens, and perhaps on Cyprus as well. The figure of Paul himself is interesting in this regard. In both profiles he is listed at the bottom of the poverty scale, and in the undisputed letters Paul records no positive contact with any of the superwealthy elites; rather, Paul records that the elites beat him and threw him in prison. In Acts, however, Paul is portrayed as interacting easily with people in the top 1 percent of the poverty scale: Sergius Paulus, Asiarchs in Ephesus, the unnamed chiliarch who arrests Paul in Jerusalem, King Agrippa II; the procurator Felix; his wife, Drusilla (who was also a sister of Agrippa II); Festus (procurator after Felix); the chiliarch Lysias; and Bernice (sister of Drusilla, sister and consort of Agrippa II, later consort of Titus until he became emperor). Whether these interactions took place in this manner is beside the point; the crucial observation is that the author of Acts portrays Paul not simply as a poor man

16. A defense of this information can be found in Friesen, "Poverty in Pauline Studies."

17. The information in tables 1.4–1.5 was worked out with the assistance of a database of the references to people in literature associated with Paul in the first century. I was able to build the database because of support in the form of a Society of Biblical Literature Technology Grant, and a Research Council Grant from the University of Missouri–Columbia.

18. This profile omits references to assemblies in Judea, Samaria, and Syria because these were not Pauline assemblies.

but as a man of the highest social skills who commands respect from some of the wealthiest and most powerful Roman imperialists.

Table 1.4. Economic Profile of Paul's Assemblies Based on Acts of the Apostles

PS	Name	Reference	Location
[1]	[Proconsul Sergius Paulus?][a]	13:6–12	Paphos, Cyprus
2–3	Dionysios the Areopagite	17:34	Athens
2–3	Not a few of the Greek men of high standing	17:12	Beroea
2–3	Not a few of the Greek women of high standing	17:12	Beroea
2–3	Women of high standing (in the city)	17:4	Thessalonica
4	Crispus	18:8	Corinth
4?	(Jailer, unnamed)	18:22–36	Philippi
4?	Lydia	16:13–15	Philippi
4	Titius Justus	18:7	Corinth
4–5	Jason	17:5–9	Thessalonica
5–6	Paul	18:3–8; 20:34	Corinth; Ephesus

[a] Sergius Paulus is in square brackets because the narrative does not clearly mark him as a participant in the assemblies. The text says that he believed and was amazed at the teaching of the Lord, but it does not record a baptism, reception of the Holy Spirit, or the response of his whole house.

To sum up, the model that informs Acts is clear. There is no explanation of unequal distribution of goods, no critique of systemic causes of poverty, and no denunciation of exploitation. The text recognizes that the earliest assemblies in Jerusalem experimented in communal property but does not explain why they did this. Instead, the author restricts such efforts in time (the early years of the movement) and in space (Jerusalem). Beyond that earliest period, the text recognizes some cases of economic need, but these can be handled through hospitality and charity. In contrast to the Letter of Jacob and the Revelation of John, this text envisions that the earliest assemblies included some of the wealthiest inhabitants of the empire.

The *Shepherd of Hermas*: God-Given Wealth

The *Shepherd of Hermas* was probably written a few decades later than the other three texts under consideration. The visions in the text appear to come from a single author during the first half of the second century, with the final form of the text taking shape by the mid-second century.[19] Moreover,

19. The *Shepherd of Hermas* is an apocalypse, but it has literary features that distinguish it from the Revelation of John. *Hermas* is much longer than Revelation and the character of the visions is also quite different. While Revelation is full of fantastic apocalyptic symbols, *Hermas* tends to report

Table 1.5. Comparison: Economic Profiles from Undisputed Letters and Acts

Names from undisputed letters of Paul	PS	Names from Acts
	[1]	[Proconsul]
	2–3	Dionysios
	2–3	Leading men of Beroea
	2–3	Leading women of Beroea
	2–3	Leading women of Thessalonica
[Chloe?][a]	4	Crispus
Gaius	4	Titius Justus
	4?	Unnamed jailer
	4?	Lydia
Erastus	4–5	Jason
Philemon	4–5	
Phoebe	4–5	
Aquila	4–5	
Prisca	4–5	
Chloe's people	5	
Stephanas	5–6	Paul
The household of Stephanas	5–6	
(Many) saints in Corinth	5–6	
Churches in Galatia	5–6	
(Many) brothers (and sisters)	5–7	
(Many) saints in Corinth	6	
The assemblies of Macedonia	6	
Paul	6–7	
Onesimus	6–7	
Those without food for the Lord's supper	6–7	

[a] The text does not clearly state that Chloe was a participant in an assembly, but I think that is the most likely inference.

the text comes from the city of Rome, so it is also distinct in its provenance.[20] The four models I am developing here therefore deal with several different decades and locations during the first hundred years of the Christian movement, and so we should not think of these four texts as points along one line of development. The four texts do not form a linear trajectory of ideas about the origins and meaning of poverty. Rather, the texts illustrate four models for analysis and for action from the early assemblies.

---

more sedate visions that function as allegories. Revelation rarely explains its symbols, but in *Hermas* the meanings of the visions are almost always stated clearly. In contrast to Revelation, where the visions tend to deal with politics, religion, and economy, the visionary allegories in *Hermas* often deal with issues of theology and personal morality.

20. Carolyn Osiek, *Shepherd of Hermas*, Hermeneia (Minneapolis: Fortress, 1999), 18–20.

In the *Shepherd of Hermas*, wealth is described as a gift from God (*Sim.* 1.9; 2.10; *Mand.* 2.4–5). The gift of wealth is not a pure blessing, however, and we need to be aware of the complexity of the theme in *Hermas*. Wealth can also bring difficulties, such as renunciation of the faith (*Sim.* 1.4–5), distraction leading to spiritual weakness (*Sim.* 2.5; *Mand.* 10.1.4), and temptation to avoid persecution (*Vis.* 3.6.5–7). Thus wealth is an ambiguous blessing in *Hermas* and must be used properly.[21]

Some of these themes can be seen in *Similitude* 1. In this section a heavenly messenger who looks like a shepherd tells Hermas a parable. In the parable, the life of a believer in the world is compared to the life of a slave of God living in a foreign city. In the foreign city (= life in this world) the slave (= a believer) should not rely on possessions or wealth, for the slave could be expelled at any time and these goods would be left behind. A proper course of action is a frugal self-sufficiency (*autarkeia*). This simple lifestyle allows one to use the remaining "foreign" wealth to help widows and orphans, which, in the logic of the parable, is equivalent to buying goods in one's native city (= heaven) that cannot be confiscated.

> Instead of fields, then, purchase souls that have been afflicted, insofar as you can, and take care of widows and orphans and do not neglect them; spend your wealth and all your furnishings for such fields and houses as you have received from God. For this is why the Master made you rich, that you may carry out these ministries for him. It is much better to purchase the fields, goods, and houses you find in your own city when you return to it. This kind of extravagance is good and makes one glad; it has no grief or fear, but joy instead. And so, do not participate in the extravagance sought by outsiders; for it is of no profit for you who are slaves of God. (Herm. *Sim.* 1.8–10)

The interpretation of the parable repeats the idea that wealth comes from God but also indicates that wealth can lead one into ultimately fruitless endeavors because wealth is transient, like life itself. Note also that the city is not described as an evil location, as would be the case in John's Revelation. Urban life is not necessarily bad, according to Hermas, only foreign and temporary. In this context, charity is the proper use of wealth. God has given people wealth precisely for this reason.

Similitude 2 works out in more detail the role of wealth in the life of the churches, actually giving credit to the rich for the accomplishments

---

21. Osiek mentions three texts in *Hermas* that talk about the removal of one's wealth; *Rich and Poor in the Shepherd of Hermas: An Exegetical-social Investigation*, CBQMS 15 (Washington, DC: Catholic Biblical Association of America, 1983), 51–52. One of the texts deals primarily with the possibility that possessions will cause someone to give in to persecution of believers (*Vis.* 3.6.5–7). The other two are enigmatic and do not agree with the general teaching in *Hermas* (*Sim.* 9.30.5; 9.31.2). These two might indicate that wealthy individuals whose riches are a temptation should remove their wealth, with the implication that those who are not tempted do not need to renounce riches.

of the poor! The agricultural practice of using young elm trees to support grapevines is compared to relations of rich and poor in the assemblies. The elm symbolizes the rich, and the grapevine symbolizes the poor. According to the shepherd's interpretation, the elm tree only appears to be fruitless. If the elm supports the vine, the vine is able to grow fruit because it is off the ground and it is able to draw moisture from the elm in times of drought.[22] "And so, when the vine attaches to the elm, it bears fruit both of itself and because of the elm. And so you see that the elm also gives much fruit—no less than the vine, but rather more" (*Sim.* 2.3b–4a). This model, then, is quite at odds with Revelation and Jacob, which portray the wealthy as oppressors, and it is more extreme than Acts, where the wealthy do have a place in the assemblies. Here in *Hermas* the wealthy are credited with producing fruit, even though the poor actually do all the production.

The call to action in *Hermas* is significantly different from that of Acts. Both texts call for charity and not for justice. The difference is that while Acts advocates hospitality and charity in the service of community, *Hermas* portrays charity as an individual act that gives material aid to the poor and helps the rich survive the final judgment.[23] This plutocentric perspective is a far cry from the other end of my spectrum. It is hard to imagine the author of Revelation embracing a macarism such as the one found in *Sim.* 2.10: "Happy are those who have possessions and understand that their riches have come from the Lord; for the one who understands this will also be able to perform a good ministry."[24]

Thus in *Hermas* we find an explanation of poverty that disenfranchises the poor. As a model for action, it holds little promise. Poverty and wealth are not simply recognized as facts of social life; they are justified as crucial components of the life of the assembly. *Hermas* suggests that the poor need wealthy people in order to meet their daily needs for material survival, and that the rich need the poor so that they can have objects for charity that will eventually get the rich into heaven. It is a dysfunctional, codependent model that condones economic inequality.

22. Osiek, *Shepherd of Hermas*, 162–64.
23. For example, Herm. *Vis.* 3.9.2–6 discusses the way in which some in the assemblies are injured by overeating (PS 4 or higher) and some are injured by not eating enough (PS 6–7). The advice given to the wealthy is that they should practice moderation and share, and thus gain a place in heaven.
24. Osiek argues that Hermas was an upwardly mobile freedman from Rome (*Shepherd of Hermas*, 20–22). James Jeffers writes that Hermas reflects a lower level of the social hierarchy (*Conflict at Rome: Social Order and Hierarchy in Early Christianity* [Minneapolis: Fortress, 1991], 116–20). For more about wealth in the congregations addressed by this text, see Harry O. Maier, *The Social Setting of the Ministry as Reflected in the Writings of Hermas, Clement and Ignatius*, Dissertations SR 1 (Waterloo, ON: Wilfrid Laurier University Press, 1991), 59–65.

Conclusion

This essay deals with a phenomenon found in all human societies: the economic deprivation of many for the benefit of a wealthy few. Every society promotes the unequal distribution of resources and attempts to justify the economic inequality. And always, somewhere in the populace, there is criticism of economic exploitation. The critiques are often suppressed by the official histories and hidden from view in public culture, but they do exist. Sometimes the critiques are related to religious considerations, and other times they are not. Patristic studies need to be more attentive to the reconstruction of these submerged perspectives.

An examination of these four particular early Christian texts yields not a unified explanation of the origins of poverty, but rather four appraisals of economic inequality. In terms of their evaluations of the origins of poverty, the responses can be placed along a spectrum, with Revelation at one extreme and the *Shepherd of Hermas* at the other. On the one side, Revelation argues that poverty was the result of imperialism and international exploitation, and that wealth was the accumulation of ill-gotten gains. At the other end of the spectrum, *Hermas* ignores the causes of poverty and focuses instead on the blessings of wealth, which came not from injustice but from God. In between these two extremes are Jacob and Acts. Jacob is closer to Revelation in its condemnation of injustice, but its perspectives are more localized and its analysis less systematic. Acts is closer to *Hermas* in that the Roman system of inequality is not critiqued and wealth is considered mostly benign.

Table 1.6. Four Models

	Revelation	Jacob	Acts	*Hermas*
Origin of poverty:	imperial system	local elites	(not stated)	God
Poor should:	denounce wealth	tolerate wealth	embrace rich	depend on rich
Rich should:	divest	correct problems	support church	earn own salvation
Goal:	purity	equality	help the needy	personal salvation

We can also locate the calls to action from the four texts along this spectrum. The texts ask whether the pious poor should denounce the wealthy (Revelation), tolerate the wealthy (Jacob), embrace the wealthy (Acts), or become dependent on the wealthy (*Hermas*). The texts raise similar questions for rich individuals. Should the wealthy seek the purity of divestment (Revelation), remain involved and make the system more just (Jacob), support the community of faith (Acts), or give alms to earn personal salvation (*Hermas*)? And finally, what about the goals of these ethical admonitions? Revelation's goal seems to be purity, while Jacob focuses more on equality, Acts on helping the needy, and *Hermas* on individual salvation.

So at the end of this inquiry we do not have an explanation of the origins of poverty. Rather, we have four theories that contradict one another in several ways. Can the contradictory theories be salutary? Perhaps. They remind us of the complexities of religious history, where the texts we categorize as one religious tradition often disagree with one another on fundamental issues. They also remind us of the ambiguous roles that religion plays in society, sometimes alleviating suffering and sometimes creating misery. And the texts suggest the beginning of a typology that might be present in other texts, for these four models are not foreign to us today. They have all played a role in the subsequent histories of Christianity. Church history is full of narratives of radical resistance to economic exploitation similar to the position of Revelation; of small-scale resistance to exploitation similar to the position of Jacob; of accommodation to exploitation as in Acts; and of Christian benefactors who use a portion of their wealth to help alleviate individual cases of misery, as in the *Shepherd of Hermas*.

But what about the future of Christianity? Which model or models might guide churches into the coming decades? Which model or models might help shape a more equitable future, where unpaid labor and unrelieved hunger and untreated disease are found only in the history books? These are questions we need to address. Where will we locate ourselves as scholars, as moral agents, as religious pilgrims? Some of the ancient texts that we study say that wealth comes from God, and some of the texts say that wealth comes from Satan. Some of the texts denounce institutional causes of poverty, and some texts see poverty as God's will.

Perhaps Dom Hélder Câmara would remind us that throughout church history some people have given food to the poor; we study them and we call them saints. But others have asked *why* the poor are still hungry and have demanded justice. Will we also study their texts? And will we call them saints as well?

2

"BE NOT ONE WHO STRETCHES OUT HANDS TO RECEIVE BUT SHUTS THEM WHEN IT COMES TO GIVING"

Envisioning Christian Charity When Both Donors and Recipients Are Poor

DENISE KIMBER BUELL

Early Christian texts of the late first to early third centuries rarely offer extended discussions of poverty and charity.[1] When the topic of poverty arises at all, it is most often in contexts advocating charity, where the addressee is sometimes described as "rich" (*plousios*), such as in the *Shepherd of Hermas* and Clement of Alexandria's *Quis dives salvetur?* also known as *Who Is the Saved Rich Person?* When the "poor" (*penēs* or *ptōchos*) are visible in early Christian texts, they are usually depicted either as the passive recipients of charity or as intercessors for their donors, active only because they receive charity. Both Clement of Alexandria and the author of the *Shepherd of Hermas* depict the relationship between rich and poor as ideally

1. For feedback on earlier versions of this essay, my thanks to Susan Holman, Laura Muench-Nasrallah, Caroline Johnson Hodge, Melanie Johnson-DeBaufre, and Elana Boehm.

complementary, with the wealthy providing material support to the poor and the poor, in turn, sustaining the rich, especially through prayer. Carolyn Osiek has shown that the recipients of charity in the *Shepherd of Hermas* are almost never described as active agents, the one exception being the striking parable of the elm and the vine, where the rich and the poor are depicted as mutually dependent, with the wealthy providing material support for the poor and the poor providing spiritual intercessors and intermediaries for the rich.[2] Clement of Alexandria writes,

> Enlist on your behalf an army without weapons, without war, without blood-shed, without anger, without stain, an army of God-fearing old men, of God-beloved orphans, of widows armed with gentleness, or men adorned with love. Obtain with your wealth, as guards for your body and soul, such ones as these, whose commander is God. Through them the sinking ship rises, steered by the prayers of saints alone; and sickness at its height is subdued, put to flight by the laying on of hands; the attack of robbers is made harmless, being stripped of its weapons by prayers; and the violence of *daimones* is shattered, reduced to impotence by confident commands. Effective soldiers are all these, and steadfast guardians, not one idle, not one useless. One is able to beg your life from God, another to hearten you when sick, another to weep and lament in sympathy on your behalf before the Lord of all, another to teach some part of what is useful for salvation, another to give outspoken warning, another friendly counsel, and all to love you truly, without guile, fear, hypocrisy, flattery, or pretense.[3]

In reflecting on how scholars interpret ancient sources, Susan Holman has observed that most scholarly works on charity and poverty in early Christianity replicate the perspective of the ancient texts; most "are in fact studies about wealth" in which "the poor are referents, not subjects."[4]

This essay poses some questions about modern interpretations of and ancient rhetoric about poverty and charity. Have we been too hasty in presuming that those exhorted to give charity are not impoverished? Have we been too hasty in attributing something akin to middle- or upper-middle-class comfort to those labeled as "wealthy" in early Christian texts? If we understand the first few generations of members of communities that we study as "early Christian" to have been largely hovering near, at, or below subsistence

2. Herm. *Sim.* 2.1–10; see Carolyn Osiek, *Rich and Poor in the Shepherd of Hermas: An Exegetical-Social Investigation*, CBQMS 15 (Washington, DC: Catholic Biblical Association of America, 1983), esp. 78–90.

3. Clement of Alexandria, *Quis div.*, 34–35; critical edition: Clemens Alexandrinus, vol. 3, *Stromata Buch VII und VIII, Excerpta ex Theodoto, Eclogae Propheticae, Quis Dives Salvetur, Fragmente*, ed. Otto Stählin, GCS (Leipzig: J. C. Hinrichs, 1909), 157–91; translation here is adapted from Clement of Alexandria, *Exhortation to the Greeks, The Rich Man's Salvation, to the Newly Baptized*, trans. G. W. Butterworth, LCL (1919; repr., Cambridge, MA: Harvard University Press, 1999), 265–367.

4. Susan R. Holman, *The Hungry Are Dying: Beggars and Bishops in Roman Cappadocia*, Oxford Studies in Historical Theology (Oxford: Oxford University Press, 2001), 12.

level, how should this affect the way we read rhetorical statements about exhortations to give alms or admonitions about the perils or obligations of a so-called rich person?[5]

To begin to answer these questions, I offer one way to rethink the rhetoric of almsgiving and charity in early Christian texts. Drawing on late first- and early second-century examples from *Didache, 1 Clement,* and *Shepherd of Hermas,* I argue that even though the rhetoric about charity creates an apparently mutually exclusive pairing—donor/recipient—some contexts allow for the possibility that the same person might in some instances be a donor and in other instances the recipient of charity. This cross-grained reading of the rhetoric offers one way to imagine the economically marginal of antiquity as active agents.

My approach has the virtue of calling attention to the possible disjunctions between rhetoric and social-material realities by suggesting that the rhetorical positioning of the recipients of alms as passive may mask the historical action of impoverished Christians as themselves engaged in poverty relief.

Methodological Challenges

Before turning to examine some ancient examples, it is important to consider briefly two kinds of challenges to the study of economic difference and poverty in early Christian texts: first, the understandings of economic difference in ancient texts and in modern interpretations; and second, the fuzziness of the language about and meanings of poverty.

Representing economic difference: Then and now

Most ancient discussions of poverty or charity address readers as if they were in a position to give alms and advocate what is often called redemptive almsgiving. In order to resist a naive reinscription of the rhetorical interests of ancient texts, we must think about what kind of communal ideals are communicated in these writings. In the case of poverty and charity, this means asking: how does a given text view economic difference and how, if at all, are

5. Even a century later, in Clement's Alexandria, his rhetorical construction of addressees—primarily male, free, slave owning, with access to various luxury goods—should not be taken as evidence that most Christians in late second-century Alexandria or even under Clement's tutelage fit this description. Nonetheless, Clement's rhetoric is often taken as evidence for the wealth of his audience. For example, L. William Countryman writes, "Much of the *Paedagogus* would be completely irrelevant if addressed to any audience *but* that of the rich. And Clement's hearers, if not necessarily the cream of Alexandrian society, were at least recognizable, by anyone's standard, as rich" (*The Rich Christian in the Church of the Early Empire: Contradictions and Accommodations,* Texts and Studies in Religion [New York: E. Mellen Press, 1980], 48–49, emphasis in the original).

economic inequities addressed?[6] Ancient texts largely construct the category of "the poor" as the "other," and most often, as Holman writes, the poor are "a passive tool for redemptive almsgiving, a signifier by which the Christian donor may gain honor and divine rewards."[7]

Even if Christian texts modify the traditional patron–client relationship to grant the poor spiritual authority, this model does not call into question economic differences as such. Texts may advocate an ethic of care for the poor, but an exhortation to give alms does not intrinsically critique economic arrangements in which some people have considerable excess while others are chronically impoverished. The model of redemptive almsgiving can and has functioned to normalize or reinforce economic disparities by allocating distinctive roles for "poor" and "rich" in the same community.

We can catch glimpses of alternative ancient possibilities as well.[8] For example, Clement's *Who Is the Saved Rich Person?* suggests that competing models for handling economic difference existed in late second-century Alexandria. Clement shapes his version of redemptive almsgiving in contrast to two positions he condemns: pandering to the wealthy and total divestment of material goods. Because we never hear the precise arguments for total divestment, we cannot know whether this view is articulated in terms of economic justice, although Clement's condemnation of the so-called Carpocratians in the *Stromateis* does hint at the possibility that this group might have advocated divestment in order to achieve economic justice.[9]

But as constraining as the ancient sources are, modern lenses have also contributed to the invisibility of the poor and have downplayed or left unexplored ancient alternatives to redemptive almsgiving. It is not only Clement who formed his views in the context of debate and competition. As L. William Countryman and Steven Friesen have both shown, modern debates about ancient poverty have been overwhelmingly determined by the struggle between Marxist and capitalist ideologies.[10] Both sides of this debate invoke

6. See contribution by Steven Friesen in chapter 1 of this volume.

7. Holman, *Hungry Are Dying*, 54.

8. Friesen (above, chapter 1) suggests that the New Testament writings the Revelation of John and the Letter of Jacob (traditionally known as James) offer such alternatives.

9. The one group that Clement associates with sharing goods in common, the Carpocratians, apparently invoke Gal. 3:28, so may also have held a comparable view about the importance of getting rid of distinctions between rich and poor (see Clement of Alexandria, *Strom.* 3.54.1–56.3; the critical edition is Clement of Alexandria, *Opera*, ed. Otto Stählin, 4 vols., GCS, 12, 15, 17, 39 [Leipzig: Hinrichs, 1905–9]). For further discussion, see Denise Kimber Buell, "'Sell What You Have and Give to the Poor': A Feminist Analysis of Clement of Alexandria's *Who Is the Rich Person Who Is Saved?*" in *Walk in the Ways of Wisdom: Essays in Honor of Elisabeth Schüssler Fiorenza*, ed. Shelly Matthews, Cynthia Kittredge, and Melanie Johnson-DeBaufre (Philadelphia: Trinity Press International, 2003), 194–213.

10. Steven J. Friesen, "Poverty in Pauline Studies: Beyond the So-Called New Consensus," *JSNT* 26, no. 3 (2004): 323–37, 358–59; Countryman, *Rich Christian*, 1–18.

ancient sources to support their positions (Acts of the Apostles for the former versus Clement of Alexandria and Cyprian for the latter). One problem with this modern debate is that it forces ancient discussions about poverty and charity in a stark binary classification: either early Christian texts promote communalism (Marxist) or they promote philanthropy (capitalist).

Since the mid-twentieth century, capitalist presuppositions have become mainstream in the academic study of early Christianity, allied with historical-critical and social scientific approaches, even as Marxist readings continue to inform liberation theology and liberation-inspired criticisms, including many feminist works. Friesen identifies the by-products of the capitalist preference to include a downplaying of poverty as an issue in antiquity, and a lack of discussion of oppression, class conflict, or exploitation.[11] In this ideological division of twentieth-century scholarship, redemptive almsgiving has received privileged attention not only as the primary mode of early Christian charity advocated by authors such as Clement; it also is allied with capitalist values of retaining wealth while supporting philanthropy, in contrast to the perceived Marxist-friendly alternative of communal egalitarianism through total redistribution of goods.

Friesen and Justin Meggitt have tried to interrupt this ideological trend in Pauline studies in part by insisting on understanding Paul and the majority of his audience as "poor," including almost all those who are asked to contribute to the collection for the "poor" in Jerusalem.[12] Meggitt dubs this model of support "economic mutualism," as a form of reciprocal giving and receiving for those living near or below subsistence level. Friesen nuances Meggitt's position by proposing a classificatory scheme to distinguish among *kinds* of poverty in Pauline communities. Most important, both stress that modern interpreters should not presume that the rhetoric of charity necessarily presumes any or many members of Jesus movement/early Christian communities with abundant material excess. Friesen's and Meggitt's works illuminate ways to imagine the impoverished as agents of charity as well as its recipients.

Language about poverty

Before turning to examine some ancient examples, it is important to note three linguistic and social factors that complicate our ability to understand

11. In addition to these factors, Friesen also persuasively notes other by-products such as an emphasis on social status as an interpretive key (of which economic means is just one factor), an increased focus on the individual, and a downplaying or denial of the relevance of historical study for the present. Friesen, "Poverty in Pauline Studies," 331–35. Please note that I have not presented these items in the order that he presents them in his article.

12. See Justin J. Meggitt, *Paul, Poverty, and Survival* (Edinburgh: T & T Clark, 1998); Friesen, "Poverty in Pauline Studies," 323–61.

language about poverty in ancient texts. First, the two most common Greek terms for the poor, *penēs* and *ptōchos*, have a range of meanings. Although *penēs* frequently connotes "the working poor" and *ptōchos* "the destitute beggar who is outside or at the fringes of society,"[13] this distinction is not absolute. And other terms, such as *endeomenos* (needy; e.g., *Did.* 4.8) and *hysteroumenos* (lacking; e.g., Herm. *Sim.* 5.3.7), are favored in some early Christian contexts.

The second challenge concerning language about poverty is that "the poor" did not constitute a social class in Greek or Roman society.[14] Early Christian writers have to negotiate this fact even as they draw on scriptures that do provide a precedent for Jewish and Christian communities to identify the poor as a distinct economic grouping requiring direct attention.

The third complicating factor arises in texts that use the "poor" as some special kind of insider, not as those simply with material needs. The blessing of the "poor in spirit" in the Gospel of Matthew, for example, clearly seeks to distinguish one kind of poor from poverty measured in other, nonspiritual, ways (Matt. 5:3). In this context the "poor in spirit" clearly means more than those who lack the means for subsistence. Nonetheless, it is difficult to declare that the use of "the poor" as an insider category in some Jesus movement and early Christian texts does not sometimes *also* indicate a lack of material resources. For example, Paul's collection for the saints (*hagioi*) (2 Cor. 8:4), if part of his remembrance for the poor (*ptōchoi*) (Gal. 2:10), suggests a convergence of economic need with insider status.[15]

Textual Analysis

We cannot be certain of the economic or spiritual standing of those who listened to the *Didache*, *1 Clement*, or the *Shepherd of Hermas*, let alone the economic or spiritual standing of those who acted in response to hearing their respective exhortations. We cannot know precisely how these hearers classified themselves or their peers as in need or as subject to admonitions to give alms. Nonetheless, these three early Christian texts offer strategies, at least implicitly, for generating funds for donations under near-subsistence conditions. In these we can glimpse the possibility of the poor donating to the poor. The late first-century treatise known as *1 Clement* and the anonymous

13. Holman, *Hungry Are Dying*, 5.

14. As Holman writes with respect to Greco-Roman culture, "While poverty was certainly a reality in the ancient world, the poor did not comprise a discrete social or political category, and poverty was *not* a criteria for assistance" (Holman, *Hungry Are Dying*, 32, emphasis in original).

15. As Friesen notes, within Paul's letters "the poor" in Jerusalem for whom Paul attempts to collect funds may have been at or below subsistence level (see "Poverty in Pauline Studies," 350–51 and 351n87).

early second-century visionary text *Shepherd of Hermas* are associated most closely with Rome, whereas the provenance of the late first- or early second-century *Didache* is less clear, but often linked with Syria.[16]

The Shepherd of Hermas

Hermas gives instructions for performing a fast specifically for raising funds for the needy: "On the day you fast, taste nothing but bread and water, calculate the price of the food you were going to eat, and give it to a widow or an orphan or needy person [*hysteroumenos*]" (Herm. *Sim.* 5.3.7).[17] A community member fasts and sets aside for donation the money one would have otherwise spent on food (5.3.5–9). It is clearly possible for a person with adequate food and/or surplus funds to generate money for donation this way; indeed, one could even argue that this practice could create a greater sense of community with those who are chronically im-poverished. But these instructions *also* make it possible for someone who is already living at or near subsistence level to participate. If one imagines a context in which the lines between donor and recipients are blurry, the injunction to fast is a strategy that enables mutual assistance, along the lines of the "economic mutualism" that Meggitt suggests characterizes Pauline communities.

In other places, *Hermas* suggests an audience composed of a broader range of means than just around the subsistence level: for example, "Some are becoming ill from too much eating and damaging their flesh while others who have no food are damaging their flesh by not having even necessary food, and their body is perishing" (Herm. *Vis.* 3:9.3). Nonetheless, this does not mean that the implied readers include only the very rich or that those with meager resources are not proactive in caring for those who are even more needy.

First Clement

First Clement offers another striking example of poverty relief that could indicate a poor donor: "We know that many among ourselves have given

16. While I am not prepared to accept Aaron Milavec's mid-first-century dating for the *Didache*, I do imagine it as a text used by Christian communities (see Aaron Milavec, *The Didache: Faith, Hope, and Life of the Earliest Christian Communities, 50–70 CE* [Mahwah, NJ: Newman, 2003]). I am not presuming that the text under consideration reflects a single community of production. Rather, I am interested in showing how the text could have been deployed and understood.

17. The critical edition of *Shepherd of Hermas* is that of Molly Whittaker, ed., *Der Hirt des Hermas*, 2nd ed. (1956; repr., Berlin: Akademie-Verlag, 1967). Translation here is by Carolyn Osiek, from *Shepherd of Hermas: A Commentary*, Hermeneia (Minneapolis: Fortress, 1999), 173. The *Didascalia* [19] and *Apostolic Constitutions* [5.1.3] offer similar instructions, although the context is to raise funds for those imprisoned as Christians.

themselves to bondage that they might ransom others. Many have sold themselves into slavery, and provided food for others with the price they receive
for themselves" (*1 Clem.* 55.2).[18] Jennifer Glancy wisely cautions that the
use of the word "many" probably overstates the frequency of this practice.[19]
She especially calls attention to the context of the passage as part of a list of
virtuous actions, sandwiched as it is between the deeds of unnamed gentile
rulers and the biblical heroines Judith and Esther. Nonetheless, it is the only
example in the list that directly engages the audience ("many among *ourselves*"); its rhetorical effectiveness relies on the plausibility of the concept
of enslavement for procuring food for others, even if not a single member
of the audience has actually done so.

Didache

The *Didache* is one of the few early Christian texts that includes direct
statements to both potential donors and potential recipients of charity.[20] It
is plausible to imagine that the same individual might be both donor and
recipient at different points in his or her life.

> Do not be one who stretches out hands to receive but shuts them when it comes
> to giving. Of whatever you have gained by your hands you shall give a ransom
> for your sins. You shall not hesitate to give nor shall you grumble when you
> give, for you shall know who is the good paymaster of the reward. You shall not
> turn away the needy [*endeomenos*] but shall share everything with your sibling,
> and shall not say it is your own, for if you are sharers in the imperishable, how
> much more in the things which perish? (*Did.* 4.5–8)[21]

In this passage, listeners are exhorted to give freely to other members of the
community, notably those characterized as "needy." The text emphasizes the

18. Critical edition: *The Apostolic Fathers*, vol. 1, ed. and trans. Kirsopp Lake (1912; repr., Cambridge, MA: Harvard University Press, 1985), 8–121; translation here closely follows Lake's.
19. Jennifer A. Glancy, *Slavery in Early Christianity* (Oxford: Oxford University Press, 2002),
82–83.
20. I agree with Milavec that the *Didache* promotes what he dubs "resource sharing" (Milavec,
Didache, xiii, xxxiv, 176–227) and that there is no evidence in the text for a central collection of funds
then distributed by centralized means or leaders (221). Although he does not view the community
as comprised of wealthy members, he does seem to view members as all having some (potential)
excess (see 180–81), a view that I would question.
21. *The Apostolic Fathers*, 308–33; translation is adapted from Lake's. I have also consulted
Milavec's edition and translation (*Didache*, 12–45). This passage is from the material known as "the
two ways." Even if this material is not original to the *Didache* but is adapted from an oral or literary
precedent, it is still important to ask about its function in this text. Much of the quotation above
appears in the *Epistle to Barnabas* 19.8–11; these statements are not clustered together in one bundle
but rather are subdivided. On the "Two Ways Tractate" and the hypothesis of an earlier, independent source, see the discussion in Kurt Niederwimmer, *The Didache: A Commentary*, Hermeneia
(Minneapolis: Fortress, 1998), 30–41.

siblinghood of insiders as a reason to share possessions, and also implies that charitable practices are to be understood as both a "ransom for sins" and a forerunner to one's own reward from the divine paymaster.

This passage can be read as presuming that the same person might be, at different times, giver and receiver of material goods. Alternatively, it could be instead admonishing one who extends a hand for payment for goods or services to also give alms.[22] Regardless, we can imagine the addressees as people living economically marginal lives, who at times may require alimentary or financial assistance from other members of the community but are simultaneously exhorted to come to the aid of others as well. Other passages support this kind of reading.

As the quotation above suggests, the *Didache* urges its audience to think of perishable goods as ultimately belonging to God. This idea appears early in the text and is repeated later when readers are commanded to bring the "first fruits" to resident apostles, teachers, or "the poor" of the community (*Did.* 13.1–7). As part of the "way of life," the *Didache* urges listeners to "give to everyone who asks" (*Did.* 1.5):

> For the father wants people to give to everyone from the gifts that have been freely granted to them. Blessed is the one who gives according to the commandment, for that one is guiltless. Woe to one who receives. If anyone takes when in need, then that one is guiltless, but if that one is not in need they shall have to given an account of why they took . . . if they are imprisoned they shall be interrogated about what they have done and shall not go free until they have paid the last penny. But concerning this it was also said, "Let your alms sweat into your hands until you know to whom you are giving." (*Did.* 1.5–6)

This passage seems first to pressure the recipient (not to take if not "in need") and then finally the giver, to hold on to alms until one "knows to whom you are giving." The view that one is guiltless if one receives when in need, but is otherwise accountable, could certainly be legible as an admonition against greed. In a context where resources are scarce the imperative to share what one has (again, interpreted as gifts from God) could also mean that many in the community could reasonably view themselves as in need; the onus is placed on the individual to strive to be a giver rather than a receiver— reinforcing the likelihood that the same person could potentially occupy both positions.

The quotation about almsgiving does not appear in other early texts and has no clear scriptural referent. Augustine quotes a similar saying as Scripture: "Let alms sweat in your hand until you find a righteous person to whom to

---

22. My thanks to Susan Holman for this observation, supported by the sense that the text could have merchants in mind.

give."[23] Augustine's saying clearly emphasizes the quality of the recipient, part of a long tradition of the myth of the "deserving poor."[24] But we should not be too quick to read Augustine back into the *Didache* by presuming that the subtext of the *Didache*'s version simply concerns the quality of the recipient. Two other factors seem at least as important. First, in a context in which one might on any given day be either a recipient or a donor, the chances are great that one's alms will be limited. An admonition to hold on to one's alms until one's palms are sweaty is intelligible in a context in which one has little to give. The agency of the donor is foregrounded.

Second, "until you know to whom you give" can have quite a different connotation than "until you find a righteous person." Already the passage has put the onus on the recipient to take only when in need.[25] Knowing to whom you give suggests a direct relationship between donor and recipient. Later in the *Didache*, readers are instructed to appoint bishops and deacons for themselves, but there is no indication that those in office are intermediaries for alms. The admonition to know to whom one gives may suggest that donors are to be more actively involved in the lives of recipients than in only giving food, clothing, money, or other goods.

Other passages in the *Didache* also make sense when interpreted in light of a communal setting in which many members are living on the margins yet are expected to contribute. The discussions of visiting and resident apostles and those who "come in the name of the Lord" include concerns about food and remuneration.[26] Exhortations to provide even limited temporary support seem directed to the community at large and not simply to members with extra resources or to officeholders. Finally, the *Didache* also specifies that, if the community does not have a resident apostle to support, its firstfruits should be given to "the poor" (13.4). The text does not clarify who counts as *ptōchos*, but it need not be interpreted as a static constituency. Rather, in keeping with my reading of the earlier ethical exhortations of the *Didache* and the communal responsibility for supporting visitors and resident spiritual leaders, some hearers of the text may have qualified as "the poor" episodically and some chronically.

23. Augustine, *Enarrat. Ps.* 102:12; cf. Niederwimmer, *Didache*, 84; see discussion on pp. 83–86.

24. For a trenchant critique of this myth in the modern American context, see Dorothy Allison, "A Question of Class," in *Skin: Talking about Sex, Class, and Literature* (Ithaca, NY: Firebrand, 1994), 13–36.

25. This emphasis continues later in the text's discussion of traveling apostles where apostles are judged by their actions—the community is expected to provide what is requested by the apostle (and even to follow the apostle's lead in the practice of the Eucharist if different from their own) but is also given instructions on how to determine whether the apostle is genuine. In the *Didache*, this comes down especially to whether the apostle asks for money or eats food that has been requested when "in a spirit" (see *Did.* 10.7–11.12, esp. 11.6, 9, 12).

26. See, e.g., *Did.* 11.6, 9, 12; 12.3–5.

Conclusion

Exhortations to give alms, at least in some contexts, do not preclude the agency of the poor. In a context of widespread poverty, almsgiving has the potential to function as a system for providing mutual support. I am not seeking to romanticize poverty or to imply that all poor Christians were almsgivers or charitable donors; rather, I am offering a fresh way to address the invisibility of the poor in scholarship and ancient texts. Moreover, I have been challenging the binary rhetoric of donor/recipient and rich/poor by interpreting them in light of a material social context in which most early Christians lived economically marginal lives.

I have shown that the model of almsgiving to address poverty could be embraced and practiced by Christians who lived near or at subsistence level. In these cases, almsgiving would function more like mutual assistance, insofar as a person might be a recipient at one time and an almsgiver at another.

Nonetheless, the model does not lend itself to a critique of economic differences. That is, even when almsgiving is legible as potentially mutual and when the poor can be interpreted as agents of charity, this does not mean that these practices in themselves embody radical critiques of economic difference. The active/passive division between giver and receiver in the almsgiving model more frequently has been used to justify and sustain economic divisions within Christian communities, rather than to serve as a basis to critique them as unjust. Further attention to submerged alternative approaches to economic difference within the Christian tradition is needed.

3

JAMES 2:2–7
IN EARLY CHRISTIAN THOUGHT

GÖRGE K. HASSELHOFF

To understand the reception and interpretation of James 2:2–7 in early Christian thought, it might be helpful to see what James has written and what the crucial points of this text are. The passage in question reads in the translation of Luke Timothy Johnson as follows:

> For if a man with gold rings and splendid clothing enters your assembly, and also a poor man dressed in filthy clothing, and you look favorably on the one wearing splendid clothing and say to him, "you sit here in a fine place," while you also say to the poor person, "you stand there, or sit below my footrest," are you not divided within yourselves and have you not become judges with evil designs? Listen, my beloved brothers! Has not God chosen the poor in the world to be rich in faith and heirs of the kingdom which he has promised to those who love him? But you have dishonored the poor person! Is it not the rich who oppress you and are they not the very ones who are dragging you into courts? Are they not the very ones blaspheming the noble name which has been invoked over you?[1]

---

1. Luke Timothy Johnson, trans., *The Letter of James: A New Translation with Introduction and Commentary*, AB 37A (New York: Doubleday, 1995), 220. All remaining translations in this essay are mine unless otherwise indicated.

The Letter of James is one of the seven "catholic" letters of the New Testament. It is not clear when the letter was written, but it seems quite obvious that it owes much to the early Jewish wisdom literature.[2]

The main point in the author's argumentation, be it James the Lord's brother or some anonymous James,[3] is that he objects to the social preference of rich people in the congregation. This position is clearly stated in 2:5: "Has not God chosen the poor in the world to be rich in faith and to be heirs of the kingdom that he has promised to those who love him?"

What influenced this early Christian strong opposition to wealth? According to recent commentators and writers on James,[4] the letter was not universally accepted as part of the New Testament canon in the ancient Christian world. The first of the Latin writers to comment on the letter as a whole was Bede the Venerable. So I first turn to Bede's commentary, which was completed around 715.[5]

Bede the Venerable's Commentary on James

Bede's commentary does not tell us *why* he wrote on the Letter of James. We do know that he wrote on all seven catholic letters and that he started that particular series with his commentary on James. The translator of the German translation, Matthias Karsten, suggests that Bede wrote for his fellow

2. Roy Bowen Ward, "Partiality in the Assembly: James 2:2–4," *HTR* 62 (1969): 87–97, esp. 89–95; Johnson, *Letter of James*, 34–46; Matthias Konrad, *Christliche Existenz nach dem Jakobusbrief: Eine Studie zu seiner soteriologischen und ethischen Konzeption*, SUNT 22 (Göttingen: Vandenhoeck & Ruprecht, 1998), 135–45; Christoph Burchard, *Der Jakobusbrief*, HNT, vol. 15, no. 1 (Tübingen: Mohr, 2000). See also Rinaldo Fabris, *Legge della libertà in Giacomo*, Supplementi alla Rivista Biblica 8 (Brescia: Paideia, 1977). Fabris's interest is, however, the explanation of James 2:12, and therefore his interpretation of James 2:2–7 is rather to show its relevance for the "law of freedom."

3. In addition to the commentaries on James, see Max Meinertz, *Der Jakobusbrief und sein Verfasser in Schrift und Überlieferung*, BibS(F), vol. 10, nos. 1–3 (Freiburg: Herder, 1905); Joseph B. Mayor, *The Epistle of St. James: The Greek Text with Introduction, Notes, and Comments and Further Studies in the Epistle of St. James* (London: Macmillan, 1913), esp. lxvi–lxxxiv; Arnold Meyer, *Das Rätsel des Jakobusbriefes*, BZNW 10 (Giessen: Alfred Töpelmann, 1930), esp. 8–108; and Wilhelm Pratscher, *Der Herrenbruder Jakobus und die Jakobustradition*, FRLANT 139 (Göttingen: Vandenhoeck & Ruprecht, 1987).

4. See François Vouga, *L'Épître de Saint Jacques*, CNT 2ᵉ série 13a (Genève: Labor et Fides, 1984), 33–34; Hubert Frankemölle, *Der Brief des Jakobus: Kapitel 1*, Ökumenischer Taschenbuchkommentar zum Neuen Testament, vol. 17, no. 1 (Gütersloh: GVH, 1994), 94–105; Johnson, *Letter of James*, 124–40; Burchard, *Jakobusbrief*, 26–30.

5. I follow the Latin text in *Beda Venerabilis Opera, Pars II Opera Exegetica 4: Expositio Actvvm Apostolorum, etc.*, ed. D. Hurst, CCSL 121:179–342 (*In Epistolas Septem Catholicas*, ed. David Hurst). Translations are those of D. Hurst, ed., Bede the Venerable, *Commentary on the Seven Catholic Epistles*, Cistercian Studies Series 82 (Kalamazoo, MI: Cistercian Publications, 1985); and Matthias Karsten, ed., *Beda Venerabilis, In Epistulam Iacobi Expositio—Kommentar zum Jakobusbrief*, Fontes Christiani 40 (Freiburg: Herder, 2000).

brethren in St. Paul in Jarrow.[6] According to Karsten, Bede's main interest was to explain who the "right teachers" are.[7] From Bede's prologue to the commentary we know that he was aware that Athanasius had written on the seven catholic letters.[8]

In the commentary itself, Bede explains James verse by verse. He does so with the help of scriptural references and explanations he found in the works of the fathers. Among the authorities he quotes are Jerome (*Adversus Iovinianum*; ad 1:14), Augustine (*Ep.* 167, ad 2:2. 10sqq.), Pope Innocent I (*Ep. 25 Ad Decentium*, ad 5:14–15), and Plinius, whom Bede calls Marcellinus Comes (ad 3:7). Needless to say, none of them had written a commentary on James that survives complete today.

On the verses in question, Bede's commentary is less original than his comments on other passages of the letter. Whereas Bede formulates his comments on verse 1 in his own words, for his explanation of verses 2–3 he refers to Augustine without giving his exact source. He states only that Augustine explained James's words that he, Bede, will now use:

> In the explanation of this thought let us use the words of blessed Augustine: If we apply (he says of this) a distinction between sitting and standing to church honors, it must not be considered a light sin to have the faith of our Lord Jesus Christ, the Lord of glory, while showing favoritism to individuals. For who would put up with having a rich man chosen to a place of honor in the Church when a poor man, more learned and holier, is rejected? If, however, it is a question of everyday seatings, who does not sin here, if indeed he sins, whenever he so judges within himself that that man appears to him better the richer he is.[9]

This explanation equates James's words with the ecclesiastical hierarchy in which it is regarded as a sin to acknowledge only the wealth of a person in church and to conclude wrongly by his or her wealth that the person is not a sinner. A poor person may, perhaps, be better educated and holier (*instructior atque sanctior*). The sin is that of making an internal judgment, namely, a judgment that someone who appears rich is also better. This interpretation follows from verse 4, which is not interpreted on its own. Concerning verse 5, Bede goes on to explain what is meant by the term "poor people" (*pauperes*).

> By the poor he means the humble and those who because of their disregard for visible things but because of their faith in invisible riches appear contemptible

6. Karsten, *Beda Venerabilis*, 34, 47–48.

7. Cf. Karsten, *Beda Venerabilis*, 56.

8. *Denique multi scriptorum ecclesiasticorum, in quibus est sanctus Athanasius Alexandrine presul ecclesie*; ed. D. Hurst, 181. On (Pseudo?) Athanasius, see below (n. 25).

9. Beda Venerabilis, *In epistulam Iacobi expositio*, ad 2.2–3 (CCSL 121:193–94), trans. Hurst, *Commentary on the Seven Catholic Epistles*, 22.

to this world. For *God,* our Lord Jesus Christ, *has chosen* such as these by say-ing, *Do not fear, little flock, because it has been pleasing to your Father to give you the kingdom* [Luke 12:32]. He chose such as these when he created poor parents for himself, by whose devotion he might be brought up on coming into the world, but nevertheless he made them famous and noble because of their anticipation of the future kingdom.[10]

In commenting on verse 7, Bede characterizes the rich (*divites*).

Here he shows more clearly who are the rich, whose humiliation and de-struction he had discussed above [James 1:10–11], those undoubtedly who prefer their riches to Christ, and further, separated from faith in him, also oppress with their power those who believe, dragging them to judgments of the more powerful and blaspheming the *name* of Christ which is *above every name* [Phil. 2:9]. That quite a few of the leading men both of the gen-tiles and particularly of the Jews did this in the apostles' time is sufficiently clearly shown both in the Acts of the same apostles and in the Letters of the apostle Paul.[11]

Concerning the rich and the poor, Bede's explanation might be summa-rized as follows: The rich are, in fact, poor people who prefer the wealth of faith to the wealth of the world, whereas the poor are those who prefer the wealth of the world and who prefer to treat believers in an atheistic and blas-phemous manner. Examples of both groups can be found in Holy Scripture, but those who are rightly rich people are all those who have lived as sincere and humble Christians.

Bede's Predecessors on the Letter of James

Bede did not rely on any commentary on the Letter of James known to us today. We know by his quotation from Augustine that he read at least *Ep.* 167, which Augustine wrote to Jerome and which is a sort of commentary on James 2:10.[12] In two places in this letter, Augustine comments on verse 3. Augustine is attempting to answer the question of how one should under-

10. Beda Venerabilis, *In epistulam Iacobi expositio,* ad 2.5 (CCSL 121:194), trans. Hurst, *Com-mentary on the Seven Catholic Epistles,* 23.
11. Beda Venerabilis, *In epistulam Iacobi expositio,* ad 2.7 (CCSL 121:194), trans. Hurst, *Com-mentary on the Seven Catholic Epistles,* 23–24.
12. Augustine writes in his second autobiography that he wrote a commentary on the Letter of James (see *Retract.* 2.32 (58), ed. Almut Mutzenbecher [CCSL 57:116]). Since this exposition is not preserved it remains uncertain whether Bede might have known it. George Lawless suggests that Augustine might have referred to his treatise *De fidei et operibus,* ed. Zycha, CSEL 41:33–97. On Augustine and the Letter of James, see also Paulus Bergauer, *Der Jakobusbrief bei Augustinus und die damit verbundenen Probleme der Rechtfertigungslehre* (Vienna: Herder, 1962).

stand the phrase, "For whoever undertakes keeping the entire law, yet fails in one thing, has become accountable for them all."[13] Does this mean that the value of a failure (or sin) is the same whether someone commits a theft or says to a rich person, "Sit here," or to a poor person, "You stay there"? Is this person also guilty of homicide, adultery, or idolatry? If not, what then is the meaning of verse 10? Augustine suggests that James's remarks on rich and poor people ought to be understood from their context within the letter.[14] Thus he quotes the first six verses and, after a short connecting remark, verses 6–9.

Augustine's words are a kind of *scriptura scripturam interpretans*. After the lengthy passage of the Scripture that interprets itself, Augustine starts with the remark, *"Videte!"* another attempt to explain verse 3. For him the contextual reading demonstrated that the lawbreakers (*transgressores*) are those who say to a rich person, "Sit here," and to a poor person, "Stand there." Lest they think it a trivial (or contemptuous?) sin (*contemptibile peccatum*) to break the law in this one matter, James goes on to say, "For whoever undertakes keeping the entire law," and so on. As long as no other interpretation of the passage can be demonstrated, Augustine concludes, breaking the law in a minor matter demonstrates that this person also breaks the law on a larger scale. The full text of Augustine's *Ep.* 167.3 reads:

> How, then, I ask you, are we to understand, "Whoever has observed the whole law, but offends on one point, has become guilty of all"? Is a person who commits theft, or even someone who says to a rich man, "Sit here," but to a poor man, "You, stand over there" [James 2:3] also guilty of murder, adultery, and sacrilege? But if he is not, how has someone who offends on one point become guilty of all? Or does what I mentioned about the rich man and the poor man not belong among those points on which, if one offends on any of them, he will become guilty of all? But we must remember the source of this statement and the ones that preceded and led up to it, on which it is dependent. It says, "My brothers, do not . . ." [etc., James 2:1–6]. See how it calls transgressors of the law those who say to the rich man, "Sit here," and to the poor man, "Stand there." And so that they would not think that it is a sin of no significance to transgress the law on this one point, it goes on and adds, "But whoever observes the whole law, but offends on one point, has become guilty of all. For he who said, You shall not commit adultery, also said, You shall not kill. If you do not kill, but commit adultery, you have become a transgressor of the law" on account of what it had said, "You are convicted by the law as transgressors." Since this is so, it seems to follow (unless one shows that it should be interpreted otherwise) that the person who said to the rich man, "Sit here," and to the poor man, "Stand there," offering more respect to

13. James 2:10 translation, Johnson, *Letter of James*, 220.
14. This attempt in itself looks quite "modern"; today it is called contextual interpretation.

the former than to the latter, should be judged an idolater, a blasphemer, an adulterer, a murderer and—not to mention all of these, which would take a long time—guilty of all serious sins, for by offending on one point he has become guilty of all.[15]

In other words, Augustine explains verse 10 ("For whoever undertakes keeping the entire law, etc.") within the context of chapter 2; he shows that by introducing the example of the rich man and the poor man, James was hinting at the general problem of breaking the law by inferring the principle of "minor" or "major" transgressions.

Augustine goes on to interpret James 2:10 in a philosophical manner, coming back to verse 3 toward the end of his letter. Here Augustine suggests an interpretation that is no longer contextual but metaphorical. He looks at the ecclesiastical hierarchy. He criticizes not the hierarchy itself but rather how members of the ecclesiastical hierarchy are selected for their posts. A person ought to be chosen not for his wealth but according to skills, even if he is the (economically) poorer candidate. And even if the scriptural passage concerns daily life, it shows that everyone is a sinner when his internal or unspoken judgment prefers the rich or wealthy person to the poor person. And that is exactly the point James had in mind when writing verse 4, "have you not . . . become judges with evil thoughts?"[16]

As noted above, Bede adopts this latter interpretation. Although it appears that Bede used only Augustine's letter to Jerome as a patristic source for his commentary on James 2, there are several other interpretations he might have used if he could have read Greek.

The Greek *catenae*, collected in the eighth century (or later), as well as other sources, tell us that a number of commentaries on James were available.[17] Two of these, lost to us today, included those of Clement of Alexandria and Origen.[18] The oldest fragments preserved in the Greek *catenae*[19] are

15. Augustinus, *Ep.* 167, ed. A. Goldbacher, CSEL 44:589, 590–91; *Letters 156–210*, trans. Roland Teske, The Works of Saint Augustine: A Translation for the 21st Century, part 2, vol. 3 (Hyde Park, NY: New City Press, 2004), 96–97. Thanks to Susan R. Holman, who checked the translation for me.

16. For the Latin text, see Augustinus, *Ep.* 167, CSEL 44:605–6, ed. Goldbacher.

17. On the *catenae*, see Karl Staab, "Die griechischen Katenenkommentare zu den katholischen Briefen," *Biblica* 5 (1924): 296–353; Hubertus R. Drobner, *The Fathers of the Church: A Comprehensive Introduction*, trans. S. S. Schatzmann (Peabody, MA: Hendrickson, 2007), 530–32.

18. According to Berthold Altaner and Alfred Stuiber, *Patrologie: Leben, Schriften und Lehre der Kirchenväter* (Freiburg: Herder, 1978), 201–2, there has never been any commentary on James by Origen. Drobner, *Fathers*, 140–43, seems to follow their position.

19. For the Letter of James I refer to *Catenæ Græcorum Patrum in Novum Testamentum, vol. 8: In epistolas catholicas et apocalypsin*, ed. J. A. Cramer (Oxford: Oxford University Press, 1844), 1ff. Nonetheless, its worth in some cases is quite doubtful; e.g., the "explanation" of 2.7 (p. 11) by Apollinarius reads more like an excerpt from another, lost treatise than from a commentary on the Letter of James. See also below on John Chrysostom and Burchard, *Jakobusbrief*, 28: "schlecht herausgegeben" ("badly edited").

by Didymus the Blind (313–398) and include his commentary on James 2:26.[20]

John Chrysostom may have provided another Greek source.[21] The *catena* preserves a comment on verse 4[22] that is attributed to him, but it remains doubtful whether he is the author of this passage. Here we read that in Christ there is neither rich nor poor, therefore people should be judged not according to their appearance but according to their internal faith. This interpretation is extended on verses 5–6 and 6–7.[23]

Hesychios of Jerusalem (d. after 450) is a third Greek writer who wrote on James. Of his comments on chapter 2, only that on verse 13 is preserved.[24] Two additional authors might be (Ps.-?) Athanasius (296–373) and Euthalius the Deacon (mid-fifth century), who both wrote a summary of the letter.[25] It may be that Athanasian summary to which Bede refers in his commentary's prologue.

The *Shepherd of Hermas* also made use of James. However, it appears that no reference to the *Shepherd* survives in any of the early commentaries on the Letter of James.[26]

Conclusion

In summary, as Bede read James, those who are truly rich are the ones who prefer the wealth of faith to the wealth of the world. And those who are truly poor prefer the wealth of the world and the atheistic and blasphemous way of treating believers. It appears that Bede took his ideas, at least in part, from Augustine's letter to Jerome (*Ep.* 167). For Augustine, the main point is that the example of the rich and the poor reveals yet another truth: that all are sinners because even in minor aspects all tend to act against the law.

Whereas the majority of early Christian literature until the fifth century does not include comments on James, we do know of Greek commentaries that survive in fragments. But only in the fragments of a commentary attributed

20. See *Didymi Alexandrini in Epistolam Beati Jacobi Apostoli brevis enarratio* (PG 39:1752B–C; preserved only in Latin translation).

21. On Chrysostom, see Rudolf Brändle, *John Chrysostom: Bishop, Reformer, Martyr*, trans. John Cawte and Silke Trzcionka, rev. notes by Wendy Mayer, Early Christian Studies 8 (Strathfield, UK: St. Pauls, 2004).

22. Cramer, *Catenae*, 10, 8–12; (Ps.?) *Johannes Chrysostomi Fragmenta in Epistolas Catholicas* (PG 64:1041D).

23. Cramer, *Catenae*, 10, 17–11, 10; PG 64:1041D–44C. A question for further research is whether Chrysostom, if he was the writer of that particular passage, might have influenced Augustine, or whether both had a common source.

24. Cramer, *Catenae*, 13, 11–4; *Fragmenta in Epistolam I [sic] S. Jacobi* (PG 93:1389B).

25. Athanasius: PG 28:405–8 (n. 52, 20 lines); Euthalius: PG 85:676C–7A (20 lines).

26. See Johnson, *Letter of James*, 75–80. It remains to be discussed whether Hermas actually read the Letter of James or whether he made use of similar sources.

to John Chrysostom do we find remarks on the rich and the poor that are interpreted in a manner similar to that of Bede and Augustine, namely, that real wealth is the true faith.

As other scholars have argued, these interpretations may suggest why it appears that it was difficult for early Christians to receive and accept this letter. Apart from writers of the "Alexandrian" school of exegesis, there were very few references to, or even commentaries on, the letter. This is usually explained by suggesting either that the identity of the author is doubtful—was he the Lord's brother?—or that his radical interpretation of the law as it concerns the deeds of believers was too difficult to accept. Was James's (implied) social criticism such a powerful influence? Does its radical critique of wealth—which ought to be opposed by true faith expressed by ethically good behavior—explain the limits of its reception? The question remains open for further study.

4

WEALTH, POVERTY, AND THE VALUE OF THE PERSON

Some Notes on the Hymn of the Pearl and Its Early Christian Context

EDWARD MOORE

The survival of Christianity in its early days depended on the aid of wealthy benefactors.[1] So Christ's exhortation to abandon all worldly possessions and follow him became rather problematic.[2] The wealthy man described in Luke 18:22–23, who could not bring himself to abandon his fortune and follow

1. See P. A. Harland, "Connections with Elites in the World of the Early Christians," in *Handbook of Early Christianity: Social Science Approaches*, ed. A. J. Blasi, J. Duhaime, and P.-A. Turcotte (Walnut Creek, CA: AltaMira Press, 2002).

2. Mark 10:21–31; Luke 12:22–31. John A. McGuckin, *The Westminster Handbook to Patristic Theology* (Louisville: Westminster John Knox Press, 2004), 360: "The Hellenistic trend to interpret literature allegorically made for a progressively 'spiritual' approach to Jesus' difficult commandments, especially when they refer to wealth and possession. One of the first examples of such an allegorizing approach appears in the evangelist's symbolical retelling of Jesus' parable of the Sower and the Seed in Mark 4. The allegorical retelling of the editor (Mark 4:13–20, as distinct from the original parable of Jesus, Mark 4:2–9) adds in the detail that the thorns that choke faith are the 'cares of the world, and the lure of wealth.' Here we see the Gospel story being reapplied for an increasingly affluent city church in the late first century."

Jesus, came to be seen as the archetypal example of unreasoning attachment to material existence, and was contrasted with the wealthy merchant who sold all he had to purchase the "pearl of great price," that is, the kingdom of heaven.[3] In the Christian gnostic *Hymn of the Pearl*[4] we find a beautiful allegory of the tension abiding between the opposing lures of material and spiritual wealth—that is, between attachment to corruptible possessions and the fluctuating fortunes of worldly life, and the knowledge of incorruptible, eternal spiritual wisdom, and one's home on high.

Hellenistic philosophers—whether Stoic, Platonic, Pythagorean, or even Epicurean—agreed on one thing: that the greatest good a human can acquire is intellectual, not material.[5] One's status in this Hellenistic world depended more on one's intellectual acumen and quality of soul than on one's material prosperity, or lack thereof.[6] However, as W. W. Tarn writes, "pity for the poor had little place in the normal Greek character."[7] The belief that poverty is a result of a curse from the gods, or the activity of a malevolent demon, went back to archaic Greece,[8] as did the consequent idea that the poor are unworthy of any "attention, solace, or compassion."[9] Christ's message in the Gospels, however, is very clear: charity toward the poor and the relinquishing of one's worldly possessions are prerequisites for salvation. Yet one finds already in the New Testament evidence of the difficulty inherent in the practical application of this injunction (e.g., James 2:1–8). In this essay, I examine the theme of the lure of poverty (worldly, illusory "wealth") and the promise of true wealth (salvation in the kingdom of heaven) as allegorized in the *Hymn*

3. Matt. 13:45–46; *Gospel of Thomas* 76.

4. Bentley Layton, *The Gnostic Scriptures* (New York: Doubleday, 1987), 366, notes that the *Hymn of the Pearl* "presents a Hellenistic myth of the soul's entry into bodily incarnation and its eventual disengagement from the body [and] does not directly demand a religious response from its reader, for it is a general description of salvation." This work survives in Greek and Syriac manuscripts of the *Acts of Thomas*, though scholars are uncertain whether it is an original feature of the Acts, or a later addition. Hans Jonas, *The Gnostic Religion*, 3rd ed. (Boston: Beacon Press, 2001), 112, classifies the *Hymn* as an example of Iranian gnostic literature. Such classifications have come into question recently, along with the designation "gnostic(ism)" itself. See Michael Allen Williams, *Rethinking "Gnosticism": An Argument for Dismantling a Dubious Category* (Princeton, NJ: Princeton University Press, 1996); and Karen L. King, *What Is Gnosticism?* (Cambridge, MA: Harvard University Press, 2003). My designation of the work as "Christian gnostic" is based on its inclusion in an apocryphal Christian text, its mythical and allegorical character, and its theme of lost and recovered knowledge (γνῶσις).

5. One of the earliest expressions of this Greek ideal is found in Heraclitus (fragment B 108, Diels-Kranz), trans. Jonathan Barnes, *Early Greek Philosophy* (New York: Penguin, 1987), 109: "Of those whose accounts I have heard, no-one has come so far as to recognize that the wise is set apart from all things."

6. See Jonas, *Gnostic Religion*, 5–6.

7. W. W. Tarn, *Hellenistic Civilization* (New York: Plume, 1974), 110.

8. See E. R. Dodds, *The Greeks and the Irrational* (Berkeley: University of California Press, 1951), 28–50.

9. McGuckin, *Westminster Handbook*, 359.

of the Pearl.[10] Also, using the later, Neoplatonic-influenced schema of the Valentinian gnostic text *The Tripartite Tractate* as an example, I consider the reaction of some early Christian theologians to the problem of wealth and poverty in a larger eschatological context, specifically relating to the value of the *person* as potentially divine.

Allegorizing Wealth and Poverty: *Hymn of the Pearl*

The basic scheme of the *Hymn of the Pearl* is a myth of lost and recovered wealth, involving a pearl of great value, properly allegorized as knowledge (*gnōsis*) of one's divine origin and status. Wealth is, in this text, identified with intellectual recognition of the soul's primordial origin in the Godhead. Poverty is ignorance of the soul's divine status. "I did not (any longer) recognize that I was a child of the (Great) King,[11] but rather acted as a servant to their [the Egyptians'] king."[12] Recognition of one's divine provenance, brought about by a call to awareness from the divine realm, then draws the soul toward remembrance of its origin, and to salvation.

> Remember that you are a child of kings.
> You have fallen under a servile yoke.
> Call to mind[13] your garment shot with gold.
> Call to mind the pearl for which you were sent on the mission to
> Egypt.
> Your name has been called [to] the book of life.[14] (*HPrl* 110, verses
> 44–47)

Poverty, the "servile yoke," here denotes not lack of material wealth but the ontological status of a soul that has lost and forgotten its true wealth. The wealth in question, of course, is not temporal or worldly wealth but the promised eschatological wealth of a soul embroiled in history and seeking repose.

The young prince who travels, at the bidding of his father, in search of the pearl of great price to the land of exile (Egypt), where it is hidden, reveals the consciousness of humanity's general lack of fulfillment with material wealth.

---

10. Layton, *Gnostic Scriptures*, 366: "For the most part, the myth of salvation is not expressed literally in [*Hymn of the Pearl*] but, rather, is hidden behind a figurative fairy tale or folktale. To perceive the myth, an ancient reader would have needed to reinterpret the tale allegorically."

11. ἠγνόησα ἐμαυτὸν υἱὸν ὄντα βασιλέως.

12. *Hymn of the Pearl* (Greek) 109:33. All quotations of the *Hymn* in this essay are from Layton's translation in *Gnostic Scriptures*, 371–75, and will henceforth be abbreviated as *HPrl* with Greek paragraph number(s) followed by the traditional Syriac version verse numbers. I have consulted the Greek version, *L'hymne de la Perle des Actes de Thomas*, ed. Paul-Hubert Poirier, Homo religiosus 8 (Louvain-la-Neuve: P. Pierier, 1981), 352–56.

13. μνημόνευσον.

14. ἐκλήθη δὲ τὸ ὄνομά σου βιβλίον ζωῆς.

Our longing for something more, something that will complete our spiritual journey, is expressed in the *Hymn of the Pearl* as the reunion of the prince (bearing the pearl, that is, Wisdom, and wearing the robe of his inheritance, that is, salvation) with his father, the king (Christ).

> Once I had put it [the robe] on, I arose into the realm of peace belonging to reverential awe.
> And I bowed my head and prostrated myself before the splendor of the father who had sent it to me.
> For, it was I who had done his commands,
> And likewise it was he who had kept his promise. (*HPrl* 113, verses 98–100)

The recovery of the pearl from the land of Egypt (allegorized as the realm of darkness and matter) signifies the recovery of the prince's inheritance. This inheritance is the spark of divine power he lost when he became enamored of material existence and forgot his home on high, the *plērōma*.

> They [the Egyptians] gave me a mixture of cunning and treachery, and I tasted their food. . . .
> And I even came to the pearl for which my parents had sent me on the mission
> But sank into deep sleep under the heaviness of their food. (*HPrl* 109, verses 32, 34–35)

We find here a mythological expression of what the Christian gnostics regarded as a universal truth: that all souls have lost their pearl, that is, their knowledge of the *plērōma*, and will achieve salvation only if they manage to recover this pearl of wisdom.[15] The one who recovers this wisdom is the wealthy man; the one who fails to recover it remains in poverty, that is, enthralled to darkness and matter, and will not be permitted to return to the realm of the blessed.

However, in the later and more developed gnostic schemas the ability to recover the pearl of wisdom had little to do with free will and personal choice, that is, the decision to respond, or not, to the call of awakening from the heavenly realm, but rather involved one's ontological status. The tripartite distinction of pneumatics, psychics, and hylics was based not on any notion of the value of material wealth and the degree of one's attachment to it, but rather on a mythopoetical schema in which certain souls were said to be saved by nature, others possibly saved (based on their actions), and finally the last, the "material"

---

15. See Kurt Rudolph, *Gnosis: The Nature and History of Gnosticism* (Edinburgh: T & T Clark, 1984), 113–17.

ones damned by nature.[16] The respective natures and fates of the "three races" is summed up in the Valentinian *Tripartite Tractate* as follows:

> The spiritual race will receive complete salvation in every way. The material will receive destruction in every way, just as one who resists him [the Logos, the savior]. The psychic race, since it is in the middle when it is brought forth and also when it is created, is double according to its determination for both good and evil.[17]

The unconditional promise of divine wealth belongs solely to the spiritual race, while the material race remains destitute, destined for destruction regardless of their actions. Only the psychic race possesses some measure of freedom and self-determination. However, in all three cases, the ontological status of souls is seen as the result of a cosmic drama having no connection to their existentiality or, in gnostic terms, cosmic life. We shall now turn to a brief discussion of the ethical import of this Christian gnostic schema, and why it was eventually rejected by the emerging Orthodox church.

Wealth, Poverty, and the Person

In the development of Christian dogma, the importance of human freedom came to the fore. Life ceased to be understood in terms of a preestablished "game plan"; rather, it began to be seen as an expression of humanity's deep desire for salvation. Humanity spoke, but its voice was nearly lost in the morass of souls vying for an expression of their historical experience. Humanity wanted to speak about itself but had not yet developed the terminology necessary to do so. Within the intellectual milieu of Hellenistic-Roman culture, the concept of the person as a unique, unrepeatable entity (*hypostasis*), rather than a functional identity (*prosōpon*), having meaning only within a sociopolitical or—as in the case of Stoicism—divinely instituted order, had not yet arisen. It was only later, in the age of the ecumenical councils, that a rigorous definition of the human person was established.[18] The reason for this, according to some Christians, was that humans had fallen into a world-centered existence, capable of expressing their existence only in and by the language and "wisdom" of the world—that is, through philosophy.

Paul's seeming denunciation of philosophy (Col. 2:8) was not an outright rejection of reflective thought; rather, it was a powerful critique of reliance

---

16. See Giovanni Filoramo, *A History of Gnosticism* (Cambridge, MA: Basil Blackwell, 1990), 56–57, 128–30.

17. *The Tripartite Tractate* (NHC I,5), 119:15–25, trans. Harold W. Attridge and Dieter Mueller, in *The Nag Hammadi Library in English*, ed. James M. Robinson (Leiden: Brill, 1978), 95.

18. See John D. Zizioulas, *Being as Communion: Studies in Personhood and the Church* (Crestwood, NY: St. Vladimir's Seminary Press, 1985), 27–65.

on human wisdom at the expense of divine wisdom, on the fruit of unaided intellectual labor, as opposed to divine revelation. Let us recall Paul's wondrous experience of the ineffable mysteries of the "third heaven":

> I know a person in Christ who fourteen years ago was caught up to the third heaven—whether in the body or out of the body I do not know; God knows. And I know that such a person—whether in the body or out of the body I do not know; God knows—was caught up into Paradise and heard things that are not to be told, that no mortal is permitted to repeat. (2 Cor. 12:2–4)

This is the experience of one eschewing worldly wealth in favor of spiritual wealth, involving mysteries beyond comprehension. The uncertainty and limitations attendant on this experience—that is, not knowing whether it was embodied or unembodied, the inability to express the mystical words, and so on—pale in comparison to the transformative revelation of paradise, which causes Paul to glory even in his infirmities (2 Cor. 12:9). The certainty of philosophical or worldly knowledge is no knowledge at all, just as worldly wealth is not true wealth, for both are destined to pass away. The promise of wealth is properly understood as a call to transcendence—of the body, the "certainty" of worldly knowledge, and so on. Paul's attitude toward philosophy did not imply a rejection of wisdom, for Christ the incarnate Logos was the manifestation of divine wisdom in a human, making possible the transformation of the human from a poverty-stricken, material existence to a wealthy, spiritual existence manifesting the image and likeness of God in creation.

Plato, writing long before Paul, defined the goal of human existence as achieving likeness to God as far as possible.[19] Later philosophers, both pagan and Christian, understood this goal as involving a training of the mind (*nous*) toward divine things, thereby regaining one's true nature as an intellectual being akin to God.[20] In our present mode of existence we are divided between worldly and spiritual life; salvation is the union of these modes in a human-divine coexistence, in which we find our "whole self." As the young prince in the *Hymn of the Pearl* exclaims after beholding the garment of his salvation, which he had left behind in his father's palace, that is, in the heavenly kingdom of his origin:

> . . . when suddenly I saw my garment reflected as in a mirror,
> I perceived in it my whole self as well.
> And through it I recognized and saw myself.
> For, though we derived from one and the same we were partially divided; and

19. ὁμοίωσις θεῷ κατὰ τὸ δυνατόν. Plato, *Theaetetus* 176b.

20. See, for example, Plotinus, *Enneades* 4.8.4.1–7, and Gregory Nazianzen, *Oration* 28 (*De theologia*) 3.3–10.

then again we were one, with a single form.[21] (*HPrl* 112, verses 76–78)

This idea of a reunification of the lower, material aspect of our nature with the higher, spiritual state of existence was essential for the development of orthodox *theōsis* ("deification") doctrine in the writings of Gregory Nazianzen, Gregory of Nyssa, and especially Maximus the Confessor.[22]

However, it would be wrong to think that the dialectic of wealth and poverty was carried out only in "mystical" or metaphysical terms. Practical concerns regarding the well-being of the poor and the responsibility of well-to-do Christians to look after their less fortunate neighbors were inextricably bound up with eschatological concerns.

Clement of Alexandria devoted an entire treatise, *Quis dives salvetur?* (discussed at length in chapter 5 in this volume) to the problem of Christian attitudes toward wealth and poverty and the ethical implications of these attitudes. According to Clement, the value of a human was to be judged not on the basis of that person's status in society, but rather within a historically minded schema inclusive of creative individuals who are shaping history in their quest for salvation. Clement did not advocate the radical renunciation of worldly wealth, as apparently called for in certain sayings of Jesus, but rather recognized the importance of a modest income for the general social welfare—provided, of course, that the poor were given the necessary aid for survival. Gregory Nazianzen, in his Oration 14, *De pauperum amore* (PG 35:857–909), also devoted himself to the task of addressing the problem of wealth and poverty within the confines of his world. According to Gregory, wealthy Christians are obligated to provide for their less-fortunate neighbors. McGuckin explains that, for Gregory,

> the poor person is de facto the image of God, intrinsically equal to all other human beings and worthy of care. Even if all the rest of human society cannot see the connection between poverty and merit (the poor man was deservedly so for most Greek society as one who had been cursed by the gods), nevertheless the Christians must begin to see and make that connection. The Christian philanthropist who supports the helpless poor, Gregory argues, at that instant acts like God (mercifully and philanthropically) and demonstrates the perfect example of true discipleship.[23]

---

21. μορφῆς μιᾶς.

22. For recent discussions of these three theologians, see Torstein Theodor Tollefsen, "*Theōsis* according to Gregory," in *Gregory of Nazianzus: Images and Reflections*, ed. J. Børtnes and T. Hägg (Copenhagen: Museum Tusculanum, 2006), 257–70; Hubertus R. Drobner, "Gregory of Nyssa as Philosopher: *De anima et resurrectione* and *De hominis opificio*," *Dionysius* 18 (2000): 69–101; Edward Moore, *Origen of Alexandria and St. Maximus the Confessor: An Analysis and Critical Evaluation of Their Eschatological Doctrines* (Boca Raton, FL: Universal Publishers, 2005), 74–97, 142–69.

23. McGuckin, *Westminster Handbook*, 361.

We find here a sociological and eschatological, not a metaphysical, distinction: people were defined no longer in terms of their supposed primordial ontological status but rather in terms of their status as potentially divine souls striving by their actions to return to their divine home with Christ and realize their likeness to God. As Maximus the Confessor writes in his *Chapters on Knowledge*:

> There is no rational soul which is by essence more valuable than another rational soul. Indeed, God in his goodness, creating every soul to his image, brings it into being to be self-moving. Each one, then, deliberately either chooses honor or accepts dishonor by its own deeds. (1.11)[24]

The tendency of the gnostics to value humans on the basis of their status as souls who live a predetermined existence, destined for either salvation or damnation and lacking true freedom of will, was rejected by emerging orthodoxy in favor of a concept of the person involving a self-perception of one's unique, unrepeatable historical existence in God's created realm.

Poverty became defined as ignorance, that is, as a lack of knowledge of one's homeland. Wealth became defined as knowledge of one's homeland. The greatest aspiration of humanity was seen as the actualization in history of the image and likeness of God—in short, the purpose for which we were placed here. In his *Oratio catechetica magna*, Gregory of Nyssa describes our original condition, as intended by God—which is also our eschatological state—as follows:

> Empowered by God's blessing, man held a lofty position. He was appointed to rule over the earth and all the creatures on it. His form was beautiful, for he was created as the image of the archetypal beauty.[25] By nature he was free from passion, for he was a copy of Him who is without passion. He was full of candor, reveling in the direct vision of God.[26] (6.104–11)[27]

Poverty is lack of this transformative vision of God. Wealth is living a life of wonder, knowing that God's love pervades all things and that we, like the prince in the *Hymn of the Pearl*, are on a journey to our Father's kingdom. In this we discover the glory of our humanity.

24. George C. Berthold, trans., *Maximus Confessor: Selected Writings* (Mahwah, NJ: Paulist Press, 1985), 130. For the Greek original, see PG 90.1087.

25. ἀπεικόνισμα γὰρ τοῦ ἀρχετύπου ἐγεγόνει κάλλους.

26. αὐτῆς κατὰ πρόσωπον τῆς θείας ἐμφανείας κατατρυφῶν.

27. Cyril C. Richardson, trans., "Address on Religious Instruction," in *Christology of the Later Fathers*, ed. E. R. Hardy (Philadelphia: Westminster Press, 1954), 280. For the Greek, see also J. Srawley, *The Catechetical Oration of Gregory of Nyssa* (Cambridge: Cambridge University Press, 1903).

TWO

EGYPT
IN LATE
ANTIQUITY

5

WIDENING THE EYE OF THE NEEDLE

Wealth and Poverty in the Works of Clement of Alexandria

ANNEWIES VAN DEN HOEK

When Augustine reflected back after many years on his conversion to Christianity and his renunciation of a public career and a lucrative marriage, he described and perhaps justified this change of course not only in highly emotional but also in highly rhetorical terms. One of the elements in his account—the famous garden scene in Milan (*Conf.* 8.6.14)—comes from an encounter he had with a fellow African shortly before. This man, named Ponticianus, was a high official at the court who had paid a visit to Augustine and his friends. During the encounter the visitor noticed, as Augustine records, a codex with the letters of Paul, something Ponticianus had not expected in the house of a professor of rhetoric. A conversation began, in which Ponticianus revealed his Christian sympathies and described how he had been inspired by Anthony, an Egyptian monk, whose work he and his companions had stumbled on during their stay in Trier. Anthony's fame had spread among fellow Christians in the West, though it had escaped the notice of Augustine and his friends up to that point. The gospel command to "go, sell whatever you have, and give to the poor" had been a key element in Anthony's conversion story and had led to his renunciation of worldly goods. Ponticianus himself had taken the command to heart, and as part of the rhetorical account of the garden scene, Augustine takes up the theme as one of the major motivations for his renunciation of a secular career and worldly expectations.

Toward the end of the fourth century voluntary renunciation of one's public career and private goods had become a recurrent theme in the discussions of the elite. For Augustine, whose family was not particularly wealthy (*Conf.* 2.3.5), this renunciation must have had a different impact than it did for some of his more richly endowed contemporaries, such as Paulinus of Nola, who belonged to the senatorial ranks and whose family owned extensive property and estates in Gaul, Spain, and Italy.[1] In the case of Paulinus, the practice of property renunciation undoubtedly had more dire consequences than for Augustine and his clan. Paulinus was well aware of the practical obstacles that people of his status faced; in his early years he had boldly taken on the difficulties, but eventually the rhetoric of his younger years seems to have faded in favor of a more cautious stance. In the carefully balanced advice that he would give to others who approached him on the thorny issue, Paulinus would emphasize *intellectual* detachment and the right use of wealth rather than complete re-nunciation. In any case, his own grand building project in Cimitile near Nola, around the shrine of St. Felix, did not lack for financial backing. Many remains of Paulinus's largess are still visible at the site today through its architecture, marble columns, decorative floors, colorful marble revetments, and so on. His poetry, moreover, celebrates the expenditure. The lavish construction of his new church, the *basilica nova*, and the reconstruction of other parts of the complex were meant, at least conceptually, to rival St. Peter's in Rome. There-fore, it remains to be seen how Paulinus's rhetoric of poverty and renunciation would have related to the reality of his ascetic community.

The idea of spreading one's wealth for the common good had a long tradi-tion among the Roman Empire's elite, who considered it a civic duty to use their riches for communal purposes. This system of patronage worked on various levels and in reciprocal ways; the beneficiaries would help to enhance the patron's status by providing certain services in the exchange of favors and benefits. In a Christian context the concept was slightly modified, but the old patterns could still shine through. Wealth should be used wisely according to God's plan and for the service of fellow Christians, but in exchange the recipients would honor their benefactors through intercessions and prayers to God. The courtyards, fountains, mosaics, and frescoes were all part of Paulinus's idea of appropriate expenditure of wealth, and no less than before did the munificence stand in direct correlation to the authority and status of the one bestowing it.

1. Dennis E. Trout, *Paulinus of Nola: Life, Letters, and Poems* (Berkeley: University of California Press, 1999); Thomas Lehmann, *Paulinus Nolanus und die Basilica Nova in Cimitile-Nola: Studien zu einem zentralen Denkmal der Spätantik-frühchristlichen Architektur* (Wiesbaden: Reichert, 2004).

This essay is, however, not about the late fourth century or the remarkable ascetic tendencies of the upper classes in Italy, Gaul, and North Africa. The reason for beginning briefly with Augustine and Paulinus is to illuminate the contradictions within the theme of wealth and poverty, since the historical information provided by the late fourth century is so much more abundant and verifiable than that of earlier times, in this case the Greek-speaking East of some two hundred years before. Moreover, in spite of the chronological and geographical differences, there are striking similarities in theological outlook and resolve between someone like Paulinus of Nola and Clement of Alexandria.

Clement, whose dates are tentatively placed at about 150 to 215, is one of the earliest authors known to have discussed questions of wealth and poverty in a comprehensive way. Historically Clement remains an elusive figure, but he left a substantial amount of writing, not all of which has survived. His official name, Titus Flavius Clemens, may give a glimpse into his background. His family descended presumably from a *libertus* of the household of (T.) Flavius Clemens, who was consul in 95 together with Emperor Domitian. If this reconstruction is correct, our Clement was at least indirectly connected with the Roman upper class across an interval of about three generations. Freed people were often successful in their entrepreneurial lives, and Clement's family seems to have done reasonably well for itself. His writings indicate that he lived the mobile life of a person of leisure, an aspiring philosopher who was able to travel to various places in the empire. He refers to a number of his teachers, although not by name, and he settled for a while in Alexandria, a great Greek city then under Roman rule, where he met a teacher whom he greatly admired. Clement's oeuvre shows that he had a keen interest in literature, whether Greek, Jewish, or Christian. It is also clear from his elegant style and the content of his discourses that both he and his readers must have been members of a highly literate elite.[2]

Clement composed a small work that is best known under its Latin title, *Quis dives salvetur?*[3] It is generally considered to be a stylized homily on the passage about the rich man in the Gospel of Mark (10:17–31). It is also the first known commentary on this passage, in which Clement addresses the hermeneutical challenge of the command: "go, sell whatever you have, and give to the poor," the very command that inspired Anthony and Augustine but did not seem to have attracted Paulinus of Nola.[4] As a reason for taking on this passage, Clement alludes to certain problems that involved the richer

2. William V. Harris, *Ancient Literacy* (Cambridge, MA: Harvard University Press, 1989).

3. "Which Rich Man Will Be Saved?" The Greek title (Τίς ὁ σῳζόμενος πλούσιος) may also be rendered as "Who Is the Rich Man Being Saved?" All translations are mine.

4. Paulinus's favorite passage was about Lazarus and the rich man; see the chapter on property renunciation in Trout, *Paulinus of Nola*, 133–59, esp. 135.

members of the community. These prosperous Christians were discouraged by the biblical command or else neglected it. Clement writes:

> The reason why salvation seems to be more difficult for rich people than for those without means is perhaps not simple but complex. For some who just listened in an offhand way to the Lord's saying that a camel slips more easily through a needle's eye than a rich person into the kingdom of heaven, despairing of themselves in the belief that they are not going to live, indulge in the world in every respect; clinging to the present life as the only one left to them, they withdraw even more from the road there (to heaven), no longer inquisitive about who the rich people are to whom the Lord and teacher speaks, neither how what is impossible among men becomes possible. Others, however, understood this rightly and properly, but neglecting the works that lead to salvation, they did not make the required preparation to attain the things of their hope. (*Quis div.* 2)

Clement makes clear that his words are directed not to every rich person in Alexandria but only to those who committed themselves fully to the Christian cause, indicating that he is preaching only to the converted: "In both cases I speak about the rich who learned about the Savior's power and his splendid salvation, but I have little concern with those who are uninitiated in the truth" (*Quis div.* 2).

Clement also implies that the rich had a kind of second-class status among Alexandrian Christians, and he admonishes the community about proper behavior toward their wealthy fellow believers; his remarks are revealing about the presence of social prejudice.

> The people who are moved by love of truth and love of their brothers and who do not behave with insolent rudeness toward the rich who are called [cf. 1 Cor. 1:24], nor, on the other hand, fawn on them for their own greed, should first remove the unfounded despair of the rich by means of scripture and show with the required interpretation of the Lord's sayings why the inheritance of the kingdom of the heavens is not totally cut off from them, if they obey the commandments. (*Quis div.* 3)

Since this and the preceding passages do not sound like literary *topoi*, they may reflect an actual situation in the Alexandrian community, at least, in the perception of the author. We get a sense that real problems and conflicts existed in this community not only about the interpretation but also about the implementation of the gospel injunction.

Clement quotes the entire pericope about the rich man (Mark 10:17–31), his most extensive biblical quotation ever (fifteen verses long), and he maintains that the passage in Mark concurs with all the other accepted gospels.[5] In Clement's view, they all show the same general tenor, although there are some small differences of wording here and there. Apparently, Clement did not want to burden his audience with too many details of New Testament scholarship. Less important to him were the textual differences between Mark, Matthew, and Luke than was the general tenor of the pericopes. He maintains that one should not understand the words in a literal way but search for their hidden meaning.

With this hermeneutical principle Clement lets his audience know from the onset what to expect. He continues operating, as it were, from a set of premises in which the search for the nonliteral or hidden meaning of the biblical words plays a primary role. Clement uses the biblical text fully, proceeding verse by verse, but his technique is to underscore his premises. For example, to illustrate his thoughts about the knowledge of God, he refers to Mark 10:18: "Why do you call me good? No one is good but God alone." This verse then triggers an elaborate discussion about the importance of the knowledge of God and how to achieve it:

> We must therefore right from the beginning store up in the soul the greatest and highest point of the teachings that relate to life, namely, to know the eternal God, giver of eternal gifts, the first, the highest, the one and good God, whom we can procure for ourselves through knowledge and understanding. (*Quis div.* 7)

Another premise is that irrational emotions and passions (*pathē*) should be mastered and, in fact, should be eliminated. Another is that perfection should be sought. These themes are omnipresent in all of Clement's writings, and he works them ingeniously into his comments on the text. In *Quis dives salvetur?* he introduces perfection by manipulating his gospel quotation. He takes a few words from the parallel pericope of Matthew and plants them into the Markan passage: "*If you want to be perfect*, go, sell what you have and distribute to the poor" (*Quis div.* 7). This interpolation gives him the possibility of discussing the meaning of perfection and being perfect.

Although many themes are touched on elsewhere in Clement's works, new elements appear in *Quis dives salvetur?* It is novel to give a full-fledged "biblical" commentary on issues of wealth and poverty, and Clement seems to be the first Christian writer to do so. His search for hidden meanings also

---

5. *Quis div.* 5: "This is written in the Gospel of Mark, and in all the other accepted [gospels] there are perhaps a few variations here and there in wording, but the passage as a whole shows the same agreement in meaning. Knowing that the Savior teaches his people nothing in a human way but everything with divine and mystical wisdom, we should not listen to the words in a carnal [literal] way but search and learn the hidden meaning in the words with due inquiry and understanding."

makes it possible for him to tame "extravagant" images, such as the camel and the needle's eye.[6]

While the biblical text provides Clement's starting point, the question remains: what does the text convey about wealth and poverty to him, and how does he interpret the passage? He is eager to diminish the text's apparently harsh implications for the salvation of the wealthy. He engages in elaborate rationalization, making considerable use of common sense. At the same time, his interpretation confronts those who maintain that the biblical command should be taken at face value and interpreted literally. Clement begins by pointing out that it is not desirable to be poor, and he does this in a way that almost suggests contempt for the poor. He also maintains that the renunciation of wealth is neither new nor inherently beneficial. He even brings out apparent contradictions in the biblical text when taken literally:

> It is not great or enviable to be without wealth except for the reason of [eternal] life.[7] In this way those who have nothing at all but are destitute and beggars for their daily needs, the poor who are cast out on the streets though they are ignorant of God and God's justice, would be most blessed, most dear to God, and the sole possessors of eternal life, simply because they are utterly destitute and live without necessities of life and because they lack even the most minimal means; nor is it something new to renounce wealth and to give it to the poor or to one's native country; many have done this before the descent of the Savior: some to have time to study letters and for dead wisdom, others for empty fame and vainglory, [I am thinking of] people such as Anaxagoras, Democritus, and Crates. (*Quis div.* 11)

Clement goes on to interpret the passage on his own terms. He maintains that the real message of the biblical command is not the visible act of throwing away one's possessions, but doing something more creative and lofty, namely, to strip the soul of its passions (*Quis div.* 14). He then turns to the negative potential of renunciation of wealth in real-life terms. Even if people shed their possessions, this may not stop their desire to have them. As he puts it:

> For there is also this possibility; someone who unburdens himself from his possessions may nonetheless still have a desire and appetite for money that absorbs him and lives in him. He may have shed the use, but being destitute and at the same time yearning for the things he squandered, he is doubly grieved both by the absence of support and by the presence of regret. For it is

6. See François Bovon, *L'Évangile selon saint Luc* (Geneva: Labor et Fides, 1991–), 235, who terms the image "extravagant." Clement harmonizes the image with the straight and narrow way as, for example, in *Quis div.* 26 end. See also Origen, *Cels.* 6.

7. Life probably means "eternal life" here. For μὴ οὐκ ἐπὶ λόγῳ, see *Strom.* 2.145.3: εἰ μὴ ἐπὶ λόγῳ πορνείας in a quotation from Matt. 31:32, which has παρεκτός λόγου πορνείας. For εἰ μή = μὴ οὐ, see LSJ μή s.v. II 3.

unattainable and impossible for someone who lacks the necessities of life not to have his thought processes break down and to find time to engage in higher things, since he is trying to provide these necessities in any possible way and from whatever source. (*Quis div.* 12)

In this view there is nothing to gain and everything to lose. "And how much more useful is the opposite, when by possessing sufficient means he does not suffer any distress and provides aid to whom he ought to? For what would there be left to share among people, if nobody had anything?" (*Quis div.* 13).

In more philosophical terms Clement points out that wealth is an *adiaphoron*, a Stoic concept that means that something is morally indifferent, thus neither good nor bad (*Quis div.* 14). It is an instrument and as such much depends on its proper use, not on wealth per se (*Quis div.* 15).[8] Clement argues that there are two kinds of wealth and poverty, just as there are two kinds of treasures, referring to the gospel saying about the good man who produces good and the bad man who produces evil out of their treasures (*Quis div.* 16). The same holds true for wealth; one kind is desirable and worth getting, the other undesirable and worthless. As for poverty, Clement explains:

> In the same way also spiritual poverty is blessed. Therefore Matthew added "blessed are the poor"—how?—"in spirit;" and again "blessed are those who hunger and thirst after God's righteousness." Wretched then are the opposite kind of poor who have no part in God and even less in human possessions; they have not tasted the righteousness of God. (*Quis div.* 17)

There are various ways in which someone can be rich: either by being frugal and saving money or else by being born to wealth. As Clement points out:

> For what wrong does one do, if, by being careful and living frugally before coming to faith, one gathered sufficient means of living? Or even less reproachable, if one was immediately established by God, the distributor of life, in a household of such people, a wealthy family, strong in funds and powerful in riches? If a person has been banished from life by being born to wealth, something beyond his will, he is rather wronged by God, who brought him into life, being granted temporary comfort but being despoiled of eternal life. Why should wealth ever have risen at all from the earth if it was a producer and patron of death? But if someone can make a U-turn[9] within the abundance of his possessions and be moderate and temperate, seeking God alone, breathing God's spirit, and living

---

8. Later, in *Quis div.* 31, Clement formulates this differently, admitting that all possessions are by nature unrighteous if used for personal advantage.

9. As G. W. Butterworth notes, κάμπτω is probably a metaphor from the horse or chariot race ("The Rich Man's Salvation," in *Clement of Alexandria*, LCL [Cambridge, MA: Harvard University Press, 1919], 265–367). See also LSJ, s.v.: "to turn or guide a horse or chariot round the turning post."

with God, he approaches God's commands as a free person, undefeated, unaffected by disease and the wounds of riches. But if not, a camel will more quickly enter through the needle['s eye] than such a rich man arrives at the kingdom of God. The camel that passes through the straight and narrow way before the rich man must have some higher meaning; this mystery of the Savior can be learned in the *Exposition of First Principles and Theology.* (*Quis div.* 26)

When rich people share their wealth, this works for Clement as a kind of monetary exchange system: "What beautiful trade, what divine business! One buys incorruptibility with money, and by giving the perishable things of the world one receives an eternal abode in exchange" (*Quis div.* 32).

The impression that these passages transmit is that Clement is primarily concerned with problems of the wealthy. Although he tries to balance his attentions evenly, it is clear that he cannot shed his own background. Even when he speaks about actual poor people, this is from a rather privileged perspective, as when he writes:

Open your heart to all who are enrolled as disciples of God without looking at their bodies with contempt, nor neglecting them because of their age; if someone appears poor, ragged, ugly, or weak, you should not be disgusted in your soul and turn away. This appearance is thrown around us from without for our entrance into the world, in order to be able to enter this school that we share; but hidden inside dwells the Father and his Son who died for us and rose with us. (*Quis div.* 33)

This perspective also becomes clear in Clement's other works, as a passage of the *Pedagogue* shows: "One should engage in wealth in a dignified manner and share humanely, not in bad taste or boastfully."[10]

The focus is clearly not on the poor but on the rich and their social obligations. It is not coincidental that Clement frequently uses the word *philanthrōpos* in this context.[11] As it was to be for Paulinus of Nola, sharing is part of a social system, in which both the rich and the poor are players; they have their own complementary roles and need each other in a system of social patronage.[12] This becomes even clearer in a passage in which Clement speaks in a rather peculiar way about poverty as "thrifty" or "miserly." After quoting a text from Proverbs (10:4) that states that "poverty humiliates a person," Clement interprets this as follows: "The biblical text means thrifty poverty, according to which the rich are poor in sharing, as if they did not possess anything" (*Paed.* 3.30.4). It is hard for a modern reader to assess

10. *Paed.* 3.34.1. See also *Paed.* 2.14.6; 2.120.5–6; 3.35.5.
11. See also *Strom.* 2.82.3 (in a quotation from Philo) and *Strom.* 2.86.3.
12. For the theme, see Susan R. Holman, *The Hungry Are Dying: Beggars and Bishops in Roman Cappadocia* (Oxford: Oxford University Press, 2001), 11.

the reality behind such a pronouncement, since it seems far removed from modern ideas of social justice and solidarity.

The passages above show that, in Clement's view, the exhortation to liquidate one's assets refers allegorically not so much to actual money as to the desire for money and immoderate attachment to it. The inner workings of the soul are more important than the human condition of poverty or wealth. When he discusses actual wealth, Clement defends it as an instrument for doing good and views the sharing of wealth as a civic if not religious duty. He maintains that rich people should set aside selfishness and spend freely on their poorer fellow believers, who in turn would intercede with God for their benefactors. It is clear that Clement cannot easily disguise his own elite background. He makes his comments with the donors, rather than with the recipients of welfare, in mind. In this respect Clement's attitude is comparable to that of Paulinus of Nola.

Clement's interpretations form a notable landmark in the reconciliation of an economic elite with a Christian community. As Elizabeth Clark remarks: "Clement gladly widens the needle's eye to welcome the rich who generously give."[13] Attitudes toward wealth (and poverty) were complex and at times problematic, as Clement observed. They will continue to be problematic both in the reception history of the biblical command and in the history of the church. The abandonment of property never became a norm for Christians, but the more radical voices did not die out either.[14]

13. Elizabeth A. Clark, *History, Theory, Text: Historians and the Linguistic Turn* (Cambridge, MA: Harvard University Press, 2004), 173. I am indebted to Liz Clark for the title of my essay and thank her for the image.

14. Two studies have made important contributions to the understanding of *Quis dives salvetur?* and its social and cultural environment. Louis William Countryman's study of the rich Christian in the early church makes Clement's work the centerpiece (*The Rich Christian in the Church of the Early Empire: Contradictions and Accommodations* [New York: E. Mellen Press, 1980]). Countryman analyzes early Christian attitudes toward wealth, almsgiving, and the religious value of wealth, and the danger of riches to their possessor and to the church. The author shows that although mixed emotions existed in early Christianity toward wealth, the abandonment of property never became a norm for Christians. Countryman signals the basic problem that the church assigned a central role to rich Christians in supporting its institutions and providing for its finances; at the same time, however, it denied them traditional rewards in return for their beneficences. The second study is a recent Oxford dissertation (still unpublished) by David O'Brien, "Rich Clients and Poor Patrons: Functions of Friendship in Clement of Alexandria's *Quis dives salvetur?*" (PhD diss., University of Oxford, 2004). O'Brien offers an extensive literary and rhetorical analysis of *Quis dives salvetur?* and approaches the subject matter from the viewpoint of patronage and friendship. O'Brien makes considerable effort to place Clement's discourse within the ambience of other Greco-Roman philosophical and cultural conventions. Particularly interesting in O'Brien's interpretation of Clement is the idea that the "poor" have a privileged spiritual status on account of their *askēsis* and *oikeiōsis* and not because of the mere fact of their poverty. The notion that Clement's approach can be seen as a precursor of the later "poor" holy man who acts as a spiritual patron is important from the point of view of the study of asceticism and spirituality.

6

CARE FOR THE POOR, FEAR OF POVERTY, AND LOVE OF MONEY

Evagrius Ponticus on the Monk's Economic Vulnerability

DAVID BRAKKE

In the popular imagination, Christian monks, at least those in the West, take a "vow of poverty," but in this case "poverty" does not mean what this volume seeks to address—that is, a lack of material resources so extreme that it degrades and even threatens human life. Rather, monastic "poverty" usually means renunciation of private property: the monk owns nothing of his or her own, but has all things in common with his or her monastic colleagues. It is likely that in fourth- and fifth-century Egypt, entering a cenobitic monastery such as those associated with Pachomius and Shenoute actually protected the monk from real poverty; the Pachomian or Shenoutean monk turned over to the monastery his or her worldly goods and could never ask for them back, but then the monk could count on adequate clothing and shelter, regular if minimal meals, and excellent health care for the rest of his or her life.[1] The

1. On food in the White Monastery, see Bentley Layton, "Social Structure and Food Consumption in an Early Christian Monastery: The Evidence of Shenute's *Canons* and the White Monastery Federation A.D. 385–465," *Le Muséon* 115 (2002): 25–55. On health care in early monasticism, see Andrew T. Crislip, *From Monastery to Hospital: Christian Monasticism and the Transformation of*

Pachomian and White Monastery federations operated as large financial enterprises that had substantial effects on local economies.[2]

In contrast, the semi-eremitical monks in the communities of Nitria, Scetis, and Kellia in northern Egypt did not take formal vows, nor did they create such large institutions. Rather, these monks supported themselves individually or in small groups clustered around a particular *abba*, and so for them the prospect of slipping from monastic simplicity into actual poverty was more real. Recent studies of the literary, archaeological, and documentary evidence from late ancient Egypt indicate that many and probably even most of these lavra monks lived fairly comfortably by ancient standards.[3] Still, unlike his cenobitic brother, who took his place in a well-structured collective, the semi-eremitical monk had to manage his own financial affairs, and thus monastic renunciation complicated his relationship to money and possessions, rather than ending it completely. The demon Love of Money or Avarice (*philargyria*) surfaces infrequently in the Pachomian literature and the works of Shenoute, but it makes regular appearances in the *Apophthegmata Patrum* and the works of Evagrius Ponticus (d. ca. 399), which concern these more loosely affiliated monks.

This essay briefly examines the values and anxieties that surround money, economic activity, and charity to the poor as they appear in Evagrius's discussions of possessions and the demon Love of Money. Evagrius's works provide a good basis for such a study because, unlike the *Apophthegmata Patrum* and other sources for northern Egyptian monasticism, his works actually originated in fourth-century Egypt; they also provide a good mix of social data and theological reflection. These works reveal that Evagrius's ideal monk lives simply, at the edge of poverty, so to speak, accumulating only enough to support himself and to provide basic hospitality to his guests; any surplus to this amount is to be given to the poor. Possessions, Evagrius argues, weigh down the monk, distract him from prayer, and exacerbate the irascible aspect of his soul. Evagrius consistently encourages generosity to the truly poor, but such generosity threatens to send the monastic donor over

---

Health Care in Late Antiquity (Ann Arbor: University of Michigan Press, 2005). When the monk Herai decided to leave the White Monastery and asked for her possessions to be returned to her, she received a blistering response from Besa, Shenoute's successor. On this incident, see Heike Behlmer, "The City as Metaphor in the Works of Two Panopolitans: Shenoute and Besa," in *Perspectives on Panopolis: An Egyptian Town from Alexander the Great to the Arab Conquest; Acts of an International Symposium Held in Leiden on 16, 17, and 18 December 1998*, ed. Arno Egberts, Brian P. Muhs, and Jacques van der Vliet, Papyrologica Lugduno-Batava 31 (Leiden: Brill, 2002), 13–27, at 22–27.

2. James E. Goehring, *Ascetics, Society, and the Desert: Studies in Early Egyptian Monasticism*, SAC (Harrisburg, PA: Trinity Press, 1999), 39–52.

3. Ibid.; Mission suisse d'archéologie copte de l'Université de Genève sous la direction de Rodolphe Kasser, *Le site monastique des Kellia (Basse-Égypte): Recherches des années 1981–83* (Louvain: Peeters, 1984), 22–23; Ewa Wipszycka, *Études sur le christianisme dans l'Égypte de l'antiquité tardive*, SEAug 52 (Rome: Institutum Patristicum Augustinianum, 1996), 337–62.

the edge of self-sufficiency into poverty—or at least some monks feared and the demon Love of Money suggested. Evagrius wants the monk to cultivate a condition of economic vulnerability, which fosters a spiritual condition of dependence on God and openness to other people.[4]

The Dangers of Possessions

As commentators have frequently noted, Evagrius does not consider any material object, including gold, evil in itself.[5] Only our thoughts about such objects can be morally evaluated. For example, angels may inspire us to ask why God created gold, to investigate why it is granular and spread through the soil (requiring that humans work hard to acquire it), and to contemplate the use of gold vessels in the worship of the Lord, as found in Exodus. These are worthy thoughts about gold. Demons, however, inspire the evil thoughts of acquiring gold and gaining pleasure from it. It is also possible for the human to think about gold without any passion.[6] So apart from any thoughts about them, material things, including gold, are unproblematic. Possessions, however, are potentially problematic, for they are not merely material things, but things defined by attitudes or thoughts that attach them to us and us to them—for example, "These items belong to me."

Evagrius frequently exhorts the monk to renounce possessions.[7] Like many Christian authors before and after him, Evagrius argues that "the person without possessions enjoys the pleasure of a life free from cares," but the person still attached to possessions suffers from continual anxieties about them.[8] The attention that possessions claim of their owner divides the monk's intellect and so distracts him from prayer and contemplation of God (*Chapters on Prayer* 17). Evagrius can employ a variety of metaphors for the danger that possessions pose to the monk, most of which convey his conviction that

4. I refer to the monk that Evagrius envisions and addresses with the masculine pronoun. Although Evagrius addresses some of his writings to female ascetics, his paradigmatic monk is male, and nearly all the monks of the semi-eremitical groups in northern Egypt were men.

5. For example, Jeremy Driscoll, "'Love of Money' in Evagrius," *StudMon* 43 (2001): 21–30, at 25.

6. *On Thoughts* (hereafter *Thoughts*) 8, in Évagre le Pontique, *Sur les pensées*, ed. and trans. Paul Géhin, Claire Guillaumont, and Antoine Guillaumont, SC 438 (Paris: Cerf, 1998). Ancient works cited without an author are by Evagrius. The reader can access most of the works cited here in Evagrius of Pontus, *The Greek Ascetic Corpus*, ed. and trans. Robert E. Sinkewicz, Oxford Early Christian Studies (Oxford: Oxford University Press, 2003). The major exception is *Talking Back*. In most cases I provide my own translation, but in others I have used Sinkewicz's and such cases are noted.

7. *Thoughts* 3, 32; *To Monks in Monasteries and Communities* (hereafter *Monks*) 25, 30; *Exhortation to a Virgin* 17; *Maxims* 3.18; *Exhortations* 1.2.

8. *To Eulogius: On the Confession of Thoughts and Counsel in Their Regard* (hereafter *Eulogius*) 12.11 (Greek text: Sinkewicz, *Greek Ascetic Corpus*, 317; translation: Sinkewicz, *Greek Ascetic Corpus*, 38).

they restrain or hold the monk back from free ascent toward his heavenly goal.[9] For example, possessions are like the cargo that sinks an overloaded ship, while the monk should be free to soar like an eagle.[10] More precisely, for Evagrius it is not the possessions themselves that weigh upon the monk, but the "thoughts of worry" and mental representations to which possessions give rise. Anxious thoughts about possessions are like a tunic that prevents a racing athlete from running freely or a chain that restrains a dog from going where he must (*Thoughts* 6, *Eight Spirits* 3). Representations form the mental pictures that obscure image-free contemplation of God.[11] And thus Evagrius, in the tradition of such Stoicizing authors as Clement of Alexandria (*Who Is the Saved Rich Person?*), can state the general principle that "the lover of money is not the one who has possessions, but the one who desires them," but with a qualification fit for the monastic context: "For the steward is, it is said, a rational money-bag" (*Gnostikos* 30).

Love of money or the desire for possessions, then, distorts the desire that derives from the concupiscible part of the soul, which Evagrius, in Platonizing fashion, pairs with the irascible part as the two sources of irrational psychic energy in the person.[12] Greedy people desire money or things rather than God and knowledge of God. But Evagrius is as much if not more concerned about how possessions distort the irascible energy that ought to be directed against the demons. To be sure, he worries that the monk desires things that he does not have, but even more, he points out that the monk becomes unnaturally aggressive out of the fear that he may lose the things he already has. If we have property, then we become like a dog that barks at and attacks people because it wants to protect its things. Possessions cause our irascibility to flare up into anger, preventing pure prayer (*Thoughts* 5). Anger that is aroused by "food, clothing, riches, and the glory that passes away," Evagrius warns, "does not depart from the heart, but rather plunges the intellect into the depths of perdition."[13]

9. Cf. Driscoll, "Love of Money," 23.

10. *The Eight Spirits of Wickedness* (hereafter *Eight Spirits*) 3.

11. On the formation of thoughts and representations and their role in preventing pure prayer, see Columba Stewart, "Imageless Prayer and the Theological Vision of Evagrius Ponticus," *JECS* 9 (2001): 173–204.

12. On Evagrius's view that the person is constituted by a rational part, an irascible part, and a desiring part, see the discussion of Antoine Guillaumont and Claire Guillaumont in Évagre le Pontique, *Traité pratique, ou le moine*, ed. Antoine Guillaumont and Claire Guillaumont, 2 vols., SC 170–72 (Paris: Cerf, 1971), 1:104–12.

13. *Antirrhetikos* (hereafter *Ant.*) 5.30, in Wilhelm Frankenberg, *Euagrius Ponticus*, Abhandlungen der königlichen Gesellschaft der Wissenschaften zu Göttingen, Philologisch-historische Klasse, n.s., vol. 13, no. 2 (Berlin: Weidmannsche Buchhandlung, 1912), 472–544; cf. *Ant.* 5.22. Evagrius attributes to John of Lycopolis the view that hatred of fellow monks based on money or food is easier to uproot than that based on a concern for reputation ("glory that comes from human beings") (*Ant.* 5.6).

Some monks become so driven by their enflamed irascibility that they take other people to court over financial issues. These monks aggressively seek to preserve their claim on things that legally should be theirs. "In our opinion," Evagrius writes, "these people are deluded by demons and make the road of the monastic life even more difficult for themselves because they are inflaming their irascibility for the sake of money while on the other hand they are endeavoring to quench it with respect to money, like someone who stabbed his eyes with a pin in order to apply salve to them" (*Thoughts* 32). The monk who engages in lawsuits over property exacerbates the very condition that the ascetic life seeks to assuage and embodies an extreme form of the defensive, even hostile, attitude that possessions create in a person. Addressing the monk who wants to file a lawsuit, however justified, to regain lost property, Evagrius recommends that he recite Matt. 5:40: "And if anyone wants to sue you and take your coat, give your cloak as well" (*Ant.* 3.39).[14] Not surprisingly, then, Evagrius concludes that the antidote to the hostility that arises from possessions is to let go of them: the monk who gives to the poor "destroys irascibility."[15]

In addition to fostering anxious thoughts, mental representations, and anger, possessions can represent a problematic ongoing connection to the monk's family and his premonastic past. Evagrius's *Antirrhetikos*, or *Talking Back*, lists at least eight thoughts that the demon Love of Money insinuates concerning the property of one's family. According to this work, monks harbor resentment against their parents for failing to leave them an inheritance or they fantasize about the inheritance that they gave up when they became monks, compare themselves to their nonmonastic siblings who enjoy material comforts, and recall the splendid house in which they lived with their parents, in comparison to which their monastic cell appears "small" and "odious." If you had not given up your family's wealth, Love of Money says to some monks, you would be able to support many of your monastic colleagues now.[16] The monk may feel inadequate, not only because his natural siblings have more money than he does, but also because they have the status and human approval that wealth and worldly success bring (*Ant.* 3.18). All these concerns reveal that the monk has not truly renounced his family and his

14. All biblical quotations are mine, translated to reflect how they appear in Evagrius's works.

15. *Monks* 30, in Jeremy Driscoll, *Evagrius Ponticus: Ad Monachos*, ACW 59 (New York: Newman Press, 2003), 46.

16. *Ant.* 3.3, 16, 18, 20, 22, 34, 36, 50. The reader should be aware of a problem in the numbering of the entries in book 3 (Love of Money) of *Talking Back*. In the Syriac manuscript that Frankenberg transcribed, there are no entries numbered 19 or 20, only one unnumbered entry between 18 and 21, and two entries numbered 27. Therefore, the unnumbered entry must be 19, and those numbered 21–26 and the first entry numbered 27 must be numbered one too high. Because of this, the entries that I refer to here as 3.20 and 3.22 appear as 3.21 and 3.23 in Frankenberg's text. My forthcoming English translation of *Talking Back* seeks to clarify this and other numbering problems in Frankenberg's text.

former life and embraced the monastic community, hence the need to truly let go of everything, not only what one has, but also fantasies about what one used to have or could have had.

On the other hand, monks can justify accumulating too many possessions on the pretext that in this way they can avoid asking their family or anyone else for financial help. Love of Money tells the monk that it would be shameful to have to rely on others for material support.[17] This suggestion is particularly insidious because, as we shall see, monastic tradition, including Evagrius, valued financial and social independence and discouraged the monk from becoming a burden to others. In response, Evagrius tells the beginning monk, "If you need food or clothing, do not be ashamed of accepting what others bring you, for this is a form of pride."[18] But Evagrius too exhibits ambivalence about accepting aid from one's natural family. In *Talking Back* one demon tells a monk, "In a dream I will entice one of your relatives or one of the rich people to send you gold," but another demonic thought "taunts us because our parents have forsaken us and they will not send us gold to meet our need." To the former monk Evagrius adduces Abram's vow not to take even "a shoe-latchet" from the king of Sodom (Gen. 14:22–23), and in response to the latter he quotes Ps. 27:10: "My father and mother have forsaken me, but the Lord has received me" (*Ant.* 3.1, 17). I suspect that Evagrius would like other monks to be the people from whom one is not ashamed to accept help, rather than one's family, who may not be reliable and from whom the monk needs to distance himself, both financially and emotionally.[19] Above all, of course, the monk ought to trust in God if he fears that he will find no benefactor "on the day of need" (*Ant.* 3.2).

Turning briefly to social history, we should note that Evagrius's comments reveal the variety of economic backgrounds from which the monks whom he knows come. Family inheritances, splendid family homes, lawsuits—these are the concerns of the well-to-do, not the poor. Indeed, just sentences after advising the novice monk not to be ashamed to accept food and clothing from others, Evagrius discourages him from acquiring a slave to serve him (*Found.* 5). Some monks received criticism from those friends and relatives to whom the monks did not give any of their (presumably substantial) wealth when they took up the monastic life (*Ant.* 4.60). Evagrius also knows monks who had been slaves themselves—and are taunted by other monks because of it—and

17. *Praktikos* (hereafter *Prakt.*) 9.
18. *The Foundations of the Monastic Life: A Presentation of the Practice of Stillness* (hereafter *Found.*) 4 (trans. Sinkewicz, *Greek Ascetic Corpus*, 6).
19. On the monk and his natural family, see David Brakke, "Making Public the Monastic Life: Reading the Self in Evagrius Ponticus' *Talking Back*," in *Religion and the Self in Antiquity*, ed. David Brakke, Michael L. Satlow, and Steven Weitzman (Bloomington: Indiana University Press, 2005), 222–33, at 227–29.

monks who are truly poor appear regularly in his writings.[20] Significantly, however, impoverished or lower-class monks are talked about more than they are addressed directly.

Evagrius knows that some semi-eremitical monks band together in collective business enterprises; thus a monk may have to handle money in behalf of not only himself but also his brothers. The ideal "steward," as we have already seen, went about his duties dispassionately, like a "rational money-bag" (*Gnostikos* 30). This responsibility carried with it dangers—the temptations to spend the money according to one's desires rather than for the group's benefit, or to fret about financial matters when funds run low—and in fact the prospect of being "a steward of God's wealth" or "an overseer of the brothers" may be an attack of the demon of vainglory (*Ant.* 3.15, 56; 7.10). Despite these demonically inspired problems, we historians might welcome this firsthand confirmation of such business alliances among the monks.

Monastic "Poverty" as the Cultivation of Vulnerability

Evagrius does often refer to the monk choosing to be "poor" (*penichros*) or to live in "poverty" (*penia*),[21] but what does he envision in practical terms? Not, surely, having absolutely nothing, and not having only the most basic necessities, for Evagrius himself clearly has a library, for example. Rather, the ideal monk seeks the kind of self-sufficiency that Athanasius had Antony model in the *Life of Antony*.[22] As Athanasius presents his story, when Antony moves to his more remote retreat, the so-called inner mountain, he at first relies on others to bring him supplies of bread. But eventually Antony plants a garden and is able to produce his own bread, and then he rejoices that he will no longer be a burden to anyone. He then grows some vegetables to provide hospitality to his guests. Antony's support of himself and his provision for guests represent strategies by which Antony configures a proper form of monastic independence from and connection to the wider society.[23] Echoing Athanasius, Evagrius instructs the monastic beginner, "Give thought to working with your hands, if possible both night and day, so that you will not be a burden to anyone, and further that you may be able to offer donations, as the holy apostle Paul advised" (meaning most likely 1 Thess. 2:9; 2 Thess. 3:8). The monk, then, should have only enough to support himself and to

20. Slaves: *Ant.* 5.44. Poor monks: *Ant.* 3.7, 9, 10, 37, 38, 40, 57.
21. *Prakt.* Prol. 6; 26; *Thoughts* 6; *Monks* 16, 26.
22. On self-sufficiency and dependence on benefactors in early Egyptian monasticism, see Daniel Caner, *Wandering, Begging Monks: Spiritual Authority and the Promotion of Monasticism in Late Antiquity*, Transformation of the Classical Heritage 33 (Berkeley: University of California Press, 2002), 41–47.
23. Athanasius, *Vit. Ant.* 50.4–6; see David Brakke, *Athanasius and Asceticism* (Baltimore: Johns Hopkins University Press, 1998), 230–33.

provide charity to others. This principle means that the monk must have a business life based on his manual labor; Evagrius worked as a calligrapher, but the weaving of baskets appears to have been the most popular monastic trade.[24] Evagrius admits, however, that buying and selling merchandise inevitably entangle the monk in sin, and so he suggests that the monk never haggle about prices and instead resign himself to taking a small loss in every transaction. Better yet, the monk should employ "some other trustworthy person" as his business agent, and so leave the haggling to him.[25]

At first glance the twin goals of self-sufficiency and charity seem clear enough, but they raise several questions and present complications that do not trouble the person who simply seeks to make himself as rich as possible. In other words, despite what Evagrius says, the renunciation of possessions does not simply eliminate cares about them; it also introduces new cares. What constitutes self-sufficiency? To what extent should the monk secure his economic future? What if he cannot support himself because of sickness or old age? And what are the limits to the monk's obligation to give to others? If giving to the poor is a good thing, would it not be better to give more, thus justifying more ambitious business activities? Questions like these provide the raw material for the demon Love of Money, perhaps the craftiest of the eight demons that make war on the Evagrian monk.[26]

As Evagrius presents it in the *Praktikos*, Love of Money preys primarily on the fragility of self-sufficiency. "Love of Money," he writes, "suggests an extended period of old age when one's hands will be too weak to work, future famines and the accompanying diseases, the bitterness of poverty, and that it is shameful to receive what one needs from other people" (*Prakt.* 9). These anxieties appear in other works as well and indicate a general insecurity about the future, and they are not groundless. *Talking Back* is peppered with references to monks who are truly impoverished because, for example, illness has prevented them from working.[27] Here these truly poor monks appear as potential recipients of the monk's almsgiving, a theme to which I will return, but such monks also provide vivid incarnations of what every monk might face. And thus Love of Money seeks to persuade the monk to work more and set aside money and provisions for the proverbial rainy day and especially for an extended period of old age. Evagrius attempts to counter such thoughts

24. Lucien Regnault, *The Day-to-Day Life of the Desert Fathers in Fourth-Century Egypt*, trans. Étienne Poirier (Petersham, MA: St. Bede's Publications, 1999), 99–102.

25. *Found.* 8 (trans. Sinkewicz, *Greek Ascetic Corpus*, 9).

26. On Evagrius's demonology in general, see David Brakke, *Demons and the Making of the Monk: Spiritual Combat in Early Christianity* (Cambridge, MA: Harvard University Press, 2006), 48–77; and Antoine Guillaumont and Claire Guillaumont, "Démon: III. Dans la plus ancienne littérature monastique," in *Dictionnaire de spiritualité ascétique et mystique: Doctrine et histoire*, vol. 3 (1957), 189–212, at 196–205. On the demon Love of Money, see Driscoll, "'Love of Money.'"

27. *Ant.* 3.7, 9, 10, 37, 38, 40, 57.

with biblical verses that encourage trust in and dependence on God—"The Lord will not withhold good things from those who walk in innocence" (Ps. 83:12 LXX)—and that stress the fleeting nature of human life—"A human being is like vanity; his days pass by as a shadow" (Ps. 143:4 LXX) (*Ant.* 3.23, 29). Place your trust in God, Evagrius says, and understand that to be human is to be contingent and insecure in the face of the future.

When Love of Money targets the monk's economic self-sufficiency, then, it exploits the temporal dimension of human life. This aspect of the demon's attack finds its summation in this passage from *Talking Back*: Love of Money "suggests to our intellect either the remembrance of money that we have renounced, or the effort that we are making to acquire things that at present cannot be seen, or the preservation and safekeeping of the things we have now" (*Ant.* 3.24). That is, Love of Money seeks to redirect the monk's attention to the past that he has left behind and to saddle him with regret; calls into question the rewards of the kingdom of God and knowledge of God that lie in the future; or encourages the preservation of what the monk has at the present time. Love of Money tries to turn economic self-sufficiency, a monastic good, into spiritual or existential self-sufficiency, the monastic vice of pride. The demon suggests that the monk should secure his future by his own efforts rather than accept his temporal nature and trust in God for his future. From this perspective, we see that the monk's economic self-sufficiency certainly has the practical aim of not making the monk a burden on others, as Evagrius says explicitly, but it also has the disciplinary goal of fostering in the monk a spiritual condition of dependence on God. Evagrius writes, "Having therefore what you need for the present time, do not worry about the future, whether that be a day, a week, or some months. When tomorrow has arrived, that time will provide what is needed, as long as you are seeking above all for the kingdom of God and his righteousness."[28] The monk should seek economic *sufficiency*, not economic *security*. Sufficiency represents a state of vulnerability.

But self-sufficiency is not the only principle guiding the monk's relationship with money; the other is charity to others. "The one who consoles the poor," Evagrius writes, "is manly in pious acts."[29] Here too Love of Money finds plenty of complications to exploit, for the monk must learn to give generously without making generosity his primary project. Already in *Foundations of the Monastic Life*, a work aimed at beginners, Evagrius must command, "Do not desire to possess riches in order to make donations to the poor, for this is a deception of the evil one that often leads to vainglory and casts the mind into occasions for idle preoccupations." Instead, he adduces for his reader the

28. *Found.* 4 (trans. Sinkewicz, *Greek Ascetic Corpus*, 6).

29. *Scholia on Proverbs* 342, in Évagre le Pontique, *Scholies aux Proverbes*, ed. Paul Géhin, SC 340 (Paris: Cerf, 1987).

widow with two mites from the Gospel of Mark (12:41–44): the monk need only give his small surplus to fulfill his charitable obligation.[30] The path that leads from charity to vainglory reappears in his *On Thoughts*, in a passage where Evagrius's seeming insight into the human capacity for self-delusion has made it a favorite of many readers:

> The demon of Love of Money appears to me to be very complex and inventive in its deceit. Often, hemmed in by extreme renunciation, it pretends to be a steward and a lover of the poor; it prepares generous hospitality for strangers who have not arrived and sends provisions to others who are absent; it visits the prisons of the city and ransoms those sold into slavery; it attaches itself to rich women and points out those persons who ought to be treated well, as it admonishes others who have a full purse to renounce. And after it has little by little deceived the soul in this way, it surrounds the soul with the thoughts of love of money and hands it over to the demon of Vainglory. That demon introduces a crowd of persons who glorify the Lord for these acts of stewardship and people who eventually talk to one another about the priesthood; then it predicts the death of the present priest and adds that someone who has accomplished so many things should not flee (from the possibility of ordination). And so the wretched intellect, entangled in these thoughts, takes issue with those persons who have not accepted (ordination) and gives gifts to and receives with courtesy those who have accepted it willingly, while it hands over to the magistrates those who disagree with it and demands that they be banished from the city. Finally, while these thoughts are circling around within (the intellect), the demon of Pride suddenly appears, forming continuous flashes of lightning in the air of the cell, letting loose winged dragons, and producing the uttermost loss of one's wits. But as for us, let us pray for the destruction of these thoughts and live in poverty with thanksgiving, "for we clearly brought nothing into this world, and we cannot bring anything out of it; since we have food and clothing, let us be content with these" (1 Tim. 6:7–8), remembering that Paul said, "Love of money is the root of all evils" (1 Tim. 6:10). (*Thoughts* 21)

The familiarity of this scenario suggests that Evagrius, like a modern psychologist, has identified the mixed motives and pleasure in virtue that run through the ego. But we should remind ourselves that Evagrius himself understands this phenomenon not in terms of mixed motives and a divided self but in terms of successive demons that cooperate in a multistage attack (Love of Money, Vainglory, Pride). His essential warning is that, although the monk is obliged to give alms to the poor, care for the poor must not become his primary project, which should be prayer and knowledge of God.[31] To become a professional philanthropist, as Love of Money suggests, opens one up to the attacks of Vainglory and Pride.

30. *Found.* 4 (trans. Sinkewicz, *Greek Ascetic Corpus*, 6).
31. Cf. Driscoll, "'Love of Money,'" 26.

Care for the poor frequently appears as a pretext for excessively acquisitive activity, but in *Talking Back* Evagrius just as often portrays monks as unwilling to give to the poor, whether these poor people are fellow monks or just poor people. There are frequent references to a general reluctance to give to the poor,[32] but Evagrius mentions specific objections as well: the poor person has other sources of financial help, while I do not; I do not have enough for both me and the poor person; the person really is not very poor or at least not as poor as others are, and besides, he is lazy and will not work; I would just make myself poor; the poor person is my enemy.[33] Here the monk calculates both the threat to his own security and the worthiness of the poor person, manifesting a defensive and judgmental posture that Evagrius seeks to undermine with biblical exhortations to trust in God and to be open to others. But even the act of giving could send the monk into regret and donor fatigue: maybe I am spending my money too freely; the recipients of my aid do not show sufficient gratitude, and I suspect that some of them may be faking poverty; those monks to whom I lend show no interest in repaying; I am doing too much "service to the brothers."[34] If self-sufficiency should foster dependence on God, but could lead to a futile attempt to achieve self-preservation through financial means, then charity to others should foster an open generosity to one's fellow humans, but could lead to a defensive judgmentalism that cuts one's self off from others. "You shall love your neighbor as yourself," Evagrius reminds his readers, and he quotes Deut. 15:7: "You shall not close your hand to your brother who is needy. You shall open your hands to him and lend him as much as he wants" (*Ant.* 3.5, 9). The closed and open hands serve as fitting images for the existential postures that Evagrius seeks to condemn and foster.

As we have seen, Evagrius's works can be charming and even amusing in their insight and circumstantiality. We have met the monk whose success at charity leads him to vainglory and eventually to demonic madness. In other places Evagrius depicts an advanced monk who inflicts his manic need to produce more income on his disciple, forcing the junior monk to perform constant manual labor and giving him no time to study the Scriptures or for meditation on monastic teachings (*Ant.* 3.4, 6). Moreover, we have seen that charity to the truly poor constitutes, along with self-sufficiency, the guiding principle for the Evagrian monk's financial life. Almsgiving, then, more than just one among many ascetic practices, provides one of the organizational principles for the semi-eremitical monastic life, according to Evagrius. To be sure, it was the large cenobitic monasteries that, thanks to their higher level of organization, could construct and staff hospitals and other institutions for

32. *Ant.* 3.5, 7, 9, 10, 27, 31, 37, 38, 40, 43, 44, 47, 48, 58.
33. *Ant.* 1.28, 49; 3.28, 57; 5.28.
34. *Ant.* 1.58; 3.12, 30, 33, 45; 5.48, 51, 57.

the poor, but the lavra-type monastic settlements had their own charitable dimension as well. Still, for Evagrius even charity for the poor is a secondary good, subordinate to the monk's goal of pure prayer and, ultimately, knowledge of the Trinity. To reach that goal, the monk must create in himself or herself a spiritual condition of reliance on God and openness to others, summed up in the virtues of *apatheia* and *agapē*. It is this spiritual vulnerability and generosity that economic vulnerability and generosity are meant to cultivate.

7

WINE FOR WIDOWS

Papyrological Evidence for Christian Charity in Late Antique Egypt

ADAM SERFASS

On August 9 in an unknown year during the late fifth or early sixth century CE, four memos were issued to Victor, an *oinopratēs*, or wine merchant, in the Egyptian city of Oxyrhynchus. Each document, known in papyrological parlance as an order-to-pay or an order-of-provision, instructed Victor to distribute wine to the widows associated with a church in the city. Three churches' widows, those of St. Victor, St. Michael the Archangel, and Sts. Cosmas and Damian,[1] were to receive one *diploun* of

References to editions of papyri and other papyrological materials (*Hilfsmittel*, papyrological congresses, etc.) follow the conventions set out in J. F. Oates et al., *Checklist of Greek, Latin, Demotic and Coptic Papyri, Ostraca and Tablets*, 5th ed., BASP Suppl. 9 (Oakville, CT: American Society of Papyrologists, 2001), now regularly updated at http://scriptorium.lib.duke.edu/papyrus/texts/clist.html. Unless designated otherwise, all translations in this study are mine.

1. In 1924, the documents were published in the condensed format employed in the "Minor Documents" section of the early volumes of the Oxyrhynchus papyri: *P. Oxy.* XVI 1954–1956. Seventy years later, P. Pruneti Piovanelli republished the texts with critical apparatus, introduction, and commentary: "Attività assistenziali a favore delle vedove (*P. Oxy.* XVI 1954, 1955, 1956)," in *Paideia cristiana: Studi in onore di Mario Naldini*, Scritti in onore 2 (Rome: Gruppo Editoriale Internazionale,

wine;[2] those of Ptoleminos's church were to receive five.[3] On January 27, 480, the *hagia ekklēsia* of Oxyrhynchus ordered Peter, *oikonomos*, or steward, of Sts. Cosmas and Damian, to provide the widow Sophia with a coat.[4] In this essay, the evidence of papyri such as these is employed to reconstruct the mechanisms by which Christian institutions in the Egyptian *chōra* aided those in need.[5] I argue that these institutions created a system of safety nets, a charitable nexus that sought to prevent individuals from slipping through the cracks. Due to constraints of space, evidence for monastic charity is not adduced in this study.[6]

Although a growing body of scholarship has examined Christian charity in late antiquity, the testimony of papyri for the phenomenon has not been widely explored by those outside the papyrological community.[7] This testimony is particularly valuable because it counterbalances the tendency of the late antique evidence for philanthropy to focus on large cities such as Alexandria, Constantinople, Jerusalem, and Antioch. Bishops of such cities may have pioneered large-scale philanthropic programs, but papyri reveal that well-organized charitable outreach was also present in the Egyptian

---

1994), 199–205 = *SB* XXII 15528–30. An English translation of *P. Oxy.* XVI 1954 appears in J. Rowlandson, ed., *Women and Society in Greek and Roman Egypt: A Sourcebook* (Cambridge: Cambridge University Press, 1998), 64. The title of this essay, "Wine for Widows," is borrowed from Rowlandson's introductory material for this translation. Except for the names of the churches, the texts of the three documents are identical. Each of the three churches is attested elsewhere: see the lists of Oxyrhynchite churches in Timm 1:283–300; L. Antonini, "Le chiese cristiane nell'Egitto dal IV al IX secolo secondo i documenti dei papiri greci," *Aegyptus* 20 (1940): 172–83; A. Papaconstantinou, *Le culte des saints en Égypte des Byzantins aux Abbassides: L'apport des inscriptions et des papyrus grecs et coptes* (Paris: CNRS Éditions, 2001), 286–88. Since the publication of these lists, the church of St. Victor has appeared in *P. Oxy.* LXVII 4617.13; 4618.1, 17.

2. The volume of the *diploun* varied from 4.5 to 8 *sextarii* (about 2.5–4.3 liters): see K. A. Worp, "A Survey of ἁπλᾶ, δι(δι)πλᾶ and τριπλᾶ Measures in the Papyri," *ZPE* 131 (2000): 146–48.

3. *P. Oxy.* LXVII 4621, published in 2001. The text, date, and hand of this document match those of the other three orders issued to Victor *oinopratēs*. A church of Ptoleminos in Oxyrhynchus is not otherwise attested.

4. *P. Wisc.* II 64 = New Docs. II 108. English trans.: Rowlandson, *Women and Society*, 63.

5. On the papyrological evidence for Christian charity, see also R. Rémondon, "L'église dans la société égyptienne à l'époque byzantine," *CE* 94 (1972): 263–65; A. Martin, "L'église et la khôra égyptienne au IVe siècle," *RÉAug* 25 (1979): 19–25; idem, *Athanase d'Alexandrie et l'eglise d'Égypte au IVe siècle (328–373)*, CÉFAR 216 (Rome: École Française de Rome, 1996), 719–34; *P. Bingen* 136; E. Wipszycka, *Les ressources et les activités économiques des églises en Égypte du IVe au VIIIe siècle*, Papyrologica Bruxellensia 10 (Brussels: Fondation Égyptologique Reine Élisabeth, 1972), 109–19. Wipszycka's scholarship on Christianity in late antique Egypt is fundamental.

6. On the subject, see E. Wipszycka, "L'attività caritativa dei vescovi egiziani," in *L'évêque dans la cité du IVe au Ve siècle: Image et autorité. Actes de la table ronde organisée par l'Istituto patristico Augustinianum et l'École française de Rome (Rome, 1er et 2 décembre 1995)*, ed. É. Rebillard and C. Sotinel, CÉFAR 248 (Rome: École Française de Rome, 1998), 78–80.

7. An exception is J. P. Thomas, *Private Religious Foundations in the Byzantine Empire*, Dumbarton Oaks Studies 24 (Washington, DC: Dumbarton Oaks Research Library and Collection, 1987), chap. 3.

chōra, the demography of which will now be sketched. There were some fifty small cities, three of which predominate in the papyrological record: Oxyrhynchus, Hermopolis, and Arsinoe. To appreciate the scale of these settlements, one might consider Hermopolis, like the other two cities a nome capital and an episcopal seat. Hermopolis was about 120 hectares in area and had a population of perhaps 25,000.[8] Beyond the cities, some 2,000 to 2,500 villages dotted the countryside. While the population of the villages varied widely, an average figure in the range of 1,000 to 1,300 people is plausible. Exceptional among villages for both the size of its population and the richness of its papyrological record is Aphrodito, a nome capital until the sixth century, which had some 15,000 residents.[9] We will see that charitable institutions in Egypt were not confined to the cities; they were scattered among the villages as well.

As a way of entering the charitable nexus just posited, let us begin by "following the wine," that is, by tracing the administrative process that benefited the widows.[10] It should first be observed that, in comparison with the order regarding Sophia's coat, the orders issued to Victor *oinopratēs* are laconic.[11] Key information is missing, including the identity of the person or persons who issued the documents. One possibility might be the *oikonomoi* of the

8. For an overview of Egyptian cities in late antiquity, see R. S. Bagnall, *Egypt in Late Antiquity* (Princeton, NJ: Princeton University Press, 1993), 45–109. On the population of Hermopolis from the late third through the mid-fifth centuries, Bagnall (ibid., 53) suggests 25,000 to 50,000, settled in some 7,000 houses; for the same city in the fourth century, A. K. Bowman suggests about 20,000: "Landholding in the Hermopolite Nome in the Fourth Century A.D.," *JRS* 75 (1985): 139. On the difficulties of estimating populations in Egypt, see D. Rathbone, "Villages, Land and Population in Graeco-Roman Egypt," *PCPhS*, n.s., 36 (1990): 103–42.

9. Rathbone ("Villages, Land and Population," 123–24) estimates the average population of a village at about 1,000; Bagnall (*Egypt in Late Antiquity*, 110) prefers 1,270. On the villages in general, see Bagnall, *Egypt in Late Antiquity*, 110–47. On Aphrodito, see L. S. B. MacCoull, *Dioscorus of Aphrodito: His Work and His World*, Transformation of the Classical Heritage 16 (Berkeley: University of California Press, 1988), 1–9; and, among his many superb studies of the village and its papyri, J. G. Keenan, "The Aphrodite Papyri and Village Life in Byzantine Egypt," *BSAC* 26 (1984): 51–63.

10. On widows in the papyri, see G. Tibiletti, "Le vedove nei papiri greci d'Egitto," PapCongr. 17, 3:985–94; and J. Beaucamp, "La référence au veuvage dans les papyrus byzantins," *Pallas* 32 (1985): 149–57. Rowlandson, *Women and Society*, gathers a number of texts related to widows. For widows as recipients of churches' charity, see briefly J.-U. Krause, "La prise en charge des veuves par l'église dans l'antiquité tardive," in *La fin de la cité antique et le début de la cite médiévale de la fin du IIIe siècle à l'avènement de Charlemagne: Actes du colloque tenu à l'Université de Paris X-Nanterre, les 1, 2 et 3 avril 1993*, ed. C. Lepelley, Munera 8 (Bari: Edipuglia, 1996), 115–26; and, at greater length, idem, *Witwen und Waisen im römischen Reich*, Heidelberger althistorische Beiträge und epigraphische Studien 19 (Stuttgart: F. Steiner, 1995), vol. 4.

11. A sample order to Victor (*SB* XXII 15530): "To Victor wine merchant. Give to the widows of St. Victor a *diploun* of wine, 1 only. Mesore 16 of the 5th indiction, beginning of the 6th." Compare with the order regarding Sophia's coat: "The holy church to Peter, steward of Cosmas. Provide to Sophia, widow, from the coats that you have for good use, one coat, 1 coat only. Farewell. In the year 156 = 125, Mecheir 1 of the 3rd indiction."

churches to which the widows were attached. But this is not the case: the handwriting in our documents indicates that the four orders-of-provision were written by the same person. It may have been a private individual: in the accounts of the Apiones, a prominent family in Oxyrhynchus, line items evince gifts to widows.[12] While this second possibility cannot be completely ruled out, a third explanation, first suggested by Roger Rémondon,[13] seems the most likely: an official working for the episcopal church of Oxyrhynchus. Bishops coordinated charitable relief in their dioceses and were charged with the support of widows.[14] The parallels between *P. Wisc.* II 64 and *SB* XXII 15529 offer the most suggestive evidence for this identification. Both documents are orders-of-provision: the former records a gift made by the episcopal church (*hagia ekklēsia*) to a widow of Sts. Cosmas and Damian; the latter records a gift to the widows of the same church, without identifying the donor. By analogy, the episcopal church, with its documented interest in the widows of Sts. Cosmas and Damian, is the logical candidate for the unidentified donor in *SB* XXII 15529 and the other three orders issued to Victor *oinopratēs*. Other orders-of-provision emanating from the *hagia ekklēsia* confirm that this church distributed wine. In one such document, Gregory, a presbyter of the *hagia ekklēsia*, instructs Menas, a wine steward (*oinocheiristēs*), to provide two *dipla* of wine to a *strōtēs*.[15]

The telegraphic style of the four orders issued to Victor begs other questions. How would Victor have ascertained the precise identity of the widows associated with a particular church so that he could arrange for deliveries to be made to individual recipients? He may have consulted a copy of the list of widows whom the church supported. Churches across the late antique Mediterranean kept such lists, and those in Egypt were no exception.[16] Or Victor,

12. *PSI* VIII 953.61, 956.43; *P. Oxy.* LVIII 3960.23, LXVII 4620.5–7 (the last text is probably Apionic). Cf. *SB* VI 9613, frag. 2.

13. Rémondon, "Église dans la société égyptienne," 265–66, who also identified the *hagia ekklēsia* as the episcopal church of Oxyrhynchus. Rémondon's interpretation is accepted by Papaconstantinou, *Culte des saints*, 280. See also *P. Oxy.* LXVIII 4702, comm. on lines 3–4.

14. Wipszycka, "Attività caritativa"; A. Martin, "L'image de l'évêque à travers les 'Canons d'Athanase': Devoirs et réalités," in Rebillard and Sotinel, eds., *Évêque dans la cité*, 59–70; Krause, "Prise en charge des veuves," 117–18.

15. *P. Oxy.* XVI 1951, with A. Serfass, "On the Meaning of *strōtēs* in *P. Oxy.* XVI 1951," *ZPE* 161 (2007): 253–59. Other orders-of-provision issued explicitly by the *hagia ekklēsia*: *P. Oxy.* VI 993, XVI 1950, *PSI Congr. XX* 17, *P. Laur.* III 95; cf. *P. Wash.Univ.* II 100. See N. Gonis, "Chronological Notes on III.–V. Century Documents," *ZPE* 123 (1998): 197n12; idem, "Notes on Oxyrhynchus Papyri III," *ZPE* 150 (2004): 199–200.

16. Egypt: *Canons of Athanasius of Alexandria: The Arabic and Coptic Versions*, ed. and trans. W. Riedel and W. E. Crum, Text and Translation Society Publications 9 (London: Williams and Norgate, 1904; repr., Amsterdam: Philo, 1973), canon 61. Some churches included all their dependents on a single list; others maintained multiple lists for their various groups of dependents (e.g., widows). On the lists generally, see inter alios J. Herrin, "Ideals of Charity, Realities of Welfare: The Philanthropic Activity of the Byzantine Church," in *Church and People in Byzantium*, ed. R. Morris,

having received a number of these orders before, simply may have known from experience the names of the widows who were eligible. This might explain why the orders are so terse; Victor was familiar with the distributions and needed only minimal instructions.[17] It is reasonable to assume that distributions to these widows were made regularly. The *Canons of Athanasius*, of Egyptian provenance and dating to the late fourth or early fifth century, enjoin bishops to give alms to those in need, including widows, on a weekly basis; generous gifts were to be made on the great feasts of Epiphany, Pentecost, and Easter.[18] Indeed, Arietta Papaconstantinou has noted that the date of the orders to Victor *oinoprates*, August 9, suggests that the wine may have been distributed to the widows in honor of the Feast of the Assumption.[19]

It is useful to discuss briefly Victor's title. An *oinoprates* is a wine merchant; the suffix *-prates* denotes an individual involved with buying and selling.[20] This occupation, strictly speaking, is distinct from that of an *oinocheiristes*, a steward or overseer of wine stores, usually those belonging to a prominent landowner. While these titles imply distinct occupations, the duties of *oinopratai* and *oinocheiristai* might overlap: for example, there is evidence of *oinocheiristai* purchasing and selling wine.[21] This information is germane to the interpretation of yet another order-of-provision from Oxyrhynchus. This document is addressed to Victor *oinocheiristes*, who is ordered (again the sender's name is absent) to give one *diploun* of wine to the widows of the *martyrion* of St. John. This document is very similar—but not identical—to

---

Society for the Promotion of Byzantine Studies Spring Symposium 20 (Birmingham, UK: Centre for Byzantine, Ottoman and Modern Greek Studies, University of Birmingham, 1990), 153–55; V. Neri, *I marginali nell'occidente tardoantico: Poveri, "infames" e criminali nella nascente società cristiana*, Munera 12 (Bari: Edipuglia, 1998), 97–102; P. Brown, *Poverty and Leadership in the Later Roman Empire*, Menahem Stern Jerusalem Lectures (Hanover, NH: University Press of New England, 2002), 64–65.

17. The writer of the four texts consistently abbreviates a number of words in the orders, including that for "widows" (χηρρ for χήραις). This may be a further indication that the distributions were regular. Because of Victor's familiarity with the distributions, it was unnecessary for the writer to spell things out. Cf. the order to provide Sophia with a coat, where the word for widow (χήρᾳ) is written in full and the widow herself is explicitly named, perhaps indicating that this was an unusual gift whose recipient needed specific identification.

18. *Canons of Athanasius*, canon 16. Martin ("Image de l'évêque," 63) calculates that about one-third of the *Canons* concern charity. On the *Canons'* dating and provenance, see Martin, "Image de l'évêque," 59–60.

19. Papaconstantinou, *Culte des saints*, 280.

20. L. Casarico, "Reportorio di nomi di mestieri: I sostantivi in -πώλης e -πράτης," *SPap* 22 (1983): 23–37.

21. T. M. Hickey, "A Public 'House' but Closed: 'Fiscal Participation' and Economic Decision Making on the Oxyrhynchite Estate of the Flavii Apiones" (PhD diss., University of Chicago, 2001), 133–35, 217; R. Mazza, *L'archivio degli Apioni: Terra, lavoro e proprietà senatoria nell'Egitto tardo-antico*, Munera 17 (Bari: Edipuglia, 2001), 146. On the lexical distinction between *oinoprates* and *oinocheiristes*, see LSJ, 9th ed., and *WB*, s.vv.; S. Daris, "Ricevuta per la consegna di vino," *ZPE* 36 (1979): 85.

the orders addressed to Victor *oinopratēs*.[22] Noting that the terms *oinopratēs* and *oinocheiristēs* are not equivalent, the editor of this text warns against identifying Victor *oinocheiristēs* with Victor *oinopratēs*. But based on the texts' similarities it seems probable that the two Victors are indeed one and the same; the same individual could easily take on the roles of both wine merchant (*oinopratēs*) and wine steward (*oinocheiristēs*) for the episcopal church of Oxyrhynchus. As a parallel, one might look to the dossier of Kyrikos, deacon and *elaiopratēs* (oil merchant) of the episcopal church of Arsinoe. Ewa Wipszycka describes Kyrikos as "chef des magasins d'huile appartenant a l'église épiscopale d'Arsinoe." In other words, Wipszycka considers the "merchant" to be acting as a "steward."[23]

Where did the church's wine come from? There are at least three possibilities. The church may have purchased the wine. This seems the least likely source, as only one papyrus attests to the purchase of wine by a church.[24] There was less need to buy wine when two other sources were readily available: the offerings of the faithful and the produce of property owned by the church. Offerings were frequently made in kind, sometimes in the form of wine. For example, the accounts of the Apiones detail the family's donations in wine and wine vinegar (*oxos*) to more than a dozen ecclesiastical institutions, in quantities ranging from six to one thousand *dipla*;[25] some of the donations were offered on a customary basis (*kata to ethos*). One account also records a blanket donation "to the holy churches and *xenodocheia* and *martyria* of the city and in the country [of Oxyrhynchus]" of 8,458 *knidia* of wine and wine vinegar—in modern metrology, more than 36,000

22. *P. Oxy.* LXVII 4622. There are differences between this order to Victor *oinocheiristēs* and those issued to Victor *oinopratēs*. According to its editor, the former document is written in a different hand, omits the word "δός," was discovered in a different excavation season, and was issued on a different month and day. A Victor *oinocheiristēs* is also attested in *SB* XVI 12608 + *BL* IX 287, from Oxyrhynchus and dating to July 11, 511.

23. The quotation is from Wipszycka, *Ressources*, 40; see also 146, and idem, "Deux papyrus relatifs à l'administration écclesiastique," *CE* 89 (1970): 142. On the dossier of Kyrikos, see now F. Morelli, *Olio e retribuzioni nell'Egitto tardo (V–VIII d.C.)* (Florence: Istituto Papirologico G. Vitelli, 1996), 28–41.

24. *P. Cair.Masp.* II 67168, in which Theodoros, bishop of the Pentapolis in Libya, arranges for the advanced purchase of 1,500 *knidia* of wine from a Pachomian monastery in the Hermopolite. There are two examples of monasteries purchasing wine: *P. Bad.* IV 55, *P. Prag.* I 45. See further G. Schmelz, *Kirchliche Amtsträger im spätantiken Ägypten: Nach den Aussagen der griechischen und koptischen Papyri und Ostraka*, Archiv für Papyrusforschung und verwandte Gebiete, Beiheft 13 (Munich: K. G. Saur, 2002), 191–93.

25. Six *dipla*: *P. Oxy.* XXVII 2480.119; 1,000 *dipla*: *P. Oxy.* XVI 2044.18, but see Hickey, "Public 'House,'" 222. The Apiones' offerings in wine to ecclesiastical institutions are tabulated in Thomas, *Private Religious Foundations*, 98–101, and Hickey, "Public 'House,'" 218–24. On the Apiones generally, see E. R. Hardy, *The Large Estates of Byzantine Egypt*, Studies in History, Economics and Public Law 354 (New York: Columbia University Press, 1931); Hickey, "Public 'House'"; Mazza, *Archivio degli Apioni*.

liters.[26] How many religious institutions were to share this vinous largesse is not clear. The other important source of wine—and of ecclesiastical revenue generally—was agricultural property owned by churches. Churches' properties were typically leased out rather than farmed directly by slaves or *coloni*. Papyri confirm that churches and other Christian institutions owned vineyards. For example, the public physician (*archiatros*) Flavius Phoibammon bequeaths, in his will, one *aroura* of vineyards, with its own irrigation equipment, to a monastery of Apa Jeremias. The hospital of Apa Dios owned thirteen-sixteenths of an *aroura* of vineyards in Aphrodito.[27] Rents and fees on vineyards might be paid in wine.[28] Since the episcopal church of Oxyrhynchus employs *oinocheiristai*, this institution may have owned vineyards.[29] So the widows may have enjoyed wine obtained through purchase or, what is more likely, through offerings, or through the yields of the episcopal church's proprietary vineyards.

As the cases of Victor *oinopratēs* and Kyrikos *elaiopratēs* indicate, churches maintained stores of goods in kind, such as wine and oil. A further observation should be made about churches' assets in grain. Of the commercial properties owned by Egyptian churches, most commonly attested are bakeries.[30] For example, two receipts attest to rent paid by a baker, Peter, for the lease of a church-owned bakery. A lease evinces a rental agreement between the episcopal church of Hermopolis and a baker.[31] Why did churches so often own bakeries? Because churches always needed bread. One might speculate that owning a bakery or keeping a baker on retainer could obviate the need to maintain separate grain stores. Rents and offerings in grain could be received directly by a bakery, where they could be stored or converted into bread, which was then employed in the liturgy or distributed to the church's clergy and dependents. Bakeries could act as clearinghouses in churches' networks of charitable distribution.

26. *P. Oxy.* LVIII 3960.20–22; in this text, one *knidion* is almost certainly equivalent to eight *sextarii* (about 4.3 liters): see introduction to text; Hickey, "Public 'House,'" 135n238; but cf. P. Mayerson, "The Enigmatic Knidion: A Wine Measure in Late Roman/Byzantine Egypt?" *ZPE* 141 (2002): 206–7.

27. Flavius Phoibammon: *P. Cair.Masp.* II 67151. Hospital of Apa Dios: *SB* XX 14669.89. 1 aroura = 0.2756 hectares.

28. E.g., *P. Mich.* XIII 667, *P. Köln* II 104.

29. So also Wipszycka, *Ressources*, 49. Oinocheiristai: *P. Oxy.* XVI 1951, LXVII 4622. A papyrus published after the text of this chapter was finalized confirms that the episcopal church of Oxyrhynchus owned vineyards: A. Benaissa, "New Light on the Episcopal Church of Oxyrhynchus," *ZPE* 161 (2007): 199–206.

30. E. Wipszycka, "L'église dans la chora égyptienne et les artisans," *Aegyptus* 48 (1968): 130–38; idem, *Ressources*, 60–63.

31. *SB* XII 10766–67; *P. Alex.* 32 + *BL* V 3, VII 4. See also the dossier of Elias, *diakonos* and *artopratēs* (baker), and Paeitos *artopratēs* for the bishop Peter: H. Harrauer, "Die Bäcker Elias und Paeitos," *APF* 37 (1991): 51–54. Furthermore, it is noted in the *Canons of Athanasius* (canon 34, trans. Riedel and Crum) that "it is not permitted unto a priest to go out on account of the bread of offering and to stand at the oven." It is tempting to infer from this canon that an oven was a common fixture of an Egyptian church, but the text does not indicate whether the church actually owned the oven in question.

Watchers for the Widows

To sum up this study so far, it has been suggested that widows, tied to particular churches in Oxyrhynchus, received recurrent distributions of wine from diocesan wine holdings at the request of an administrator of the city's episcopal church. It is now time to turn to the other order-of-provision adduced in the opening of this essay. Here the widow Sophia is to receive a coat, a gift appropriate to the season as the document is dated to late January. The *hagia ekklēsia* is explicitly identified as the sender of the order, which is directed to the *oikonomos* of Sts. Cosmas and Damian. This official is assumed to have a store of coats ready for just such a request. This is not surprising; churches are known to have stockpiled clothes for charity. In 303, civil officials inventoried the possessions of a church in the North African village of Cirta and discovered, among other items, "82 women's tunics . . . [and] 47 pairs of women's shoes."[32] These items were surely meant for distribution to women supported by the church.

The provision of a coat to an individual widow seems likely to have stemmed from a special request rather than a regular distribution. Sophia might have voiced her need at one of the regular distributions or meals that were held for widows and other dependents.[33] But what if she were housebound or frail? Who watched over the churches' widows? Members of the clergy, of course, visited widows; indeed, in Alexandria, certain clergy were specially appointed to look after them.[34] There is suggestive papyrological evidence that in Egypt the care of some widows was assumed by a group of laywomen known as *hai pros chērais*, which we might translate as "the women for the widows."[35] Very little is known about these women, who appear in only two papyri, but we might speculate that they not only would have visited the widows but also would have acted as intermediaries between the widows and churches, thereby seeing to the widows' special needs, like that of a coat. The oversight of widows and of other groups of dependents also might have been assumed by other laypeople, especially by the members of the churches' lay

32. Optatus Appendix 1.3 = J.-L. Maier, *Le dossier du Donatisme*, TU 134 (Berlin: Akademie-Verlag, 1987), 1:219, with n. 59. English trans. from M. Edwards, ed., *Optatus: Against the Donatists*, Translated Texts for Historians 27 (Liverpool: Liverpool University Press, 1997), 154.

33. *Les canons d'Hippolyte: Édition critique de la version arabe, introduction et traduction française*, ed. R.-G. Coquin, PO, vol. 31, no. 2 (Paris: Firmin-Didot, 1966), canon 35; cf. 5, 32; *Canons of Athanasius*, canon 16; cf. 6, 61, 70; Athanasius *H. Ar.* 13.3, 61.2 (Opitz II 1.5:189, II 1.6:217).

34. οἱ πεπιστευμένοι τὰς χήρας κληρικοί, Athanasius, *H. Ar.* 61.2 (Opitz II 1.6:217).

35. *SB* XII 10926.17, *P. Bad.* IV 97.21 + *BL* VI 9. On *hai pros chērais*, see E. Wipszycka, "Les confréries dans la vie religieuse de l'Égypte chrétienne," PapCongr. 12, 511–24, at 524. A revised version of this study appears in idem, *Études sur le christianisme dans l'Égypte de l'antiquité tardive*, SEAug 52 (Rome: Institutum Patristicum Augustinianum, 1996), 257–78.

confraternities, or *philoponeia*.[36] In late antique sources, *philoponoi* are characterized by their zealous attendance at church services and their charitable works. Papyri confirm that *philoponeia*, like their better-known medieval counterparts, drew their members from all strata of society. On the one hand, a Hermopolite *philoponeion* was led by a man of the highest senatorial rank (*gloriosissimus*); on the other, a list of *philoponoi* enumerates among others three farmers, two tailors, an embroiderer, a carpenter, a cantor (*psaltēs*), and a merchant.[37] Confraternities elsewhere were open to women, but there is, as yet, no papyrological evidence for female *philoponoi*.

Charitable Institutions

The existence of *philoponoi* and *hai pros chērais* indicates that laymen and laywomen played a role in the philanthropic enterprise. Another important role was played by specialized institutions dedicated to those in need, charitable foundations such as *nosokomeia*, *xeneōnes*, *hospitia*, *xenodocheia*, and *gērokomeia*. The papyrological evidence for these charities has never been the subject of a full-length study.[38] In preparing the following discussion, I compiled a database of more than sixty papyri in which references to charities or their employees are found.

A charitable foundation does not appear in a securely dated papyrus until 502, in a lease of a dining room in Oxyrhynchus. The room was located in a particular quarter of the city named for a *xenodocheion Aollou*.[39] References to charities do not become common until the middle of the sixth century

36. On the *philoponeia*, see Wipszycka, "Confréries"; *P. Sorb.* II, introduction, pp. 76–77; J. Russell, *The Mosaic Inscriptions of Anemurium*, Österreichische Akademie der Wissenschaften, Denkschriften, Philosophisch-Historische Klasse 190 (Vienna: Verlag der Österreichischen Akademie der Wissenschaften, 1987), 61–64; P. J. Sijpesteijn, "New Light on the ΦΙΛΟΠΟΝΟΙ," *Aegyptus* 69 (1989): 95–99; Papaconstantinou, *Culte des saints*, 279–80.

37. Hermopolite: *P. Lond.Copt.* I 1013, with *P. Sorb.* II, introduction, p. 76. List of *philoponoi*: *SB* XX 14105 = *P. Lond.* III 1071b desc.

38. Previous compilations and treatments of the papyrological evidence include Wipszycka, *Ressources*, 115–19; *P. Bingen* 136; H. R. Hagemann, "Die rechtliche Stellung der christlichen Wohltätigkeitsanstalten in der östlichen Reichshälfte," *RIDA*, ser. 3, 3 (1956): 275–80; K. Mentzou-Meimari, "Ἐπαρχιακὰ εὐαγῆ ἱδρύματα μέχρι τοῦ τέλους τῆς Εἰκονομαχίας," *Byzantina* 11 (1982): 295–306; G. Husson, "L'hospitalité dans les papyrus byzantins," PapCongr. 13, 174–77; W. F. G. J. Stoetzer and K. A. Worp, "Zwei Steuerquittungen aus London und Wien," *Tyche* 1 (1986): 195–202; P. van Minnen, "Medical Care in Late Antiquity," in *Ancient Medicine in Its Socio-cultural Context: Papers Read at the Congress Held at Leiden University, 13–15 April 1992*, ed. P. J. van der Eijk, H. F. J. Horstmanshoff, and P. H. Schrijvers, Clio Medica 27 (Amsterdam: Rodopi, 1995), 1:161–66.

39. *P. Oxy.* L 3600.12–13. This *xenodocheion* was in existence for more than sixty years, as it is attested again in 566 (*PSI* VI 709.15–16 + *P. Oxy.* L 3600, comm. on line 12) and in a text dating to the sixth or seventh century (*P. Lond.* V 1762.12 + *BL* VIII 193, X 108). In literary sources there are attestations of Egyptian charitable institutions dating from before the sixth century: Mentzou-Meimari, "Ἐπαρχιακὰ εὐαγῆ ἱδρύματα," 295–306; *RE*, 9a.2:1494–95, s.v. ξενοδοχεῖον.

and coincide with the promulgation of extensive legislation by Justinian regarding them.[40] Egyptians were acquainted with Justinian's new laws. In a recently republished will, the testator leaves a legacy to a hospital and then threatens his or her heiress, Christodora, by quoting from Justinian's first *Novella*, which promises disinheritance to an heir who fails to pay, within a year, the legacies outlined in a will.[41] According to another *Novella* of Justinian, charities (*euageis oikoi*) may be divided into two categories. On the one hand were charitable institutions administered by bishops and their deputies. On the other hand were institutions founded, funded, and administered by private individuals.[42] A recent and generally superb study of hospitals in late antiquity has suggested that private hospitals predominated in late antique Egypt, and that they functioned, for the most part, independently of local ecclesiastical authorities.[43] But agnosticism is perhaps in order regarding the question of whether private foundations outnumbered ecclesiastical foundations in Egypt. In most of the papyri in which charities appear, it is difficult to determine definitively whether a particular foundation is under direct ecclesiastical control or under the control of private individuals.[44] Furthermore, private charities were independent from ecclesiastical authorities only to a degree. Imperial law did vouchsafe to founders certain privileges over their institutions, such as the right to select their administrators and to transmit their charities' management to heirs. But from the middle of the fifth century, canon and civil law extended bishops' oversight of the private charities in their dioceses.[45] To illustrate this point, one may return to the example of Flavius Phoibammon, the *archiatros* mentioned above. In his will, Phoibammon transfers the management of a hospital, the oversight of which he had himself inherited from his father, to his brother John. According to Justinianic law, should John mismanage the hospital, he could be removed by the local bishop, who would assume control of the institu-

40. 551: *P. Oxy.* XIX 2238; 565/66: *P. Oxy.* XXVII 2480.44; 566: *PSI* VI 709; 566/567: *PSI* VIII 953 + *BL* V 125. On Justinian's legislation regarding charitable institutions, see Hagemann, "Christlichen Wohltätigkeitsanstalten," 272–83; and idem, *Die Stellung der Piae Causae nach justinianischem Rechte*, Basler Studien zur Rechtswissenschaft 37 (Basel: Helbing & Lichtenhahn, 1953).

41. *P. Bodl.* I 47 = *P. Grenf.* I 62 = M. Amelotti and L. Migliardi Zingale, *Le Costituzioni giustinianee nei papiri e nelle epigrafi*, 2nd ed., Legum Iustiniani Imperatoris Vocabularium, Subsidia 1 (Milan: A. Giuffrè, 1985), 77–78. Cf. *CJ* 1.3.45.

42. *Nov.* 120.6, with Hagemann, *Stellung der Piae Causae*, 49–58.

43. Van Minnen, "Medical Care," 162–63: "Most Egyptian hospitals are institutions independent of ecclesiastical institutions with an endowment from private individuals and occasional gifts (*prosphorai*) from other sources" (162).

44. There are exceptions: see, e.g., *P. Oxy.* XIX 2238; *P. Sorb.* II 19 A26, 31 20; *P. Cair.Masp.* II 67151. On the difficulty of ascertaining from the sources whether a particular religious foundation was private, see also Thomas, *Private Religious Foundations*, 3–4.

45. Thomas, *Private Religious Foundations*, 37–58; T. S. Miller, *The Birth of the Hospital in the Byzantine Empire*, rev. ed., Henry E. Sigerist Supplements to the Bulletin of the History of Medicine, n.s., 10 (Baltimore: Johns Hopkins University Press, 1997), 100–105.

tion and nominate a substitute administrator.[46] An activist bishop, ready to define mismanagement in the broadest of terms, might have watched John like a hawk. To put it another way, the independence enjoyed by a particular charitable institution surely had much to do with the proclivity of the local prelate. Some heirs were indeed negligent in discharging their responsibilities with regard to religious foundations (*CJ* 1.2.15, 1.3.45). Phoibammon tries to forestall such a scenario when he warns John that, should he mismanage the hospital, God will take note.[47] Justinian legislated closer ties between the private founders of charities and prelates: the former were to secure episcopal approval before building, and the latter were to preside over liturgical rites at the construction site.[48] Ideally, clergy and donors would work together when planning new foundations. An example of such cooperation may be found in a fascinating but lacunose letter, dating to the sixth or seventh century, in which a count (*komēs*) addresses a cleric, almost certainly a bishop, regarding the construction of a new hospital. The count will cover the costs of building, but the cleric will oversee construction. The count pointedly refers to the foundation as *to ho[s]pi[ti]n sou*: your, that is, the cleric's hospital.[49] Despite the private funding, the church will be in charge.

Like churches, charities received their income from offerings and rents. Regular offerings were made to local charities by the Apiones: for example, a receipt issued by Menas, *notarios* of the Apion family and *oikonomos* of the *nosokomeion* of Abba Elias, records a gift of 371 *artabas* of wheat to that institution. This is a large gift, more than 14,000 liters of grain. This charity, one suspects, was entirely funded by the Apiones; Menas's double title strengthens this assumption. More modest gifts are also attested, like the seven *artabas* that the Apiones gave to the *nosokomeion* of Leukadios.[50] Charities owned houses and agricultural properties and, like other Christian institutions, were willing to issue emphyteutic leases, long-term agreements that offered rights to the leaseholders, such as the capacity to transmit the lease to heirs, that approached those of ownership.[51] Because charities' immovable property was generally inalienable—though there were loopholes in this ban—their landholdings essentially functioned as endowments and provided regular income in the form of rents. Some institutions came to own

46. *P. Cair.Masp.* II 67151; *CJ* 1.3.45.3; *Nov.* 131.10.

47. *P. Cair.Masp.* II 67151.195. On the will, see also van Minnen, "Medical Care," 164–66; Mac-Coull, *Dioscorus of Aphrodito*, 50–54; Hagemann, "Christliche Wohltätigkeitsanstalten," 276.

48. Thomas, *Private Religious Foundations*, 42–43; Hagemann, "Christliche Wohltätigkeitsanstalten," 272–73.

49. *P. Bas.* 19 + *BL* I 433, III 7: τὸ ὁ[σ]πί[τι]ν σου. Textual problems with this papyrus make the interpretation offered here probable, but not entirely sure.

50. Abba Elias: *P. Oxy.* XVI 1898. Here, one *artaba* (*kankellos* measure) equals about thirty-nine liters. Leukadios: *P. Oxy.* LXI 4131.

51. Emphyteusis: *Stud.Pal.* III 47, 314. Other rental receipts and leases: *PSI* IV 284, *SB* I 4869, *BKU* III 348. Houses: *Stud.Pal.* VIII 791, 875.

landholdings of some significance. The hospital of Apa Dios owned more than twenty-five *arouras* of vineyards, orchards, and arable land in Aphrodito.[52] The most telling document regarding the prosperity of a particular institution is a "declaration" (*homologia*) issued by an official of the *nosokomeion Basileou Antinoou*, acknowledging that the charity had received a refund in its taxes (*dēmosia*) for the second indiction of one pound of gold (seventy-two *solidi*). This implies that the institution was annually paying more than seventy-two *solidi* in taxes, a considerable sum. This is by far the largest fiscal payment made by a charity in the papyri.[53]

Charities employed a variety of people. They were administered by officials known as *oikonomoi*, *nosokomoi*, or *epitropoi*, who in turn might be aided by assistants (*dioikētai*) and property managers (*pronoētai*); there is an example of an official with the dual title of *pronoētēs* and *nosokomos*.[54] Deacons are attested, especially in service of the *nosokomeion megalon* of Arsinoe; in one case, an official bears the compound title of deacon and *nosokomos*. Nurses (*hypourgoi*) appear in two documents, and public physicians (*archiatroi*) are associated with two hospitals, which bolsters the claim that Justinian reassigned these physicians to work in Christian hospitals.[55] Of particular interest is an Oxyrhynchite *nosokomeion* that employs a female *oikonomos*, named Maura, who is the only female administrator of a charitable institution known from Egypt.[56] The papyri are far more informative about charities' finances and administration than about the care they provide, but a recently published text does detail one aspect of their work. The document, written by the administrator of a *xenodocheion*, lists distributions of grain. Among the beneficiaries are "the children of Daniel," who receive one-and-one-half *artabas*; the "bride of a baker" (*nyphē* [sic] *kathar[ourgou]*), one-and-one-half *artabas*; the wife of a courier, eleven *artabas*; and the daughter of a doorman (?), three and one-twelfth *artabas*.[57] The editor of the text plausibly

---

52. *SB* XX 14669.86, 89, 120, 142, 144; the hospital also appears in *PSI* IV 284.

53. *CPR* XXII 2; the editor compiles comparative data about taxes paid by other charitable foundations. The foundation's importance as a landholder is confirmed in *P. Sorb.* II (introduction, p. 78).

54. Oikonomoi: *PSI* IV 284; *P. Oxy.* XVI 1898 (and *notarios* for the Apiones), LXI 4131, *P. Vind. Worp* 15; *P. Haun.* III 64. Nosokomoi: *P. Bad.* IV 95; *Stud.Pal.* VIII 1090, X 16, 245 (?); *P. Lond.Copt.* I 1077; an ex-*nosokomos* appears in *P. Ryl.Copt.* 224. Epitropos: *P. Oxy.* XVI 2058.131. Dioikētēs (and reader): *P. Bad.* VI 173. Pronoētai: *P. Lond.Copt.* I 1077; *P. Lond.* III 1324 (p. 276); *Stud.Pal.* III 314 + *BL* VIII 438. Pronoētēs and nosokomos: *Stud.Pal.* III 47 + *BL* VII 255. Deacons: *Stud.Pal.* VIII 791, 875; *CPR* IV 198 (?); *SB* I 4903 (?), with Wipszycka, *Ressources*, 117; deacon and *nosokomos*: *SB* I 4668.

55. Hypourgoi: *P. Lond.* III 1028 (p. 276), *CPR* XII 9. Archiatroi: *Stud.Pal.* X 251 (but cf. *BL* VI 195); *P. Cair.Masp.* II 67151, with Miller, *Birth of the Hospital*, 48–49.

56. *P. Oxy.* LXI 4131.

57. *P. Bingen* 136. The first item: νύφη [sic] καθαρ[ουργοῦ]. For the last item mentioned, the text reads "(καὶ) (ὑπὲρ) Μαρία θυρ(ωροῦ) Πέτρε" (line 9; see comm. ad loc.). The editor translates as "und für Maria, Türhüterin des Petros." Since there are, to my knowledge, no other attestations of "doorwomen" (E. Wipszycka, "Les ordres mineurs dans l'église d'Égypte du IVe au VIIIe siècle,"

suggests that these women and children are widows and orphans supported by the *xenodocheion*, which is seen here operating as a source for charitable distributions in kind.

How often do charities appear in the papyrological record? It should first be noted that the terminology employed for these institutions is not always a sure guide to the services they provided; for example, in Greek, *xeneōn* was originally synonymous with *xenodocheion* (guest house), but later came to mean hospital.[58] The hospital of Apa Dios in Synoria is in one document called a *xeneōn* and in another a *xenodocheion*.[59] That said, most commonly attested are *nosokomeia*. These institutions (or their *nosokomoi*) appear in thirty-four documents, in a few of which multiple *nosokomeia* are listed. *Xenodocheia* appear in eighteen documents, in a few of which, once again, multiple such institutions are named. *Xeneōnes* appear in five documents, *hospitia* in five, and a fragmentary text provides the only papyrological testimonium of a *gērokomeion*. To my knowledge, poorhouses, orphanages, and other such institutions do not appear in papyri.[60] Most foundations were located in or near cities, but at least four charities, and perhaps more, were located in villages or smaller settlements.[61] While Wipszycka is right to point out that urban residents, with their proximity to prosperous episcopal churches, had readier access to support than those

JJP 22 (1992): 181–215 = *Études sur le christianisme*, 225–55, at 252–54), perhaps θυρ(ωροῦ) Πέτρε should be read as a patronym: "Maria, daughter of doorman Peter."

58. On the terminology, see Miller, *Birth of the Hospital*, 23–29; V. Nutton, *Ancient Medicine* (London: Routledge, 2004), 308.

59. *Xeneōn*: *SB* XX 14669; *xenodocheion*: *PSI* IV 284. Alternatively, there may have been two sister institutions in Synoria bearing the name of Apa Dios, one a hospital (*xeneōn*) and the other a hostel (*xenodocheion*).

60. Monasteries, however, might act as de facto orphanages. Extant are a number of Coptic legal documents by which parents donate their children to the Theban monastery of St. Phoibammon: see now A. Papaconstantinou, "Notes sur les actes de donation d'enfant au monastère thébain de Saint-Phoibammon," *JJP* 32 (2002): 83–105, and idem, "ΘΕΙΑ ΟΙΚΟΝΟΜΙΑ: Les actes thébains de donation d'enfants ou la gestion monastique de la pénurie," in *Mélanges Gilbert Dagron*, Travaux et mémoires 14 (Paris: De Boccard, 2002), 511–26.

61. (1) Ibion Sesymbotheos, a village in the Hermopolite nome: *SB* XVIII 13770 + M. Drew-Bear, *Le nome hermopolite: Toponymes et sites, ASP* 21 (1979), s.v. Ἰβιὼν Σεσυμβώθεως. (2) Synoria, a village in the Panopolite nome: *PSI* IV 284; *SB* XX 14669.86, 89, 120, 142, 144 + J. Gascou and K. A. Worp, "The Panopolitan Village ΣΥΝΟΡΙΑ," *ZPE* 112 (1996): 163–64. (3) Ptolemais, a village in the Arsinoite (there were multiple villages by that name in the nome): *Stud.Pal.* X 219 + Calderini, *Diz.geogr.* and supplements, s.v. Πτολεμαΐς. (4) the *epoikion* or *ktēma Leōnidou* in the Oxyrhynchite: *P. Oxy.* XVI 1910.r4 + P. Pruneti, *I centri abitati dell'Ossirinchite: Repertorio toponomastico*, Papyrologica Florentina 9 (Florence: Edizioni Gonnelli, 1981), s.v. Λεωνίδου. Other candidates: (5) Leukadios, *P. Oxy.* LXI 4131 + Pruneti, *Centri abitati*, s.v. Λευκαδίου. (6) Spania: an *epitropos* of a *xenodocheion* resides in this Oxyrhynchite village, which may indicate that such an institution was there located: *P. Oxy.* XVI 2058.131 + Pruneti, *Centri abitati*, s.v. Σπανία. (7) *Nosokomeion* "in the plain" (ἐν πεδίῳ): *SB* I 4869. See also van Minnen, "Medical Care," 162; Husson, "Hospitalité," 176–77. For the presence of charities in small settlements in Syria, see Nutton, *Ancient Medicine*, 307.

who lived elsewhere,[62] it is important to note that charitable institutions were located in the countryside as well.

The most valuable evidence for the penetration of charitable institutions in Egypt derives from an enormous, yet incomplete, cadastre that records taxes in wheat paid on properties in the Hermopolite nome (*P. Sorb*. II). The cadastre dates to either 618/619 or 633/634 and thus offers a snapshot of landholding patterns in an area of approximately 440 square kilometers on the eve of the Arab conquest of Egypt. Christian institutions occupy, to paraphrase the text's editor, an enviable position as landowners.[63] The cadastre evinces the simultaneous existence in the region of twenty-nine churches, twenty-five monasteries, and, more importantly for our purposes, one *diakonia*, seven *philoponeia*, and seven hospitals, two of which specialized in the treatment of leprosy. If the region's population is estimated at 40,000, a high figure, then there was one hospital for every 5,700 residents.[64] Six other Hermopolite hospitals are known from other documents, so this ratio is likely to have been even lower. Indeed, Peter van Minnen notes that the "ratio may have been lower than anywhere else at any given time before the Industrial Revolution."[65] Charitable institutions had saturated this particular area of Egypt.

Conclusion

In this study, the mechanisms of Christian charity in late antique Egypt have been surveyed from the ground up. Although the great cities of the eastern Mediterranean are considered the grand theaters of late antique philanthropy, a survey of the papyrological evidence reveals a responsive system of Christian charity in the small cities and even, to some degree, in the villages of the Egyptian *chōra*. Episcopal churches superintended philanthropic networks, in which ecclesiastical revenues, often in the form of goods in kind, were regularly distributed to those in need. Laymen and women acted as go-betweens, bridging the gap between the needy and the church administrators who aided them. Charitable institutions, funded through gifts and rents, provided specialized care to the sick, to travelers, to the aged, and

62. Wipszycka, "Attività caritativa," 75–78.

63. "L' 'Église,' sous ses diverses modalités, occupe dans notre livre une position, sinon dominante (loin de là), du moins enviable," *P. Sorb*. II, introduction, p. 57.

64. Van Minnen, "Medical Care," 161–62, whose analysis of *P. Sorb*. II informs this entire paragraph. (Note, however, that *P. Sorb*. II evinces seven hospitals [introduction, pp. 78–79], not eight as suggested by van Minnen.) For this calculation to be truly meaningful, however, it would be necessary to know how many beds each hospital had.

65. Van Minnen, "Medical Care," 162.

to others. Living in the ancient Mediterranean was a dangerous business, but the Christians of Egypt tried to minimize the peril.[66]

66. How effective the Christians were at succoring the marginalized remains an open question: see, e.g., the pessimistic perspective of Krause, "Prise en charge des veuves," 124–25. As a coda to this study, it is worth noting that some of Egypt's charitable institutions survived well into the Islamic period: e.g., a *nosokomeion* was operating in Arsinoe as late as 678 (*SB* I 4668), and a *xenodocheion* is probably attested (the reading is not sure) in a papyrus dating to the year 706 (*P. Lond.* IV 1441.77). On Christian hospitals operating under Islamic rule, see P. Horden, "The Earliest Hospitals in Byzantium, Western Europe, and Islam," *Journal of Interdisciplinary History* 35 (2005): 361–89, esp. 369.

8

RICH AND POOR IN SOPHRONIUS OF JERUSALEM'S *MIRACLES OF SAINTS CYRUS AND JOHN*

SUSAN R. HOLMAN

The Christian healing shrine of the Diocletianic martyr-saints Cyrus and John at Menouthis in Egypt lies deep underwater today, six kilometers off the coast of Alexandria, in Aboukir Bay, buried by geologic and climatic changes that occurred some time after the eighth century CE.[1] The shrine's foundation is traditionally attributed to Cyril of Alexandria in the early fifth century as part of a campaign to counter pagan pilgrimage to the nearby healing sanctuary of Isis.[2] In this essay I discuss the only text we have that describes the shrine, Sophronius of Jerusalem's *Miracles of Saints Cyrus and John*, or *Thaumata*, a seventh-century collection of seventy short stories of miraculous healings, in light of the author's social context and known theo-

---

1. The area is currently being excavated by a French-Egyptian team headed by Franck Goddio (http://www.underwaterdiscovery.org/Sitemap/Project/CanopicRegion/Default.aspx; accessed July 3, 2006). Yvonne Stoltz of Oxford University is studying the gold and jewelry remains associated with the pilgrimage shrine.
   2. This is debated. See below.

logical agenda.[3] This essay looks particularly at Sophronius's four story-sets that seem clearly, if rhetorically, to connect a rich person in the text with another who is poor.

Incubation healing shrines are traditionally associated with Asclepius,[4] and Patricia Cox Miller notes as one of the "ironies of history" that Asclepius "lived on in Christianity in the cult of the saints."[5] Thecla, for example, is known to appear wearing Asclepius's mantle.[6] Both Asklepieia and early Christian healing sanctuaries consisted of a shrine that served for liturgies and also as a sleeping place for the sick; both included images of the divinely inspired healer(s) and often their patrons, votive thank offerings in shapes related to the diseased organ or method of healing, and stelae or other written records that give the names, hometowns, and healing stories of those who experienced cure at the site. Christian healing shrines were also characterized by relics and regular liturgical worship services. In Constantinople six churches were associated with Saints Cosmas and Damian, and pagans often slept in the shrine on Fridays for the all-night *pannychis* when, at the "sixth hour," sacred wax that figures in many different forms in healing stories[7] was

3. The full Greek title of the text is Διήγησις θαυμάτων τῶν ἁγίων Κύρου καὶ Ἰωάννου τῶν σοφῶν ἀναργύρων. The critical edition of the Greek is Natalio Fernandez Marcos, ed., *Los Thaumata de Sofronio: Contribucion al estudio de la incubatio cristiana* (Madrid: Instituto "Antonio de Nebrija," 1975). The *editio princeps* of the Greek text with its Latin version, translated by Anastasius Bibliothecarius in about 857, is in Angelo Mai, ed., *Spicilegium Romanum* (Rome, 1840), 3:97–669. For a recent study on Anastasius's translation, see B. Neil, "The Miracles of Saints Cyrus and John: The Greek Text and Its Transmission," *Journal of the Australian Early Medieval Association* 2 (2006): 183–93. The most complete study on Sophronius remains that of Christoph von Schönborn, *Sophrone de Jérusalem: Vie monastique et confession dogmatique*, Théologie historique 20 (Paris: Beauchesne, 1972). For textual history and a consideration of Sophronius's rhetorical style, see John Duffy, "Observations on Sophronius' *Miracles of Cyrus and John*," *JTS*, n.s., 35 (1984): 71–90. All translations are mine unless noted otherwise. For a recent translation of the entire text see now Jean Gascou, trans., *Sophrone de Jérusalem: Miracles des saints Cyr et Jean (BHG 477–79)*, Collections de l'Université Marc-Bloch-Strasbourg: Études d' archéologie et d'histoire ancienne (Paris: De Boccard, 2006). I am very grateful to Alice-Mary Talbot for her assistance in accessing Denise Peltier's French translation (*Récit des miracles des saints Cyr et Jean: Traduction et commentaire* [Paris: Université de Paris, 1978]); Daniel Caner, who first suggested I read the *Miracles*; and Pauline Allen, Bronwen Neil, and Phil Booth for their critique and helpful suggestions. Errors that remain are mine.

4. A recent study is that of Bronwen Lara Wickkiser, "The Appeal of Asklepios and the Politics of Healing in the Greco-Roman World" (PhD diss., University of Texas at Austin, 2003).

5. Patricia Cox Miller, *Dreams in Late Antiquity: Studies in the Imagination of a Culture* (Princeton, NJ: Princeton University Press, 1994), 117.

6. See Gilbert Dagron, *Vie et Miracles de Sainte Thècle: Texte grec, Tradition et Commentaire*, Subsidia Hagiographica 62 (Brussels: Société des Bollandistes, 1978), 103–8, for discussion; here cited in Miller, *Dreams in Late Antiquity*, 117.

7. E.g., salve, balm, wafers; perhaps also used to form candle offerings in the name of the saints. For the role of scent in the wax and oil used at such shrines, see now Béatrice Caseau, "Parfum et guérison dans le christianisme ancien et byzantin: Des huiles parfumées des médecins au myron des saints byzantins," in *Les Pères de l'Église face à la science médicale de leur temps*, ed. Véronique

distributed to those present.[8] Congregants used this service to relate their healing stories to one another.[9] Pagan gods were sometimes believed "hidden" behind the Christian identities as, for example, the belief that Cosmas and Damian were Castor and Pollux in disguise. Both pagan and Christian healers addressed universal issues; "the fundamental success of Cosmas and Damian is not that they were successors to Castor and Pollux, but rather that Asclepius and Castor and Pollux and Cosmas and Damian, and all the possible healers, responded to two constants: human misery and unshakable faith in the heavenly *euergetēs*."[10] Sophronius's text dates late in this tradition of incubation shrines, but it reflects the centuries-long continuity of religious healing themes and practices.

Sophronius and the Legend of Saints Cyrus and John

The author of the *Miracles of Saints Cyrus and John* is usually identified with the Sophronius who was John Moschus's traveling companion[11] and later a mentor to Maximus the Confessor. Sophronius was a native of Damascus and was trained in classical rhetoric. He met John Moschus[12] while living at the monastery of Theodosius in Palestine, under the abbot Theodore.[13] Sophronius

---

Boudon-Millot and Bernard Pouderon, Théologie Historique 117 (Paris: Beauchesne, 2005), 141–91; and Susan Ashbrook Harvey, *Scenting Salvation: Ancient Christianity and the Olfactory Imagination* (Berkeley: University of California Press, 2006).

8. *Miracles of SS Cosmas and Damian, Mir.* 30; the critical Greek edition is Ludwig Deubner, *Kosmas und Damian: Texte und Einleitung* (Leipzig: Teubner, 1907). For French translation, see A.-J. Festugière, "Saints Côme et Damien," in *Sainte Thècle, Saints Côme et Damien, Saints Cyr et Jean (Extraits), Saint Georges*, ed. and trans. A. J. Festugière, Collections grecques de Miracles (Paris: A. et J. Picard, 1971), 85–213, where the reference to wax in *Mir.* 30 is at 171. For pagan participation, see *Mir.* 10.

9. "Those who had received a cure from the saints related how they had obtained it and there was truly just cause for delight and for building of morale in these stories, each person imagining more than hearing what someone said" (Virgil S. Crisafulli and John Nesbitt, trans. and eds., *The Miracles of St. Artemios: A Collection of Miracle Stories by an Anonymous Author of Seventh-Century Byzantium*, Medieval Mediterranean 13 [Leiden: Brill, 1997], 25); see also (to which Crisafulli and Nesbitt refer here) H. Delehaye, "Les recueils antiques des miracles des saints," AnBoll 43 (1925):1–85, 305–25.

10. Festugière, "Saints Côme et Damien," 94–95.

11. John dedicates the *Spiritual Meadow* to Sophronius, calls him a "sophist," speaks of his later choice for the monastic life, and mentions him as present in chapters 69, 77, 92, 102, 110, 113, 135, 157, and 162.

12. John Moschus's death, while he and Sophronius were in Rome, is variously dated to September of either 619 or 634, depending on one's interpretation of "the eighth indiction." On their friendship, see also H. Chadwick, "John Moschos and His Friend Sophronius the Sophist," *JTS*, n.s., 25 (1974): 41–74.

13. The monastery of Theodosius was the largest coenobium in the Judean desert, built in about 479 by a monk from Cappadocian Caesarea on the south bank of the Kidron Valley, six miles from Jerusalem; at Theodosius's death, his successor, (another) Sophronius, was an Armenian from Sebaste who died in 542. According to Theodore of Petra's *Life of Theodosius* (H. Usener, ed., *Der*

and Maximus met (according to the tenth-century Greek *Life of Maximus*) as exiles in a North African monastery, probably in Carthage, between 627 and 633.[14] In his letter to Peter the Illustrious, Maximus calls Sophronius his "blessed lord, father and master, the lord abbot, Sophronius who is truly prudent (*sōphrona*), a wise advocate of truth and an invincible defender of divine dogmas."[15] In another letter, Maximus refers to the "venerable monks exiled in Africa, above all the blessed servants of God, our fathers who are called the *Eukratades*," which Christoph von Schönborn notes most likely refers to the circle of John Eukratas, meaning John Moschus.[16] Judith Herrin notes that "John Moschos, . . . Sophronios, Maximos, and his faithful assistant Anastasios were probably the last generation of eastern monks to practice the traditional *xeniteia*," or rootless wandering from one community to another, "a choice that became a necessity during the Persian and Arab invasions from about 604."[17] As Sophronius wandered, he wrote, in addition to the *Miracles of Saints Cyrus and John*, a *Life of St. John the Almsgiver*,[18] a number of still extant sermons,[19]

---

heilige *Theodosius, Schriften des Theodoros und Kyrillos* [Leipzig: Teubner, 1890]), the monastery included workshops, hospices, and hospitals, a home for aged monks, and a place for monks who had lost their sanity. By 542 it housed about four hundred monks and had five churches: Greek, Armenian, Bessarion-speaking, one for insane monks, and one to the Virgin. For archaeological details see Yizhar Hirschfeld, *The Judean Desert Monasteries in the Byzantine Period* (New Haven: Yale University Press, 1992), 15, 34 (photo), 49, and passim.

14. Andrew Louth, *Maximus the Confessor* (London: Routledge, 1996), 5–6, points out that in the Syriac *Life of Maximus* (whose author is hostile to Maximus but a more contemporary witness in time), it is Maximus who influenced his "Origenistic" abbot, Sophronius; see Sebastian Brock, "An Early Syriac Life of Maximus the Confessor," AnBoll 91 (1973): 299–346, esp. chap. 7ff. The Syriac text gives Maximus's birth name as Moschion.

15. Maximus, PG 91:533A, arguing against monophysitism. My translation but cf. Schönborn, *Sophrone de Jérusalem*, 75.

16. The *Eukratades*: Maximus, PG 91:461A; for the link with John Moschus see Schönborn, *Sophrone de Jérusalem*, 75.

17. Judith Herrin, *The Formation of Christendom* (Princeton, NJ: Princeton University Press, 1987), 210–11.

18. Sophronius and John Moschus's *Life of John the Almsgiver* (Chalcedonian patriarch of Alexandria from 610 to 619) makes up the first fifteen chapters in the extant *Life*; for critical ed. see Delehaye, "Recueils antiques des miracles des saints," 5ff; for discussion and ET see Elizabeth Dawes and Norman H. Baynes, "St. John the Almsgiver," in idem, *Three Byzantine Saints: Contemporary Biographies Translated from the Greek* (Crestwood, NY: St. Vladimir's Seminary Press, 1977), 195–206, followed by Leontius of Neapolis's "Supplement," 207–62.

19. For *Orations* 1–10 see PG 87c:3201–3364 (*Or.* 1–9), PG 87c:4001–4 (*Or.* 10). For translations, see now Jeanne de la Ferrière and Marie-Hélène Congourdeau, *Les pères dans la foi* (Paris: Migne, 1999) [seven homilies]; and Antonino Gallico, ed. and trans., *Sofronio di Gerusalemme: Le Omelie* (Rome: Città nuova editrice, 1991). *Oration* 10, which exists only in an unedited fragment, is the only one to mention the Arabs. John Duffy, who is preparing a critical edition of the homilies recently identified fragments from a previously unknown sermon "On the Circumcision " that he argues is Sophronian on the basis of grammatical style: John Duffy, "New Fragments of Sophronius of Jerusalem and Aristo of Pella?" short communication, Fifteenth International Conference on Patristic Studies, Oxford, 6–11 August, 2007.

letters, epigrams and liturgical texts,[20] and poems.[21] It was also Sophronius who, as bishop of Jerusalem, opened that city's gates in surrender to the Arab caliph, Omar, in 638,[22] probably dying soon afterward. The *Miracles of Saints Cyrus and John* probably dates between 610 and 615, while Sophronius's friend John "the Almsgiver" was the Chalcedonian patriarch of Alexandria.[23] The Greek text has survived in only one manuscript, dated to the tenth century.[24]

The legend of the shrine's foundation comes from the *Vita* of the saints (PG 87c:3677–96) that accompanies Sophronius's *Thaumata* and is attributed to Cyril (ca. 427/428). Seeking relics for his campaign against Isis, Cyril was divinely directed to the two sets of bones, buried together in the Church of St. Mark in Alexandria. He prayed, and their identity was revealed. According to his narrative, the martyr-saint Cyrus had been a physician of low social status martyred in Alexandria during the Diocletianic persecution, and his companion, John, was a Roman soldier converted by Cyrus's life and witness and martyred with him.[25] The pair's arrest and martyrdom came when

20. John Moschus's and Sophronius's monastic interviews probably inspired, either as fact or literary fiction, the sixth- or seventh-century *Narration of the Abbots John and Sophronius.* For discussion, see Robert F. Taft, SJ, "The Βηματίκιον in the 6/7th c. *Narration of the Abbots John and Sophronius (BHGNA* 1438w): An Exercise in Comparative Liturgy," in idem, *Divine Liturgies–Human Problems in Byzantium, Armenia, Syria and Palestine* (Aldershot: Variorum, 2001), reprint IX.

21. Sophronius, *Anacreontica*, PG 87:3733–3838. For translations of *Anacr.* 19 and 20, see Herbert Donner, *Die anakreontischen Gedichte Nr. 19 und Nr. 20 des Patriarchen Sophronius von Jerusalem,* Sitzungberichte der Heidelberger Akademie der Wissenschaften, Philosophisch-historische Klasse 10 (Heidelberg: Carl Winter, 1981). For selections in English, see John Wilkinson, *Jerusalem Pilgrims before the Crusades* (Warminster, UK: Aris and Philips, 2002), 157–63. Texts traditionally attributed to Sophronius but now regarded as pseudonymous include the *Life of Mary of Egypt* (PG 87.3697–3726) (Schönborn, 116) and the *Life* of the martyr Anastasius, now attributed to George of Pisidia (Bernard Flusin, *Saint Anastase le Perse et l'histoire de la Palestine au début de VIIe siècle,* Monde byzantin [Paris: Éditions du C.N.R.S., 1992], 2.381 ff.).

22. According to the *Chronicle of Theophanes* 339, Sophronius surrendered the city in exchange for a promise of immunity for all of Palestine to avoid a repetition of the bloodshed caused by the Persian entry in 614; see also Schönborn, *Sophrone de Jérusalem,* 83–98. Schönborn suggests March 11, 639, for the date of Sophronius's death. For a fictional account from a Muslim perspective, see Kanan Makiya, *The Rock: A Tale of Seventh-Century Jerusalem* (New York: Vintage, 2001).

23. Here I follow P. A. Booth (pers. comm.). *Mir.* 11 speaks of him as "presently" leading the church in Alexandria. Marcos dates the text before 614 since it does not mention the Persian invasion of Jerusalem in that year. Schönborn and Duffy simply date it after 610. Booth argues for 610–615 since Sophronius hints he is writing in Alexandria and the anonymous prologue of the *Meadow* says that he and John Moschus left Alexandria when they learned of the Persian invasion.

24. *Vaticanus Graecus* 1607. For textual history and a consideration of Sophronius's rhetorical style, see Duffy, "Observations."

25. A wall fresco discovered in 2001, at the Church of the Holy Virgin in Deir al-Surian (Wadi al-Natrun, Egypt), depicts a physician identified as "Ο ΑΓΙΟΣ ΑΠΑΚ [. .]" [sic] which the excavators believe to be that of our Cyrus ("Abba Kyr"). The inscription is on a layer dated before 800 CE (when Syrian monks arrived at the site). For online image and site report with discussion, see Karel C. Innemée and Lucas Van Rompay, "Deir al-Surian (Egypt): New Discoveries of 2001–2002," *Hugoye* 5, 2 (July 2002), at http://syrcom.cua.edu/Hugoye/Vol5No2/HV5N2InnemeeVanRompay.html;

they accompanied three virgin girls (Theoctista or Theopista, Theodota or Theodora, and Theodosia or Theodoxia) and their mother, Athanasia, to Alexandria.[26]

Not knowing which bones were Cyrus's, Cyril kept the pair together and "placed their relics under the protection of the monks of the old Pachomian monastery at Tabennisi, who sent a delegation to Menouthis to take charge of the devotions there"[27] and translated them to the newly established Christian shrine at Menouthis.[28]

There is some debate about whether the shrine was actually founded by Cyril or under the later patriarchate of Peter Mongus as a probably monophysite foundation; the description of the Christian destruction of the Isis sanctuary during Peter's episcopate, in about 489, preserved in Zacharias Scholasticus's *Life of Severus*, where Pachomian monks help to destroy the sanctuary,[29] does not mention the shrine of Cyrus and John. Suggesting a middle way through these debates, Dominic Montserrat considers it most likely that "the shrine was indeed established during the reign of Theodosius, but fell into abeyance after the family of patriarch Cyril lost influence when he was succeeded by Dioscorus in 444 CE. After being deprived of funds for almost 50 years, the shrine was revived in the last decade of the fifth century to combat the vital paganism that still existed."[30] The region is still identified as "Aboukir," the place of "Abba Cyr."

---

accessed July 11, 2006. The restored image (fig. 2) shows Cyrus, holding medical instruments, paired with Abba Pisentios, a sixth-century bishop of Koptos; the letters "APAK [. .]" are not visible in the published photo. The excavation also uncovered several other frescoes of physician-saints, including a large and prominent fresco of a physician-saint treating a blind supplicant; several frescoes of soldier-saints are also present.

26. Sophronius, *Laudes* 18 (PG 87c:3399–3402).

27. John A. McGuckin, *Saint Cyril of Alexandria: The Christological Controversy: Its History, Theology, and Texts* (Crestwood, NY: St. Vladimir's Seminary Press, 2004), 18, referring to Cyril, *Homiliae diversae* 18 (fragment), PG 77:1099–1106; the reference to "Tabennesiote" monks of the Metanoia monastery in Canopis is at PG 77:1099C.

28. The translation is celebrated on June 28, while the martyrs' festival is celebrated on January 31, a tradition noted in the thirteenth-century Alexandrian Synaxary attributed to Michael, bishop of Atrib and Malig; see Iacobus Forget, *Synaxarium Alexandrinum*, CSCO: Scriptores Arabica series 3, vols. 18–19 (1921–1922), where the Egyptian calendar date for the translation is Abīb 4 (19:201) for the festival is *Amšīr* 6 (18:475); for the Alexandrian Synaxary, see also CSCO 47–49, 67, 78, 90. Stephen J. Davis summarizes the establishment of the site in relation to Theophilus's influence on Cyril's policies in his book *The Early Coptic Papacy: The Egyptian Church and Its Leadership in Late Antiquity*, Popes of Egypt 1 (Cairo: American University in Cairo Press, 2004), 73–74.

29. Zachariah Scholasticus, *Vie de Sévère*, trans. M.-A. Kugener, PO 2 (1907), esp. 14–43, recently discussed in Edward Watts, "Winning the Intracommunal Dialogues: Zacharias Scholasticus' *Life of Severus*," *JECS* 13 (2005): 437–64, esp. 442 and 456–59.

30. Dominic Montserrat, "'Carrying on the Work of the Earlier Firm': Doctors, Medicine and Christianity in the *Thaumata* of Sophronius of Jerusalem," in *Health in Antiquity*, ed. Helen King (London: Routledge, 2005), 232–33. Montserrat summarizes the controversy in more detail in idem, "Pilgrimage to the Shrine of SS Cyrus and John at Menouthis in Late Antiquity," in *Pilgrimage and*

Sophronius and His Miracles in Theological Context

From the shrine's foundation, Cyrus and John were viewed not only as healers but as "doing battle for the Christian religion."[31] Like John Moschus, Sophronius was a devoted Chalcedonian Christian and supporter of John the Almsgiver. Opposed to all "heterodoxy," he particularly condemned "Julianites," who were adherents to a position among "monophysite" Christians in Egypt advanced in the sixth century by Julian of Halicarnassus, once a friend and disciple of Severus who, like Severus, was banished to Egypt. While Severus became "the symbol of opposition to the Fourth Council"[32] and sought to be faithful to (and was ever viewed by his followers as embodying) the Christology of Cyril of Alexandria, Julian became known for "aphthartodocetism," the teaching that Christ's physical body was from conception incapable of corruption. Severus condemned aphthartodocetism as docetic reductionism. Whatever Julian's true views,[33] for Sophronius "Julianites" were heretics whose illnesses particularly betrayed the corruption of their souls.

While the Julianite controversy was a century old when Sophronius came to Menouthis, another christological controversy was brewing even as he was gathering these stories. Indeed, he was to play a key role in this "monoenergist" controversy, and his writings were to serve as authoritative for the (ultimately) "official" condemnation of both monoenergism and the later "monotheletism" (the view that Christ had "one will") at the sixth ecumenical council of 680–681. While monoenergism plays little part in Sophronius's text about Cyrus and John, the context of this controversy may have influenced its ultimate distribution and use.

Summarized briefly,[34] the monoenergist controversy began in about 616, when Emperor Heraclius (610–641) and Sergius, patriarch of Constantinople, encouraged the idea of one "energy" or activity in Christ as a potential solution to the Chalcedonian-Monophysite division. The idea gained impetus in the 620s and took official shape in 633, in the Alexandrian *Pact of Union* under Cyrus, patriarch of Alexandria. Sophronius launched the attack on monoen-

---

Holy Space in Late Antique Egypt, ed. David Frankfurter (Boston: Brill, 1998), 257–79, esp. 261–66. See also Sarolta Takács, "The Magic of Isis Replaced or Cyril of Alexandria's Attempt at Redirecting Religious Devotion," *Poikila Byzantina* 13 (1994): 489–507; and Christopher Haas, *Alexandria in Late Antiquity* (Baltimore: Johns Hopkins University Press, 1997), 169–70, 327–29. For another recent view of this debate, see Jean Gascou, "Les origines du culte des saints Cyr et Jean," online at http://halshs.archives-ouvertes.fr/docs/00/05/91/74/PDF/introcyretjean.pdf, accessed 10/27/07.

31. PG 77:1105; McGuckin, *Saint Cyril*, 19.

32. Aloys Grillmeier and Theresia Hainthaler, *Christ in Christian Tradition*, trans. Pauline Allen and John Cawte (Louisville: Westminster John Knox Press, 1995), vol. 2, part 2, p. 2.

33. Grillmeier (ibid., 2.2, p. 80) believes that Severan polemic misinterpreted them.

34. For a general overview, see Pauline Allen and Bronwen Neil, *Maximus the Confessor and His Companions: Documents from Exile* (New York: Oxford University Press, 2002), 1–21.

ergism in his *Synodical Letter*, issued at his election as bishop of Jerusalem in 634,[35] a letter he sent with his envoy, Stephen of Dora, to Rome.

The relics of Cyrus and John were transferred to Rome in the summer of 634. Bronwen Neil suggests that it is entirely possible that "the text of the *Miracles* may have accompanied the relics . . . underlining the orthodoxy of these two Alexandrian martyrs, in stark contrast to the heresy recently embraced by the Alexandrian patriarch Cyrus."[36] While Honorius, bishop of Rome (625–638), originally accepted monoenergism, Sophronius's *Synodical Letter* quickly persuaded him otherwise, and his successors at Rome would all consistently reject it.[37] Several years later Maximus the Confessor would write an extended treatise against the patriarch Cyrus's monoenergist arguments.[38]

While the use of the *Miracles* may have been influenced by the later controversy, Sophronius says that he wrote it as a thank offering after being cured at the shrine of an eye ailment.[39] Indeed, compared to other miracle texts from Christian incubation shrines, the text is unusually rich in social details, and its style considered far more sophisticated than Moschus's *Spiritual Meadow*. In chapters structured as liturgical events, Sophronius tells his readers each patient's social, economic, and religious status, occupation, family relations, and relations with others famous in the region or mentioned elsewhere in the text, and describes in detail their illness, attempted cures or authorities consulted prior to their visit, the narrative of their oneiric interviews with, and waking responses to, the saints, prescriptions for cure, and final results. The suggestion of an explicit liturgical context is evident in the summons,

35. For the synodical letter addressed to Pope Honorius and Sergius, patriarch of Constantinople, see Rudolf Riedinger, ed., *ACO*, series 2, vol. 2, part 1, pp. 410 (l. 13) to p. 495 (l. 11) (Berlin, 1990). Pauline Allen is preparing a new translation and study of this text and a monoenergist dossier. The *Synodicon* (PG 87c:3147–3200) is discussed in Schönborn, *Sophrone de Jérusalem*, 199–224; see also Sophronius's letter to Bishop Arcadius of Cyprus calling for a council with a short treatise against the monothelite controversy, in M. Albert and C. von Schönborn, eds., "La lettre de Sophrone de Jérusalem à Arcadius de Chypre," PO 39 (Turnhout, 1978). For the synod's activity see also S. Brock, "An Early Syriac Life of Maximos the Confessor," esp. chaps. 10–14. Maximus's criticism of Sergius's monothelite analysis of the Gethsemane prayer, "Not my will but thine be done," followed the list of six hundred patristic citations that Sophronius had compiled, according to his deacon, Stephen of Dora (Mansi 10:896A). Photius may refer to these in *Bibliotheca* 231 when he mentions a *florilegia* "from the witnesses of diverse holy Fathers" that followed in his copy of Sophronius's *Synodical Letter* (Schönborn, *Sophrone de Jérusalem*, 100–101).

36. Neil, "Miracles of Saints Cyrus and John," 188.

37. The Lateran Synod of 150 bishops in Rome in 649, which opposed imperial monotheletism, sparked Maximus the Confessor's trial in Constantinople and ultimate martyrdom; dyothelite orthodoxy ultimately championed in the sixth ecumenical council of 680–681, where Sophronius's *Synodical Letter* of 634 was (and is still) in the official documents.

38. Maximus Confessor, *Ambigua* 5, trans. in Louth, *Maximus the Confessor*, 171–79.

39. Henry Chadwick, "John Moschos and His Friend Sophronius the Sophist," *JTS*, n.s., 25 (1974): 59, suggests that "it is probable that Sophronius' decision to renounce the world was taken in consequence of his cure at Menuthis."

at the end of each story, to sing a hymn praising God's power in the saints. John Duffy has said of the *Miracles* that it is

> a work . . . which, if treated with patience as a historical document, has much to offer readers who are interested in topics as varied as lexicography, biography, Christian incubation, heretical sects, medicine and magic, liturgy, and Alexandria in the late sixth century. . . . Its rhetorical nature . . . [is] a far cry from the style of . . . John Moschus. . . . But in this respect it might be true to say that it is John, rather than Sophronius, who is unusual. . . . [Sophronius] was a rhetorician to the fingertips.[40]

Rich and Poor in the *Miracles of Saints Cyrus and John*

The collection includes a number of stories about individuals who are specifically identified as poor or rich. In four of these narratives the healing account of the rich person seems intentionally connected, at least rhetorically, with a (usually otherwise unrelated) healing story of a poor person. A comparison of Sophronius's text with those of other Christian incubation shrines from the same period, particularly three similar stories from the *Miracles of Saints Cosmas and Damian*, reveals Sophronius's particular monastic interests and perspective on theological and physical wholeness.

Sophronius's four story-pairs of rich and poor are contained in *Mir.* 17, 18, 24, 28, and 46. Although Sophronius's rhetorical fondness for comparing details from two stories is not limited to comparing and contrasting rich and poor,[41] where such comparisons contrast economic differences they may offer an insight into his critique of the social and religious interplay of rich and poor in his society.

John Chrysones and the Beggar Paul

Miracles 17 and 18 tell two otherwise independent stories, one of a rich but pious cripple named John "Chrysones" ("the golden," or "man of gold") and the other of a poor beggar named Paul. In 17.1, Sophronius writes, "Let us also remember John, but not because he was a noble and counted amongst those who take pride in their wealth; for it was hence that he was called *Chrysones*, a name forced upon him by both his assets and his position. For he would have been called a poor man rather than *Chrysones*, if it were not for the fact that he received his health from the saints, a possession far brighter than

---

40. Duffy, "Observations," 71, 76.

41. For example, *Mir.* 19 and 20 (two women with similarly "incurable" diseases, cancer and "hydrops"); *Mir.* 49 (two unrelated thieves with similar methods); *Mir.* 11 (two deacons both named John); *Mir.* 26 and 27 (Theodora and the homonymous Theodore, who both swallow toxic substances and are cured by similar episodes of saint-induced vomiting).

gold."[42] Sophronius's deliberate linking of this story with the next is evident in 18.1–2, where he introduces the beggar, Paul, by writing:

> After the rich *chrysonēs* John comes the poor [*penēs*] Paul in our narrative, a penniless beggar [*ptōchos te lian kai achrysos*], who in his haste to be associated with John thought that if he could gain some connection to him he would also perhaps gain some benefit from him, just as we see poor people doing in the marketplaces, when they approach and then follow the wealthy from behind, in the hope that they might chance upon some of their crumbs which have fallen through Christ-loving compassion. And this is what Paul now proceeds to do, and perhaps he obtains such a desire, for John was not unfamiliar with love for the poor [*philoptōcheias*].

An infection in John's legs had putrefied so that the cracked skin was separating from the bone, the flesh rotting little by little while "envelopes of skin" fell to the ground. Feeling cheated by his physicians, the rich man came to the shrine resigned either to die or to receive a divine remedy. The saints appear to him in a dream and tell him to grind together a mixture of salt and cumin and to remodel his legs with the paste. After waking, he obeys, the putrefaction stops, and he is healed, "cheered by the effects of cumin and salt." John's healing is consonant with monastic apophthegmata in its deceptively simple story, humble remedy, and happy ending.

Paul's experience, however, is more difficult. He comes to the shrine exhausted from lack of sleep and howling in agony from pains in his head. Using "charm and delight," the saints induce sleep and use his dream, too, to order his treatment. He is told that when he awakes, he must go out from the sanctuary through a certain door, follow the wall, and strike hard on the jaw the first person he meets.

Put off by bizarre instructions to externalize his own pain so violently, Paul does nothing until the dream recurs three nights in a row.[43] Finally persuaded, he follows directions and immediately meets a soldier in a foul mood who is carrying a cudgel. Obediently, Paul punches him on the jaw. The soldier, not surprisingly, retaliates, bringing his weapon down on Paul's head, knocking him to the ground and cracking open his skull. Out of the wound spurt "blood and worms," Sophronius writes, "all the worms that were found in his head." But far from dead, Paul stands up, returns to the shrine in "new and perfect health," praises the martyrs, celebrates God, and goes

42. Translations here from *Mir.* 17 and 18 are by P. A. Booth (pers. comm.).
43. Triple revelation was a commonplace, though in the early-sixth-century *Questions and Responses* 418, of Barsanuphias and John, Barsanuphias cautions that "the one who appears to us once in the form of a lie, can also do the same three times and many times. Therefore, do not be ridiculed, but pay attention to yourself" (John Chryssavgis, trans., *Letters from the Desert: Barsanuphias and John*, Popular Patristics Series (Crestwood, NY: St. Vladimir's Seminary Press, 2003), 128–29.

on his way. While he may or may not have found the remedy to his poverty, Sophronius adds, he certainly was healed of his disease (18.2).

Paul is not alone in experiencing healing through violence at the shrine.[44] Nor is such a bizarre encounter easily pigeonholed as a tall story from antiquity. The Southern Baptist writer Will Campbell describes an oddly similar account in his childhood memoirs, recounting a fight between two of his brothers in the poor South during the Depression. When one is struck by a whirling metal water bucket and falls to the ground, "screaming and with convulsion-like movements," the boys wonder at his exaggerated reaction until they see the wound that has been burst open by the blow:

> Summer boils . . . were common to us all. They probably resulted from a poor diet. . . . A big one had plagued Joe for weeks . . . every day it got a little bigger until it was nearly the size of a lemon. And about the color. The . . . water bucket had . . . well-popped [it] for sure. The hard ball of pus, hard as green apple, was hanging out of its nest by yellow and red strings of corruption. The hole it had left in the skin was a nasty sight but the pressure it had relieved made Joe quick to forgive.[45]

In both tales incidental violence leads to exquisite and curative relief from a deeper, agonizing ailment. In both tales, the religious author gives significance to the role of human agency in an ironic and paradoxical process of relationships vital for a healing that takes everyone by surprise.

The two Julianas

Miracles 24 tells of two women named Juliana, "of the same name but not the same illness nor the same social rank" (24.1). Sophronius emphasizes their alikeness and differences. Like John and Paul, both are residents of Alexandria. One was famous for her wealth; the other had poverty as her companion. One had a lung disease;[46] the other was blind. One consulted many physicians; the other had no money for medical care. Both had an incurable ailment (24.2).[47] Sophronius draws further here on imagery from another story, *Mir.* 29, in which a rich woman, Athanasia, suffers an affliction that keeps her bent to the ground. The very symptoms that Athanasia displays while seeking healing mirror the posture that the wealthy consumptive Juliana will accept as her cure. As with John and Paul, the two Julianas have no direct contact or relationship in the text. The rich Juliana arrives

---

44. In *Mir.* 23 Gennadios, another poor man, is healed by fresh camel dung and a blow on the head from the exasperated camel driver. In *Mir.* 41 and 59, patients are healed by striking their heads on the pavement before the saints' shrine.

45. Will D. Campbell, *Brother to a Dragonfly* (New York: Seabury Press, 1977), 41.

46. ἡ μὲν δεινῶς ἠσθένει τὸν θώρακα καταφορητικῇ διαθέσει δουλεύουσα (24.2).

47. Ἔσχον δὲ κοινὸν τῶν παθῶν τὸ ἀνίατον (24.2).

in the church on a litter and is placed in the most eminent spot, directly in front of the saints' relics. In contrast the poor, blind Juliana, who "lived by the work of her hands,"[48] lies outside, before the porch, like the poor and miserable Lazarus who was given a place in the bosom of Abraham (24.4). Yet the saints, Sophronius says, "showed themselves equally to the two women, correcting one of her pride, consoling the humility of the other, but healing both" (24.4). They instruct the rich woman to take up her litter and lie among the crowds of supplicants on the ground. They instruct the poor woman to roast and grind crocodile skin into a powder and to apply it to her eyes. Each follows instructions; each is healed. The stories suggest a certain value for social parity. The rich woman moves (literally) down from her bed elevated before the place of honor at the shrine, to sleep on the ground. But the poor woman's cure uses the product of a beast that lived on an even lower level than the patient—in the water, crawling on its belly: a reminder, whatever the medical reputation of its skin, of her own "higher" position as a human. One woman is healed by casting off (luxury) and moving down; the other is healed by applying her skills of "working with her hands" to appropriate a new substance and raise her hands, applying the reptile's skin to her eyes. One is healed by emptying, the other by filling. Neither changes her social status, but each finds healing in action that affirms moral ideals of ascetic labor and humility.

Nemesion and Photeinos

Eye ailments were common in the ancient world, and in *Mir.* 28 both supplicants are blind. These are also the only two who meet in the story, and, as with Paul, it is the poor man who initiates the relationship. *Mir.* 28 is also one of the few where the saints refuse to heal, since the (rich) patient refuses to change his religious beliefs.

Nemesion, an ex-eparch, calls himself a Christian but in fact is an expert in Greek astrology, a loyal determinist who looked to the stars for fate. They are stars he can see no longer. Sophronius emphasizes the irony: Nemesion believes in fate, realizes that physicians cannot heal him, yet seeks a cure that will defy fate itself. Day after day, Nemesion retains his private beliefs as he prostrates himself before the shrine, shouting and praying for help, reaching out with his hands to touch the holy place. But the martyrs are no fools, and he remains blind.

Among other blind supplicants at the shrine is one named, ironically, Photeinos, "a very poor man who sold his fruit" in front of a nearby sanctuary dedicated to the "three holy children."[49] This sanctuary may have been that which Apollinarius, patriarch of Alexandria (d. 568), had founded with

---

48. Ἰουλιανῇ δὲ τῇ πενιχρᾷ καὶ χερνίτιδι ταῦτα φανέντες εἰρήκασιν (24.5).
49. τοῦ νεὼ τῶν ἁγίων τριῶν παίδων (28.9).

a relic of the hand of one of the "three holy children" of Dan. 1:6, Hananiah, Mishael, and Azariah, especially as it is said that Apollinarius incorporated into this shrine Cyrus's medical workshop (*ergastērion*).[50]

Recognizing the beggar's loyalty, Cyrus and John appear to him as soon as he falls asleep. They instruct him to find Nemesion and to have the rich man place his hands on Photeinos's eyes. Like the beggar Paul, however, Photeinos is acutely aware of the social distance between himself and Nemesion, and requires a strategy. He speaks to "the appearances" or shadows of people around him. They lead him to the place where Nemesion is zealously praying and place him directly in front of him. The rich man finds himself touching not relics but a beggar who stands deferentially in the place of the saints. In that sacred moment Photeinos—but not Nemesion—regains his sight.

Though the rich man remains blind, his persistent arrogance is evident in how he commemorates this event. After Photeinos, praising God and the saints, returns to selling fruit, Nemesion, "who had no dream of a miracle," says Sophronius, "decorated with a mosaic a side of the wall of the shrine. He there represented Christ, John the Baptist, Cyrus the martyr, and himself proclaiming the grace that had been manifested there" (28.12).[51] Persisting in heterodoxy, unable to persuade the saints to heal him, Nemesion could at least use the shrine to present himself for posterity in their holy company.

Tribunus and the monk

The fourth story, *Mir.* 46, concerns two blind men who were not from Alexandria. The details of wealth and poverty in this story are more subtle. One man, identified as Tribunus, came from Mareotis, the site of the sanctuary of St. Menas, "the pride of all Libya" (46.1).[52] The other is a poor Pachomian monk who is not named.

50. Peltier, *Récit des miracles*, 92n1, citing *BHG* 2:469.C2–4. Given Cyrus's and John's association with the three virgin girls (see above), they are thus doubly associated with "three children."

51. John the Baptist was a dominant figure in the late fourth-century Christianization of the Menouthis site. Rufinus says (*HE* 11.27–28) that Cyril's uncle and predecessor, Theophilus, bishop of Alexandria when the Serapeum at Canopis was destroyed, and who also founded the "Church of the Evangelists" at Menouthis, built a church and martyrium to house the Baptist's relics on either side of the former Serapis shrine between 390 and 400. For discussion see Norman Russell, *Theophilus of Alexandria,* Early Church Fathers (NY: Routledge, 2007), 7–11. Zachariah of Mitylene's Syriac *Chronicle* 5.6 mentions a church of John the Baptist at Alexandria in the sixth century, where the (Chalcedonian?) monk John, who (briefly) undermined Peter Mongus in his bid for episcopal office, was a presbyter and "also one of the Tabennesiots" (F. J. Hamilton and E. W. Brooks, trans., *The Syriac Chronicle Known as That of Zachariah of Mitylene* [London: Methuen, 1899], 116).

52. For the *Miracles* of St. Menas, see, e.g., James Drescher, trans., *Apa Mena: A Selection of Coptic Texts Relating to St. Menas* (Le Caire: Societé d'archéologie copte, 1946); John Duffy and Emmanuel Bourbouhakis, "Five Miracles of St. Menas," in *Byzantine Authors: Literary Activities and Preoccupations: Texts and Translations Dedicated to the Memory of Nicolas Oikonomides* ed.

It is unknown whether the man from Mareotis was a Roman military tribune by occupation or if Tribunus was simply his name. John Duffy argues for its being a proper name; *Tribounos* is not common but does occur, and "one of the features of Sophronius' *Miracles* is that, with only a couple of exceptions, all the subjects of cures . . . are identified by name."[53] While I am inclined to agree—since indeed there is only one other story (*Mir.* 64) where the patient is *not* named—to interpret it here as an occupation might in fact fit Sophronius's rhetorical pattern for this particular story, where the second of the contrasted pair is indeed nameless, and each man is identified dominantly by his primary religious location. An allusion to military status for one so closely aligned with the shrine of St. Menas might also logically follow from the legends of St. Menas as a native Egyptian conscripted as a soldier under Diocletian.[54] Even if Tribunus was indeed his proper name, Sophronius might well be intentionally ambiguous, given his pattern of teasing as much double meaning as possible from his stories.

Of particular interest here is this story's curious deference to other holy places. As Dominic Montserrat has noted, Cyrus and John, more than any other healing saints, limit their work and power within the physical boundaries of their "home" sanctuary.[55] They may heal or not heal, but they rarely make referrals. Yet in these two dream interviews, the blind men are both given exactly the same orders: each is told to travel to Jerusalem and there, like the man in the Gospel, wash in the Pool of Siloam. This is one of the few stories (with *Mir.* 39 and 44) where supplicants are told to find their healing outside the boundaries of the shrine complex. Was this instruction meant to minimize friendly rivalry, to express professional deference to Menas and to the Pachomian community? The reader is not told.

For the Libyan, both prescription and cure are easy. He arrives at Menouthis "brimming with a faith similar to that of the man born blind." Receiving the prescription, he travels to the holy city without any additional comment, washes, and is cured. Despite the saints' diplomatic diversion, he returns to

John W. Nesbitt (Boston: Brill, 2003), 65–81; and E. A. Wallis Budge, *Texts Relating to Saint Mêna of Egypt and Canons of Nicaea in a Nubian Dialect* (London: British Museum, 1909).

53. Duffy, "Observations," 87.

54. See, e.g., Stephen J. Davis, *The Cult of St. Thecla: A Tradition of Women's Piety in Late Antiquity*, Oxford Early Christian Studies (Oxford: Oxford University Press, 2001), 121.

55. Montserrat, "Pilgrimage to the Shrine," 270. P. A. Booth, who graciously shared with me his relevant dissertation chapter, qualifies this centralizing theme by emphasizing that "the dominant emphasis on the physical presence of the patient at the shrine does not inhibit a parallel representation of the omnipresence of the martyrs' power" ("Monasticism and the Church: Sophronius Sophista's *Miracles of Cyrus and John*," in idem, "John Moschus, Sophronius Sophista and Maximus Confessor between East and West," PhD diss., University of Cambridge, 2008, manuscript p. 51). See now also P. Booth, "Saints and Soteriology in Sophronius Sophista's *Miracles of Cyrus and John*," in P. Clarke and T. Claydon, eds., *The Church and the Afterlife*, Studies in Church History 45 (Oxford: Oxford University Press, forthcoming).

Menouthis, redirecting his religious loyalties from St. Menas to Cyrus and John, and spends "the rest of his life near them until he died; a good example of the gratitude one ought to show in regard to our benefactors" (46.3).

It was not unusual to find supplicants traveling between Mareotis and Menouthis. A Coptic manuscript preserves the story of a bricklayer, whose bricks St. Menas miraculously turned to gold. Afraid to show the bricks in his own village, where people know he is poor, he visits the goldsmiths at "Apa Apakyri," who make it into fine vessels that he in return donates to the shrine of St. Menas.[56] This story suggests possible trade dynamics between the two shrines and offers a glimpse of the alleyways in which fruitsellers like Photeinos might peddle their wares to visitors and pilgrims.

The blind monk in *Mir.* 46, however, differs from the Libyan by his stated poverty and his implicit loyalty to his home community. During *his* incubation conversation, when told to go to Jerusalem, he reminds the saints that the man born blind in the Gospels just happened to live in Jerusalem, but he has no travel funds and the Pool of Siloam is quite a jaunt. What, he asks politely, might the saints suggest to resolve this small fiscal obstacle?

As with Photeinos, here again the community becomes involved on behalf of the poor man. The martyrs instruct the monk to find a certain Thomas, steward of a nearby warehouse, and tell him that the martyrs have ordered him to pay the monk's traveling expenses to Jerusalem.[57] As Photeinos did, here again the poor man seeks help from strangers of higher status who have connections to the shrine, human patronage sought deferentially. Like Photeinos, the monk obeys. He receives his cash, journeys to Jerusalem, and is healed. We do not know what happens after his healing, but it is less likely he faced divided loyalties. The Pachomian monastic community had a long heritage of loyalty to the cult of Cyrus and John. If he was part of the local monastery at Canopis that Theophilus established twenty years before Cyril "founded" the shrine,[58] this might explain why he could easily visit Cyrus and John with empty pockets, while the Libyan, coming from some distance, did not.

Directing these two men to Siloam does not just minimize competitive loyalties. It also explicitly points to Christ as the higher, and ultimate, source of all healing, a theme Sophronius emphasizes throughout his text. Health, defined as much by "orthodox" theology as by physical restoration, is above all a proper relation to Chalcedonian authority, Christ, and the liturgy.

---

56. Found in Cod. M585, part of a Coptic monastic library discovered in the Fayum in 1910. I here rely on the translation of Drescher, *Apa Mena*; for the reference to Apa Apakyri, see pp. 154–55.

57. Thomas's power to write an "order of provision" for aid to the poor suggests documents comparable to those Adam Serfass describes for widows elsewhere in chapter 7 of this volume.

58. Davis, *Coptic Papacy*, 74.

If Tribunus was not a military man, the reader cannot assume he was a man of substance, but Sophronius does describe several people who walk a long way to Menouthis due to poverty, and in each case (but not this one), emphasizes their destitution or exhaustion upon arrival. Thus the Libyan's ready ability to travel on to Jerusalem, still blind and needing particular assistance that he does not expect from the saints, suggests that he did possess more economic resources than many, and far more than his monastic counterpart, whose poverty is noted. The story also reiterates Sophronius's thematic concern with social equity: both are empowered to the same cure. The poorer man presumably remains a monk, just as the healed Juliana and Photeinos also return to their lowly occupations. But the Libyan makes a significant shift in his lifestyle—moving from his home in Libya to serve at Menouthis. This would fit Sophronius's tendency to show the saints often asking more of their rich supplicants than they do of those from the poor and lower classes. Despite the uncertainties of class issues in this story, it contains the same key themes we find in Sophronius's treatment elsewhere of rich and poor.

The *Miracles* in Social Context

A comparison of this text with other Christian incubation healing narratives from the same period suggests several similarities and differences. Most obviously, of course, Cyrus and John, like the other saints at such shrines, use dreams to communicate with their patients. Unlike most, however, they use dreams almost exclusively to give orders; patients are virtually never healed *during* dreams with Cyrus and John. Healing depends on waking obedience to medicinal and theological instructions. This is unlike the *Miracles of St. Artemius*, from the same period, in which most patients are passively cured during sleep. Further, Cyrus and John are like Cosmas and Damian in that both pairs are *anargyroi*, "silverless" or "unmercenary" saints who heal for free, while Artemius's patients were expected to bring an offering and to work in the shrine while awaiting their cure. Those who serve Cyrus and John at Menouthis apparently work only after their healing, and only as an expression of gratitude, not to pay a debt. All three of these texts differ from both the *Miracles of St. Thecla*[59] and those of St. Menas, where healing is only a small component in a range of other social functions that more often include miraculous revelations of justice and political order.[60]

59. Cf. Davis, *Cult of Saint Thecla*; on Thecla in Egypt, see pp. 81–145; on Thecla and Menas, see pp. 120–25. For more on her fifth-century cult narratives, see Dagron, *Vie et Miracles de Sainte Thècle*; and Scott Fitzgerald Johnson, *The Life and Miracles of Thekla: A Literary Study* (Cambridge, MA: Harvard University Press, 2006).

60. For example, Duffy and Bourbouhakis's collection ("Five Miracles of St. Menas") contains only one story of physical healing; the others concern justice in the context of greed and lust.

Varieties of healing in Sophronius

The stories that Sophronius chooses to tell suggest that healing at Menouthis was a complex process. The "standard" therapies of holy oil and wax, *myron* and *kērōtē*, are used in only a few cases and are usually combined with other instructions. Getting healed by these saints is tough work, and most cures involve suffering and difficult moral lessons. The poor like Paul may experience this as yet another of life's inevitable encounters with physical pain. The rich and heterodox can expect some intentional humiliation. Gesios, for example (*Mir.* 30), was a crypto-pagan physician who scorned the shrine until he became paralyzed and his colleagues convinced him to seek its aid. He is healed only after he obeys instructions to spend several days crawling around the sanctuary on his hands and knees, a donkey's saddle on his back and a bell around his neck, led by a servant, and shouting out, "I am a fool!"[61] Heterodox supplicants—identified variously as crypto-pagans, Judaizers, or non-Chalcedonians—could expect theological dialogue as part of their nightly visitations. In several cases patients argue with the saints for days or weeks before they either convert and are healed or leave as they came.

Cyrus and John might also use their dream appearances to provide therapeutic consolation. Martyria, for example (*Mir.* 21), who comes howling with visceral pain, is said to be a victim of evil people with impious intentions who take malignant pleasure in afflicting their subjects.[62] The saints sit down beside her bed kindly, tenderly ask her to tell her story, then merely breathe gently into her mouth. The next morning she runs to the latrines, evacuates a four-inch worm, and is healed. Her symptoms might hint at domestic or psychological distress, and her healing demonstrates "mercy by the grace and love of Christ." *Mir.* 41 may also hint at domestic abuse, in which eight-year-old Menas was visited by a "demon" one night who wrenched out his tongue and then beat him in the face. He is healed during play with other children at the shrine by a simple child's fall on the marble flagstones in front of the sanctuary. Such stories reflect a world characterized by violence, church politics, poverty, and social injustices, and ruled by unpredictable natural catastrophes, human agency, and grace.

Sophronius's discussion of the contrast between rich and poor is more complex than the simple equation that one often finds in earlier Christian texts on poverty and wealth, where the rich-poor dynamic is part of a narrative about divestment, the "Christ-poor," or redemptive alms. The dynamics between Sophronius's characters do not neatly fit into the second-century interdependence of vine and elm tree of the *Shepherd of Hermas* (*Sim.* 2).

---

61. Sophronius says that Gesios's treatment was severe not because he was a physician but because he was not a true Christian.

62. ἐκ περιεργίας καί τινων μοχθηρίας καὶ ἄθεον κεκτημένων προαίρεσιν, καὶ φιλοτιμουμένον κακῶς πρὸς τὸ οὕτως ἀφειδῶς λυμαίνεσθαι τὸ ὁμόφυλον (21.1).

Nor are any of these poor identified as in Matt. 25:31–46 with Christ. The rich who come to this particular shrine are not consistently—indeed are not in any case in this text—healed by engaging in conscious generosity to the poor at the shrine. In the only story where a rich man (Nemesion) takes an active part in healing a poor man (Photeinos), the rich man is *not* healed. These stories emphasize rather the poor's dependence on the social network of religious communities. Photeinos is healed because others at the shrine lead him to Nemesion. The blind monk is healed because Thomas believes the saints expect his alms in such a way. Paul is healed by placing himself literally "under" the power of a local authority at the border of the *temenos* and then defines the order of his place in the communal narrative, to follow that of the *philoptōchon* John. Sophronius the monk may be critical of the inherent pride that usually accompanies wealth, but he focuses neither on alms nor on divestment, but on humility and equality. Rich and poor must come to the saints with an attitude of faith, a willingness to be changed, and prepared to obey. The diseases of the poor are never related to moral faults.[63] If the poor teach, they most often teach only the reader through Sophronius's rhetoric. While none of these four story-pairs concern the Severan heresy, they are inseparable from the author's broader concern with orthodox piety.

The miracles of Saints Cosmas and Damian: A brief comparison

Sophronius knew at least some of the miracles of Cosmas and Damian. He explicitly defends their similarities to his own narrative, since all the miracles come from the same source, "Christ our God," who is master to all the healing saints and who accomplishes these wonders through them (*Mir.* 30.13–14). Thus it is particularly interesting to compare three stories about rich and poor from the Cosmidion in Constantinople with Sophronius's text.

The *Miracles of Saints Cosmas and Damian* exists in six different series, totaling forty-eight stories. Three of these (*Mir.* 12, 34, and 39) contain similar accounts of a rhetorical and therapeutic dynamic between rich and poor supplicants.

Miracles 12 describes an example of hospice care for women.[64] A "very pretty" woman named Martha, whose family had a special devotion to Cosmas and Damian, has spent her youth "in bodily disorder, by ignorantly arousing lustful acts, and in debauchery" (*Mir.* 12.1) before repenting of her sins. Afflicted in her head with some pain or distress, she comes to the shrine and immediately begins to serve the poor while awaiting healing. She gives generously of her goods to the poor and sets up housekeeping in a part of the atrium,[65] where she is welcomed and cares for other women suffering

63. This is also true in his healing stories of children.
64. Festugière, "Saints Côme et Damien," 120–25.
65. ἐν τῇ κορτίνῃ (Deubner, *Kosmas und Damian*, 129, line 20).

"the afflictions of the enemy." One night the saints visit her, hold her head in their hands, and heal *half* of her disorder. She is distressed at the partial healing, but hope and loyalty keep her at the shrine a little longer; she prays for complete healing while continuing her ministry to the other women.

As Martha is serving and eating among these women, a demon in a patient named Christine is overcome with erotic love for Martha, to the point of wishing to enter her.[66] The saints, ever on the alert and considering her philanthropy, visit Martha again, heal her remaining affliction, warn her about Christine, and tell her to go home. They order her not to allow Christine into her house no matter how urgently she requests it, since "the impure spirit in her has a passion for you and is plotting to possess you" (*Mir.* 12.84). Martha is also told not to approach the place where Christine holds discourse, in the colonnade to the left of the narthex, but to hurry home in peace in the name of the protomartyr Stephen.[67] Indeed, Christine arrives at dawn, and her demon cries out all day to be let in, while Martha refuses. At some point during this noisy assault on Martha's new boundaries, Christine recovers her reason.

The allusion to Martha's immoral past, the "impurity" of demons, the use of *erōs*, and the demon's fanatically insistent demand to "enter into" (*eiserchomai*) Martha,[68] all serve to construct possession as what the male author clearly understands as a sexual scenario, one that is blamed on the erotic desire of Christine's "evil spirit" rather than on Christine herself. The power competition between the two women nonetheless threatens Martha such that in this (her) account, it requires physical boundaries to protect not only her soul but also her philanthropic space. Christine, even "sane," continues to beg for Martha's usual assistance, arguing that she is not responsible for the demon's desires. But Martha persists in refusing her, and the story's retelling at the shrine's liturgy would have reiterated her moral fortitude.

The text does not say that Martha is rich, but it seems evident in light of her extended generosity and family's public loyalty to the shrine. While the complex sexual narrative about Christine does not obviously relate to wealth-poverty dynamics, it does suggest (as in Sophronius) a rich patient faced with a particularly difficult moral challenge as part of the healing process. This

66. τὸν ἐνοικοῦντα ἐν μιᾷ γυναικὶ πασχούσῃ ὀνόματι χριστίνῃ δαίμονα εἰς ἔρωτα κατ᾽ αὐτῆς ἔτρεψεν, ὥστε εἰς αὐτὴν χωρῆσαι (*Mir.* 12; Deubner, *Kosmas und Damian*, 130, lines 75–77).

67. *Mir.* 12, lines 88–89 in the Deubner edition, says that "this woman" (presumably Martha) was wife of one of the clergy of the church of the holy St. Lawrence; Festugière ("Saints Côme et Damien," 123n47) notes a tradition that the relics of St. Stephen were deposited in the basilica of St. Lawrence.

68. See esp. *Mir.* 12, lines 95–105. While the sexual threat is not specified as homoerotic love between the two women, since it is driven by a demon and defined in terms of male sexuality, the story (and the Greek's lack of gender specificity in describing Martha's youthful sins) may hint at the possibility for such an interpretation.

story also offers an example, rare in these texts, of a rich woman serving the sick poor, and (unlike Sophronius), one whose healing is linked with alms.

In the second story, *Mir.* 34, a rich lawyer, Victor, prays night and day for healing from incurable cancer. Using his faith to effect two healings in one cure, Cosmas and Damian tell him in a dream to seek out the poor butcher Hesperos, who lies in the right colonnade near their reliquary, and demand a shave. Hesperos lies at the shrine because a paralysis has made it impossible for him to work. When Victor demands his barbering services, Hesperos objects: he knows nothing about barbering, has never been a barber, and is paralyzed! Desperate after three days of begging, Victor seizes Hesperos and insists. Startled, the paralytic reaches under his mattress for the little scissors he uses to keeps his rags mended and finds there a complete shaving kit. With much pain and difficulty he shaves Victor, and both are healed.

But the story does not end here. The saints tell Victor, "If you were healed by worldly doctors, wouldn't you joyously reward them for their services? But because you receive this grace from a lowly poor man, and God visits and heals you in this way, will you despise the state of the beggar? Go, give him fifty *nomismata*, for he prays for you with fervor, and because of him all turned to good for you" (*Mir.* 34.75–80). The saints order the former butcher to use his new tools to become a barber.[69] The rich man goes home and the poor man, doubly enriched, becomes the shrine's master-barber.

In the third story, *Mir.* 39, a rich man, an imperial official from the palace, lies in the shrine near two poor men, one a beggar who flaunts his indigence to survive, and the other a stage mime who is ill. One night, when the beggar finds himself spontaneously cured, the saints threaten the mime that he will be healed only if he gives the healed beggar his tunic. The mime obeys, to discover that he is still sick and the night is very cold. He spends the next few days applying his theatrical eloquence to curse the saints. The rich man nearby sees all and does nothing.

The saints intervene, ordering the rich man to ask the mime to slap him ten times on the cheek. Insulted, he grumbles, "Better to die at home than live with such an outrage." But after three visitations, he acquiesces. But the mime demurs. "Look at me!" he says. "I followed instructions and now I am ridiculously naked, and still sick; don't listen to them." Finally desperate, the rich man pays the mime for his punitive services: two new robes after the first slap and one hundred pieces of gold after the last, the payment saving face for both. "Thus," the story concludes, "the saints cured three ills in one move: sickness [*nosos*], poverty [*penia*], and pride [*phronēma*]" (*Mir.* 39.134–35).

---

69. It is unclear if they mean his former begging or his former butchering. Several other stories in the *Miracles of Saints Cosmas and Damian* reflect an encouragement to abandon meat consumption.

These relationships between rich and poor in the Cosmidion stories are more explicitly interactive than those in Sophronius and include economic exchanges, although Cosmas and Damian are also *anargyroi*. On the one hand, the rich at the Cosmidion do not hesitate to serve the poor with money and material aid, and alms are explicitly praised. The monastic Sophronius, on the other hand, mentions money only in conjunction with false doctors who waste it and rich men for whom it is a snare. The rich and the poor at Constantinople talk together, lie near one another, watch, and even argue and shout at one another. Yet in these Cosmidion stories, the saints speak at most length with the rich, while Sophronius includes extensive dialogue between the saints and those who are poor. We know what Cosmas and Damian say to Martha but not the poor women she serves. Victor receives detailed instructions, but the only words to the paralytic are the warning after his healing. In the triple healing, the beggar is healed without any apparent dialogue, and it is the mime who argues with the saints over giving up his cloak. The mime's winnings may support Wendy Mayer's suggestion in chapter 10 of this volume that the poor who worked at offering theatrical entertainment were valued more than beggars since they labored for their alms. Thus the Cosmidion stories appear to reflect a survival economics different from Sophronius's dominant concern for social equity and theological dialogue, while Sophronius says little of alms.

Conclusion

In modern healing, medicine is divided into two distinct categories: "allopathic" medicine, which prides itself on "rational" or "scientific" evidence and action, and "alternative" medicine, based on what is commonly regarded as more "subjective," sometimes dismissed as quackery. This division did not exist as such in the ancient world, despite the obvious competition among physicians. Ancient "Hippocratic" medicine coexisted with a wide range of other theorists, healing shrines, folk beliefs, known and suspected frauds, well-meaning ignorance, and doctors who applied an eclectic combination of approaches. In general, what was considered most appropriate for each patient might differ depending on the ailment, the location, the weather, and many other factors. Religious and material realities were understood as related pieces in a whole cosmic body. Eclecticism seems the rule by the fourth century, when collections or *compendia*, such as that of Julian's physician, Oribasius, were more common than rigid medical "schools" of particular theories. Practitioners in "Asclepian" or "Hippocratic" medicine often appealed to humoral or causation theories in the "natural" world that might be manipulated by various physical substances, but various ritual elements and explanations based on demonic or spiritual factors were an intrinsic part of the conversation.

The apparent shift at incubation sanctuaries over time, "from supernatural surgery to more earthly kinds of physical therapy," which Patricia Cox Miller has identified as a Greco-Roman development at Asclepius shrines, may be evident in the pragmatic and earthy healing practices at Menouthis by the seventh century. Nevertheless, pagan or Christian, such healings retained divine significance as "the oneiric gifts of a god."[70] The healing shrines of Christian martyr-saints expressed this divine power over the body. As Peter Brown puts it, "behind the now tranquil face of the martyr, there lay potent memories of a process by which a body shattered by drawn-out pain had once been enabled by God's power to retain its integrity."[71] And behind the power of the shattered, martyred saints, Sophronius emphasizes, is the ultimate healing, "re-membering" power of "Christ our God." Julianite heretics could be healed in body only when they changed their views about the mutable body of Christ. At Menouthis this "re-membering," for both rich and poor, was anything but restful. Seeking integrity for their own pain and disintegrating bodies, supplicants came to the shrine as a last resort. They were accosted with whole body experiences of stench, shouting, perspiration, bloody effusions, liturgy, and incense, interrupted with urgent visits to the latrines, the therapeutic experience something between a counseling session and hardcore evangelistic propaganda. Within this setting, Sophronius deliberately uses rich-poor contrasts in these stories to emphasize the role of humility and interdependence in a therapy of orthodox social justice. The healing texts represent liturgy itself in their reverential engagement with the divine and their moral lesson in the very public praise and hymns ordered at the end of each story. While the focus on rich and poor is only one part of the text, these four story sets offer a glimpse into late antique Christian views on the intersection between disease, theology, liturgically embodied images, and the role of the sacred in physical need.

70. Cox Miller, *Dreams in Late Antiquity*, 114–15.
71. Peter Brown, *Cult of the Saints: Its Rise and Function in Latin Christianity* (Chicago: University of Chicago Press, 1981), 80.

Part Three

JOHN CHRYSOSTOM, THE CAPPADOCIANS, AND FRIENDS

9

THIS SWEETEST PASSAGE

Matthew 25:31–46 and Assistance to the Poor in the Homilies of John Chrysostom

RUDOLF BRÄNDLE

I stand before you today as an ambassador to represent a just cause." In this way John Chrysostom begins the sermon about mercy that he preached to his congregation one winter Sunday at the Great Church in Antioch.[1] Vividly he describes how—on his way to the church via the agora and through the narrow streets of the old town that lies on the island in the Orontes—he saw many beggars lying there, "some of whom had been robbed of their hands, others of their eyes, and still others completely covered with running sores and unhealable wounds." As their ambassador and on their behalf he stands before his congregation and asks for mercy: *eleēmosynē*. No other term can better describe the greatest concern of John Chrysostom. He knew that in this

I would like to thank Rev. Dan Holder, who translated this text into English. The translation of the quotations from the works of John Chrysostom is based on the *Nicene and Post-Nicene Fathers* (*NPNF*) series; the nineteenth-century English has been moderately brought into line with today's language. All references in the notes to homilies in J.-P. Migne's Patrologia graeca (PG) are those of John Chrysostom unless noted otherwise. All translations from the Greek are mine unless noted otherwise.
    1. *De eleemosyna* (PG 51:261–72).

127

he was like his Lord. "For great indeed was His regard for philanthropy and mercy," says John in his seventy-ninth homily on Matthew's Gospel, which relates to the passage 25:31–46 (*Hom. Matt.* 79.1 [PG 58:717]).

Antioch was a dazzling town, which Libanius praised in his great Oration.[2] John Chrysostom was also proud of his hometown—not, however, because of the splendor of its buildings, the world famous two miles of the colonnade, and the splendid Daphne suburb,[3] but rather because it was here that Christians received their name (Acts 11:26). The modern church was, however, unworthy of the great beginnings of the faith. For John Chrysostom the Christians were too much given over to the joys of this life and too committed to riches.

John sharply criticized the excesses of wealth. The prosperous citizens had great palaces with marble pillars and halls, decorated with statues and frescoes. Some of the walls were covered with gold, and gold could even be found on the roofs.[4] The splendor of the houses was matched by the luxury of the furnishings. The Antiochian upper class also showed their wealth in clothing and jewelry. John spoke pointedly on this in one of his baptismal classes: "Countless poor people have to go hungry so that you can wear a single ruby."[5] Alongside the great luxury of the rich stood the destitution of the poor. In a sermon on 1 Corinthians, John vividly contrasted the rich man, who after taking his bath, dressed comfortably in warm clothes and hurried home to a festive meal in the family circle, with the beggar, who crept through the streets driven by hunger and cold and finally spent the night on a dirty pile of straw (*Hom. 1 Cor.* 11.5 [PG 61:93]). John irritated the rich by preaching about almsgiving.[6] They asked, "How long will you not cease from continually introducing poor men and beggars into your sermons, prophesying disaster to us and our own future impoverishment, so as to make beggars of us all?"[7] In her essay in this volume (chapter 10), Wendy Mayer gives us a vivid description of the wide range of social conditions in Antioch.

John Chrysostom, who had been presbyter and preacher at the Great Church, also known as the Golden House, since the beginning of 386, was not

2. "Libanius' Oration in Praise of Antioch," trans. with intro. and comm. by Glanville Downey, *Proceedings of the American Philosophical Society* 103 (1959): 652–86.

3. Glanville Downey, *Antioch in the Age of Theodosius the Great* (Norman: University of Oklahoma Press, 1962).

4. Rudolf Brändle, *Matt. 25:31–46 im Werk des Johannes Chrysostomos*, Beiträge zur Geschichte der biblischen Exegese 22 (Tübingen: Mohr Siebeck, 1979), 89n109.

5. *Catech. illum.* 1.15 (FC 6/1, 136); see also 1.17 (138–40).

6. Still worth reading today is the 1960 Bonn dissertation by Otto Plassmann, *Das Almosen bei Johannes Chrysostomos* (Münster: Aschendorff, 1961).

7. *Hom. 1 Cor.* 30.5 (PG 61:256), trans. T. W. Chambers, *Library of the Nicene Fathers,* 12:180, as quoted in Peter Brown, *The Body and Society: Men, Women and Sexual Renunciation in Early Christianity* (New York: Columbia University Press, 1988), 310.

prepared to accept the structural poverty in Antioch.[8] He did not consider poverty and riches to be ordained at creation. He was convinced that God had not created one rich and the other poor. To be honorably rich was not possible. The roots of wealth necessarily lay in some injustice (*Hom. 1 Tim.* 12.3–4 [PG 62:562–63]). In a sermon on 1 Corinthians, John argues that being rich itself is not a sin. It is a sin, however, not to share one's riches with the poor (*Hom. 1 Cor.* 13.5 [PG 61:113]). In his fight for more just and humane relations, he is carried along by the great utopian vision of a society of people living in unity and peace—a society of people, who like the early Jerusalem church, cast out the *anōmalia* of inequality from their midst, who relate humanely to one another, who live without those luxuries that other people have to pay for, and take monks as an example to follow in their lives. The Christian house should become like a church or a monastery. Peter Brown puts this well by saying that John strove toward "the creation of a new form of urban community through the reform of the Christian household."[9]

The Christian father as head of the house should go to the service with his family on Sunday and afterward discuss at home what they had heard. The poor should be invited for meals. The whole family should spend night watches in prayer, and so the house would become a church (*Hom. Act.* 26.4 [PG 60:203]). In many different ways John tried to demonstrate to his listeners that the perfect life could be reached not only in monastic solitude but also in the middle of a city. In his fifty-fifth homily on Matthew's Gospel he quotes the hymn the monks used to thank God after meals and suggests to his congregation that they meditate on it and pray it diligently at the table.[10]

John's suggestion of setting up a holy collection in the same way that Paul collected money for the poor is typical of the man and his concern (*Eleem.* 4 [PG 51:266]). John recommended setting this up in a place of prayer. First alms should be given and then prayer made.[11] In this way the person praying possesses a weapon against the devil, gives wings to his prayer, and hallows his house, "having stored up food there for the King."[12] As a guide for donations, he suggested a tenth of all income and returns (*Hom. 1 Cor.* 43.4 [PG 61:374]). One sleeps better with a collection box beside the bed, he says: "Make your house a church and your little box a treasury." In his exposition of 1 Cor. 16:2, John follows this sentence with an astounding statement, un-

---

8. Peter Brown distinguishes between the poverty, e.g., in Cappadocia, which was caused by the drought and the bad harvests that followed, and the "poverty built into the structures of urban life," in Antioch. Brown, *Body and Society*, 310.

9. Brown, *Body and Society*, 309; see also Claudia Tiersch, *Johannes Chrysostomus in Konstantinopel (398–404)* (Tübingen: Mohr Siebeck, 2000), 72.

10. *Hom. Matt.* 55.5 (PG 58:545); see also *Hom. Rom.* 24.3 (PG 60:626).

11. *Hom. 1 Cor.* 43.4 (PG 61:372–73). In the same context John mentions the custom of hanging the Gospel next to the bed.

12. *Hom. 1 Cor.* 43.4 (PG 61:373). John here gives a good example of his use of Matt. 25:31–46.

paralleled, as far as I am aware, among the other church fathers: "Dedicate your wealth to God and become a self-ordained steward for the poor. Love to your fellow man assigns this priesthood to you."[13] In his moving twentieth homily on 2 Corinthians, John says that despising money warms love and makes one generous, giving one priestly dignity: *hierōsynēn*. Such a priest sacrifices on an altar deserving more awe than the altar of the church, for that merely receives the Lord's body, but this one is in itself the body of the Lord. The living altar of the body of Christ is to be found everywhere in the city, and every poor believer is such an altar.[14]

Before we look more closely at the role played by Matt. 25:31–46 in John Chrysostom's exhortation, further aspects of the ethical preaching of our presbyter should be mentioned. Particular emphasis is given to the idea of *koinon*. John is convinced—and here he is at one with the Cappadocian fathers—that God has given the earth to humankind as a common table, so that they can learn from this to have other things in common as well. Because of this, "community of property more than private possession is the valid form of living, and is also in accordance with nature"; "this state (community of property) therefore is rather our inheritance, and more agreeable to nature."[15] All people share the same nature, so all have a right to help when they are in need. John formulates this concisely: "When it comes to doing good, let every human be your neighbor" (*Exp. Ps.* 143.3 [PG 55:461]). He concludes from the parable of the Good Samaritan: "So you too, if you see any one in affliction, do not be curious to enquire further. His being in affliction gives him a just claim to your help. For if when you see a donkey choking you lift him up without inquiring whose he is, you certainly ought not to be over-curious about a person. He is God's, whether he is a heathen or a Jew; since even if he is an unbeliever, still he needs help."[16] As is to be expected from this, John is in no way exclusive in applying "the least" in Matt. 25:40–45 to brothers and sisters in the faith. "Through our help to the hungry, strangers, the sick and prisoners, we become God's friends. If we do good, we make God our friend. He voluntarily becomes our debtor."[17] God likes people to whom he is in debt.[18]

John used his entire range of vocabulary and all the brilliance of his rhetoric to bring his congregation to greater solidarity. Central for John is the

---

13. αὐτοχειροτόνητος οἰκονόμος πενήτων. Ἡ φιλανθρωπία ταύτην σοι δίδωσι τὴν ἱερωσύνην (*Hom. 1 Cor.* 43.1 [PG 61:368–69]).

14. *Hom. 2 Cor.* 20.2–3 (PG 61:539–40); see also *Hom. Matt.* 45.3 (PG 58:474–75).

15. "Magis ergo communitas, quam proprietas sorte data nobis fuit, et secundum naturam est" (*Hom. 1 Tim.* 12.4 [PG 62:564]).

16. *Hom. Heb.* 10.4 (PG 53:88); see also *Hom. Rom.* 22.2 (PG 60:611).

17. *Hom. Heb.* 25.1 (PG 63:174); *Hom. 1 Thess.* 2.4 (PG 62:405–6); see also *Hom. Rom.* 7.1 (PG 60:453).

18. *Hom. Rom.* 15.6 (PG 60:548).

performance of *eleēmosynē*, a word from which the English word "alms" developed. However, *eleēmosynē* includes far more for John than alms. For him it is a behavior of loving openness to fellow humans and can be expressed in varying acts of compassion. It may include the kind word just as much as material help. *Eleēmosynē* is a power that leads God to people and people to God.[19] John calls on his people to love *eleēmosynē*. For if she once knows us, he says, the Lord will also know us; if she denies us, the Lord will also deny us and say: "I never knew you."[20] John, who was living as an ascetic, valued *eleēmosynē* more highly than any form of abstinence. For through mercy and compassion, not through asceticism, we can become like God.[21] The voice of the Lord—"Come, O blessed of my Father, inherit the kingdom prepared for you from the foundation of the world"—is heard by those who have fed the hungry Christ, even if they have lived in the state of matrimony.[22]

The church in Antioch at the time of John Chrysostom's ministry was involved in extensive social work. From his sermons we learn that the Great Church was surrounded by a wall. Here were the buildings with importance for the work of the church: a hostel for strangers and four dining halls.[23] Outside the walls lay a hospital for the incurably sick (*Stag.* 3.13 [PG 47:490]). Those widows in need of support by the church were entered in a register (*Hom. Matt.* 66.3 [PG 58:630]). The priest or deacon charged with these lists was responsible for ensuring that no unworthy widows, or others who could live from their own means, tainted the table of the poor. "Who would take the responsibility of using money entrusted to him to give to Christ for people who blaspheme the name of Christ?"[24] The Antiochian church financed this work with the income from its property. It had attained great wealth through a number of pious trusts around the end of the fourth century. John was concerned by this development. He saw the danger that the servants of the church could be kept from their real duties by the administration of these goods.[25]

Interestingly we hear nothing more of this worry in Constantinople. This could be connected to the fact that John as bishop of the capital now had the

19. Rudolf Brändle, *John Chrysostom: Bishop, Reformer, Martyr*, Early Christian Studies 8 (Strathfield, Australia: St. Pauls, 2004), 39.

20. *Hom. Philem.* 1(arg.).3 (PG 62:182); see also *Hom. Heb.* 32.3 (PG 63:223–24).

21. *Hom. 2 Tim.* 6.3 (PG 62:634). Basil the Great also valued mercy more highly than asceticism; see his homily *In divites* 3 (PG 31:283); see also Gregory of Nyssa, *De pauperibus amandis* Or. 1, ed. Adrianus van Heck, *Gregorii Nysseni Opera*, vol. 9, fasc. 1 (Leiden: Brill, 1967), 95.

22. Matt. 25:34; *Hom. 2 Cor.* 4:13, h. 1.6 (PG 51:277).

23. Malalas, *Chronographia*, ed. Ludwig August Dindorf (Bonn: Weber, 1831), 318, line 6, cited in Downey, *Antioch*, 26.

24. *Sac.* 3.12.17–20, based on *Sur le sacerdoce: Dialogue et homélie*, trans. Anne-Marie Malingrey, SC 272 (Paris: Cerf, 1980), 202.

25. Brändle, *Matt. 25:31–46*, 109–13.

final responsibility for the social work of the church.[26] John cut the budget of
the bishop's household and put the money saved in this way into an already
existing *nosokomeion*.[27] This one hospital could not cover the great needs
of the whole population of the capital, however, so Bishop John had various
new hospitals erected.[28] Yet opposition grew against his project to erect a
leper colony outside the city. The landed proprietors whose villas adjoined
the piece of land proposed for the project protested.[29] Immediately after John
Chrysostom was exiled, the rich citizens stopped the work on the planned
leper colony.

We will now turn to the sermon on Matt. 25:31–46, or more precisely John's
argumentation from this passage, or from single elements of it. The sermon
may be placed in the context of John Chrysostom's fight against poverty. He
introduces the seventy-ninth homily on Matthew's Gospel with the words
"unto this sweetest passage of Scripture [*tēs perikopēs tēs hēdistēs*], which
we do not cease to continually repeat, let us now listen with all earnestness
and compunction." The sermon is dedicated to Matt. 25:31–46 (*Hom. Matt.*
79.1 [PG 58:717]). These verses from Matthew constantly accompanied the
great preacher in his Antiochian period (386–397). He takes up this passage
in about 170 quotations and 220 allusions.[30] In these he makes free use of the
biblical text. This is evident in that the number of allusions greatly exceeds
the number of quotations. In the allusions he reproduces the biblical text in
a wide variety of expressions, comparisons, and illustrations and makes it
fruitful for his congregation. The traces of Matt. 25:31–46 can be found in all
the forms of Chrysostom's writings. However, this passage and its exposition,
or more precisely its use, has its own place in the great series of homilies
from the Antiochian years. A large proportion of important references to this
passage from Matthew are found in the homilies on Matthew's and John's
Gospels, and on the Epistle to the Romans.

John generally closes his sermons with an extensive exhortation, of which
the inner connection to the expounded Bible text can often be only guessed.
This observation is confirmed by the examination of the quotations from
and allusions to Matt. 25:31–46. A large proportion of the references are
found in the concluding parts of the homilies that serve the exhortation in
a particularly distinctive sense. The interpretation of the Matthew passage

26. Ibid., 118–20.
27. Palladius, *Dial.* 5.132–33; for translation, see SC 341:122.
28. Palladius, *Dial.* 5.134–39; on the founding of church hospitals, see Gilbert Dagron, *Naissance d'une capitale: Constantinople et ses institutions de 330–451* (Paris: Presses Universitaires, 1974), 510–11.
29. Ps.- Martyrius, *Oratio funebris* 63. For text and Italian translation, see *Oratio funebris in laudem Sancti Iohannis Chrysostomi: Epitaffio attribuito a Martirio di Antiochia*, ed. Martin Wallraff, trans. Cristina Rizzi, Quaderni della Rivista di Bizantinistica 12 (Spoleto: Fondazione Centro italiano di studi sull'Alto Medioevo, 2007), 119.
30. Brändle, *Matt. 25:31–46*, 9–74.

and the countless allusions to single aspects of this text in the homilies of John Chrysostom are to be seen in the context of his emphasis on the full incarnation of Jesus Christ.[31] The great preacher paints the hungry, thirsty, naked, stranger, sick, or imprisoned Christ most impressively before the eyes of his congregation: Christ walks through the streets of our city today, meeting us daily in the form of the miserable beggar. He has made human destitution his own. He sees what is done to the poor as done to him. Two passages are particularly noteworthy.[32] The discussion below considers each of these in turn.

Homily 50 on Matthew

The first is found in the fiftieth homily on Matthew's Gospel, where Chrysostom expounds on the passage Matt. 14:23–36, which concerns Jesus walking on the water, the sinking Peter, and the healing of many who were sick (PG 58:503–8). Toward the end of the second paragraph he leads us from verse 36 (touching the edge of Jesus's garment) to the Eucharist: "For indeed His body is set before us now, not His garment only, but even His body; not for us to touch it only, but also to eat, and be filled" (PG 58:507). In the third paragraph the preacher emphasizes the presence of Christ at his supper: "When therefore you see the priest delivering it to you, do not see it as the priest doing so, but as Christ's hand that is stretched out." Taking part in the Eucharist places us under an obligation to live better lives. "What excuse shall we have then, if when feeding on such food, we commit such sins? When eating a lamb, we become wolves? When feeding a sheep, we spoil by violence like the lions?" (PG 58:508). The pursuit of wealth is not consistent with the mystery of the Eucharist.

This leads us to the point he is making by alluding to Matt. 25:31–46. The central idea in this passage is Chrysostom's conviction that it is more important to help Christ in the poor than to honor him with precious communion vessels (PG 58:508). The table at the first communion was not silver, nor was the cup gold: "Would you do honor to Christ's body? Do not neglect Him when naked; do not, while here you honor Him with silken garments, neglect Him outside. For He that said: 'This is my body' and by His word confirmed the fact, this same said: 'You saw me hungry and perishing with

31. David Sutherland Wallace-Hadrill, *Christian Antioch: A Study of Early Christian Thought in the East* (Cambridge: Cambridge University Press, 1982), esp. 151–64: "Antiochene theology and the religious life."
32. Others that might also be considered include *Hom. Matt.* 45.2–3 (PG 58:473–76); *Hom. Matt.* 50.3–4 (PG 58:507–10); *Hom. Matt.* 88.3 (PG 58:778ff.); *Hom. Jo.* 25.3 (PG 59:151ff.); *Hom. Jo.* 27.3 (PG 59:160–62); *Hom. Jo.* 59.4 (PG 59:326–28); *Hom. Act.* 45.3–4 (PG 60:317–20); *Hom. Rom.* 7.9 (PG 60:453ff.); *Hom. Rom.* 15.6 (PG 60:547ff.); *Hom. 1 Cor.* 10.3 (PG 61:85ff.); *Hom. 2 Cor.* 20.3 (PG 61:539ff.).

cold and nakedness and did not feed me' and 'Inasmuch as you did not do it
for one of the least of these, you did not do it for me.'"

In the fourth paragraph of the homily, Chrysostom expands this idea
still further. Consecrated gifts have their place, but God loves almsgiving
better.

> For what is the use of his table being full of golden cups while he perishes
> with hunger? First fill him who is hungry, and then abundantly deck out his
> table also. Do you make him a cup of gold, while you fail to give him a cup of
> cold water? And what is the use of that? Do you provide cloths bespangled
> with gold for his table, while you fail to give himself so much as the necessary
> covering? (PG 58:509)

Once again John comes back to his central idea: "Let this then be your
thought with regard to Christ also, when He is going about a wanderer, and
a stranger, needing a roof to cover Him; and you, neglecting to receive Him,
decorate a pavement, and walls and capitals of columns, and hang up lamps
by means of silver chains, but Himself bound in prison you will not even
look upon?"[33] Once again, Chrysostom underlines that he has no intention
of preventing anyone from giving to the church. It is important, however, to
make the point that no one is blamed for not bringing gifts for the church
building, but those who unmercifully ignore the suffering of their fellow humans will be punished with eternal fire. The fellow human is a temple of God,
and this temple is far more important than the temple of the church building.
Toward the end of the sermon, Chrysostom takes up Mark 14:7—"For you
always have the poor with you, and you can show kindness to them whenever you wish; but you will not always have me"—in a very original way. He
interprets it as a reminder that we will not always have the hungry Christ
with us—only during this earthly life (PG 58:510). In an interesting discussion, he comes to the conclusion that the words were actually intended only
for the woman in Mark 14, and that Christ in reality and truth will remain
with us always, according to his promise (Matt. 28:20), and even unto the
end of the world—in Chrysostom's view, that is, obviously as a poor person.
Behind the words with which he brings the discussion to a close—"Let us
not then bring forward these things now, which were spoken because of the
situation at the time"—shines the glint of a reproach that may possibly have
been brought against Chrysostom. Could it have been held against him who
always emphasized with vehemence that Christ is present now in the poor,
that according to Mark 14:3–9 we no longer have Christ (as a person suffering poverty) among us?

33. PG 58:509. On the problem of church valuables versus human destitution, see also Jerome,
Epist. 58.7 (CSEL 54:536–37).

To conclude his sermon, John draws on three other Bible quotations to prove that almsgiving cleanses us from sins (Luke 11:41), is better than sacrifices (Hosea 6:6), and opens heaven (Acts 10:4). This passage from the fiftieth homily on Matthew shows Chrysostom's art of speaking in all its glory. The preacher gives expression to his conviction that Christ is present today in the Eucharist and in our fellow humans with a fullness of expressions, illustrations, and quotations. Here Chrysostom allows us to feel the greatness of the power that for him comes out of Matt. 25:31–46.

Homily 16 on Romans

The second text for discussion here is found in the sixteenth homily on the Epistle to the Romans.[34] Chrysostom closes the fourth paragraph with a quotation from Rom. 8:38–39. The two following paragraphs of this sermon then revolve around the love of Christ. Chrysostom emphasizes that Paul speaks about his great love to Christ only after he has already spoken about the love with which God surrounds us. Nothing can distract Paul from the love of God or love to God.

> For he loved Christ not for the things of Christ; rather, for Christ's sake [he loved] the things that were his, and to him alone he looked, and the one thing he feared was falling from his love for him. . . . And we set more store by things of mire and clay than by Christ. . . . For he [Paul] for Christ's sake does not think anything even of a kingdom; but we think slightingly of [Christ] himself, yet things of his we make great account of—and would that it were even of things of his! But now it is not even this; but with a kingdom held out to us, we let that alone, and keep pursuing shadows and dreams all our days. (PG 60:546; trans. *NPNF*[1] 11:457, alt.)

Chrysostom argues that we completely fail to take money lightly for God's sake or for our own, and that we are like animals with our eyes turned downward and not looking up to heaven (PG 60:547). He follows this idea with a passage strewn with allusions to Matt. 25:31–46. The ideas follow one another so thick and fast that it is almost impossible to grasp them all and order them systematically. God gave his Son for you, says the preacher, but you can watch him perishing of hunger and remain cold and unmoved. He was given for you, sacrificed for you, and it is for you that he goes around hungry. You should give him something of what belongs to him, to be able to make use of it yourself, and you give him nothing. In the following sentences Chrysostom expands on what he was merely hinting at here: "For He was not satisfied

34. *Hom. Rom.* 15.6 (PG 60:547–48); English translation in *NPNF*[1], vol. 11 (Grand Rapids: Eerdmans, 1975), 457–58.

even with death and the Cross only, but He took up with becoming poor also, and a stranger, and a beggar, and naked, and being thrown into a prison, and undergoing sickness, that so at least He might win you." Christ suffers today, and his suffering today is directed toward the salvation of humankind just as was his suffering on the cross. Chrysostom's use of direct speech for Christ makes a strong impression. In a long string of sentences Christ speaks of his suffering on the cross and his suffering in the poor today.

> I was naked on the cross for you; or if not this, I am now naked through the poor. I was then bound for you, and still am so for you, that whether moved by the former ground or the latter, you might be minded to show some pity. I fasted for you, again I am hungry for you. I was thirsty when hanging on the cross, I am thirsty also through the poor, that by the former as also by the latter I may draw you to myself, and make you charitable to your own salvation. (PG 60:547–48; trans. *NPNF*[1] 11:458, alt.)

Chrysostom brings a series of arguments to win his listeners for mercy: he appeals to compassion, the smallness of the demand, the reward in heaven, the thought of the common human nature of Christ and his hearers, and the remembrance of the passion of Christ on the cross. Christ does not demand riches, or to be released from his chains. He is satisfied with a piece of bread, something to wear, or a visit. For this he promises us heaven. It is important homiletically and pastorally that John emphasizes that Christ could give us the heavenly crown without having experienced our help first. "I would like to be a debtor to you, that the crown may give you some feeling of confidence [*parrēsia*]" (PG 60:548). Finally, John says: Before the theater of the whole of humanity, Christ wants to point you out as the one who fed him. He is not ashamed to acknowledge that we clothed him in his nakedness and fed him in his hunger.

At this point the preacher was interrupted by loud clapping.[35] Chrysostom brought this show of approval to an end with the challenge to put what had been said into practice, and not to leave it simply as a matter for applause.

Conclusion

In conclusion, I suggest that the passage Matt. 25:31–46 is the integrative force behind the central thoughts of John Chrysostom's theology.[36] His decisive theological ideas collect and order themselves around the power emanating from this passage as though crystallizing around a nucleus. I

35. On this behavior, see Brändle, *Matt. 25:31–46*, 196–97.
36. See also Peter Klasvogt, *Leben zur Verherrlichung Gottes: Botschaft des Johannes Chrysostomos* (Bonn: Borengässer, 1992), 156–57, 160–64, 215–16.

discussed this question intensively in 1979, and it is a great pleasure to be able to unfold these ideas once again after a quarter of a century. I do it the more gladly because I am as convinced as ever of the unchanging relevance of the words of the risen Judge to the current situation of humanity. Here, however, I would like to focus on one idea that is particularly important. In the thought of John Chrysostom the idea of the body of Christ—which also includes his explanations of the Eucharist—is closely connected to John's reading of Matt. 25:31–46. This is also valid for his understanding of *sōtēria* as the goal of God's working and also of human life. John Chrysostom's thoughts on redemption are particularly impressive. Redemption for him is not limited to what happened on the cross. Redemption is not something finished, but rather something that continues to happen in our everyday life. John formulates this conviction with the help of statements taken from Matt. 25:31–46. Continual meditation on this passage allowed John's conviction to grow that the Risen One was not only giving us a steady stream of impulses to help the poor but was also promising us his helping presence. For he who feeds the hungry, gives drink to the thirsty, clothes the naked, and visits the sick and imprisoned comes into contact with Christ the Redeemer. Out of love, Christ is prepared to be fed by his servants. He is hungry so that we do not need to starve. It is for our salvation that Christ goes naked.

In a homily on John's Gospel Chrysostom says: "Gladly He goes hungry so that you may be fed; He goes naked so that He may provide you with the opportunity to be rewarded with a garment of incorruption."[37] And in a sermon on Romans: "For it is here that He is thirsty, here that He is hungry. He is thirsty, since He thirsts for your salvation; and it is for this that He even begs; for this that He even goes about naked, negotiating immortal life for you."

In the forty-fifth homily on Matthew's Gospel, the preacher says of the risen Christ:

> He (Christ) clothed you with a garment of salvation [Isa. 61:10], and clothed you by Himself; do you at least clothe Him by your servant. He made you glorious in Heaven, do you deliver Him from shivering, and nakedness, and shame. He made you a fellow-citizen of angels, do you grant to Him at least the shelter of your roof, give house-room to Him at least as to your own servant. (*Hom. Matt.* 45.3 [PG 58:474–75]; trans. *NPNF*[1] 10:287, alt.)

And again in the sixteenth homily on Romans, John Chrysostom speaks with moving intensity of the redeeming work of the Lord, who is present among us in the poor. He puts the suffering of Christ in his passion and his suffering today in the closest possible relationship to each other. His suffering today, like his suffering then, is for our salvation. Christ is poor, a stranger, homeless, bound with chains, sick "that so at least He might win you." His

37. *Hom. Jo.* 27.3 (PG 59:161).

suffering on Calvary and his suffering today are both directed to this: "that whether moved by the former ground or the latter, you might be inclined to show some pity.[38] Because nothing is so close to the heart of the Lord as our salvation, he leaves nothing undone and finds nothing too lowly to help us toward this. He becomes poor that we through his poverty might be rich."[39] Once again, John Chrysostom allows the risen Christ to speak directly to the church:

> For it is no costly gift I ask, but bread and lodging, and words of comfort. . . . Be softened at seeing me naked, and remember that nakedness with which I was naked on the cross for you; or, if not this, then that with which I am now naked through the poor. . . . I would like to be a debtor to you, that the crown may give you some feeling of confidence [parrēsia]. This is why, though I am able to support myself, I come around begging, and stand beside your door, and stretch out my hand, since my wish is to be supported by you. For I love you greatly, and so desire to eat at your table, which is the way with those who love a person. And I glory in this. (Hom. Rom. 15.6 [PG 60:547–48]; trans. NPNF¹ 11:458, alt.)

With his bold interpretation of the Matthew passage, John Chrysostom has found a new approach to soteriology. Unfortunately for the church, this was not developed further by later writers, and even today is little taken into account. Instead, the charge of moralism is raised again and again against the great preacher. Yet for John there is a close connection between soteriology and ethics. This connection allows for a new understanding of his statements about the relationship between grace and faith, and again between faith and works, which is normally interpreted as an uninspired synergism. Through his soteriological interpretation of Matt. 25:31–46 he assures the preeminence of grace. For it is out of grace that the risen Christ comes to us today in the poor, out of love to us that he suffers in and with them, and out of grace that he accepts what we give to suffering humans as given to him and promises us great reward for our small deeds. Works for John are not elements separable from faith, but they are far more: a concrete form of faith. Good deeds are a step in the direction of the experience of faith, signs of a true life already grasped.[40] Indicative of this view are the words with which John follows a quotation from Matt. 25:34–35 in a homily on 1 Timothy: "The living differ from the dead, not only in that they behold the sun, and breathe the air, but in that they are doing some good" (Hom. 1 Tim. 13.3 [PG 62:567]).

---

38. Hom. Rom. 15.6 (PG 60:547).

39. Hom. Rom. 15.6 (PG 60:548); 2 Cor. 8:9; see also Hom. Matt. 5.5 (PG 57:61). On the whole paragraph, see Brändle, Matt. 25:31–46, 55–57, 340–42.

40. On the problem of synergism in John Chrysostom, see Rudolf Brändle, "Synergismus als Phänomen der Frömmigkeitsgeschichte, dargestellt an den Predigten des Johannes Chrysostomos," Oikonomia 9 (1980): 69–89, 113–21.

No other church father opened himself with similar intensity to the force of this parable from Matthew. The most comparable teaching is found in the Cappadocian fathers, who were also moved by human suffering to underpin their exhortations with Matt. 25:31–46.[41] It is interesting to note that Origen, who was admired and imitated, interpreted Matt. 25:31–46 quite differently. For him this text is not, or at least not mainly, directed toward practice. This simple exposition, the "vulgarior traditio," can be considered outdone by the "interpretatio subtilior." He feeds Christ, who eats and drinks the righteousness and truth of believers. We clothe the freezing Christ by receiving the garment of wisdom from God with the aim of teaching others.[42]

41. On the interpretation of the Cappadocians, see Brändle, *Matt. 25:31–46*, 348–52.

42. On the exposition of Matt. 25:31–46 by Origen, see Rudolf Brändle, "Zur Interpretation von Matth. 25,31–46 im Matthäuskommentar des Origenes," in *Studien zur Alten Kirche* (Stuttgart: Kohlhammer, 1999), 21–28.

10

POVERTY AND GENEROSITY TOWARD THE POOR IN THE TIME OF JOHN CHRYSOSTOM

WENDY MAYER

In a recent article I set out to establish a baseline for a study of the shape and role of poverty in society in the cities of Antioch and Constantinople, as viewed through the writings of John Chrysostom.[1] The seminal work of Evelyne Patlagean and Peter Brown, who both discuss a major change in the social imagination in regard to public generosity (*euergetism*) between the fourth and seventh centuries CE,[2] provides an important framework for the tentative interpretation of those results. Patlagean's work, along with that

1. Wendy Mayer, "Poverty and Society in the World of John Chrysostom," in *Social and Political Life in Late Antiquity*, ed. William Bowden, Adam Gutteridge, and Carlos Machado, Late Antique Archaeology 3 (Leiden: Brill, 2006), 465–84. The research on which that article and the present essay are based has been generously funded by the Australian Research Council.

2. Evelyne Patlagean, *Pauvreté économique et pauvreté sociale à Byzance, 4e–7e siècles*, Civilisations et Sociétés 48 (Paris: Mouton, 1977); Peter Brown, *Poverty and Leadership in the Later Roman Empire* (Hanover, NH: University Press of New England, 2002). Brown further develops a thesis first explored in detail by Michael De Vinne, "The Advocacy of Empty Bellies: Episcopal Representation of the Poor in the Late Roman Empire" (PhD diss., Stanford University, 1995).

140

of Paul Veyne,[3] is foundational in identifying and outlining a transformation from the dominant Greco-Roman civic model of the community (in which one's status as citizen or noncitizen determined one's participation in civic benefits) to an economic model of the community that becomes prevalent by the end of late antiquity. Throughout these centuries the traditional Greco-Roman model of winning prestige by displaying public generosity toward the citizens of the *polis* through building programs and the sponsorship of entertainment slowly shifted to a point where a primary focus of publicly expressed giving became the "poor."[4] Brown explains this change via the emerging role of the Christian bishop, who adopts the poor and models himself as their patron and champion, in the process giving rise to "love of the poor" as a new civic virtue.[5]

My own study of the picture of poverty that emerges at the end of the fourth century as viewed in the writings of John Chrysostom adds support to these models, but also nuances them. Of particular importance in this nuancing is the role played by the rise of asceticism in this changing dynamic. While concern over "wealth" and "poverty" as the current benchmarks of societal and self-definition permeates John's homilies, at the same time it is also clear that at this point in time the notion of giving to the economic poor is *not* well established in the minds of lay Christians, but is still largely overshadowed by a "civic" model of benefaction. John *wants* the members of his congregations to subscribe to a view of society in which giving alms to the economic poor is of both personal and social benefit, but the frequency of his advice in this regard is a reasonably clear indication that they do not. What does seem to have gained a hold in their minds is a concept of giving to the voluntary poor, that is, the ascetic, if not yet as a civic virtue, then certainly as an action that brings personal benefit. This is a notion of giving to the "poor" that takes little account of economic status.[6] John is at pains to point out that the two forms of generosity are not the same and to discourage his audience from giving to ascetics, simply because they *are* ascetics, if it is also the case that they are economically comfortably off (*Hom. Phil.* 1 [PG 62:188, 29–48]). In this

3. Paul Veyne, *Le pain et le cirque: Sociologie historique d'un pluralisme politique*, L'Univers historique (Paris: Seuil, 1976).

4. See Patlagean, *Pauvreté*, 126, where she argues that the eminent secular donors of the classical era became ascetic donors in late antiquity, choosing poverty, celibacy, and ascetic generosity as part of a new Christian interpretation of the concept of "citizen." See also Susan R. Holman, *The Hungry Are Dying: Beggars and Bishops in Roman Cappadocia* (New York: Oxford University Press, 2001), 17.

5. For a critique of the approach to poverty taken by Patlagean, Veyne, Brown, and other earlier scholars, see Holman, *Hungry Are Dying*, 5–12.

6. Gildas Hamel, *Poverty and Charity in Roman Palestine, First Three Centuries C.E.*, Near Eastern Studies 23 (Berkeley: University of California Press, 1990), 223–24, notes the emergence of this trend in the third century among Hellenistic Christians, and at pp. 195–97 offers a tentative explanation of its origins.

same period, at the institutional level organized care by the church for the economic poor within a range of categories (such as orphans, widows, and lepers) is well established, with the bishop explicitly characterized by John, in at least one Antiochene sermon, as "patron of the poor."[7] These findings raise the question of whether what we observe at Antioch and Constantinople in John Chrysostom's time includes a development that eventually faded and thus left no trace by the sixth and seventh centuries, or whether, and far more likely, another strand must be added to the models of Brown and Patlagean. In this expanded model, transformation from a civic to an economic model of community occurs not just via the emergence of the bishop as "governor of the poor" and via the transformation of prominent secular donors into ascetic benefactors, but also via the gradual redirection of public generosity from the citizens of the earthly *polis* toward the voluntary poor. Living "the life of the angels," these ascetic individuals are virtual citizens of the eternal *polis*, heaven.

It is this different valuing of economic and voluntary poverty that lies at the heart of understanding the shifting roles of wealth and poverty in society from the fourth century onward. Setting aside the theological underpinnings of these two ways of viewing and responding to poverty for others to investigate, in this essay I explore further the relative valency of these two concepts of poverty in the context of generosity toward the poor by teasing out the relationship in John Chrysostom's time between the private individual, asceticism, wealth, and economic poverty. I begin by examining how poverty, in whatever way it was defined, fitted into the life of the ascetic in John's different communities. This then leads us to explore how lay Christians responded to ascetics and to the poor in general, and then to ask what prompted their various responses and how this related to prevailing notions of poverty and generosity. Along the way we will touch on a number of theories that have recently been proposed in this regard.

Voluntary Poverty, Personal Wealth, and Generosity

One way in which to understand how poverty fitted into the life of the ascetic in John's time is to consider two cases, one from Constantinople and one from Antioch, in which the ascetics in question came from a background of considerable wealth. In this way we can test how asceticism shaped their response to wealth and determine to what extent concerns about "poverty" framed their newly adopted lifestyle.

7. *Hom. Matt.* 18.23 (PG 51:23, 19–23). On the location of this homily among those delivered following the riots in 387, see Andrius Valevicius, "Les 24 homélies *De statuis* de Jean Chrysostome: Recherches nouvelles," *RÉAug* 46 (2000): 83–91.

Example 1: Olympias

The first case is that of Olympias, a young woman with vast assets at her disposal. She was widowed during the reign of Emperor Theodosius I and, according to Palladius, fought to retain control of her fortune and her independence when those assets were placed under the control of the urban prefect Clementine by imperial directive, on her rejection of an arranged second marriage.[8] She embraced the ascetic life and was ordained a deacon of the Great Church at Constantinople (the order in which this occurred is not clear), and was active as a patron in Constantinople during the episcopates of Nectarius and of John Chrysostom, his successor. She died in 408, after being exiled to Nicomedia in the aftermath of John's own exile to Armenia in mid-404.

For Olympias, widowhood and asceticism were in essence synonymous. A pragmatic effect of the ascetical widowed state in her particular case was sustained personal control of her assets, enabling her to function as a significant patron of the Christian community. According to the sources, she donated to the Great Church at Constantinople estates in Thrace, Galatia, Cappadocia Prima, and Bithynia, while still retaining houses in prime positions within Constantinople itself, plus estates in its suburbs.[9] After giving away an additional 1,000 *litra* of gold and 2,000 *litra* of silver to the church, she retained sufficient wealth to pay John's private expenses and support his ministry for at least eight years, up to and including his ransom of captives from exile.[10] She gave money and lands to client bishops, among them Amphilochius of Iconium, Gregory of Nazianzus, and Epiphanius of Salamis, and food and lodging to yet other bishops, including Theophilus of Alexandria, Acacius of Beroea, and Severian of Gabala. She also supplied food and lodging to visiting priests, ascetics, and virgins, among them the fifty Egyptian monks, the Tall Brothers.[11] In one of the houses she retained, adjacent to the Great Church, she founded and supported a community of virgins, which comprised female relatives, fifty maidservants from within her household, and numerous women of senatorial status, totaling some 250 ascetic women.[12] What is of interest in the way the sources portray her piety and generosity by citing these statistics is not the vast amounts of wealth she gave away, but the assets and wealth that she retained, to the extent of continuing financial support for John Chrysostom into the second or third year of his exile.[13]

---

8. Palladius, *Dial.* 17, ed. A.-M. Malingrey, SC 341 (1988), 344–46, repeated in *Vita Olymp.* 4, ed. A.-M. Malingrey, SC 13bis (1968), 412–14.

9. *Vita Olymp.* 5 (SC 13bis:416–18).

10. *Vita Olymp.* 8 (SC 13bis:422); Sozomen, *HE* 8.27.8, ed. G. C. Hansen, *Historia ecclestica*, Fontes Christiani 73, 4 vols. (Turnhout: Brepols, 2004), at 4:1,048–50.

11. Palladius, *Dial.* 16–17 (SC 341:324, 348).

12. *Vita Olymp.* 6 (SC 13bis:418).

13. *Vita Olymp.* 8 (see n. 10).

During her own trial at Constantinople late in 404, she was still considered wealthy enough to sustain a substantial fine.[14]

We see similar models of wealthy aristocratic women who embrace a life of virginity and philanthropy without reducing themselves to economic poverty in three generations of women from the Anician family in Rome (Proba, Juliana, and Demetrias).[15] The account that Sozomen supplies of Nicarete, one of John's supporters, underscores this fundamental lack of association between personal economic poverty and asceticism, at least at the elite level. There Nicarete is described as a member of the aristocracy in Bithynia, who had dedicated her life to virginity. As a consequence of her vulnerability as a single woman (we are not told whether she was a widow or unmarried), a large part of her inheritance was confiscated. The intended impression here is an involuntary reduction to poverty. Again, what is significant is not what is taken or given away but what remains. Despite her relative poverty, through her frugal management of the assets still under her control Nicarete was able to run her household and still give generously to others.[16]

What we fail to see in these examples is an expectation that ascetic women must give their wealth away in order to pursue a rigorous *askēsis*. What we see instead via their ascetic female members is a shift in the object of the generosity of these elite families from civic benefaction (that is, the building of public baths and theaters, or sponsorship of games) to the building of churches,[17] the founding of ascetic communities,[18] the provision of hospitality for bishops and ascetics,[19] and the provision of care for those in need. For

14. Sozomen, *HE* 8.24.7 (ed. Hansen, 4:1036).

15. On Demetrias, see Bronwen Neil, "*On True Humility*: An Anonymous Letter on Poverty and the Female Ascetic," and on Juliana and Proba, see Geoffrey Dunn, "The Elements of Ascetical Widowhood: Augustine's *de Bono Viduitatis* and *Epistula* 130," both in *Prayer and Spirituality in the Early Church*, ed. Wendy Mayer, Pauline Allen, and Lawrence Cross (Strathfield: St. Pauls Publications, 2006), 4:233–46 and 247–56.

16. Sozomen, *HE* 8.23.4–7 (ed. Hansen, 4:1030–32).

17. On Demetrias's building of a basilica to St. Stephen in the mid-fifth century, see Neil, "*On True Humility*," 245. Empress Eudoxia is said to have sponsored the construction of a basilica at Gaza, as well as a hospice for travelers. See Mark the Deacon, *Vita Porphyrii* 53, ed. H. Grégoire and M.-A. Kugener (Paris: Société d'édition Les Belles Lettres, 1930), 43–44. On the latest opinion regarding the date of the Greek recension of the *Vita*, see Jeff Childers, "The *Life of Porphyry*: Clarifying the Relationship of the Greek and Georgian Versions through the Study of New Testament Citations," in *Transmission and Reception: New Testament Text Critical and Exegetical Studies*, ed. J. W. Childers and D. C. Parker, Texts & Studies, 3rd series (Piscataway, NJ: Gorgias Press, 2006), 4:154–78. On Eudoxia as an ecclesiastical patron, see Wendy Mayer, "Doing Violence to the Image of an Empress: The Destruction of Eudoxia's Reputation," in *Violence, Victims and Vindication: Shifting Frontiers V*, ed. Hal Drake (Aldershot: Ashgate, 2006), 205–13, esp. 208–9.

18. On Proba's founding of a community of ascetic women in Rome, see Jerome, *Epist.* 130.7, ed. I. Hilberg, CSEL 56 (1918): 182. Demetrias, Melania the Younger (Gerontius, *Vita Mel.* 1.22, ed. D. Gorce, SC 90 [1962]: 172), and Paula (see below) all established or sponsored communities.

19. Like Olympias at Constantinople, at Rome Juliana also provided hospitality for clergy. See John Chrysostom, *Ep.* 169 (PG 52:709).

women at this level, asceticism is associated not with the blanket disposal of wealth but with a shift from generosity toward citizens of the *polis*, to giving generously to the church and its clients, contributing via the church and the poor to the spiritual capital in heaven. It is not that they continue to possess wealth, but rather what their attitude toward it and the use they make of it is. This point is explicitly made by Augustine in his advice to the widowed ascetic Juliana.[20] For the successful ascetical widow, love of wealth must be quashed along with love of marriage. Generosity is to be directed to helping the needy rather than squandered on rich clients. It is alms given to the poor that add to the heavenly treasure. Another thread that we see run through these stories is the domestic shape this particular form of asceticism adopted, something to which Ramon Teja and Mar Marcos point in their comparison of Olympias and the wealthy Roman matron Paula. Both Paula and Olympias (and Proba and Juliana likewise) model their communities as large aristocratic households.[21] Olympias locates her community in a large house she has retained, on prime real estate, adjacent to the Great Church. The membership of her community centers around a core group of her female relatives and slaves. Paula, as Teja and Marcos point out, also modeled her community on the household, stratifying it so that it resembled society in microcosm. Although women of the middle and lower classes were also present, each class functioned within the community in different ways. These observations provide an important caveat. Administration of these ascetic communities and their wealth was kept in house, as it were, with the aristocratic private household both literally and conceptually providing a basic model.

I have labored these points because the sources, in their enthusiasm for the piety of these women and in their desire to exaggerate and extol their *askēsis*, can give the impression that wealth was of little account in their lives and that what wealth they did have was expended on unconditional care for others to the point of exhaustion. This disjunction between impression and reality is highlighted by Palladius's account of Olympias's reaction when Emperor Theodosius initially confiscated her assets. He quotes her as thanking the emperor for his virtue in taking away the burden of her wealth and asking only that he amplify the benefit by distributing the whole to the poor and the churches. By this means she herself will be freed of the burden

---

20. Augustine, *Vid.* 21.26 (*NBA* 7/1:208): "In uobis autem amor diuitiarum simul frigescat cum amore nuptiarum, et pius usus rerum, quas possidetis, ad spiritales delicias conferatur, ut liberalitas uestra magis ferueat adiuuandis egenis quam ditandis auaris. In thesaurum quippe caelestem non mittuntur dona cupidorum, sed eleemosynae pauperum, quae in immensum modum orationes adiuuant uiduarum"; and see Dunn's comments in "Elements of Ascetical Widowhood," 252.

21. "Modelos de ascetismo femenino aristocrático en la época de Juan Crisóstomo: Constantinopla y Palestina," in *Giovanni Crisostomo: Oriente e Occidente tra IV e V secolo*, XXXIII Incontro di Studiosi dell'Antichità Cristiana, Augustinianum 6–8 maggio 2004, Roma, SEAug 93 (Rome: Institutum Patristicum Augustinianum, 2005), 619–25, esp. 625.

of vainglory (*kenodoxia*) that accompanies the giving away of it.[22] This is the reaction that the sources prime us to expect of a rich young widow who has dedicated her life to virginity. The reality is quite other. As we saw, on regaining control of her wealth, while she distributes some to the churches and poor, she does not distribute all, while it is the honor that accompanies that generosity (the very vainglory that she reportedly seeks to avoid) that is a foundation in the anonymous *Life of Olympias* (*Vita Olympiadis*) of her ascetic reputation.[23]

Example 2: Flavian

A similar paradox comes to light in regard to Flavian, the bishop under whom John served during his presbyterate at Antioch. Praised for his ascetic rigor by John in his debut homily,[24] Flavian, we learn from another sermon John preached at Antioch, came from a wealthy aristocratic background[25] and had inherited a property that he used to house the poor (here identified as *xenoi*, resident aliens).[26] John holds up Flavian as a compelling and observable example of almsgiving (*eleēmosynē*). Yet even as he extols him for the generous use to which this house is put (it might as well, he says, be called the residents' as Flavian's, to such an extent do they have the run of it), it is clear that Flavian retains ownership. It is he who runs the hostel, who provides a variety of care, and whose estate presumably bears the burden of the day-to-day running costs. He acts as a private benefactor in this instance and has not turned the property and its income over to the church. An explanation that suits the cases of both Flavian and Olympias, as well as those of Proba, Juliana, Demetrias, and Paula, is that at this period inherited property continued to be thought of as an indisposable family asset, even after the current heir adopted the ascetic life. What is important here is again not the possession of property, but its proper use. As John says in this sermon, what we own is ours most of all when we consistently use it not for

---

22. Palladius, *Dial.* 17 (SC 341:346, 167–75); *Vita Olymp.* 4 (SC 13bis:414, 13–20): "Πρέπουσαν βασιλεῖ καὶ ἁρμόττουσαν ἀρετὴν ἐπισκόπῳ εἰς ἐμὲ τὴν ταπεινὴν ἐπεδείξω, δέσποτα, κελεύσας παραφυλαχθῆναί μου τὸ βαρύτατον φορτίον, περὶ οὗ ἐφρόντιζον, ὅπως διοικηθῇ· μεῖζον δὲ ποιήσεις, προστάξας αὐτὸ τοῖς πενομένοις καὶ ταῖς ἐκκλησίαις διασκορπισθῆναι. Ἐγὼ γὰρ ἀπηυξάμην πάλαι τὴν ἐκ τῆς διανομῆς κενοδοξίαν, ὅπως μὴ ἀμελήσω τοῦ τῆς φύσεως πλούτου, ἐλιττομένη περὶ τὴν ὕλην."

23. *Vita Olymp.* 13–15 (SC 13bis:434–40).

24. *Sermo cum presbyter fuit ordinatus*, ed. A.-M. Malingrey, SC 272 (1980), 404, 166–69.

25. Flavian's aristocratic background is explicitly mentioned by Theodoret, *Hist. Eccl.* 4.25.5, ed. L. Parmentier and G. C. Hansen, GCS, n.s., 5 (1998), 264: Φλαβιανὸς δὲ ὁ ἄριστος ἐξ εὐπατριδῶν, while John emphasizes in *Sermo cum presbyter* (404, 169) that he was raised in a wealthy household.

26. *Sermo Gen.*, ed. L. Brottier, SC 433 (1998), 170, 261–71. On the Antiochene provenance of this sermon, see Wendy Mayer, *The Homilies of St John Chrysostom: Provenance; Reshaping the Foundations*, OrChrAn 273 (Rome: Institutum Pontificum Orientalium Studiorum, 2005), 341–42.

ourselves but for the poor.[27] In Flavian's case, it is not just any poor, however. His generous hospitality is conditional, directed specifically at those driven to Antioch from elsewhere on account of the true (= Nicene) faith.[28] We will set the implications of this aside for the moment.

Voluntary and Involuntary Poverty

Having established that at this point in time the generous use of *personal wealth* for the benefit of the poor is an ascetic virtue, it is important next to consider in what way *personal poverty* could be a compatible ascetic virtue. What meaning does the term "voluntary poverty" have, if there is no requirement for the new ascetic to dispose of economic capital? Once again I turn to the case of Olympias. One point is immediately clear. The poverty that is adopted by rich aristocratic widows like Olympias, Proba, and Juliana, or by a virgin like Demetrias, is not economic. They do not reduce themselves to indigence. Rather, the indigent, the economic poor, are one of the objects of their largesse. If we are to determine whether the term "poverty" has meaning in the context of their private ascetic practice, we must look elsewhere for our definition. For Augustine, Juliana was to extinguish all love of wealth, which would lead her to use her money fruitfully and for spiritual benefit.[29] As Geoffrey Dunn points out in his recent study of Augustine and ascetical widowhood, in his advice to Proba, Augustine tempers his focus on prayer with advice about wealth. Although it was her wealth that provided the leisure for her life of prayer, the latter could be enabled only by detachment from her possessions. Wealth, Augustine advises, is to be held in contempt and indifference and used personally for no more than keeping the body healthy.[30] Proba is to live as if she herself is poor, so that her mind will be focused on spiritual things.

Olympias exhibits the same detachment, the same virtual poverty, in her own life. According to Palladius, she observed a vegetarian diet and tended to bathe only if forced to do so out of ill health.[31] In his eighth letter to her from exile, in an attempt to combat her despair, John Chrysostom discusses at great length the various virtues she has mastered in her virginity, through which she has quashed all elements of luxury and achieved freedom from the passions.[32] Highlighted is her *enkrateia* in regard to diet. She drinks

27. *Sermo Gen.* (SC 433:170, 272–75).
28. SC 433:170, 267–68.
29. See n. 20.
30. See Dunn, "Elements of Ascetical Widowhood" (n. 15), 253, on Augustine, *Ep.* 130, citing 130.2.5, 130.3.7, 130.10.19, and 130.13.24.
31. Palladius, *Dial.* 17 (SC 341:346, 181–82); *Vita Olymp.* 13 (SC 13bis:434, 19–21).
32. *Ep.* 8, ed. A.-M. Malingrey, SC 13bis (1968): 176, 12–14.

and eats only enough to keep herself alive.[33] She has mastered the practice of keeping vigil to the point where staying awake all night has become a natural habit.[34] Her dress is simple and without style.[35] Denial of luxury, living an intentionally "poor" life, detaching oneself from one's wealth, however, is insufficient if it fails to go hand in hand with the proper use of what one is denying. In summarizing her virtues, John not only refers to her perpetual contests of endurance, her patience, her fasting, her prayers, her holy vigils, and her *enkrateia*, but culminates the list with her generosity and hospitality. From her childhood to the present she hasn't stopped following the injunction in Matt. 25:34–37 (to care for Christ when she saw him hungry, thirsty, sick, naked, and in prison).[36] What John praises in Olympias is what Augustine expected of Juliana and Proba, namely, that sexual continence was an underlying discipline, and that what truly exemplified ascetical widowhood was a life of prayer and fasting, accompanied by almsgiving. This view of what comprises ascetic virtue differs significantly from that which John expresses in his treatise *On virginity*, where, in the list of the true ornaments of virginity (fasting, holy vigils, mildness, moderation, poverty, courage, humility, and endurance), generosity and hospitality are noticeably absent.[37] There poverty is a purely private discipline, detached from the public exercise of giving to the poor and providing housing for the stranger. If we set aside for the moment the question of the relationship between personal poverty and the generous use of personal wealth,[38] what can be glimpsed here is an understanding of what it means within the ascetic context to be poor. "Poverty" is a voluntary detachment from wealth, leading to the removal of all luxury from one's life. This is to the point not just of moderation (which is listed in *On virginity* as a separate virtue), but of complete simplicity. It is a poverty that is not a reduction to the point of neediness (as is often the case for the economic poor), but rather a removal of all that is superfluous. One eats only what one needs to survive, one wears only what one needs to preserve modesty, one bathes only as often as one needs to sustain health. What distinguishes the voluntary poor from the involuntary poor in this regard is that the first can deny all of these essentials (food, clothing, and private or public baths) precisely because they have unrestricted access to them. It is in this sense that the ascetic life can be described as a state of voluntary poverty, and

33. *Ep.* 8 (SC 13bis:176, 15–17).
34. *Ep.* 8 (SC 13bis:176, 19–240).
35. *Ep.* 8 (SC 13bis:178–80, 6.a).
36. *Ep.* 8 (SC 13bis:198, 9–17).
37. *De virginitate*, ed. H. Musurillo and B. Grillet, SC 125 (1966), 326, 1.6–11.
38. The audience of *De virginitate* is uncertain. If John is addressing virgins of a broader range of economic backgrounds, it may be that the ministries of generosity and hospitality remain unmentioned, since not all the women to whom the treatise was addressed would be able to participate.

why, for the ascetics of this time and those who admired them, personal wealth and voluntary poverty were entirely compatible.[39]

That this view of poverty holds true not just for rich aristocratic women devoted to asceticism but also for rich aristocratic men is supported by our second example, the bishop Flavian. In his praise of Flavian's virtues in the homily preached on the occasion of his own ordination to the rank of presbyter, John Chrysostom focuses on Flavian's *enkrateia*, which, he says, is all the more remarkable because he was raised in a wealthy and luxurious household. His control of his stomach, his dismissal of excess, and his despisal of a luxurious diet are all to be admired.[40] There would be nothing remarkable, he says, in an impoverished person attaining such a level of severity and restraint.[41] This is a more direct statement of the same point that John makes to Olympias, but he also takes it one step further. The person raised in poverty lives in a persistent state of *enkrateia*, but by default. It is in the element of choice, in the capacity to live with wealth but dismiss it, that the greater ascetic virtue lies.[42] This additional point moves us a step beyond the conclusion drawn at the end of our discussion of Olympias. For the ascetic, personal wealth and voluntary poverty are more than simply compatible. Rather, the one needs the other, if it is to be remarkable.

Differing Views of Poverty

Now that we have gained some understanding of what it means to adopt a life of voluntary poverty in the time of John Chrysostom, the next point to consider is the relative valency of voluntary and involuntary poverty in society, bearing in mind that we are talking about a very specific period in time and two very specific cultural settings. What we are interested in here is the respective moral values placed on voluntary and economic poverty. What aspects of these render a person morally appealing or unappealing? To recover a sense of this, we will look at how different people reacted to the ascetics they encountered or to the economic poor who surrounded them in society, and then try to analyze the underlying value judgment.

39. For the background to the development of a Christian discourse in which wealth and property were seen as neutral and emphasis was placed rather on its "proper use," see Hamel, *Poverty and Charity*, 232–35.

40. *Sermo cum presbyter* (SC 272:404, 166–69).

41. *Sermo cum presbyter* (SC 272:404, 169–406, 173).

42. It is likely that the Stoic notion of wealth as an "indifferent" underlies this reading, which would also help to explain why it is the use to which wealth is put, not wealth itself, that is significant for ascetic virtue. On the role of *askēsis*, the "passions," and "indifferents" in the Stoic pursuit of happiness via virtue, see Dirk Baltzly, "Stoicism," in *The Stanford Encyclopedia of Philosophy*, ed. E. N. Zalta (Winter 2004), http://plato.stanford.edu/archives/win2004/entries/stoicism/ (accessed October 2005).

The most visible of the economic poor and those who provoked a strong reaction are the beggars. These are individuals or family groups who were structurally poor, that is, without resources and unable to secure their livelihood through their own labor.[43] The structurally poor who lacked family networks for support were heavily reliant on charity for survival. Noncitizens were especially vulnerable. The common reaction to people who begged for food, money, or clothing ranged from simple avoidance to hostility and suspicion. At what is most likely Constantinople, on being solicited, passersby habitually backed away or quickly replied, "I don't have anything on me."[44] At Antioch the beggars' lack of employment was a source of criticism; not only did people refuse to give them money, but they also abused them to their faces for being lazy.[45] There is a strong underlying sense here that the beggar exhibits negative moral behavior.[46] A common response to poverty in general was the argument that poor people have a choice and could better their lot, if they really wanted to, which ties into the idea that poverty and laziness are to be equated and adds the idea that poverty is a personal responsibility (*Hom. Phil.* 9 [PG 62:251, 35–41]). Criticism could extend to allegations of criminal behavior. In *Hom. Matt.* 35, a homily of uncertain provenance, the rich commonly assume that a poor person who is young and healthy must not only be lazy but be a runaway slave who has abandoned his or her master (PG 57:409, 43–46). In *Hom. Heb.* 11, another homily of uncertain provenance, John addresses at great length the belief that beggars are fraudulent (PG 63:94–96). The criticism here is that if one gives beggars clothing, they will turn around and sell it (PG 63:94, 34), or that they present a false appearance, that is, that their material condition is by no means as extreme as they would have it appear (PG 63:94, 31–32 and 45).[47] That John admits that beggars do exaggerate their appearance to provoke pity is irrelevant here (PG 63:94, 45–50).[48] What is significant is the belief that begging and criminality are closely associated. This is not always the case,

43. For a definition of structural poverty, see Anneliese Parkin, "Poverty in the Early Roman Empire: Ancient and Modern Conceptions and Constructs" (PhD diss., Cambridge University, 2001), 26–27.

44. *Hom. Act.* 8 (PG 60:70, 31–33 and 71, 19–20). On the provenance of this homily, see Mayer, *Homilies of St John Chrysostom*, 330–31.

45. *Hom. princ. Act.* 2 (PG 51:85, 4–15; Mayer, *Homilies of St John Chrysostom*, 368–69). Cf. *Hom. Heb.* 11 (PG 63:94, 24–26), where the same response to the homeless poor is said to be typical. In *De eleemosyna*, another Antiochene sermon (Mayer, *Homilies of St John Chrysostom*, 368), John condemns his audience for interrogating beggars about their country, life, morals, pursuits, and state of health (PG 51:269, 23–28), which implies concerns both about citizenship and capacity to work.

46. See *Hom. princ. Act.* 2 (PG 51:85, 8–11), where the moral judgment itself is criticized: οὐκ ἐποίησέ σε κατήγορον κακία, ἀλλὰ ἰατρὸν κατέστησε συμφορὰ . . . οὐκ ἵνα κακίζῃ τρόπον, ἀλλ᾽ ἵνα λύσῃ λιμόν.

47. Cf. *Hom. Act.* 45 (PG 60:320, 15).

48. Cf. *De eleemosyna* (PG 51:269, 28–31).

however. There is at least one circumstance in which the response is quite different. When beggars sought attention by resorting to street theater, they could quickly attract a crowd of both men and women who would stay for a while, enjoy the show, and respond by giving the performer bread, a coin, or some other item (*Hom. 1 Thess.* 11 [PG 62:465, 30–37]). The reaction here is the opposite of that to the beggar who solicits directly. There is no criticism and no resistance. In fact in *Hom. 1 Cor.* 21, John accuses the onlookers of giving silver coin specifically for the purpose of encouraging the beggar to perform again (PG 61:177, 54–58).[49]

The response to the voluntary poor could also range from positive to negative. In the same homily where John discusses the allegation that beggars are fraudulent, he takes his audience to task for having the same reaction to ascetic men (*monazontōn andrōn*) who ask for food and shelter (*Hom. Heb.* 11 [PG 63:96]). What is significant here is that the negative reaction attaches to the action—the soliciting—not to the type of poverty (i.e., voluntary or economic). The response is indiscriminate. The same person who interrogates the structural poor when they beg interrogates the voluntary poor when they solicit. An ascetic male who begs is fraudulent, that is, not a true ascetic— the underlying idea being that a true ascetic is either rich in reality or at least self-sufficient. Libanius, responding to ascetic men in and around Antioch from a non-Christian perspective, likewise considers their actions fraudulent. The ascetic men exhibit moderation only in respect of their dress.[50] They wear black, eat, drink and sing hymns excessively and hide it all underneath an artificial pallor.[51] Although their appearance communicates that they lead a life of contemplation and moderation, their actions are assumed to exhibit an excess that is at odds with that *askēsis*. The corollary of this point of view can perhaps be seen in *Homiliae in epistulam ad Philippenses* 1, where John is at pains to explain that giving to ascetics is of benefit only if the ascetic in question is poor. It is giving to the poor that is important, not giving to the ascetic (PG 62:188, 29–48). That John needs to say this implies both that giving to ascetics who were poor was not something that people would readily do, and that giving to ascetics who were comfortably off was a practice sufficiently well established that it needed to be discouraged as not being in the spirit of almsgiving. It also confirms that, in most people's minds, voluntary poverty is to be admired only when it is clearly distinguished from economic poverty.

What we begin to see behind these responses is a view of the world in which destitution or neediness holds a negative connotation, to the point of being

49. On the Antiochene provenance of this homily see Mayer, *Homilies of St John Chrysostom*, 368–69. Cf. *Hom. Rom.* 4 (PG 60:420, 58–421, 7), where slaves sent out of the house on an errand by their masters are said to be habitually distracted by beggars who perform conjuring tricks in the agora.

50. *Or.* 2.32, in *Libanii opera* (1903), 1:249.

51. *Or.* 30.8, in *Libanii opera* (1906), 3:91.

associated with criminal behavior, while the kind of poverty that is simple but self-sufficient can be seen as appealing but is at the most basic level at least free from negative association. It is at this point that my argument becomes frankly speculative, partly because our understanding of the relative valency of these two kinds of poverty in the early Christian world is in its infancy, while study of the origins of this worldview in the earlier Greco-Roman world is also underdeveloped. What is emerging from the research by Kavita Ayer of Macquarie University, Sydney,[52] is that the language used by the elite to describe poverty distinguished two types.[53] As she explains in her analysis, one is defined by words such as *paupertas*, *simplicitas*, and *frugalitas*, which, while it can be evoked in opposition to wealth, does not describe those who possess nothing or are in need. It describes rather a state in which one does not crave any more than one has, and is the domain of respectable citizens. A person in this state possesses property, if little, and his or her respectability lies in the possession of enough, rather than excess. Exploiting this discourse, Cicero draws an explicit link between the philosopher and this particular kind of poverty, which serves to elevate that profession's moral status. While the late republican authors utilize this construction to contrast a simple and austere past with a debauched present as part of their moralizing discourse, what is of interest here is both the idea of nobility attached to this type of poverty and the explicit link between it and the philosophical life. It is my suspicion that this discourse continues to influence the early Christian world via *paideia*, at least in elite circles, and that the substratum of Stoic philosophy that lies beneath asceticism is instrumental in attaching moral superiority to the Christian philosophic or ascetic life.

The second type of poverty that Ayer finds distinguished within late Roman republican discourse is defined by words such as *inopia*, *egestas*, and *mendicitas*, and describes a state of destitution or neediness. This is not a state of having little but enough, but rather a state of having not enough and needing to take from others for survival. Where the first type of poverty is linked to the virtues, this poverty is virtually a vice. Within the moralizing discourse of the late republic, the *egentes* pose a threat to social order and become characterized more or less as part of the criminal class.[54] Where Ayer's interest in these constructions lies in how they were utilized for political and

---

52. "Measuring Worth: Articulations of Poverty and Identity in the Late Roman Republic" (PhD diss., Macquarie University, 2006). Ayer takes up the terminology and discourses that receive mention in Parkin, "Poverty in the Early Roman Empire," parts 1–2 (esp. p. 153), and extends her analysis of them and their Stoic underpinnings considerably further. I am indebted to her for the summary of her findings that follows.

53. For the argument that two types can likewise roughly be distinguished in terminology in use in the Greek-speaking world of the first three centuries, see Hamel, *Poverty and Charity*, 167–77; and Holman, *Hungry Are Dying*, 4–5.

54. Hamel, *Poverty and Charity*, 194, alludes to the existence of a similar discourse in the classical Greek world.

private ends and in how their articulation shaped identity, my own interest lies in how this same or a very similar discourse can be seen to underpin the response to economic poverty that we have just explored. The same idea that destitution is dishonest and poses a threat to social order informs the ways in which in John's time we see people responding to beggars, while Libanius's hostile response to male ascetics can now be read in part as a resistance to the Christian adoption of a simplicity that is seen to be the natural province of the Greek philosopher.

While understanding these readings of poverty helps us to comprehend exactly what John needed to target in his own discourse on wealth and poverty, we still haven't reached an understanding of why these moral constructions of poverty had valency in the first instance in the society of John's time. The key here may lie in the idea that destitution is something that threatens society. The theory of limited good that emerged within the discipline of social anthropology in the 1960s argues that in certain types of societies everything, both material and nonmaterial, is viewed as finite.[55] That this theory can successfully be applied to communities of the Greco-Roman world in the early Christian period has been argued by New Testament scholars[56] and has been applied directly to an analysis of engagement with the supernatural within fourth-century Syrian and Palestinian society,[57] a study that includes the city of Antioch and draws in part on the writings of John Chrysostom. While there must remain reservations, since the original theory was developed to explain a "classic" peasant society, and we are operating here within a more complex urban rather than village setting, with the full range of social strata from imperial officials and local aristocracy to unemployed resident aliens, the theory does offer an attractive explanation.[58] If people who are approached by a beggar believe that both what

55. See George M. Foster, "Peasant Society and the Image of Limited Good," *American Anthropologist* 67 (1965): 293–315; and idem, "A Second Look at Limited Good," *Anthropological Quarterly* 45 (1972): 57–64. For the range of criticisms that initially greeted this model, see J. R. Gregory, "'Image of Limited Good,' or Expectation of Reciprocity?" *Current Anthropology* 16 (1975): 73–92.

56. E.g., Bruce Malina, *The New Testament World: Insights from Cultural Anthropology* (Atlanta: SCM, 1981); *Using the Social Sciences in New Testament Interpretation*, ed. Richard L. Rohrbaugh (Peabody, MA: Hendrickson, 1996); and J. H. Neyrey and R. L. Rohrbaugh, "'He must increase, I must decrease' (John 3:30): A Cultural and Social Interpretation," *CBQ* 63 (2001): 464–83.

57. See Silke Trzcionka, *Magic and the Supernatural in Fourth-Century Syria* (London: Routledge, 2007).

58. In its broad aspects, the Roman agrarian economy operates in a way not dissimilar to the peasant society that Foster describes. On the close relationship between town/city and country in late antiquity, see Peter Garnsey and C. R. Whittaker, "Trade, Industry and the Urban Economy," in *The Cambridge Ancient History*, vol. 13, *The Late Empire, A.D. 337–425*, ed. Averil Cameron and Peter Garnsey (Cambridge: Cambridge University Press, 1998), 312–37, at 326–27, and esp. 333. See, moreover, Foster, "Second Look," 59, where he argues that "some degree of Limited Good behavior is present in *every* society" (his emphasis), and that societies rather represent a continuum in which the poles are "more limited" and "less limited."

they possess and what is available within their society is limited, then they also believe that the act of giving without return dangerously diminishes their own resources. Generosity toward others is desirable only if one receives something else in return. If reciprocity is a key concept within this framework, it is easy to see how the person who needs to take from others to survive is accorded the same social value as a thief, and how his or her actions are conceived of as socially destabilizing. It also helps to explain why beggars who entertain are not perceived in this way, since they are providing a service in return for the money and food that they receive from their audience. This theory also fits well with the notion of simple self-sufficiency as a virtue, since such people, by neither seeking to gain more than they have nor requiring assistance from others, exhibit behavior that is ideal for the preservation of social order. This in turn helps to explain why so much of John's argument in promoting *eleēmosynē*, or almsgiving directed toward the economic poor, is about the benefit received by the giver.[59] He needs to persuade his audience that giving to the economic poor is not, in reality, a one-way street that results in deficit.

Within such a worldview, the voluntary poor whose "poverty" conformed to this ideal of noble self-sufficiency were held up to admiration. This is more clearly expressed in the writings of John Chrysostom's near contemporaries, including Augustine and Nilus of Ancyra.[60] There we see the explicit development of a Christian discourse about poverty and asceticism that drew freely on this tacit value system. As Dan Caner has so carefully documented, this discourse disenfranchised the ascetic who embraced radical freedom from possessions (*aktēmosynē*) in favor of total devotion to prayer by exploiting notions of idleness to create a rhetoric of suspicion. That negative appraisal was cemented in place by the promotion of an alternative model of asceticism, characterized by moderate freedom from possessions and by a provision for one's own modest needs through manual labor. By drawing on these implicit negative and positive notions of poverty, with their assumed negative or positive social consequences, this discourse was able to apply the label of legitimacy or illegitimacy and thus frame the one form of asceticism as heretical, the other as orthodox.[61]

59. See, e.g., *Hom. Matt.* 66/67 (PG 58:631, 20–30) (the benefit is spiritual: the beggar asks God in prayer to be merciful toward the person who gives him food, and battles on that person's behalf against demons); *Hom. 1 Thess.* 11 (PG 62:466, 17–60) (the beggar benefits the rich simply by existing; he educates the rich morally); *Hom. Jo.* 25/24 (PG 59:152, 15–39) (the person who gives to the poor lends to Christ and earns interest in heaven). For the same argument expressed variously by other representatives of the ecclesiastical establishment, see De Vinne, *Advocacy of Empty Bellies*, 84–114.

60. See, e.g., Augustine, *De opere monachorum*, ed. F. Tempsky, CSEL 41 (1900), 529–96; and Nilus of Ancyra, *De voluntaria paupertate ad Magnam* (PG 79:968–1060).

61. Daniel Caner, *Wandering, Begging Monks: Spiritual Authority and the Promotion of Monasticism in Late Antiquity* (Berkeley: University of California Press, 2002).

Generosity toward the Poor

The next question to be explored is how these particular ways of viewing and valuing poverty informed the way in which generosity toward the poor was effected (or avoided) within society. Since the change in the social imagination that Patlagean observes is specifically related to public benefaction, the role at this time of the patron-client relationship, which fits into notions of reciprocity, and which in turn is related to the acquisition of honor, is likely to be important. If we return to Olympias, we note that as a wealthy patron her generosity was spread over two broad areas, the churches and the poor, the poor being both voluntary and economic. Notable among the clients of her generosity were bishops, the Nicene church at Constantinople, and visiting priests, on the one hand, and her own ascetic community, countless ascetics and virgins,[62] and the structurally poor,[63] on the other. When Empress Eudoxia, an important patron of Nicene Christianity at Constantinople,[64] is praised by John, we see a similar spread. She is described as "mother of churches, nourisher of monks, patron of ascetics, and the staff of beggars."[65] These two women should, however, be seen as exceptional in encompassing such a broad range of clients, by virtue of their unique social and financial standing. Few had the resources or the status to compete with them. In less extreme but nonetheless elite cases, we see individuals such as Flavian, himself an ascetic and bishop, at Antioch providing care for the poor who had fled for the sake of orthodoxy from elsewhere and had no personal networks for support. At Constantinople, Nicarete, another well-off ascetic, used her remaining resources to support her own ascetically transformed household, as well as supplying hands-on medical care for the impoverished. When the fifty Egyptian monks arrived as petitioners at Constantinople, it was to such women as Nicarete and Olympias to whom John turned for assistance, asking them to use their private resources to provide for the monks' needs beyond the lodging provided by the church in a hostel attached to St. Anastasia.[66] In a letter from exile, John commends the lay Christian and tribune Marcianus for his personal care for orphans and widows at Constantinople, in alleviating

---

62. Palladius, *Dial.* 17 (SC 341:348, 201–5). Cf. *Vita Olymp.* 13 (SC 13bis:434, 4–9), where the list of recipients of her generosity includes, somewhat anachronistically, monasteries and *koinobia*.

63. John Chrysostom, *Ep.* 8 (SC 13bis:198, 9–17).

64. See Mayer, "Doing Violence," n. 17.

65. *Sermo post reditum a priore exsilio* 2 (PG 52:446, 15–17: τὴν μητέρα τῶν Ἐκκλησιῶν, τὴν τροφὸν τῶν μοναζόντων, καὶ προστάτιν τῶν ἁγίων, τῶν πτωχῶν τὴν βακτηρίαν). See, however, Sever Voicu, "La volontà e il caso: La tipologia dei primi spuri di Crisostomo," in *Giovanni Crisostomo: Oriente e Occidente* (see n. 21), 101–18, at 105–6, who points to inauthentic expressions within the homily and prefers to locate it among the spuria manufactured in the period following John's death. Regardless of who authored the homily, it points to a tradition that framed Eudoxia in this light and that cannot have been promulgated without some basis in fact.

66. Palladius, *Dial.* 7 (SC 341:150, 87–91).

their poverty and becoming their protector in the months following John's expulsion from the city.[67] What we see here is care for the poor, of whatever variety, in the hands of the elite, who furnish that care from their own private resources. In about half the cases we have just considered, the patrons are themselves members of the voluntary poor.

The redistribution of wealth from individuals at this social level is unlikely to have been viewed as destabilizing the social order, especially if, as we observed earlier, their generosity stopped short of taking away their own self-sufficiency. These are, after all, the traditional patrons in society and are expected to spend large sums regularly on public generosity. The question remains, however, whether generosity toward the poor was widespread among the elite, particularly among those who were not obligated to care for the poor as part of their *askēsis*. That this is unlikely to have been the case, and that suspicion of the economic poor prevailed, is suggested by the response to poverty that John tackles at Antioch in *Hom. 1 Cor.* 21. There the rich who wallow in ostentatious display of their personal wealth (in contrast to those who detach themselves from it) argue that the church has considerable assets and that care for those in need is its responsibility (PG 61:179, 12–49).[68] John's response is that the church is obliged to possess what it does precisely because of the rich citizens' stinginess. If the rich were in general unwilling to give to the economic poor, were they any more inclined to give to the voluntary poor, who were held in higher value? As we saw in *Hom. Phil.* 1, where John is at pains to explain that giving to ascetics is of benefit only if the ascetic in question is poor (PG 62:188, 29–48), there is a suggestion that generosity toward the poor of this kind was better established. As argued earlier, that John needs to engage with this issue implies both that giving to ascetics who were poor was not something that people would readily do, while giving to ascetics who were comfortably off was a practice sufficiently well established that it needed to be discouraged.

We need to consider, however, that our sources, with their emphasis on elite patrons, provide us with only a fragmentary picture of which poor were cared for and by whom. In an attempt to expand our view, it is useful to turn to the case of the monk Isaac. This is the same Isaac who became John's enemy and brought charges against him at the Synod of the Oak. As Dan Caner has shown, where Isaac fits into our model is as an ascetic without substantial assets of his own but, as the most respected of the Nicene monks

---

67. *Ep.* 122 (PG 52:676). Cf. *Ep.* 217 (PG 52:731), in which Valentinus, another individual of high rank, is said to be an enthusiastic patron of the poor and is exhorted to extend his support to a crisis situation involving widows and orphans. Regarding the status of both Marcianus and Valentinus, see Roland Delmaire, "Les 'lettres d'exil' de Jean Chrysostome: Études de chronologie et de prosopographie," *RechAug* 25 (1991): 71–180, at 140 and 169.

68. See further ll. 49–52, alluding to institutional care by the church for the poor, the sick, and enrolled widows.

at Constantinople, with considerable status.[69] What is of interest here is that he attracts the patronage of two men of senatorial rank, Victor and Saturninus,[70] who vie with each other to provide him with housing. Isaac also attracts the support of a number of other prominent members of the imperial administration (*V. Isaacii* 4.16–17). While Isaac nourishes his patrons with spiritual food and supports them in prayer, they support the monks under his care, along with the destitute in the street, whose cause he brings to their attention (*V. Isaacii* 4.16). What we observe here rather than patronage by rich ascetics is patronage by the rich and elite of an ascetic and via that ascetic of other ascetics and the structural poor. The ascetic here is not rich and so does not provide for the poor from his own assets, but becomes instead the conduit for the flow of material assistance from the rich. Given the date of the lives that inform us of Isaac's story,[71] it is possible that what we view here is a later model imposed on the early fifth century. Given the way in which it bears significant parallels with a model of care for the poor that Susan Ashbrook Harvey has described for late fourth- to early fifth-century Syria,[72] however, and given Isaac's own Syrian origins, it is more likely to reflect a genuine social dynamic. Harvey points out that while elsewhere in the Roman Empire ascetic communities were expected to be economically self-sufficient, in the Syrian Orient a different pattern emerged. There it was local civic communities who supplied the financial means for the ascetics who lived in and around them. The more extreme ascetics, totally dependent on others, were not a drain on society, however, but became the linchpin in what she terms an economy of exchange.

> In turn, the ascetics could offer an economic service in response to the dependency of their vocation on the civic population. For the monastic communities and ascetic virtuosos both served as locations in which wealth was donated, negotiated, and redistributed throughout local regions. The poor and needy came to monasteries or to holy individuals seeking assistance and relief of the most concrete kind: food, clothing, shelter. Ascetics or monasteries did not so much produce these goods as they received them, in various forms and kinds, from the better off, the wealthy, and the fortunate. These brought their bounty to be dispensed appropriately.[73]

Like Symeon and other virtuoso ascetics from Syria, Isaac at Constantinople likewise functions as the linchpin in an economy of exchange. When we

---

69. Caner, *Wandering, Begging Monks*, 190–99.

70. *V. Isaacii* 4.15, ed. R. P. D Cardono, *Acta SS Maii* (1866), 7:251F.

71. The *V. Hypatii* by Callinicus dates from the mid-fifth century (ed. G. J. M. Bartelink, SC 177 [1971]: 11–12), the anonymous *V. Isaaci* from the sixth or seventh century.

72. Susan Ashbrook Harvey, "Praying Bodies, Bodies at Prayer: Ritual Relations in Early Syriac Christianity," in *Prayer and Spirituality*, 149–67.

73. Ashbrook Harvey, "Praying Bodies," 159.

consider this model of care for the poor within a system in which reciprocity, patronage, status, and honor are significant, everyone's needs are neatly
taken care of. The rich gain status, as well as spiritual benefit, from taking on
as client a respected member of the voluntary poor. The ascetic gains honor
through exhibiting one of the ascetic virtues, by taking on as clients other
voluntary poor and the destitute. In an exchange of this kind nothing is given
or taken without receipt, and the social order remains undisturbed.

Conclusion

The implications of the thesis presented in this essay are several. In a society
where voluntary poverty holds positive moral value and economic poverty
is seen as socially destabilizing and negative, it is inevitable that, under the
influence of a religion that valued care for the poor, care for the voluntary
poor would emerge as more attractive. There was an inherent value as patron
in taking on a client who contributed to the social capital (whether spiritually or through his or her own clients), as opposed to taking on as client an
individual who, through his or her need to take to survive, threatened the
stability of society. In attempting to persuade laypeople that they should give
generously to the economic poor, John Chrysostom, like many other preachers of his time, was battling against a widespread and persistent belief system
that engendered suspicion and resistance. At the same time, there is a clear
connection between *askēsis*, at least for the rich ascetic, and patronage of at
least some sectors of the economic poor.

The question that has not been explored here is how within the framework
of the discourse on poverty prevalent in society this came to be acknowledged as a virtue. In this respect it is important to acknowledge that when
we attempt to examine the role of poverty and generosity toward the poor,
we face a number of different discourses: John's distinctive discourses as
priest and bishop on economic and on voluntary poverty, with their own
particular theological underpinnings; the moral discourse about "poverty"
prevalent in society; and the discourses that arose from within the pursuit of
asceticism in its various forms that came with their own specific theological
and philosophical background. We need to engage both singly and in various
combinations with all three categories of discourse if we are to grapple seriously with the topics of wealth and poverty in early Christianity.

11

Poverty and Wealth as Theater

John Chrysostom's Homilies on Lazarus and the Rich Man

Francine Cardman

"There was a rich man" wearing purple garments every day, covering his soul with cobwebs, scented with perfumes, but stinking inside, setting an expensive table, feeding parasites and flatterers, fattening the slave, his flesh, but allowing the mistress, his soul, to perish from hunger. His house was decorated with garlands, but the foundation was dusty with sin. His soul was buried in wine. There that rich man was, you see, with his expensive table, his wine bowls wreathed with garlands, and his company of parasites and flatterers, the evil theater of the devil, the wolves which seize many of the rich, which purchase the destruction of the wealthy by the fullness of their own bellies, which spoil wealth by excessive honor and flattery.[1]

John Chrysostom's impassioned tirades against the theater as a central social institution in late antiquity are, as Blake Leyerle has demonstrated

Research for this essay was funded in part by a Henry Luce III Fellowship in Theology from the Association of Theological Schools.

1. *Laz.* 6.5 (PG 48:1032), in John Chrysostom, *On Wealth and Poverty*, trans. Catharine Roth (Crestwood, NY: St. Vladimir's Seminary Press, 1984), 106. All translations of this text are from Roth unless noted otherwise. Chrysostom's six homilies on Lazarus and the rich man have been preserved in a manuscript series of seven homilies under that title, the fifth of which took up a different topic; the seven homilies are found in PG 48:963–1054.

in *Theatrical Shows and Ascetic Lives*, equaled only by his own extensive deployment of theatrical language, imagery, and technique in his preaching and teaching. "The theater's celebration of display made it a symbol of the cultural reproduction of late antique society," Leyerle argues, and an object of Chrysostom's vehemence.[2] It is display, coupled with a nearly infinite capacity for self-deception, that arouses Chrysostom's ire at the practice of spiritual marriage, the focus of Leyerle's study, and makes it an apt target for a theatrically constructed attack. Display and deception, as evident in the description of the rich man quoted above, are central to Chrysostom's analysis of poverty and wealth in late fourth-century Antioch. Here too theater provides him with a rhetoric for preaching. This essay builds on Leyerle's argument and extends it to a consideration of the rhetorical staging of poverty and wealth and of rich and poor in Chrysostom's homilies on Lazarus and the rich man.

Setting the Stage

If theater serves to reproduce antique culture by teaching its canon to the unlettered and affirming and inculcating its values, whenever Christians attend the theater they are drawn into a competing community and way of life.[3] Chrysostom's repeated complaints against absent or inattentive members of his congregation, eager to rush off to the shows—even those accompanying the catechumens during Lent repair to the racetrack soon afterward—are indicative of the powerful lure of this formative public institution.[4] Vice and deception are everywhere at the theater: in the players, the stories, and the deportment of the audience. Appearance masquerades as reality, ostentation is the order of the day, and passion is unrestrained. Thus theater and spectacles deform both character and community, even as preaching in the Christian assembly tries to form and reform them.

2. Blake Leyerle, *Theatrical Shows and Ascetic Lives: John Chrysostom's Attack on Spiritual Marriage* (Berkeley: University of California Press, 2001), 4–5.

3. Leyerle notes that the fourth-century Roman calendar of Philocalus (354 CE) designates 177 days of the year for plays in the theater, spectacles, and horse racing, and cites Paul Petit, *Libanius et la vie municipale à Antioche au IV siècle après J.-C.* (Paris: P. Geuthner, 1955), who argues that there may have been spectacles every Saturday in Antioch (*Theatrical Shows*, 14–15). Thus competition for the attention of Chrysostom's congregation would have been formidable.

4. *Laz.* 7.1 (PG 48:1045), 125: "Simply following some habit they applaud what we say . . . and afterwards run back to the race-course." See also the homily *Contra ludos et theatra* (PG 57:263–70), recently translated by Wendy Mayer and Pauline Allen, *John Chrysostom* (London: Routledge, 2000), 118–25. In the sixth baptismal catechesis from the Stavronikita manuscript, Chrysostom decries the declining numbers in church so soon after Easter: Antoine Wenger, *Huit catéchèses baptismales inédites*, 2nd ed., SC 50 (Paris: Cerf, 1970), 6:1. Wenger (215n2) argues that those absent—"some" (τινές)—are longtime members, since Chrysostom would have been explicit if neophytes had been so negligent so soon after their baptism. Paul Harkins makes a similar point in St. John Chrysostom, *Baptismal Instructions*, trans. Paul Harkins, ACW 31 (New York: Newman, 1963), 6:1 (262n6).

As Leyerle has shown, Chrysostom uses a "rhetorical strategy of accommodation," employing the language and devices of the theater to keep his flock from frequenting the entertainment.[5] He follows this strategy in his homilies on Lazarus and the rich man, redirecting his congregation to the theater of poverty and wealth, refocusing their understanding of what they see there, and reforming their practice in regard to the poor. What is striking in these homilies is not so much that he uses the methods of theater for his own ends, but that he casts so much of his theological and pastoral argument in terms of theater. Chrysostom sees—and wants his audience to see—rich and poor, almsgiving or the refusal of it as part of a personal and historical drama that itself participates in a larger, eschatological drama of salvation and condemnation. Before that final act, however, the story plays out in the city and especially the marketplace.

In what follows, I examine Chrysostom's preaching of poverty and wealth—Lazarus and the rich man—in terms of seeing the story, discerning the meaning, and playing within the play, concluding with some critical observations about the implications of Chrysostom's rhetorical strategies in these homilies.

Seeing the Story

Chrysostom engages in theater while preaching on wealth and poverty, deploying its visual and verbal devices, setting the stage, directing the gaze, and unfolding a narrative that engages his audience. Like theater, his homilies have stock characters: the rich man and the poor man, either as types or as personified by Dives and Lazarus, who have themselves become types; the virtuous man who suffers unjustly in this life, most often Job; the vain woman, either Job's wife or Jezebel, making cameo appearances; and cosmic interlocutors, the devil or God, who either deceive in this life or make all things clear through judgment in the next. Chrysostom tells and retells their stories, drawing his audience in through the familiarity of the biblical characters and the recognition created by his vivid descriptions of rich and poor. Pity and terror also have their place, evoked by the plight of the poor and by the prospect of judgment that lies ahead for all.

Chrysostom's preaching on the rich man and Lazarus is strikingly visual, setting scenes, bringing characters before the eyes of his congregation, and drawing the congregation into the story by asking them to *see* it. "Do you not seem to see [*horan*] the whole situation as if it were present?" he asks in the first homily; "you saw [*eidete*] him at the gate of the rich man; see [*blepete*] him today in the bosom of Abraham," he urges at the beginning

---

5. Leyerle, *Theatrical Shows*, 12.

of the second.[6] Chrysostom's depictions of rich and poor are at once stereotypically simple and strategically complex, perhaps even ambiguous. They raise questions about the nature of the gaze he asks his audience to direct toward these characters, as well as about the response he hopes to elicit from them.

The characters

First, consider the rich man. Whether describing the rich man who ignored Lazarus or a generic rich man, Chrysostom can be scathing in his representation of a life lived in luxury and ostentatious display. Set pieces on the rich man's table, his entourage of friends, servants, and hangers-on, and his brutal dealings with the poor appear several times in the homilies on Lazarus and the rich man. This summary portrayal from the seventh homily is typical:

> Remember with me that rich man, the one who wore purple and fine linen every day, who dined lavishly, who fed parasites and flatterers, who served out a lot of undiluted wine, who yielded himself to gluttony and great luxury every day. . . . Everything flowed easily to him as if from a spring—he had many servants, immeasurable luxury, health of body, plenty of money, honor from the mass of people, praise from the flatterers, and nothing up to that time to give him grief.[7]

The nameless rich man entered by the wide gate and walked an easy road, nowhere encountering difficulties, never noticing the waves of evil drowning him, the wicked desires tearing him apart, or the delusion that had overwhelmed his reasoning. If they think this man is lucky, Chrysostom warns his audience, they should wait until the end of the story.

The rich man's behavior toward Lazarus is depicted harshly. He is inhumane, beastly, living in wickedness; he held Lazarus in contempt and neglected him, never giving alms to him or anyone else; he is hard-hearted,

---

6. *Laz.* 1.7 (PG 48:972), 23; *Laz.* 2.1 (PG 48:981), 39. The pairing of ειδετε. . .βλεπετε occurs six times in eight lines at 2.1. See also *Laz.* 6.3 (PG 48:1031), 103: "If you agree, let us bring into our midst first the person who is punished hereafter, but enjoys luxury here."

7. *Laz.* 7.3 (PG 48:1048), 131. Similarly in *Laz.* 6.5 (PG 48:1033), 106: "There that rich man was, you see, feeding parasites and flatters, making his house a theater, weakening everyone with wine, passing his time in great prosperity." See also *Laz.* 1.9 (PG 48:975); 1.10 (PG 48:976–77); 1.11 (PG 48:979); 6.3 (PG 48:1030); and 6.4 (PG 48:1032). The generic rich man is greedy and unsatisfied, yearning for others' property (*Laz.* 2.1 [PG 48:982]), robbing widows and orphans (*Laz* 4.4 [PG 48:1011] and 6.3 [PG 48:1030]); the greedy rich "are a kind of robbers" (*Laz* 1.12 [PG 48:980], 36).

Cf. descriptions of the rich in the homilies *On the Statues*, which were occasioned by a popular revolt in Antioch in 387: e.g., *Ad populum Antiochenum de statuis* 2.5 (PG 49:39), 2.7 (PG 49:44); the luxury of the rich leads to a panoply of sins (*Stat.* 15.11 [PG 49:159]).

never moved to pity.[8] Depending on his particular brand of beastliness he could rightly be considered a wolf (rapacious), a lion (savage temper), or a cobra (deceitful), rather than a human.[9] Worse than all these, however, is that he did not, would not, see Lazarus, though he was lying at his gate. The rich man walked by him "like a stone, shamelessly and mercilessly."[10]

Next, consider Lazarus. "His appearance was pitiful, as he was overcome by hunger and long illness."[11] He lay at the rich man's gate "like a living corpse," his poverty and illness surpassing all other. "Did you see," Chrysostom asks, "both poverty and disease besieging his body to the extreme degree?"[12] So weakened was he by illness and hunger that he could not keep away the dogs that licked his sores (Laz. 1.9 [PG 48:976] and 7.3 [PG 48:1049]). Suffering from "hunger and extreme poverty, afflicted by continuous illness and sores," Lazarus lacked even basic sustenance and longed for the crumbs from the rich man's table; his poverty "surpassed all other poverty at that time."[13] Physical proximity to the rich man forced Lazarus to perceive his own misfortunes more clearly, the great discrepancy between his virtue and goodness and the rich man's wickedness heightening his anguish. Nevertheless he did not blaspheme, complain, or become discouraged.[14] Chrysostom applauds the patient silence of poor people like Lazarus, noting that it can move those who are better off to give alms, while pestering can harden their hearts:

> But when we see those who need help standing by in complete silence, uttering no sound, not complaining though never satisfied, but merely appearing to us in silence . . . we become ashamed at the excess of politeness and are moved to pity.[15]

To this rather distant depiction Chrysostom adds some poignantly human touches. He observes that Lazarus's sufferings were exacerbated by his loneliness—"no friend, neighbor, or relative, not even any onlooker" offered him comfort as so many passed by him at the rich man's gate ("drunkards and merrymakers," Chrysostom calls them).[16] To make his distress even worse,

8. Laz. 1.6–7 (PG 48:970–72); 2.4 (PG 48:987); 6.5 (PG 48:1033); and 7.3 (PG 48:1048); see, e.g., Roth, 131.

9. Laz. 6.5 (PG 48:1034).

10. Laz. 1.10 (PG 48:976), 30.

11. Laz. 1.6 (PG 48:971), 22.

12. Laz. 1.9 (PG 48:975–76), 29.

13. Laz. 7.3 (PG 48:1049), 132; Laz. 1.9 (PG 48:975), 29.

14. Laz. 1.9 (PG 48:975); also 6.5 (PG 48:1034), 108: "he did not say what most poor people would say," i.e., he did not question God's providence; cf. Laz. 3.7 (PG 48:1002), Lazarus as witness that poverty and other evils cannot make a virtuous person blaspheme. For Job, see Stat. 5.1 (PG 49:70).

15. Laz. 1.6 (PG 48:971), 22; however, this did not tame that "savage" rich man.

16. Laz. 1.9 (PG 48:976), 30.

"he could not observe another Lazarus" in whom he might find consolation and companionship through common affliction.[17] He did not have the hope of resurrection to comfort him, and he suffered the judgment of those who thought he must have deserved his misery.[18]

Seeing is crucial to Chrysostom's preaching of the rich man and Lazarus. Again and again Chrysostom calls on his congregation to see the plight of both Lazarus and the rich man, and to pay attention to the crucial role that seeing and not seeing play in the condition of each. Being unable to see another like himself increases Lazarus's suffering; the prospect of being seen by the rich man who had the means to relieve his poverty is a potential source of temporary salvation from his material misery, while being rendered invisible by him is deadly. For the rich man, refusing to see the poor Lazarus continually before his eyes is sinful and will lead to condemnation if he does not change his ways. By bringing the story of Lazarus and the rich man to life before his congregation, Chrysostom aims to make the poor visible, challenge the sensibilities of the rich, and move the rich to act mercifully and thereby save themselves as well.

The gaze

Like theater, preaching is words made flesh. Though he lacks players and a stage, Chrysostom nevertheless makes the drama of Lazarus and the rich man present to his congregation's eyes and ears through the classic rhetorical device of *ekphrasis*—drawing a picture with words, painting a story.[19] At one point in the homilies he even asks his congregation to paint the parable on the walls of their hearts.[20] What kind of picture does Chrysostom paint? What sort of flesh does he conjure as he preaches?

Some basic terms of the portrayals are set by the biblical narrative itself—the rich man's purple cloak and his sumptuous feasting; Lazarus's sores and the dogs attending him. But other elements are entirely Chrysostom's: assumptions extrapolated from the story and enlarged, or details imported from late fourth-century Antioch—the drunken debauchery of the rich man's household and hangers-on, for instance, or the sociology of urban begging. Simply by preaching he is asking his audience to see Lazarus, the rich man, and the other characters in the same way he does.

Chrysostom depicts Lazarus and the rich man at the extremes of wealth and poverty, excess and deprivation. He offers far more detail in the portrayal

17. *Laz.* 1.10 (PG 48:977), 31; also 1.12 (PG 48:981). In contrast, Chrysostom notes that his audience can find comfort in their troubles by looking at Lazarus.

18. *Laz.* 1.10 (PG 48:977).

19. My colleague John O'Malley drew my attention to the function of *ekphrasis* in these homilies; see his analysis of its reappropriation in Renaissance preaching: *Praise and Blame in Renaissance Rome: Rhetoric, Doctrine, and Reform in the Sacred Orators of the Papal Court, c. 1450–1521* (Durham, NC: Duke University Press, 1979), 61–70.

20. *Laz.* 4.2 (PG 48:1008).

of the rich man, his household, and his hangers-on than in his painting of Lazarus in his abjection. Insistence on the extremity of Lazarus's suffering replaces the kind of "thick" description evident in other homilies in which Job or beggars in the marketplace figure prominently. The biblical narrative supplies Chrysostom with considerably more material for depicting Job than it does for Lazarus, while "a Mediterranean discourse on the poor" shapes his representation of urban beggars.[21] Thus he describes Job naked on his dunghill, "streaming with gore from every part, and his flesh gradually wasting away."[22] He regards with awe the blood-stained body, "battered" by the adversary, "perforat[ed] . . . with ulcers of every kind," its ribs "pierced . . . in every direction." The devil's violent treatment of Job "made him more *conspicuous* to us; and through that piercing he gave to all the privilege to *look into* his interior and to *discern* completely the whole of his wealth."[23]

Similarly, in a homily on almsgiving, Chrysostom brings before his audience a crowd of beggars, recounting how they had "elected" him to plead for them in church, not by votes but by the "pitiful and most bitter spectacles" they presented as he walked through the marketplace:

> I saw in the middle of the streets many outcasts, some with severed hands, others with gouged-out eyes, others filled with festering ulcers and incurable wounds, especially exposing those body parts that, because of their stored-up rottenness, they should be concealing.[24]

With an eye for detail, even if exaggerated, he describes how they manage to get by in the city during the summer, but in the winter are doubly under siege "by the famine that devours the viscera from within and the frost that freezes and deadens the flesh from without."[25] An equally pathetic description of a "generic" poor man appears in the first homily of the Lazarus series, when in the midst of berating the rich for their luxury (in this case their beds), Chrysostom summons the image of the poor man who "has thrown himself on a pile of straw by the door of the bath-house, wrapping the stalks around him, shivering, stiff with cold, pinched with hunger."[26]

---

21. Vividly exaggerated descriptions of extreme poverty had become part of this discourse by Chrysostom's time: Peter Brown, *Poverty and Leadership in the Later Roman Empire* (Hanover, NH: University Press of New England, 2002), 64; see also 45–55 for a discussion of more nuanced social gradations than the extremes of destitution and excessive wealth.

22. *Stat.* 5.1 (PG 49:69), translation adapted from the "Oxford Library of the Fathers" by W. R. W. Stephens, *NPNF*[1] 9:371.

23. *Stat.* 5.1 (PG 49:70), trans. Stephens, 372; emphasis mine.

24. *De eleemosyna* 1 (PG 51:261), St. John Chrysostom, *On Repentance and Almsgiving*, trans. Gus George Christo, FC 96 (Washington, DC: Catholic University of America Press, 1998), 131.

25. Ibid., 132.

26. *Laz.* 1.8 (PG 48:973), 26.

As a counterpoint to this rhetoric Chrysostom attacks the callousness of the rich who attempt to judge the worthiness of beggars by assessing the causes of their poverty. He chastises his hearers for their hard-heartedness and urges them to give alms simply because of the need that presents itself.[27] Otherwise, this kind of public scrutiny leads some to inflict injury on themselves and others "to simulate physical disabilities, so that by dramatizing their misfortunes they may deflect our cruelty and inhumanity."[28] Chrysostom attempts to redirect his congregation's gaze away from rationalizing poverty or interrogating it and turn their sight instead toward recognizing the human need of the poor person before their eyes.

Throughout the Lazarus homilies, Chrysostom asks his audience to *see*: to picture Lazarus and the rich man as individuals, brought before their eyes by the preacher's descriptions. He asks them to observe how the two men see or do not see each other, at the rich man's gate in this world and across the great chasm that separates them in the next. And, crucially, he asks his congregation to see even more deeply, to perceive the drama as a whole and discern its meaning, not only for Lazarus and the rich man but for themselves.[29]

Discerning the Meaning

Despite the physicality of Chrysostom's descriptions of Lazarus, the rich man, and other rich and poor people, the figures lack depth. Ultimately they are important not in themselves but for what they represent. This problematic is inherent in both preaching and theater, especially classical theater in which the actors wear masks. Seeing the story is an important step in Chrysostom's homiletic appropriation of theater, but it is only the first step; seeing the meaning is the second and more significant step in his rhetorical strategy.

As Chrysostom makes the story of Lazarus and the rich man visible in his preaching, he is preoccupied with two levels of meaning: teaching his audience how to distinguish appearance from reality in this life, and showing them how this reality translates into the life to come. Chrysostom shares the question of appearance versus reality with others in the ancient world (Platonists, Stoics, Epicureans, each with their particular perspective on the

27. *Laz.* 2.5 (PG 48:989), 52–53, "need alone is the poor man's worthiness."

28. *Eleem.* 6 (PG 51:269), 147; cf. the famous description in *Hom. 1 Cor.* 21.5–6 (PG 61:177) of beggars doing violence to their bodies in order to gain attention and alms.

Chrysostom indicts the rich who spend their time in theaters and useless gatherings yet demand an accounting from "that miserable and wretched man, who spends all day begging in tears" (*Eleem.* 6 [PG 51:269], 147).

29. Chrysostom uses verbs for seeing (βλέπω, ἔιδω, ὁράω, θεωρέω) more than ninety times in the course of the Lazarus homilies, urging the congregation to see, noting what they see now or have seen, hoping that they will see aspects of the story and its meaning; at times one of these sight words is simply used in narrating a biblical story or everyday event.

topic), his interpretation of the reality of poverty and wealth having especially strong affinities with Stoic ethics.[30] Throughout these homilies he contrasts inward and outward reality, reversing popular sentiment in regard to who is really rich and really poor; who is really merciful and who is not; who is really suffering or really fortunate and who is not; what is really punishment and what is reward; and what is really happening when one gives alms to the poor or does not. Display and deception, masking and unmasking are recurrent themes in his narrative of poverty and wealth.

Theater as revelatory

Theater is not just a way for Chrysostom to get his meaning across; it is part and parcel of that meaning. He uses theater as an explanatory model that provides an analogy for understanding appearance and reality and also serves as a means in itself for revealing truth.[31] Appropriation of the theatrical model is the goal of Chrysostom's rhetorical strategy in these homilies. He brings Lazarus and the rich man before his audience's eyes, then invites them to see more clearly, to look behind appearances for the deeper meaning of the story. Grasping that the story is theater is the first step; applying that understanding to life as a whole is the second. What transpires in the world of theater and in the theater of the world is revelatory if one knows where and how to look: at the end of the story, at the inner reality of things. "For just as on stage actors enter with the masks of kings, generals, doctors, teachers, professors, and soldiers, without being anything of the sort, so in the present life poverty and wealth are only masks."[32] At the end of a play the players remove their costumes, the characters disappear, and the actors appear for who they are. "So also now when death arrives and the theater is dissolved, everyone puts off the masks of wealth or poverty and departs for the other world."[33] Judgment follows, the situation is reversed, and all is made known.

---

30. Stoic arguments abound in regard to the nature of poverty and riches, as well as the way each relates to freedom and slavery, the good life and misery. For some parallels with Chrysostom, see, e.g., Seneca, *Ep.* 110 ("On True and False Riches"), 115 ("On the Superficial Blessings"), LCL 77:265–77 and 319–31; Epictetus, *Discourses* 3.9 (need for possessions as poverty); 3.26 (longevity of beggars); 4.9 (miseries of wealth), LCL 218:62–71, 226–41, 390–97.

31. Theater as revelatory model is presented in two extended analogies, each comparing the world to a theater and pointing to the reversal of perception and reality that occurs when masks come off at the end of the play: *Laz.* 2.3 (PG 48:986) and 6.5–6 (PG 48:1034–36). In contrast, see Chrysostom's tirade against the theater in *Against the Games and Theaters* in Mayer and Allen, *John Chrysostom*, 118–25; even there Chrysostom is able to reverse and strategically appropriate theater for his own purposes: "Does the populace that loves Christ, the simple spiritual theater, allow this?" *Contra ludos et theatra* (PG 56:264), trans. Mayer and Allen, 119. For analysis of Chrysostom's views on theater, see Leyerle, *Theatrical Shows*, 42–75.

32. *Laz.* 2.3 (PG 48:986), 46.

33. Ibid., 47.

Chrysostom explicates the model in the sixth homily, connecting the two theatrical worlds for his congregation:

> In a theater of this world at mid-day the stage is set and many actors enter, playing parts, wearing masks on their faces, retelling some old story, narrating the events. . . . Evening overtakes them, the play is ended, the truth appears. So it is also in life and its end. The present world is a theater, the conditions of men are roles. . . . [W]hen the play is ended, when the masks are removed . . . [then] each person is judged with his works.[34]

He goes on to reveal his strategy and his intent.

> I want to set before you the masks of two roles from the theater. I have handled two masks, cutting a path for you with these two, and giving you a starting point. I have broadened your understanding by explaining the present life, so that each of you may learn to distinguish reality.[35]

What his audience learns is that outside the theater, at the end of the day, the seemingly free person is a slave and the slave can be nobler than a free person; it is the virtuous who are fortunate, not the wealthy, the wicked who are miserable, not the poor.[36] They learn the definition of wealth and poverty: "The rich man is not the one who has collected many possessions, but the one who needs few possessions; and the poor man is not the one who has no possessions, but the one who has many desires."[37] Ultimately the audience learns what the rich man learns: that Lazarus's body may be covered with sores, but his soul is more precious than gold, while the rich man's soul is full of sores. They learn that "just as the poor man lived in starvation of nourishment, so the rich man lived in starvation of every kind of virtue."[38] In short, if the preaching is effective, they learn to see and, in seeing, they learn to avoid the rich man's end.

Judgment as theater and theodicy

In teaching his congregation how to see the reality of Lazarus and the rich man, Chrysostom trains their gaze on the end of each. They see Lazarus borne up by angels, resting in the bosom of Abraham: "The angels received

34. *Laz.* 6.5 (PG 48:1035), 109.
35. *Laz.* 6.6 (PG 48:1035), 110.
36. *Laz.* 6.5–6 (PG 48:1035); also 6.6 (PG 48:1037) and 1.12 (PG 48:980).
37. *Laz.* 2.1 (PG 48:982), 40; ibid., "We are accustomed to judge poverty and affluence by the disposition of the mind, not by the measure of one's substance." See also *Laz.* 4.2 (PG 48:1008), "what we see is a shadow and not factual truth," 83; 6.8 (PG 48:1039), the rich man's luxury and possessions were a dream and a shadow.
38. *Laz.* 1.11 (PG 48:980), 35.

Lazarus—angels after the dogs, after the rich man's gate the bosom of Abraham, after hunger limitless prosperity, after tribulation perpetual comfort."[39] They then immediately see the rich man suffering: "But poverty received the rich man after his wealth, after his rich table punishment and retribution, after his comfort unbearable anguish."[40] They also see the two men regarding each other from a great distance, their situations reversed. Now the rich man sees Lazarus clearly, whom he had refused to see or show mercy; now Lazarus can no longer offer him the mercy his alms would have brought, for now there is an unbridgeable chasm between them. The rich man suffers in hell what Lazarus suffered in this world, his anguish greater because he will forever have before his eyes the abundance he lost for himself.[41]

The drama of the rich man's transition from death to judgment, his evident fear and shame, and his ensuing torment (Chrysostom notes repeatedly that the man is "on the grill") is grim enough to silence the audience. Chrysostom urges his congregation to consider further what the day of judgment, that "terrible day," will be like for them: "There will be endless ages, rivers of fire, threatening anger, powers dragging us to judgment, a terrible judgment seat, an incorruptible court, and the deeds of each one set before our eyes, no one to help . . . what will we do then?"[42] In these homilies, Chrysostom plays to his audience's fear. But when he treats the Sermon on the Mount in his homilies on Matthew, he plays to their desire for reward and acclaim. While advising against vainglory and giving alms to be seen before others, he assures them that if they want spectators for their deeds, they already have "the God of all." If they wait a little until the day of judgment, they will have "the whole universe" as spectators in "this our theater."[43]

In addition to motivating his congregation to virtue, whether through fear of punishment or desire for reward, the theater of judgment offers Chrysostom a way to answer the age-old question of why the virtuous suffer. He constructs an extensive calculus of suffering, reward, and punishment, relating actions and experiences in this life to their consequences in the next, and he explicates the workings of this calculus in his preaching of Lazarus and the rich man. Some are punished in this life only; some are punished both

39. *Laz.* 6.6 (PG 48:1036), 110.

40. Ibid.

41. Chrysostom depicts this scene twice, in *Laz.* 2.3–4 (PG 48:985–87) and 6.6 (PG 48:1035–36), reprising it in the final homily, 7.3–4 (PG 48:1050–52), where he observes that the rich man's plight is his own doing: "he has betrayed himself" (7.4 [PG 48:1051], 136). Cf. 3.9 (PG 48:1005), after death nothing can help the man "who has been betrayed by his own life" (76).

42. *Laz.* 6.1 (PG 48:1028), 98; also *Laz.* 2.4 (PG 48:987), 49, there will be "no need of witnesses, accusers, evidence, or proof; the deeds themselves just as we have done them appear before our eyes." See *Stat.* 20.2 (PG 49:200): sins will be exposed to the eyes of all.

43. *Hom. Matt.* 19.2 (PG 57:276); also 20.1–2 (PG 57:288): they should wait and display their victory to God, who will reward them permanently.

here and hereafter; and some are punished only in that other life.[44] By showing that even Lazarus is not without some sin and the rich man not without some modicum of good, he can blunt the force of arguments about unjust suffering or undeserved prosperity in this world. He acknowledges frankly that the suffering of the righteous in this life can go beyond the measure of their sins, in which case, he argues, they should be understood as having "a surplus of righteousness" reckoned to them.[45] "In summary," he notes, "every punishment, if it happens to sinners, reduces the burden of sin, but if it happens to the righteous, makes their souls more splendid."[46] Chrysostom astutely uses these calculations to instruct his congregation in how to see through appearances and find the true meaning of things.

Playing within the Play

This glimpse at the calculus of punishment and reward introduces another dimension of the theater of poverty and wealth: the meaning of almsgiving and the consequences of refusing to show mercy to the poor. Here the language of the marketplace dominates but does not replace the language of theater.

Exchange and refusal

References to future reward and punishment abound in the homilies on Lazarus and the rich man. Implicit in the expectation of judgment, reward, and punishment is the practice and perspective of exchange: in exchange for good deeds and a virtuous life, one will receive heavenly rewards, while wicked deeds and vicious living will be exchanged for punishment. Chrysostom explicitly uses such marketplace language in regard to charity, almsgiving, and mercy toward the poor to show his audience how rich and poor are involved in a complex material and spiritual exchange in this life and the next. This rhetorical strategy parallels his appropriation of theater language and works well within it.[47] In the first homily, Chrysostom chides his congregation for using the language of the marketplace in reference to reward and punishment. He points out that Lazarus never used such language:

44. *Laz.* 3.4–8 (PG 48:996–1004) and 6.3 (PG 48:1031).
45. *Laz.* 6.9 (PG 48:1042), 124.
46. *Laz.* 3.8 (PG 48:1004), 73.
47. Blake Leyerle, "John Chrysostom on Almsgiving and the Use of Money," *HTR* 87 (1994): 41–43, takes Chrysostom's use of marketplace language as an expression of mutuality and an attempt to create a new economic and ecclesial community of rich and poor. While I agree that this is his rhetorical goal, I find the language of exchange far less mutual, especially within the theatrical context of these homilies, than does Leyerle.

He did not say to himself anything like what many people are likely to say, that if this rich man when he departs to the other world, receives punishment and retribution, he has made one for one, but if he enjoys the same honors as here, he has made two for nothing.[48]

Lazarus may not use such expressions, but Chrysostom's congregation does, bringing the language of the marketplace, the racetrack, and the theater into the church and even into their houses. Such language, he insists, "is a mark of extreme disbelief, of real mania, and of a childish disposition."[49] But he uses it himself, without apology, to refute their notion that the rich man could at least "make one for one," asking his audience instead if the brief time a person has to use his riches (even if granted an impossible thousand years) can begin to compare to the negative return he would receive in punishment that is everlasting.[50]

Chrysostom continues to employ marketplace language in the Lazarus homilies and elsewhere to explain the meaning of almsgiving. As a central category of exchange, almsgiving represents a material and spiritual transaction between rich and poor. This idea is not unique to Chrysostom—it goes back at least as far as Hermas—but it takes on a greater degree of complexity in the framework of theater and Chrysostom's focus on distinguishing appearance from reality.[51]

The second homily on Lazarus and the rich man offers several examples of such transactions. There is a simple level of exchange, in which those who give to the poor will themselves attain abundance, the material gift leading to a spiritual reward. At the level of divine intent, it is God who has created the context for exchange and set the conditions for almsgiving, reward, and punishment. Here the poor themselves can become the medium of exchange, as when Chrysostom imagines God chastising the rich man and explaining why he will spend eternity contemplating Lazarus, rewarded and at rest.

I sent the poor man Lazarus to your gate to teach you virtue and to receive your love; you ignored this benefit and declined to use his assistance toward your

48. *Laz.* 1.11 (PG 48:978), 32–33.
49. Ibid., 33.
50. Ibid., 33–34.
51. Marketplace or exchange language is even more abundant in other of Chrysostom's homilies. Alms given to the poor are kept on deposit by Christ, transferred to heaven, received back at one's judgment, *Stat.* 2.5–7 (PG 49:39–43) and cancel sins, *Stat.* 2.7 (PG 49:43). God is the debtor of the almsgiver, *Hom. Matt.* 15.9 (PG 57:235); 15.11 (PG 57:238); and 19.4 (PG 57:277). Heaven is a commercial enterprise (ἐμπορία) and a business (πραγματεία), *Paenit.* 3.2 (PG 49:294). For early use of exchange language, see Herm. *Sim.* 2, in Carolyn Osiek, *Shepherd of Hermas: A Commentary*, Hermeneia (Minneapolis: Fortress Press, 1999), 161–64.

salvation. Hereafter you shall use him to bring yourself a greater punishment and retribution.[52]

At the same time, the very existence of rich people can be ascribed to divine causality. The rich were given greater material resources precisely so they could distribute them to the needy. In this sense they are stewards of God's money, not their own, and will be punished (another exchange) just like thieves if they do not show mercy to the poor. If the rich use their goods sparingly, "as belonging to others," and give to those in need, their goods may actually become their own on the day of judgment (another exchange).[53]

In the end, Chrysostom locates the ultimate basis of all such exchange in the theater of judgment and salvation. If the rich show mercy to the unfortunate, they will receive mercy from God and enjoy the divine philanthropy. But if they demand that the poor demonstrate their worthiness in order to receive alms, they will "lose the philanthropy from above."[54] At the conclusion of this homily, Chrysostom reiterates the centrality of exchange for the salvation of the rich:

> I beg you, remember this without fail, that not to share our own wealth with the poor is theft from the poor and deprivation of their means of life; we do not possess our wealth but theirs. If we have this attitude, we will certainly offer our money; and by nourishing Christ in poverty here and laying up great profit hereafter, we will be able to attain the good things which are to come.[55]

Melding the marketplace with the theater of salvation creates an appeal to self-interest designed to catch the attention of the rich and turn their gaze at least to the preacher, if not to the poor.

The preacher's gaze

As Chrysostom preaches, he too is engaged in an exchange. At the end of the first homily he encourages the congregation to "examine carefully all the wealth which comes from this parable"—and, presumably, from his preaching on it.[56] As he instructs his congregation in how to see and understand the biblical narrative, he directs his gaze at them, reinforcing and at times revising how *he* sees and understands *them*. He asks for his audience's attention and comments on their responses, hoping to move them by his words

52. *Laz.* 2.4 (PG 48:987), 48.
53. *Laz.* 2.4–5 (PG 48:988), 49–50. See also *Laz.* 3.10 (PG 48:1006), goods given as alms vouch for a person on the day of judgment; *Stat.* 2.6 (PG 49:42), goods given as alms become one's possessions at judgment; *Hom. Matt.* 20.2–3 (PG 57:288–89).
54. *Laz.* 2.6 (PG 48:990), 53.
55. *Laz.* 2.6 (PG 48:991–92), 55.
56. *Laz.* 1.12 (PG 48:982), 38.

to change their hearts and lives so that in the end they might come to the true and final good that God has revealed through Lazarus. Spontaneous interchange between preacher and congregation is common in this period; less common, I think, is the preacher's self-reflective commentary on what he wants to teach, how he is teaching it, and whether his preaching is having any effect.

Chrysostom's thinking out loud about his preaching is a visual as well as a verbal event, a performance of the message he wishes to convey to his audience. He is aware of that performance, of its inherent dangers and limitations. "I want to teach," he insists, "not simply to put on a display."[57] He knows the power of his words—he sees it in the faces of the congregation, he feels it in their applause and in their silence. When he shocks them into silence with the vivid description of the rich man being led away to judgment, he acknowledges their response and explains his intent.

> Are you listening to this in silence? I am much happier at your silence than at applause; for applause and praise make me more famous, but this silence makes you more virtuous. I know that what I say is painful, but I cannot tell you how great a benefit it contains.[58]

He brings them fear, he says, to prepare their salvation.[59] If the rich man had received such good advice, he would not be roasting in hell now!

Posing the rhetorical question in the sixth homily of how he helps his congregation by preaching, Chrysostom replies that, "I help if anyone hears me." Like the sower in the parable, he has scattered so much seed that some harvest must be forthcoming—a half, a third, a tenth, even just one person, someone must be listening. "I will not stop speaking," he avers, "even if there is no one at all who listens."[60] Yet alongside this extravagant, even spendthrift account of preaching, Chrysostom suggests a more direct kind of exchange in the practice of preaching. At the beginning of the second homily, he notes with approval the good will with which the congregation had received the previous sermon; given such a favorable response, he says, he will go on to the next part of the story.[61] At the beginning of the seventh homily, however, he threatens to halt his efforts, since some of them have "forgotten everything and surrendered themselves again to the satanic spectacle of the races." He chastises them at some length but nevertheless takes up the story once more and revisits its ending in the hope that, with Lazarus, they too might

---

57. *Laz.* 6.6 (PG 48:1042), 123; see Leyerle, *Theatrical Shows*, 63–67, for Chrysostom's critique of rhetorical display and excess in preaching.

58. *Laz.* 2.3 (PG 48:985), 44.

59. *Laz.* 6.1 (PG 48:1028).

60. *Laz.* 6.2 (PG 48:1029), 99–100.

61. *Laz.* 2.1 (PG 48:981).

choose the narrow gate and pass through it to the wide place of comfort and blessing.[62]

Conclusion

The theater of poverty and wealth, the calculus of punishment, and the language of exchange reveal inherent tensions in Chrysostom's rhetorical strategy of accommodation. These tensions generate ambiguities that, I would argue, reduce Chrysostom's effectiveness in moving his audience to show mercy to the materially poor. Despite the power of his preaching, or perhaps because of it, the same ambiguities are still evident today in the ways in which Christians see, understand, and act in relation to poverty and wealth, poor and rich.

As Chrysostom teaches his congregation to see the poor, he also unwittingly teaches them to objectify the poor. His descriptions of Lazarus and the rich man in these homilies, and of Job or of beggars in the marketplace in others, have an element of spectacle about them that draws the eye but reduces the object of its gaze. To be sure, neither Lazarus nor the rich man are merely caricatures. There is approval and condemnation, sympathy and distance, intimacy and objectification in Chrysostom's depictions of them. They are human enough to hold the audience's attention. But they are also types—of rich and poor, of virtue and vice—and as types they are distanced from the human reality from which they are drawn. Something dehumanizing happens when Lazarus and the rich man become objects of pity and terror, tools of a strategy for persuading the rich to give alms and the poor to endure their plight in patient silence.[63] Because types train the gaze and define what is seen, they make it dangerously possible to ignore the reality of actual rich and poor people and to see them instead as means to an end. In response to his preaching, Chrysostom's congregation may perhaps become more generous, but will they become more humane?

When joined to objectifying characterizations and typology, the calculus of reward and punishment serves to reinforce the status quo even when it succeeds in moving the rich to give alms. Real riches and real poverty, Chrysostom argues, are made fully known only in the theater of judgment and salvation, but they can be recognized already in this world by those trained in virtue. The poor man who is spiritually wise (i.e., virtuous) will not be harmed by his poverty, even though his body suffers, nor will the spiritually wise rich man be harmed by his wealth as long as he is its master, not its slave. The rich man's and the poor man's suffering or fortune in this

---

62. *Laz.* 7.1 (PG 48:1044), 126; the scolding extends to 1047.
63. Because Lazarus does not complain in his extreme sufferings, there is no excuse for the poor to complain that they have to beg for a living, *Laz.* 2.1 (PG 48:981–82).

life is only apparent; each will receive his due in the theater of eternity. In the meantime, the material condition of each may require modification, but not reversal or renunciation.

The objectifying language of exchange merges almost seamlessly with the calculus of reward and punishment to transform the poor into commodities for the benefit of the rich. Thus Chrysostom can castigate the rich man for neglecting and refusing to see Lazarus, a pearl in the mud outside his gate, a treasure chest with thorns above and pearls beneath it, a gold coin in the furnace—valuable and overlooked objects, but objects nonetheless.[64] Though far from Chrysostom's intention, his seemingly uncritical appropriation of the rhetoric and practice of the marketplace undercuts his far more challenging vision of money and goods as held on loan, and of the rich as robbers if they do not share them with the poor.

In the homilies on Lazarus and the rich man, Chrysostom preaches poverty and wealth as theater. The story of the rich man and Lazarus is itself theater, a narrative in which the characters are not who they seem, their reality revealed only in their ends. Chrysostom's preaching of this story is also theater, an extended performance in which he endeavors to draw his audience from the deception of appearances to the truth of reality, from the theater of the world to the theater of salvation. The interaction of preacher and audience in this process is itself theater, an integral part of the earthly and eschatological drama, as they negotiate their roles and, when all goes well, turn their gaze toward the same salvific end.

But Chrysostom's congregation in late fourth-century Antioch is not the only audience in this multitiered theater, which extends through the centuries to our own world of poverty and wealth, appearance and reality, exchange and refusal, commodification and compassion. We too have to look more intently and learn to see more clearly how the story is playing itself out today in our rhetoric and in our practice.

---

64. *Laz.* 6.5 (PG 48:1033 and 1034); see also Chrysostom's disapproving observation that the rich man ignored Lazarus like a stone (n. 10, above). Roth's translation of χρυσίον ἐν καμίνῳ as "a gold coin beside the road" (108) appears to be mistaken; "a gold piece (or, gold coin) in a furnace" seems preferable, both as the only translation of the word in lexicons and as consistent with Chrysostom's other uses of καμίνῳ in his homilies (eighty-eight times), including *Laz.* 1.11 (PG 48:978, 9), a person lying in a furnace.

12

WEALTHY AND IMPOVERISHED WIDOWS IN THE WRITINGS OF ST. JOHN CHRYSOSTOM

EFTHALIA MAKRIS WALSH

As a preacher, teacher, and rhetorician, John Chrysostom had much to say about the society of his day. A frequent topic was the role of widows in the church and society. In this essay I reflect on what he wrote about the situation of both wealthy and impoverished widows in late fourth-century Antioch, and also on the importance of widows in his life, in his theology, and in his understanding of Christian teaching (*didaskalia*)—his primary concern as a preacher.

I briefly note some of Chrysostom's major works on widowhood, showing that he saw virtuous widows as major paradigms of how Christians should live. He claimed that those who taught by example, like the scriptural widows—the Old Testament widow of Sarephtha of Sidon in 1 Kings 17:7–25 and Luke's New Testament widow who gave her last two coins to the collection tray (Luke 21:1–4)—were models of behavior for all Christians, not only widows or women. They were much greater than those who, like himself, taught by words, and they were more worthy of being emulated.[1] It was not virginity that was the primary virtue, but caring for others. I also suggest that in addition to soteriological and practical rationales for the importance of widows,

---

1. *In Heliam et viduam* (PG 51:337).

Chrysostom had an apologetic one in using widows as major paradigms. They could provide evidence of the superiority of Chrysostom's church to competing churches and to non-Christians.

Widows and Christian Behavior

Chrysostom used 1 Tim. 5 as his overriding principal of how widows and all Christians should behave, as he frequently explained, that is, bringing up children, being hospitable to strangers, washing the feet of saints, and relieving the afflicted.[2] The key words echoed throughout his writing were benevolence, hospitality, and charity (*philophrosynē, philoxenia, eleēmosynē*).[3]

In his extensive discussions of 1 Tim. 5 it can be seen that Chrysostom was not discussing an order of widows, which was a thing of the past, and "in a desolate state;" as Chrysostom wrote.[4] Rather, he was focusing on widows who were eligible by their poverty for the church dole and also both poor and wealthy widows who were living on their own. The word for widow (Greek *chēra* or Latin *vidua*), it should be noted, described any woman without a husband, some of them barren women, cast off because of their childless state, and others who never married. Chrysostom explained that it was not enough to have lost a husband to be considered a widow, but as with virgins other qualities were required, including "blamelessness and perseverance, patience with chastity."[5]

Chrysostom made a distinction between the destitute (*penēs*) and the needy (*ptōchos*). A destitute widow with children was a "widow, indeed," or true widow (*penichēran*).[6] But a wealthier widow with no children could also be a "widow, indeed," because having no maternal bonds to keep her tied to the world, she could devote her attention to God's things. Widows with children should repay their debt to their parents, presumably dead, by bringing up and educating their own children in God.[7] In a sermon on 1 Tim. 5:9, Chrysostom claimed that rearing children was the greatest of the virtues, "and that is what Paul asked first of the widow."[8] In another homily Chrysostom even refuted the Pauline injunction against women teaching in the church, by linking the widowed mother's and her children's salvation—and that of all people—to her successful job in teaching and rearing children.[9]

2. *Hom. 1 Tim.* 14 (PG 62:568, *NPNF*[1] 13:454); *Hom. 1 Thess.* 6 (PG 62:433, *NPNF*[1] 13:350–51).

3. *In illud: Vidua eligatur* (PG 51:326).

4. *Hom. 1 Cor.* 36 (PG 61:312, *NPNF*[1] 12:219–20).

5. Ibid.

6. *Hom 1 Tim.* 15 (PG 62:570, *NPNF*[1] 62:450); *Hom. 1 Tim.* 13 (PG 62:517, *NPNF*[1] 13:450–51); *De eleemosyna* (PG 49:264–65); *In Ss. Petrum et Helium* (PG 64:751).

7. *Hom. 13 in 1 Tim.* (PG 62.517, *NPNF*[1] 13:450).

8. *In illud: Vidua eligatur* (PG 51:331).

9. *Hom. 1 Tim.* 9 (PG 62:545, *NPNF*[1] 13:436).

Not only could the poor widow's example and behavior lead to her own and her children's salvation, but she could also be the cause of her own benefactor's salvation. The widows were thus patrons, or benefactors (*prostates*), of all to God,[10] with God serving as the widows' patron. Without widows there could be no perfecting the fullness of the church.

Chrysostom warned that there was "frequent mention in the Scriptures of widows and orphans, but people took no account of this." He explained how those who assisted widows could store up a future reward. "Not small is the power of the widow's tears, it is able to open up Heaven itself. . . . For not here, alone, but there also will they be our defenders cutting away most of our sins by reason of our beneficence toward them and causing us to stand boldly before the judgment seat of Christ."[11]

Again Chrysostom explained, "Would you like to know how much power the widow has? And where her patronage shows itself? Not by earthly chief and king, but the heavenly King himself. . . . Let us not ignore widowed women, but in every effort for her show care . . . the widow being our protector and suppliant."[12] The role of patron, an important social and political responsibility, was normally assumed by men in the fourth century, it should be noted.

Chrysostom claimed also that a widow, by the state of widowhood, was espoused to Christ, citing Ps. 68:5: "I am the defender of the widows and the father of the orphans."[13] Widows, he wrote, were so powerful and important in the eyes of God that the most vicious criminals and murderers were forgiven their sins if they had helped widows who had been treated unjustly.[14]

Chrysostom even maintained that those who ministered to the poor were holier than those who held the office of priest and were equal (*isos*) to God. "And instead of wearing a plate bearing the name of God, he becomes equal to God. For the merciful man is wrapped in the robe of loving kindness, which is holier than the sacred vestment and is anointed with oil not composed of material elements, but produced by the spirit."[15]

Chrysostom's comments in a homily on 1 Cor. 12 present another perspective on the situation of the most impoverished widows, who prayed night and day in the church. He holds that their role is vital: "For as bishops, presbyters and deacons and virgins and continent people enter into my enumeration when I am reckoning up the members of the church, so also do widows."[16] Chrysostom defended them against criticism by some Christians who apparently did not approve of their begging for alms in the church. The widows'

10. *In illud: Vidua eligatur* (PG 51:323).
11. *Hom. Jo.* 70 (PG 59:385–86, *NPNF*[1] 14: 259).
12. *Hom. 1 Thess.* 6 (PG 62:433, *NPNF*[1] 13:350–51).
13. *Hom. 1 Tim.* 15 (PG 62:579, *NPNF*[1] 13:459).
14. *In illud: Vidua eligatur* (PG 51:322).
15. *Hom. 2 Cor.* 20 (PG 61:539–40, *NPNF*[1] 13:374).
16. Ibid. (PG 61:254, *NPNF*[1] 12:179).

choice to do so in church, he explained, was far superior to their going out on the streets, where they would be in danger. They and other beggars in the church "could have chosen to live otherwise by becoming pimps and panderers and by other ministrations not only to live, but to live in luxury, but that it was their choice to perish in hunger rather than dishonor their own life and betray their salvation." The widows' decision to follow the better course of action made them models worthy of imitation and gave them a great position in the church.[17]

Two Biblical Widows

The impoverished widow of Sarephtha was given royal treatment by Chrysostom as surpassing Abraham in her hospitality and outstripping all others renowned for hospitality.[18] Even poor widows with children were not exempt from offering hospitality.

> She is no poorer than the widow with a little flour and a cup of oil who gave hospitality to the great prophet—for there also there were children, but neither the lack of material things, nor the misfortune of hunger, nor approaching death, nor the effort of children on widowhood, nor anything else was an impediment to the hospitable woman. It is not wealth, but the desire to provide charity and compassion. That is what counts. God defines not by the measure of what is given, but by the extent of the one who gives.[19]

The widow of Sarephtha of Sidon, a poor foreigner and barbarian, exemplified the correct attitude and response for all Christians. Chrysostom often presented widows as an illustration of what he claimed to be the first and greatest of all virtues, the rearing of children, but that is not at first glance the case for the widow of Sarephtha. What he emphasized was her hospitality and her willingness to sacrifice her many children and herself to death in order to provide food to the starving prophet when he arrived at her door—not knowing who Elijah was, and that he was sent by God. Of course, that was the spiritual message to be taught to one's children. One should sacrifice everything for another in need.

The widow of Luke 21:1–4, who gave her last two coins to the collection tray, was often paired with the widow of Sarephtha. Chrysostom cited Luke 4:25 and Matt. 10:11 to confirm the widows' greater merit as the rationale for Elijah's being sent to the widow of Sarephtha's house. Like her, Luke's widow was a symbol of unselfish love and generosity, and Chrysostom exhorted his

---

17. *Hom. 1 Cor.* 30 (PG 61:255, *NPNF*[1] 12:179).
18. *Hom. 2 Cor.* 19 (PG 61:534, *NPNF*[1] 12:371); *In sanctos Petrum et Heliam* (PG 50:732).
19. *In illud: Vidua eligatur* (PG 51:222–24).

audience to similar good works. But we are given little specific information about her.[20] In discussing the varying degrees of poverty among widows, he noted that many widows, however poor, had houses and other property at their disposal. He chided his audience: "She is not more poor or more destitute than the widow who gave the two coins. Poor though she be, she has a house, she does not lodge in the open air . . . not even in that case is she debarred from bringing up children, lodging strangers, relieving the afflicted."[21]

Widow Typology

Chrysostom did not explicitly use the resurrection typology when he might have in his numerous comments on the widow of Sarephtha. It is interesting that in the original Old Testament account she was presented as having one child, a son, and Elijah was the focus of the story, when he resurrected the widow's dead son. Chrysostom made no mention of this episode. He did use the resurrection typology as proof of the resurrection in some of his martyrdom writings, but in regard to widows Chrysostom seemed most concerned about making the point that even poor widows with children were not exempt from providing hospitality.

The widow of Sarephtha was depicted as a recipient of God's blessings offered by Elijah. But she was also referred to as one who offered blessings. Chrysostom frequently urged parents to invite widows to their children's wedding celebrations so that the widows might offer their beneficent blessings. Christ should be invited in the person of widows and other poor people, rather than the evil and corrupt who sing hymns to Aphrodite.[22]

Chrysostom also identified widows with martyrdom. They wore crowns like the martyrs and were of equally great worth.[23] It is worth noting that the cult of the Maccabees, which featured the sacrificial death of seven sons, was very popular in Antioch in the fourth century. Chrysostom himself wrote three homilies about the martyred boys and their widowed grandmother, or mother, as he elsewhere explained her marital and maternal status. "Listen mothers . . . emulate the courage of the woman, the tender love to the grandchildren. Thus they nurtured children, for it is not bearing that makes a mother, for this is from nature, but for a mother to nurture—this is by choice."[24] This example showed that widows could be raised up by surpassing the limitations of their own maternal nature. They could follow the model of Luke's widow and the Maccabean widow by not fearing death, and by their willingness to

---

20. *In Heliam et viduam* (PG 51:351); *In illud: Vidua eligatur* (PG 51:332).
21. *Hom. 1 Tim.* 14 (PG 62:572, *NPNF*[1] 13:454).
22. *In illud: Propter fornicationes autem* (PG 51:212).
23. *In illud: Vidua eligatur* (PG 51:321–23); *De Maccabeis* 1 (PG 50:623).
24. *De Maccabeis* 1 (PG 50:621); *De studio praesentium* 5.3 (PG 63:488).

sacrifice their children and their own lives for the truth and for strangers. The widows' freedom to decide how to live and behave was the important point.[25] Chrysostom lauded the widows and claimed that unlike pagan games that excluded widows, old people, and others, Christianity permitted widows to play and win in this competition and rise above nature.

Chrysostom did not fully follow the widow-as-altar typology found in the *Didascalia apostolorum*, the *Apostolic Constitutions*, and other early church writings. But his image of the poor (including widows) clinging to the altar doors in the homily on 1 Cor. 12 mentioned above does suggest this sacrificial aspect,[26] as does his description of the poor in the city as the altar.[27]

Comparing Widowhood with Virginity

Still another example of Chrysostom's belief in the importance of widows as exemplars is found in his comparison of virginity to widowhood. Usually in his writings on virginity he proclaimed the superiority of ascetic life, claiming that as virginity was superior to marriage, so too was widowhood to second marriage, suggesting that virgins are more virtuous than widows. Nevertheless, Chrysostom rated the superiority of almsgiving as performed by the widows over the ascetic practices of virgins.

> For he who has learnt to give to him that needs will in time learn not to receive from those who have to give. This makes men like God. While virginity and fasting and lying on the ground are more difficult than this, but nothing is so strong and powerful to extinguish the fire of our sins as almsgiving. It is greater than all other virtues. It places the lovers of it by the side of the King himself, and justly. For the effect of virginity, of fasting, of lying on the ground is confined to those who practice them, and no other is saved thereby. But almsgiving extends to all and embraces the members of Christ. [It is] . . . the mother . . . of that love, which is characteristic of Christianity. . . . It is . . . the ladder fixed to heaven; it binds together the body of Christ . . . for they will readily incline to almsgiving, like the widow, and they have no occasion for enmity toward their neighbor and they will enjoy freedom in every respect.[28]

Wealthy Widows, Childless Widows

Wealthy widows were expected to maintain the same high standard as impoverished widows. Here again the emphasis was rearing, teaching, and caring

25. *De sanctis Bernice et Prosdoce* (PG 50:633); *De Maccabeis* 2 (PG 50:623).
26. *Hom. 1 Cor.* 30 (PG 61:255, *NPNF*[1] 12:179).
27. *Hom. 2 Cor.* 20 (PG 61:539–40, *NPNF*[1] 12:374).
28. *Hom. Tit.* 6 (PG 62:698, *NPNF*[1] 13:542, alt.).

for their children, as well as caring for others. It is likely that Chrysostom's direct personal experience with wealthy widows shaped his strongly pro-widow views. His mother, Anthusa, was widowed at a young age. Chrysostom described the financial and marital predicament of this affluent young widow with children, adding "she held on in the midst of the storm and uproar, and did not shun the iron furnace of widowhood." The reason for not remarrying was the necessity of caring for children, especially, she noted, a son who "fills her with a thousand alarms and many anxieties every day."[29]

In a homily on 1 Thess. 4, Chrysostom dismissed a rich widow's concern for the financial and social status of her orphaned children as a lack of faith, for they had God for their Father. Widows should enlist them in the ranks of the heavenly king's army. He summarizes the wealthy widow's complaints:

> A multitude of troubles rushes in upon me. I am exposed to all who are willing to injure me. Those of my servants who formerly feared me now despise me and trample upon me. If anyone has been benefited, he has forgotten the benefit he received from him; if anyone was ill-treated by the departed, to return the grudge against him, he lets loose his anger upon me.[30]

According to Chrysostom, however, anxiety over such matters signifies lack of faith.

Chrysostom was not only concerned about widows with children; he also pointed out the unique possibilities for a childless widow, whom he identified as a widow indeed,

> because she is more highly approved and has a greater opportunity of pleasing God, because all her chains are loosened. . . . You are separated from your husband, but are united to God. . . . She stands at the other side of the King and acts as his fellow minister . . . and achieves an equal standard of virtue.[31]

Chrysostom's concern for wealthy, childless widows, their apologetic significance, and the role they should play in the church can also be seen in his lengthy letter to the young widow of a high government official. He counseled her not to remarry but rather to focus her energies and money on serving the church and the kingdom of Heaven, as had her husband, Thesarius, a devoted Christian. Chrysostom again detailed the problems of widowhood.

---

29. St. John Chrysostom, *De sacerdotio*, ed. A.-M. Malingrey, SC 272 (Paris: Cerf, 1980); English translation in Margaret Schatkin and Paul Harkins, *St. John Chrysostom, Apologist*, FC 73 (Washington: Catholic University of America Press, 1985); St. John Chrysostom, *Six Books on the Priesthood*, trans. G. Neville (London: SPCK, 1964), 34.

30. *Hom. 1 Thess.* 6 (PG 62:432, *NPNF*[1] 13:349).

31. Ibid. (PG 62:434, *NPNF*[1] 13:351).

Widows have greater labor to undergo than priests, being encompassed on many sides by a variety of business both public and private. For as an unfortified city lies exposed to all who wish to plunder it, so a young woman living in widowhood has many who form designs upon her on every side, not only those who aim at getting her money, but also those who are bent on corrupting her modesty. . . . Thus [widowhood] is a state which seems to be not reproached, but admired and deemed worthy of honor among men, not only among us who believe, but even among unbelievers.[32]

In another treatise Chrysostom also noted the freedom that a wealthy widow would have if she did not remarry. He elaborated on the difficulties in the marriage of a rich widow to a wealthy or highly placed official who believed that a husband's position as the first human created in Eden gave him precedence over his wife. Chrysostom asked, "Who would prefer this slavery to freedom?" "One should look not at the effort, but the reward of widowhood," he cautioned.[33]

The Situation in Antioch

From Chrysostom and other sources of the period, it can be seen that there was much need for philanthropic activity. Antioch suffered earthquakes, droughts, wars, migrations, riots, and changes in imperial laws on families and property that resulted in a large group of destitute people. Antioch had a population of some 100,000 Christians, with equal numbers of pagans and Jews.

There were more than three thousand widows and virgins supported by the church, but there were many more needy widows and orphans in the city— too many for the church to support, Chrysostom wrote.[34] He described the "great crowd of widows arrayed in a dark mourning robe . . . resulting from the wars with the barbarians overrunning our territory."[35] He noted also that in addition to the war being fought with the barbarians, there was also in Antioch a camp of the poor, and a war that was being waged for the people by the prayers of the poor. He repeatedly urged wealthy widows, and even those much less affluent, to provide care for poor widows and their children and to open their homes to strangers and those in need. His reason for urging widows not to remarry was not so that they would abstain from sex but

32. *Ad viduam juniorem* 2, in *Jean Chrysostome: À une jeune veuve; Sur le marriage unique*, ed. B. Grillet and G. H. Ettlinger, SC 138 (Paris: Cerf, 1968); *NPNF*[1] 9:122.

33. *De non iterando coniugio* (PG 48:6), St. John Chrysostom, *On Virginity; Against Remarriage*, trans. Sally Shore (Lewiston, NY: Mellen Press, 1983), 140.

34. *Hom. Matt.* 66 (PG 58:630–31, *NPNF*[1] 10:407).

35. *Ad viduam juniorem* 5, *NPNF*[1] 9:125.

because the virtuous widows' love and care of others exemplified the kind of Christian activity that mattered most.[36]

Chrysostom was critical of the city because it was wealthy enough to "nourish the poor of ten cities." And he frequently admonished people to take care of their own widows and not leave their care to the church. But he was more critical of the church because it did not provide care for widows and the poor adequately. He faulted the wealthy and especially the clergy for being overinvolved in financial matters and remiss in what he considered their primary duties. Thus occurs "the great neglect of scriptures, remissness in prayers, and indifference to other duties." This included helping the injured, strangers and "taking part with the widows."[37] He explained that because of the indignities that impoverished widows normally experienced and their pathetic state, it was necessary that church funding be not interrupted but distributed regularly. It required the bishop "to combine prudence and wisdom and skill in the art of supply, so as to dispose the affluent to emulate him."[38]

Chrysostom also pointed out the more stringent requirements for widows than for bishops—"Widows have greater labor to undergo, being encompassed on many sides by a variety of business both public and private"—and that widows shared responsibility with bishops.[39]

Competition with Christians and Non-Christians

Chrysostom's use of the once-married widow as an exemplary model could be used as an argument for the moral value of Christian tradition, as David Hunter has explained.[40] Alan Natali too has written of the fierce competition between pagans and Christians on the topic of euergetism and moral protection of the population.[41] John Leibeschuetz has noted the particularly Christian aspect of charity and benefactions directed to the poor, and that "pagan patronage was not so comprehensively defined."[42]

Chrysostom pointed out the Christian apologetic aspect of the "good widow" model when he related a story about his former "Stoic" teacher, presumably Libanius. Upon learning that Chrysostom's mother was a widow,

36. *De non iterando coniugio*, in Shore, trans., *On Virginity; Against Remarriage*, 122.

37. *Hom. Matt.* 85 (PG 58:761–62, *NPNF*[1] 10:509–10).

38. *De sacerdotio* 3 (SC 272:208, *NPNF*[1] 9:56).

39. *In illud: Vidua eligatur* (PG 51:321–22).

40. David Hunter, "Libanius and John Chrysostom: New Thoughts on an Old Problem," StPatr 22 (1989):129–35.

41. Alan Natali, "Christianisme et cité à Antioche à la fin du IVe siècle d'après J. Chrysostome," in *Jean Chrysostome et Augustin*, ed. C. Kannengiesser (Paris: Beauchesne, 1975), 41–59.

42. J. H. W. G. Leibeschuetz, *Barbarians and Bishops: Army, Church, and State in the Age of Arcadius and Chrysostom* (Oxford: Clarendon, 1990), 250.

Libanius praised her remaining a widow as advantageous for her children and exclaimed, "What fine women these Christians are."[43]

In addition to differences with the "pagans," there was also bitter contention, disarray, and schism in Antioch with its three contending bishops, Paulinus, Meletius, and Vitalis. Chrysostom frequently and strongly spoke against those who "meddled" in forbidden knowedge of the divine nature.[44] And throughout his work he argued against the Manichaeans, who denied that the Old and New Testaments were in agreement and focused on the importance of virginity, fasting, and constant prayer.[45] Chrysostom, however, looked to the Old Testament as well as the New for the correct Christian examples and rejected Greek types. His view was that widows, not virgins, exemplified the church's mission in fulfilling Christ's and the church's teaching of love and care for the less fortunate.

Chrysostom thus used the widow of Sarephtha of Sidon and Luke's widow not only to provide a model of proper Christian behavior but also to show the relationship of the Old Testament to the New. Chrysostom cited Paul's comments about widows in 1 Tim. 5:10 to make the connection between the Old and New Testaments' dispensation and to prove the superiority of the New Testament as a new creation.[46]

The widow of Sarephtha's warm hospitality to the Old Testament prophet Elijah was prophetic of the rejection of Christ by the Jews and his acceptance by the gentiles, and "she became higher than all because she had had not received either the promise or the blessing." She was prophetic of those barbarians and pagans who received the prophets Joseph, Moses, Jothan, David, Saul, and Anthus, all of whom had been rejected by the Jews. "So that when you see Christ then being accepted by the gentiles . . . having examined closely the types above, you will not marvel at the truth of the matter."[47]

In his final years in exile, Chrysostom corresponded with the wealthy deaconess Olympias, who had previously assisted him in Constantinople. Widowed at a young age with no children, she had devoted her wealth and life to the church in Constantinople. The correspondence reveals a deep appreciation of her personal, philanthropic, and political efforts on his behalf—work that had engaged her before and after his exile, and in this correspondence he cites Luke's New Testament widow as a model.[48]

43. *Ad viduam juniorem* 2 (SC 138:120).

44. Richard Lim, *Public Disputation, Power, and Social Order in Late Antiquity* (Berkeley: University of California Press, 1995), 174–77; *De incomprehens.* 2.75–80. Cf. J. Daniélou, "L'incompréhensibilité de Dieu d'après Saint Jean Chrysostome," *RSR* 37 (1950): 176–94.

45. *Hom. Matt.* 16 (PG 58:247, *NPNF*[1] 10:109–10); *Hom. Matt.* 62 (PG 58:599–600, *NPNF*[1] 10:384); *Hom. Eph.* 23 (PG 62:164–65, *NPNF*[1] 13:164–65).

46. *In Heliam et viduam* (PG 51:338–39).

47. *In sanctos Petrum et Heliam* (PG 50:732); *Hom. Gen.* 42 (PG 54:393–94; FC 82:423–35); *In Heliam et viduam* (PG 51:341).

48. St. John Chrysostom, *Lettres à Olympias*, ed. A.-M. Malingrey, 2nd ed., SC 13bis (Paris: Cerf, 1968).

Much more might be said about the huge amount of material available on widows and widowhood in John Chrysostom's writings. It is possible to conclude that widows and orphans were an important part of pastoral activities and theology in the late fourth-century church in Antioch, and that their care was a soteriological, practical, and apologetic concern for this saint and monumental church father, who called himself the ambassador of the poor. His writing on women without husbands is of as much interest and relevance today as it was sixteen hundred years ago.

13

THE HELLENIC BACKGROUND AND NATURE OF PATRISTIC PHILANTHROPY IN THE EARLY BYZANTINE ERA

DEMETRIOS J. CONSTANTELOS

I n a letter to Arsacius, the chief priest of Galatia in Asia Minor, Julian, the emperor of the early Byzantine Empire (361–363), complained that Arsacius and other priests of the Hellenic religion there had failed in their duty to practice philanthropy. "The Hellenic religion does not yet prosper as I desire, and it is the fault of those who profess it," Julian writes. The worship of the gods is not enough. Worship must be accompanied with benevolence to strangers and the poor, with care to the hungry, with the establishment of hostels (*xenōnes*) where strangers may find shelter. "Our philanthropy," Julian adds, "should benefit not only our own people but also others in need."

Julian continues to write "that the impious Galilaeans support not only their own poor but also ours." He reminded Arsacius to teach his fellow priests to pursue benevolence, because what the Galileans were practicing "was a Hellenic tradition of old." He concludes by saying, "Let us not allow others to outdo us in good works."[1] Elsewhere Julian writes that the virtue of

---

1. Julian, *Ep.* 22, in *The Works of the Emperor Julian*, ed. and trans. Wilmer Cave Wright, LCL 157 (London: W. Heinemann, 1923), 3:66–72.

generosity and other humane qualities "exist in an admirable degree among all the Greeks . . . they are hospitable to strangers; . . . all the Greeks generally, but among them the Athenians above all." He adds that he spoke from his own experience.[2]

In what sense did Julian use the term *philanthrōpia*? The original meaning is "love for the human being" (*anthrōpos*). In the course of centuries the term *philanthrōpia* has become a synonym to *agapē*, love, charity, benevolence, good will, unselfishness.

The questions are, Was Julian right in stressing that the Christian practice of philanthropy was not an innovation, that it was a tradition in practice among the ancient Greeks? Or was he advocating an imitation of Christian philanthropy of his time?

Sozomen, the fifth-century ecclesiastical historian, writes that Julian was deeply grieved that the efforts of paganism in the fourth century were totally ineffectual, and that he was determined to introduce into pagan temples the order and discipline present in the Christian communities, to establish hostels for the relief of strangers and the poor, and to energize philanthropic activities for other purposes. He adds that in this manner Julian strove to ingraft the customs of Christians on paganism.[3] Julian's contemporary and fellow student in Athens, Gregory the Theologian, also indicates that Julian admired Christian philanthropy and advocated its practice by the pagans in imitation of Christian practices.[4]

In his criticism of Julian, however, Gregory objected to ancient Greek religious beliefs but defended Hellenism and its language, thought, and culture. He stressed that what separated him from Julian was religious faith, but not culture—Hellenism (*to hellēnizein*) belonged to both. Along with the growth of Christianity, we find several forms of old religious beliefs that prospered, including ethical teachings and philosophical ideologies. Ancient ideas were fossilized but gently and imperceptibly transmitted and adopted by Christianity and medieval culture, both Greek and Latin.

In searching for the background of the social thought and the nature of patristic philanthropy, we need to take into account the Hellenic cultural and intellectual climate in which church fathers were born and nurtured. It is in the continuity of Hellenic culture, its language and philosophy, social practices and ethical values that pagan Julian and Christian Gregory converged.

A study of classical culture, including the postclassical, conventionally called Hellenistic, and its relationship with early and medieval Christianity is an absolute necessity. While the marriage between Greek *logos* and Christian *pistis* was consummated in the fourth and fifth centuries and set the

2. Julian, *Misopogon*, in *The Works of Emperor Julian*, ed. and trans. Wilmer Cave Wright, LCL 29 (London: W. Heinemann, 1913) 2:448–52.

3. Sozomen, *HE* 5.16, trans. *NPNF*[2] 2:337–38.

4. Gregory, *Contra Julianum imperatorem* 1.111.

standards for the later Byzantine centuries, the romance between the two can be traced back to Paul, the Apostolic Fathers, and the apologists. Let us turn back to Julian.

Julian was born in Byzantium, studied in Athens, and was well informed of private and social values and practices of the ancient Hellenes. Did he imitate Christians, or was he trying to revive a tradition that had declined? He was a living witness of an ancient religion in decline but also a witness of practices of the old culture that had survived. Julian acknowledged that Christians practiced what they preached. The question is, was it the practice of philanthropy that made Christianity attractive to the masses of people, or was it the influence of Constantine's conversion that contributed to the rapid growth of Christianity that was achieved in the fourth century? For nearly three hundred years Christians were a minority in the Roman Empire. In the opinion of modern scholarship, Christians made up no more than 10 percent in the Latin West, and perhaps no more than 15 percent in the Greek East.[5] Within seventy years, however, from 313, when the Edict of Milan was issued, to the laws of Theodosius I in 380, Christianity became the dominant and, soon after, the official state religion. Constantine's conversion and religious policies contributed greatly to the Christianization of the empire. "The example of the Emperor becomes a rule for his subjects" as Photius wrote a few centuries later.[6] In this essay I focus specifically on this developing transition from Hellenic ethical principles, from Hellenic to Christian *philanthrōpia*.[7]

5. Ramsay MacMullen, *Christianity and Paganism in the Fourth to Eighth Centuries* (New Haven: Yale University Press, 1997), 68–73, 151.

6. Photius, *Epistles*, ed. Ioannis N. Valettas (London, 1861), and PG 102:51; cf. para. 44.

7. Although I discuss Jewish attitudes of philanthropia and charity toward the non-Jewish stranger here only very briefly, the interested reader may wish to consult the following sources that are readily available in English: Marianne Palmer Bonz, "The Jewish Donor Inscriptions from Aphrodisias: Are They Both Third-Century, and Who Are the *Theosebeis*?" *Harvard Studies in Classical Philology* 96 (1994): 281–99; Rabbi Avrohom Chaim Feuer, *The Tzedakah Treasury: An Anthology of Torah Teachings on the Mitzvah of Charity—To Teach and Inspire* (New Rochelle, NY: Mesorah Publications, 2000); Gildas Hamel, *Poverty and Charity in Roman Palestine, First Three Centuries C.E.*, Near Eastern Studies 23 (Berkeley: University of California Press, 1990), 164–221; Susan R. Holman, *The Hungry Are Dying: Beggars and Bishops in Roman Cappadocia* (New York: Oxford, 2001), 43–48; Rabbi Yisrael Meir Kahan (the "Chafetz Chaim"), *Ahavath Chesed: The Love of Kindness as Required by God*, trans. Leonard Oschry, 2nd ed. (Jerusalem: Feldheim, 1976); Lothar Ruppert, "The Foreigner and Association with Foreigners in the Old and New Testaments," in *To Hear and Obey: Essays in Honor of Fredrick Carlson Holmgren*, ed. Bradley J. Bergfalk and Paul E. Koptak (Chicago: Covenant Publications, 1997), 151–63; Moshe Weinfeld, *Social Justice in Ancient Israel and in the Ancient Near East* (Minneapolis: Fortress Press, 1995). For the medieval period, see Mark R. Cohen, *Poverty and Charity in the Jewish Community of Medieval Egypt* (Princeton, NJ: Princeton University Press, 2005); and idem, *The Voice of the Poor in the Middle Ages: An Anthology of Documents from the Cairo Geniza* (Princeton, NJ: Princeton University Press, 2005).

The Hellenic Background

The principles of *philanthrōpia, agapē, dikaiosynē* (justice), *eleos* (mercy), *philoxenia* (hospitality), *aretē* (virtue), and *isonomia* (equality under the law) were not abstract ideas but realized experiences in the history of ancient Hellenism. Their practice, of course, was conditioned by changing political, social, and institutional developments. Demosthenes, the Athenian orator (384–322 BCE), declared that "the laws ordain nothing that is cruel or violent or oligarchic and provisions are made in a democratic and philanthropic spirit."[8]

Inspired by the ethical teachings of Socrates of Athens (469–399 BCE), Zeno of Cyprus (335–263 BCE), the founder of Stoicism, taught that the only real good (*agathon*) is virtue (*aretē*) and that the only real evil is moral weakness. Stoicism, whose influence on the religions of late antiquity is acknowledged by many scholars, emphasized the practical concerns of ethics, including the application of compassion and philanthropy. Under the influence of Stoicism, Greek *philanthrōpia*, as well as other principles of private and public ethics, transcended ethnocentric concerns. What was practiced in the past as public responsibility for civic and cultural objectives was extended now to include compassion and mercy toward all humans. Stoics subscribed to the belief that all belonged to one humanity.

Was the conversion to Christianity a logical, rational choice? Was it based on spiritual reflection or on selfish impulses for the benefit of future gains? Dependence on culture was a powerful principle that linked one generation with the next. Early Christians accepted Christ without rejecting their cultural heritage. Culture determined what people wanted, how they thought, felt, interacted, and acted. Affinity and cultural flexibility influenced the development from ancient Hellenism to Christian Hellenism, from pagan Roman to Christian Roman.

Thus in searching for the Hellenic background and the nature of patristic philanthropy, we should look to the mind, motivation, and traditions that shaped the thought and *diakonia* of the fathers. We need to enter into the non-Christian and the Greek Christian mind if we are to discern whether there is continuity or discontinuity between the two. When Christians spoke of *philanthrōpia, agapē, eleos,* and *storgē,* they spoke as receivers from a society that preexisted. They subscribed to a new faith, but they lived in an old culture. I wonder which is more powerful and influential, faith or cultural traditions?

On the one hand, there is little doubt that early Christian philanthropy derived much inspiration from the teachings of the Old and New Testaments.

8. Demosthenes, *Against Timocrates* 24.1, trans. J. H. Vince, LCL 299 (Cambridge, MA: Harvard University Press, 1935); cf. Demosthenes, *On the Crown*, trans. C. A. Vince and J. H. Vince, LCL 155 (Cambridge, MA: Harvard University Press, 1926), 108–12.

On the other hand, inspiration was also derived from the established ethos of the culture in which Christians lived and worked. When one religion replaces another, the underground belief and inherent psychological and mental ethos survive and contribute to the emergence of an interrelationship, to a thread that is woven and establishes bonds between the old and the new. The patristic thought and philanthropic activity of the fourth century, which established the standards for later Byzantine thought and praxis, was the work of spiritually careful and thoughtful church leaders who worked toward a synthesis between the new faith and the old culture.

The ancient Greeks practiced philanthropy as benevolence and humanitarianism as a natural bond of love for the common good, as outlined below. It was in this sense that the term *philanthrōpia* was used by Xenophon, Plato, Aristotle, Demosthenes, Isocrates, Diogenes Laertius, Hippocrates, and Plutarch. However, the term *philanthrōpia* was introduced as a theocentric concept by Aeschylus. The Divinity, or God, is philanthropic toward humanity; humanity, in turn, should imitate the attributes of the Divinity. As a theocentric concept, it reaches out for the human, which appropriates and puts it into practice. Thus *philanthrōpia* becomes also anthropocentric. Aeschylus reminds us that Prometheus, the demigod, decided to bring to earth fire and empower humans with knowledge and skills because of his great *philanthrōpia* for the future of humankind. He was bound to a crag and had his liver eaten daily, an image often identified with crucifixion, because of his love for humans.[9] Centuries later, Paul of Tarsus wrote that the *philanthrōpia* of God for the salvation of humankind became manifest through the incarnation of God's Logos (Titus 3:4). In both cases, the torment of Prometheus and that of Jesus the Christ were identified with their *philanthrōpia* for humanity.

The Divinity's love for humankind is expressed through other terms: *agapaō, agapē, agapētos,* and *phileō, philios, philotēs,* from which we have the term *philanthrōpia—philein ton anthrōpon,* to love the human being. While *agapaō* and *agapē* are rarely used in the Homeric epics and the later Greek literature, *phileō, philos, philotēs* appear four times as often as *agapaō, agapē.* It is in the postclassical literature of both Greeks and Greek-speaking Jews—the Septuagint, the New Testament, the papyri, Plutarch, and others— that *agapē* and *philanthrōpia* appear as synonyms.

Even in the so-called Koine Greek and the Christian patristic language, *philanthrōpia* as a theocentric concept appears more frequently than agapē. In Liddell and Scott's, as well as Lampe's, classical and patristic dictionaries of the Greek language, *philanthropeō, philanthrōpia,* and their derivatives cover two and a half large columns. Both terms were used to stress that humans

9. διὰ τὴν λίαν φιλότητα βροτῶν, Aeschylus, *Prometheus Bound* 123; cf. 11, 28, φιλανθρώπου τρόπου.

must imitate the Divine and extend their love not only to kin and friends but to all in need of love, whether in expression of word or in practical application. The word *philanthrōpia* became a standard term in the transition between pagan and Christian Hellenism—intentionally appealing to the past in Christianity's self-presentation. In Homer's *Odyssey*, "a stranger in need," a *xenos*, a suppliant, was held to be equal to a brother. A stranger must be received with philanthropy because he or she was God's agent—usually sent by Zeus.[10]

Centuries later Plato emphasized that the virtue of *philanthrōpia* in practice cultivates the human ethos, refines the human character, and promotes friendship. As the Divinity's *philanthrōpia* is manifest in various ways, humans must practice *philanthrōpia* to achieve inner satisfaction and to improve society. The *dōrētēs*, the philanthropist, benefits twice—first, because of the inner satisfaction that comes with giving, and second, because he (or she) is helping fellow humans.

Plato's emphasis on the need for *philanthrōpia* did not remain a philosophical yearning. He condemned the existence of poverty, which he considered an impediment to a happy society. "There must be no place for poverty in any section of the population, nor yet of opulence, as both breed either consequence." In a democracy poverty is not disgraceful but as a source of illiberality and evil becomes an impediment to innovation and progress. In a genuine democracy "neither is a man rejected because of weakness, poverty or obscurity of origin, nor honored by reason of the opposite."[11]

Aristotle, Plato's disciple, stressed the importance of justice, condemned poverty, and emphasized that extremes of wealth and poverty could undermine democracy. The only way to prevent social conflicts and civil wars is to establish just balance and fair distribution of goods and resources. Aristotle's *Nicomachean Ethics*, book 5, outlines Aristotle's views on philanthropy, social justice, and relative or proportionate equality under the law based on social status; Aristotle's *Politics* 3.1–10 offers a similar discussion. Beliefs and teachings like those of Plato, Aristotle, and Zeno were inherited and sustained habitually and unreflectively. Few are the cases of people who change religious allegiance because of intellectual or spiritual questioning. Those Greeks who converted to Christianity came from a climate where the teachings and the practices of the ancient Greeks were familiar to them. Were Plato's teachings on virtue, justice, and soul less Christian than the teachings of the Scriptures? "Asclepius is good for the body but Plato for the immortal soul," writes Plato's disciple Heraclides of Pontus.[12] Was Aristotle's

10. Homer, *Odyssey* 19.17; 23.214. See also *Iliad* 24.464.

11. Plato, *Republic* 8.552c; 14.421; *Laws* 5.744; *Protagoras* 319d; *Menexenus* 238d; in *Plato: The Collected Dialogues*, ed. and trans. Edith Hamilton and H. Cairns, Bollingen Series 71 (Princeton, NJ: Princeton University Press, 1985).

12. Heraclides Ponticus, *Epigrammata* 7.108.

emphasis on relative social justice, his views that material insufficiency hinders democracy and is a cause of social uprisings and the root of civil wars, less Christian than the ethics of the Bible?

Whether for selfish or patriotic reasons there were many philanthropists in Athens and in other Greek city-states. Solon, Pisistratus, Themistocles, Callias, and Cimon were highly regarded for their philanthropies. For example, Plutarch writes that Solon's father was a wealthy man but that he used much of his wealth for philanthropies and the common good, to the extent that Solon inherited little, and when impoverished, he was embarrassed to seek assistance and was forced to turn to trade and earn a living from an early age (*Solon* 2). Athenians, such as Cimon, Ephialtes, and Aristides, were not only outstanding civil servants but also popular because of their philanthropic policies.

Philanthropy was not practiced by Athenians only. For example, it was customary for Cretans to honor strangers by giving them first place at dinner. The *xenos* is still the unknown god in Crete, writes N. Kazantzakis; the ethics of *philoxenia* is sacred to the present day in the Greek world.[13] But giving in ancient Greece was not done without any discrimination. It was given to those who were regarded as deserving it. Idle beggars were turned away. Plutarch relates that when a beggar asked for charity from a Spartan, the Spartan answered: "If I were to give to you, you would become poorer. Your present miserable condition was caused by the first person who gave to you and made you lazy."[14] Concerning discrimination in giving, as we indicated before, Aristotle writes that to give away money is an easy matter and in any man's power, but to decide to whom to give it and how large and when, and for what purpose and how, is neither in every man's power nor an easy matter (*Nicomachean Ethics* 7.3.14–4.6 and 8.9.5–14.4). Hence, to achieve such excellence is rare, praiseworthy, and noble.

Pisistratus, the Athenian archon, enjoyed the reputation of a man moderate in his way of life and generous toward his fellow citizens. He had no fences around his properties and had no guards around his gardens. Anyone who wanted to pick crops and fruits from his estates was free to do so. Cimon was also highly praised for his magnanimous and philanthropic attitude toward his fellow Athenians, the poor in particular. Cimon had stationed no guards in any of his fields and gardens, so that any citizen who wanted could go in and receive. Furthermore, he had an open house, preparing plain meals for many, inviting the poor people in particular to dinner. He would distribute money to the poor every day and provide for the burial of others. If he saw someone badly dressed, he would give him money to buy better clothes.

13. Nikos Kazantzakis, *Anaphora ston Gkreko: Mythistorēma*, 3rd ed. (Athens: H. Kazantzakē, 1965), 373.
14. Plutarch, *Apophthegmata Laconica* 56 (235D10–E1).

In brief, the needs of the suffering were a matter of both private and public, personal and collective responsibility, individual and community benevolence. If the standard of measuring the value of a culture is not the military power or the magnitude of scientific achievements but the extent of reverence, compassion, justice, and philanthropy, ancient Greek culture deserves high grades. Thus when Plutarch writes that Cimon's *philanthrōpia* surpassed even the traditional *philanthrōpia* of Athens, he drew from the history of Athens and his own observations.[15] The spirit of material generosity (*euergetism*) among the ancient Greeks was always related to religious faith and practice.[16]

Were the *chorēgoi* of the postclassical Hellenic era less philanthropic than those of the Christian church? The *chorēgoi*, known also as *euergetai*, assumed the expenses for schools, athletic competitions, and public events, such as liturgies for the *penētes*, the poor, but also for the *metoikoi* (the resident aliens). Some *chorēgoi* were motivated by altruistic, humanitarian, or patriotic spirit. Others, however, made their philanthropies not for a gain in heaven or eternal salvation, but for self-display and vainglory. In a sense the *chorēgoi* can be designated as philanthropists.[17]

Hellenic women were also greatly involved in philanthropic activity. For example, Nausicaa and her mother, Arete, are the first classical examples of feminine philanthropy of pre-Christian Hellenism. Naked and exhausted from his struggle against the waves, the long-suffering Odysseus is lying on the beach. Nausicaa, who was first to see him, was not ashamed because of his nakedness, nor did she become frightened seeing his sea-buffeted body. Immediately she felt that a fellow human had need of help. And spontaneously, with true sympathy and affection, she called her friends and handmaids who were playing on the shore:

> "Come, this unfortunate came here shipwrecked
> and we must save him, because Zeus
> sends the poor and foreigners," shouted Nausicaa.
> "Well come, girls, give him to eat—water for the stranger
> and wash him in the river, in a place sheltered from the wind."
> And the girls stood and one pushed the other
> and to a shady place they led the divine
> Odysseus . . . they placed clothing near him
> a cup full of oil and they invited him
> to wash in the river stream. . . .

15. ἡ δὲ Κίμωνος ἀφθονία καὶ τὴν παλαιὰν τῶν Ἀθηναίων φιλοξενίαν καὶ φιλανθρωπίαν ὑπερέβαλεν, Plutarch, *Cimon* 10.1–6.

16. S. R. F. Price, "Between Man and God: Sacrifice in the Roman Imperial Cult," *JRS* 70 (1980): 41. Cited by MacMullen, *Christianity and Paganism*, 184n37.

17. For the role of the *chorēgoi*, see Peter James Wilson, "Choregia," in *OCD*, 323–24.

> And Nausicaa emphasized: "Cheerful must be
> the little that you give."[18]

Nausicaa carried out a divine order and in a spontaneous manner, natural, disinterested, and cheerful. This same kind of philanthropy was shown by her mother, Arete, when Odysseus arrived at their home. This kind of philanthropic ethos was inherited by the classical age, and in later centuries other women found prototypes in the persons of Penelope, Nausicaa and Arete, including Isodice, wife of the most philanthropic Cimon; Agariste, mother of the famous Pericles; and Elpinice, wife of the peacemaker Callias.[19]

Centuries later, in the drama *Alcestis*, Euripides makes *philoxenia*—philanthropy—a presupposition of salvation and emphasizes that the heroic Alcestis sacrificed herself to save her husband and to secure the happiness of her children. She was perceived as a prototype of a devoted wife and affectionate mother, whose philanthropy is considered by Plato and a series of tomb epigrams as an example worthy of imitation. "By her sacrifice, Alcestis showed that true human kinship is the natural bond of love."[20] For this reason, centuries later Christianized Hellenism adopted many of the spiritual and moral values of ancient Hellenism. The Homeric aforementioned advice to "be like a brother to the stranger and suppliant" finds its echo in "I give hospitality to the stranger so that God will not become a stranger." "A stranger and a poor person are God's bread," the Greek Christian fathers will say later. And the ancient Greek moral principle that "man resembles God when he does the good" will be repeated later by Gregory the Theologian and other fathers with the words, "Nothing relates man more to God than benevolent acts."[21]

In later Greek antiquity—the so-called Hellenistic era, following the death of Alexander the Great—many women devoted their personal time and money for the common good and philanthropic purposes. For example, an inscription of the second century BCE praises the generosity of one Euxenia, probably the granddaughter of the great Philopoemen, general of the Achaean federation from Megalopolis. Euxenia built a temple that served as a hostelry for visitors and strangers to rest. Furthermore, she used much of her personal wealth to benefit Megalopolis, her birthplace.

---

18. Homer, *Odyssey* 6.206–12, 214–16, with Nausicaa's reply at 6.208. Some translations render δόσις as "kindness," which misses the meaning. A freer translation might be, "The little that you may give should be given cheerfully."

19. D. J. Constantelos, "Women and Philanthropy in the History of Hellenism" [Greek], in idem, *The Byzantine Legacy in the Orthodox Church* (in Greek: *Byzantinē Klēronomia*) (Athens: Damaskos Publications, 1990), 117–27.

20. Bruce S. Thornton, *Eros: The Myth of Ancient Greek Sexuality* (Boulder, CO: Westview Press, 1997), 182–83; D. J. Iakovou, "Alkisti, of Euripides," *Ellēnika* 36 (1985): 244–45.

21. Gregory Nazianzus, *Hom.* 14.27 (*De pauperum amore* 27), PG 36:892C–893A.

In the same category of benefactors of communities, individuals, and citizens also belongs Menodora from Silliounta of Pisidia. Menodora was praised because she distributed large quantities of wheat to her fellow citizens and donated 300,000 denarii for assistance and support of orphaned children there. Atalanta also, from Teremesso of Asia Minor, promised to distribute wheat annually for the "mass of people," a promise that she kept in the time of famine. Atalanta also benefited the city and its citizens in several other ways—with gifts to the poor, loans, and the building of stores in the city. And Artemis from Sardis, wife of Platonianus, was honored by fellow citizens with a statue, because she had spent her personal wealth for establishments for the common good.[22] In brief, classical scholars remind us that ancient Greek social thought is ethical in nature. "The ethical strongly permeates all the Greek writings."[23]

The Platonic and Aristotelian ideas, which stressed that "something divine is present in man," first contributed to the belief of the naturalness of the ethical impulse and of care for people in need. Later, both Stoicism and Cynicism emphasized the role of *philanthrōpia*, based on the recognition of the kinship among humans. Justice exists by nature; thus humans are altruistic by nature.[24] Humanistic values were promoted, forgiveness was emphasized and revenge was condemned.

The philosopher Epictetus relates a story that illustrates this point. He writes of a young man who had blinded the Lacedaemonian leader Lycurgus in one eye. When he was handed over to Lycurgus by the people, Lycurgus did not punish him but educated and counseled him to become a good person. The young man was brought before the Lacedaemonian assembly in the theater to hear the verdict of punishment. As the people looked and wondered, Lycurgus turned to them and said: "This man, when you surrendered him to me, was insolent and violent. I give him back to you free and reasonable."[25] *Philanthrōpia* began as a theocentric concept in Aeschylus, and it continued to be practiced as both a religious and a cultural inheritance. *Philanthrōpia* continued to be an essential virtue in the postclassical era of Hellenism. The cosmopolitan philosophies of Stoicism, Cynicism, and even Epicureanism implied compassion and concern for the fellow human being. When Diogenes the Cynic was asked where he came from, he answered that

22. Constantelos, "Women and Philanthropy."

23. Joseph B. Gittler, *Social Thought among the Early Greeks* (Athens: University of Georgia Press, 1941), 13.

24. Hilda D. Oakeley, *Greek Ethical Thought* (Freeport, NY: Books for Libraries Press, 1971), 147–51; A. Laks and M. Schofield, eds., *Justice and Generosity: Studies in Hellenistic Social and Political Philosophy; Proceedings of the Sixth Symposium Hellenisticum* (Cambridge: Cambridge University Press, 1992), esp. the studies by J. L. Moles and M. Schofield, 129–58, in particular 140–41; and 191–212, especially 204–5. See also John Ferguson, *Moral Values in the Ancient World* (London: Methuen,1958), 102–17.

25. H. Schenkl, ed., *Epicteti Dissertationes* (Teubner, 1894), *Peri philias*, para. 5.

he was a *cosmopolitēs*, a "citizen of the world." It has been rightly observed that Diogenes' cosmopolitan ideas, which emphasized the oneness of humanity, rested on the concept of *philanthrōpia*, the belief that human beings should care for one another. Centuries later, Diogenes of Oinoanda (second century CE), who represented basic teachings of Epicureanism, identified the good person with the one who practiced philanthropy. When he was asked who is a good man (*chrēstos anthrōpos*), he answered, "the man who helps philanthropically" (*philanthrōpōs boēthein*). Our people, he writes, are not people of the same race, but those who are philanthropists.[26] Church fathers trained in the Greek classics could not have ignored the ethical teaching of their own intellectual background. Basil of Caesarea, addressing himself to Christians, said, "We should feel shame at the stories about the philanthropy practiced among the Hellenes. There is a law among them providing the enjoining of the whole community at a single table and food in common."[27]

The Early Christian Background

In addition to the Hellenic thought and practice of philanthropy, we need to consider the teachings of the Bible on charity. The influence of the Hebrew Bible on Christian social ethics is well known. The emphasis on charity, love for a *xenos*, that we find in the Pentateuch (Torah) might refer to needy members both inside and outside the covenant community.[28] The neighbor could be a fellow Israelite (Deut. 15:7–11; Lev. 19:17–18), but a "stranger"—a foreigner in need of philanthropy—might be a member of a foreign people (such as Egyptians or Babylonians) who are in Israel temporarily; the Hebrew Bible uses the terms *nokri* or *zar* for these foreigners. Or the stranger might be a *ger*—a term that included non-Jews who settled in the country for a certain period—or a *tosab*, a so-called sojourner. While the first two groups of strangers are dwelling among the Israelites temporarily, the *ger* and the *tosab* are more permanent strangers, usually with restricted rights (for example, servants, slaves, or others who are not permitted to own land).

Distribution of alms to the poor of the fellow Israelites was perceived as an act that pleased, and would bring rewards from, God. The ethical teachings of the Old Testament were addressed to a covenant people and were intended to serve the needs of a defined society. The command, "Open wide your hands to the poor and needy neighbor in your land" (Deut. 15:11; Lev. 19:1–37), was intended for charity within the Hebrew community, help for the poor of Israel, but might also include non-Jews.

26. Diogenes Laertius 6.2.63. See also John Linton Myres, "Diogenes the Cynic" in *OCD*, 473.
27. Basil, *Homilia dicta tempore famis et siccitatis* 8, PG 31:325.10–12.
28. See, e.g., Ruppert, "Foreigner and Association with Foreigners."

Much on philanthropy in the Talmud builds on the principle that such charity begins at home. One's first obligation was to care for fellow Jews. For Moses Maimonides (1135–1204), "the greatest form of charity, which is unsurpassed by any other, is to give a helping hand to a Jew who is on the verge of financial ruin . . . in other words, support him before he falls and becomes needy."[29] But Talmudic and Tannaitic literature did not limit philanthropy to coreligionists, stating explicitly that God "is gracious and gives his bounty as a free gift both to those who know him and to those who do not. So shall you give free gifts."[30] And modern Jewish scholars of social justice in ancient Israel point to the Gospel teaching in Matt. 25 (the duty to feed the hungry, give drink to the thirsty, clothe the naked, visit the sick, and care for prisoners) as a tradition that drew on Jewish norms.[31]

While Greek Christians therefore shared certain philanthropic values and concerns with their Jewish contemporaries, they also looked back to classical and Hellenistic Greek authors for such ideals as forgiving one's enemies, which, for example, was considered a divine and typically Athenian virtue by Socrates and Plato, down to Libanius in the fourth century CE.[32] The church, especially after the reign of Constantine, placed more emphasis than its pre-Christian Greek culture on philanthropy toward the poor, widows, orphans, strangers, and sick. The Christianization of the empire led the church to set new standards and new methods in its philanthropic ministries.[33]

To what degree were Christianity's teachings about philanthropy and attitudes toward poverty and social ethics different from those that prevailed in the Greco-Roman world? Several early church fathers emphasized that philanthropy became a distinction for Christians and the means by which Christianity was able to attract people to its fold. To be sure, there were other motives for the acceptance of the new religion: the need to belong, for one. The poor and rootless were attracted to an ideology that stressed, "There is no longer Jew or Greek, there is no longer slave or free, there is no longer male and female; for all of you are one in Christ Jesus" (Gal. 3:28; see also Col. 3:11). In the Byzantine era—especially in the thought and ethical teachings of church fathers such as Gregory the Theologian, John Chrysostom, Maximus the Confessor, and others—church fathers emphasized the practice of *philanthrōpia* in imitation of God's *philanthrōpia*.

29. Rambam, "Laws of Gifts to the Poor," chap. 10, Halachah 7, as quoted in Feuer, *Tzedakah Treasury*, 55.

30. Quoted in Kahan, *Ahavath Chesed*, 97.

31. See, e.g., Weinfeld, *Social Justice*, 19.

32. A. H. M. Jones, *The Later Roman Empire, 284–602* (Norman: University of Oklahoma Press, 1964), 1:970–71; cf. Ramsay MacMullen, *Christianizing the Roman Empire* (New Haven: Yale University Press, 1984), 52–56.

33. See Peter Brown, *Poverty and Leadership in the Later Roman Empire* (Hanover, NH: University Press of New England, 2002), 1–73.

A God of sacrificial love demanded a sacrificial love from his followers, because "God so loved the world that he gave his only Son, so that everyone who believes in him may not perish but may have eternal life" (John 3:16). Christianity, at least in theory, removed boundaries and broke down racial and ethnic fences (Gal. 3:28). While philanthropy in the Greco-Roman world was often practiced as a social obligation of the individual citizen, intended to serve and improve the community (such were the donations of the *chorēgoi*), philanthropy as an expression of love and empathy from person to person was never absent. However, it was in Christianity that the poor man or woman was discovered as a person (*prosōpon*), equal to the wealthy and the prominent. Philanthropy was advocated as selfless love for the individual person. In its theology, philanthropy went beyond Jews, Greeks, and Romans. It stressed that "love is of God; everyone who loves is born of God and knows God. Whoever does not love does not know God, for God is love" (1 John 4:7–8). God's love requires that people love one another (1 John 4:11). There is no better account of the nature and the fruits of Christian charity than 1 Cor. 13. *Agapē* is defined as the love of God expressed through the God-made-human evident in Christ and as people's love of neighbor, the solvent of hatred of the enemy. It was on the basis of Christian theology that Paul encouraged the practice of *diakonia* and conducted collections for the poor in Jerusalem. However, the *diakonia* of the early church was highly motivated by what Christ had taught. The philanthropic theology of the fathers and the philanthropic *diakonia* of the church in history was greatly influenced by the sacrificial love of Christ (John 3:16) and also by his teaching, as in Matt. 25:34–40:

> Come, you that are blessed by my Father, inherit the kingdom prepared for you from the foundation of the world; for I was hungry and you gave me food, I was thirsty and you gave me something to drink, I was a stranger and you welcomed me, I was naked and you gave me clothing, I was sick and you took care of me, I was in prison and you visited me. . . . Truly I tell you, just as you did it to one of the least of these who are members of my family, you did it to me.

The words of Christ about the last judgment (Matt. 25:31–46) motivated many Christians to practice philanthropy, either in obedience to Christ or because of fear of the consequences to those who do not care for the poor.

Patristic Thought and Witness on Philanthropy

I do not know a better definition of *philanthrōpia* in early Christian literature than the one that appears in the pseudo-Clementine homilies, whose authorship is dated to the third century CE. We read there:

The greatness of *philanthrōpia* lies in the fact that it means love [*storgē*] toward anyone, whatever one may be as a person, including physical appearance . . . *philanthrōpia* loves and benefits every person because every person is a human being [*anthrōpos*] apart from personal beliefs . . . the philanthropic person does good even to enemies . . . every person is neighbor to every person and not merely to this or that person. For the good and the bad, the friend and the enemy, are alike human beings. It behooves, therefore, the person who practices philanthropy to be an imitator of God, doing good to the righteous and the unrighteous, as God Himself graciously gives His sun and His heavens to all in the present world.[34]

The *Epistle to Diognetus* is another important source illustrating the kind of God Christians worshiped and were instructed to imitate. The unknown author exhorts Diognetus to embrace the Christian faith, that it may lead him to love a God who would inspire imitation and to achieve happiness.[35] Happiness, he writes, is not a matter of dominating one's neighbors, or in the desire to possess more than the weak, or in wealth or in power exercised over those under one's authority. One cannot imitate God in such ways, since those ways are foreign to God's greatness. An imitator of God is one who takes up another's burden, or desires to help another in need from one's own abundance, or shares the blessings received from God with those less fortunate, and so one becomes a "god" to them in their need. *Philostorgia* (heartfelt love) and *philanthrōpia* are central in the thought of the author.

Several early church fathers wrote about the practice of philanthropy by the church. Irenaeus of Lyons relates that in the second century many non-Christians went to Christian meeting places expecting to see miracles, and some saw that Christians "heal the sick by laying hands on them, and drive out demons." In praise of the Christian impression on nonbelievers, Irenaeus claimed, "We even raise the dead, many of whom are still alive among us, and completely healthy."[36] The miraculous element was one of the reasons that Christianity was popular in cities such as Alexandria, Antioch, Carthage, Corinth, and Thessalonica.

Other early Christian writers attributed the popularity of Christianity to philanthropic activity. Christians contributed money voluntarily to a common fund to support orphans, widows, the sick, and the destitute; to bring food and medicines to needy people; and to buy coffins. They dug graves to bury strangers, the poor, and even criminals.[37]

34. Ps.-Clement, *Hom.* 12.25–26; cf. Clement of Alexandria, *Stromateis* 2.23.
35. *Epistle to Diognetus* 8–10. See also *The Constitutions of the Holy Apostles* 4, in *ANF* 7, 443–44.
36. *Adversus Haereses* 2.32.4.
37. Tertullian, *Apology* 39, ed. and trans. T. R. Glover, LCL 250 (Cambridge, MA: Harvard University Press, 1931), 173–82.

Early Christians impressed non-Christians with their altruism and defiance of death. An account attributed to the physician Galen relates that "the people named Christians have contempt for death, they are characterized by self-control in sexual matters, they possess self-discipline in matters of food, drink and a keen pursuit of justice." Galen was no friend of Christians, and the comments attributed to him carry a special weight.[38]

The altruistic behavior of Christians toward non-Christians created an animosity against them and often ridicule. Their expression of love among themselves, which they extended to others who were poor, sick, and in need, also made them admirable. Tertullian adds, "What marks us in the eyes of our enemies is our practice of *philanthrōpia*—love: 'only look,' they say, 'look how they love one another.' "[39]

Early Christianity attracted many people of all social and intellectual backgrounds for a variety of reasons, to the extent that the Roman government became alarmed. Tertullian relates, "The outcry is that the state is filled with Christians—that they are in the fields, in the cities, in the islands . . . both men and women, of every age and condition, even high rank, are going over to profess Christian faith."[40]

While there were many seekers after God, the majority of the early Christians were those who sought miracles and healing, as Irenaeus suggests, and also those who were poor and destitute. Both canonical and apocryphal literature emphasized the need for philanthropy, equality, and service to the needy. In addition to the well-known teachings of Christ in Matthew's gospel (Matt. 25:31–46), the *Gospel of Truth*, one of the noncanonical writings, urges "those who have stumbled to extend their hands to those who are sick; feed those who are hungry; give rest to those who are tired; and raise up those who wish to rise" (33.1–7). Christ was depicted as a miracle worker who heals the sick, a savior from illness.[41]

The tradition of the early church carried into the post-Constantinian era. In addition to the early Christian experience, the church of the fourth century and beyond was guided by two other forces in its philanthropic activity. Christians had come to appreciate the moral teachings of their intellectual background and also the attitude of Christian emperors.

38. R. Walzer, *Galen on Jews and Christians* (London: Oxford University Press, 1949), 15.

39. Tertullian, *Apology*, op. cit. 39, p. 176.

40. Tertullian, *Apology* 1, p. 4. An excellent study on what attracted Jews and gentiles to Christianity in the first three centuries is Dionysios G. Dakouras, *Conversion to Christianity of Jews and Gentiles according to Christian Sources of the First Three Centuries* [Greek] (Athens: A. N. Sakoulas, 1988).

41. See *Gospel of Truth* 32.35–33.30; an English translation is available in Bart D. Ehrman, ed., *Lost Scriptures: Books That Did Not Make It into the New Testament* (New York: Oxford University Press, 2003), 50.

Church fathers such as the Cappadocians, whose writings and pastoral examples became prototypes for later clergy, were well read in the Greek classical authors Plato, Aristotle, and Zeno, who emphasized the morality of philanthropy and justice, as discussed above.

As Christians, the emperors patronized philanthropic activity. Constantine delegated to a number of bishops the distribution of grain and other necessities to people in need. The bishops exhorted the whole church to philanthropic activity,[42] which was not limited to distribution of goods to the poor, but also included care for orphans, widows, and the elderly. Almsgiving was an expected duty of every believer.

The devotion of the early postapostolic church to philanthropic *diakonia* is attested by several sources, Christian and non-Christian alike. The principles of philanthropy and social work were highly emphasized by the *Didache*. For the author of the *Didache, philanthrōpia* needs to be practiced in imitation of Christ: "Since we have the Lord Jesus Christ as our teacher, we ought to follow his teachings. He rejected comfort, wealth, power, glory; and out of obedience to the Father and his *philanthrōpia* for us, he suffered persecution, ridicule and ultimately crucifixion on our behalf." Thus care for orphans and widows, shelter for strangers and travelers, bread for the hungry, drink for the thirsty, clothes for the naked, visits to the sick, help to prisoners, and daily almsgiving were highly recommended by Clement of Rome, Ignatius of Antioch, Polycarp of Smyrna, Tertullian of Carthage, and others who took seriously the admonitions of Christ.

It was after the fourth century, when the persecution under Diocletian ceased and the Roman Empire adjusted to the realities of Christianity's popularity—and the church's adjustment to the secular world—that Christian philanthropy was institutionalized, especially after Constantine's reign. The church either took the initiative to build or was charged with the supervision of hospitals, orphanages, *gerokomeia, ptōcheia, xenotapheia*, reformatory institutions, and other social welfare services built by emperors or individuals.

Examples of institutions mentioned in fourth-century sources are the *xenodocheion*, a hospice supported by bishops, and the monastic communities, which received pilgrims and the poor. In her pilgrimage to the Greek East, the Latin nun Egeria, or Aetheria, was received very hospitably by the monks who offered her and her companions every courtesy in their *xenodocheion*.[43] In the same century Basil of Caesarea confirms that a *xenodocheion* provided services for sick people. He urged those who served the sick in the *xenodocheion* to serve them with a good disposition, as if the sick were brothers of the Lord.

42. Eusebius, *Life of Constantine* 1.43.
43. Egeria [Aetheria], *Diary of a Pilgrimage*, trans. George E. Gingras (New York: Newman Press, 1970), 51–167.

Philanthropic *diakonia* was no longer just almsgiving from person to person; it was also services through philanthropic organizations. Patristic sources indicate that Christians were not concerned with what non-Christians thought of them. They did not try to persuade in order to attract pagans and other nonbelievers but to emphasize the superiority of Christianty, which preached equality, justice, and love to all. They believed that Christianity wins more adherents by the philanthropic life of the faithful than by a discussion of its merits. It impressed even its enemies, such as Lucian, Galen, and Emperor Julian.

The philanthropic *diakonia* was evident not only in the church but also as practiced by members of the imperial court, wealthy individuals, and monastic communities. *Philanthrōpia* was considered one of the necessary virtues of the emperor. Basil of Caesarea's concern with both the theology of the Trinity and care for the poor and hungry is one example of how patristic theology did not divorce faith and spiritual life from involvement with social issues and problems. Patristic thought emphasized that "nothing makes man liken himself to God more than doing good [*to eupoiein*]" (Gregory of Nazianzus, *Or.* 14.27), a principle that echoes the ancient Greek admonition that "to give aid to all in need . . . through your own generosity, is to achieve immortality."[44]

In the course of time, the church developed a theology of philanthropy on the basis of its Christology and its ecclesiology and eschatology. The ecclesiological basis for philanthropy in *diakonia* was the belief that the church is the Christ perpetuated unto the ages, that it is a community whose task is to rebuild society on new foundations. The liturgies and sacramental services, patristic writings, and hagiology express the belief that Christians are members of a "holy nation," "a kingdom of God" on earth. They must therefore adopt, consecrate, become involved with, and administer social services. Christian philanthropy expanded from almsgiving to a wide variety of community social services through institutions.

As a result, in the early Christian societies of both the Greek East and the Latin West, *philanthrōpia* assumed an integrated and far-reaching meaning, its application directed to the humblest and the poorest. *Philanthrōpia* extended to the underprivileged, as it proclaimed freedom, equality, and brotherhood, transcending sex, race, and national boundaries. Thus it was not limited to equals, allies, and relatives, or to citizens and civilized men, as was most often the case in other ancient societies.[45]

44. A. R. Hands, *Charities and Social Aid in Greece and Rome* (Ithaca, NY: Cornell University Press, 1968), 56.

45. See D. J. Constantelos, *Byzantine Philanthropy and Social Welfare*, 2nd ed. (New Rochelle, NY: A. D. Caratzas, 1991); and idem, *Poverty, Society and Philanthropy* (New Rochelle, NY: A. D. Caratzas, 1992).

In the case of the imperial authority, philanthropy was also expressed in the form of legislation intended to protect what today are called human rights. This included measures to avoid imposition of the death penalty as far as possible without endangering public welfare; improve the legal position of women (for example, in cases of child custody, inheritance, and property ownership); protect poor peasant farmers against the encroachments of rich landowners; and recognize slaves as people rather than property (for example, by according to them the right to marry and enjoy the legal benefits of lawful marriage). This list could be expanded. These measures were far from perfect, but they do suggest that the Byzantine Empire was concerned with human dignity. Church fathers emphasized the worth of every human, that every person carries the image of God, is destined to achieve the likeness of God. John Chrysostom illustrates this when he writes:

> I have no contempt for anyone, for every person is worthy of our attention as a creation of God, even the lowest among the slaves. I am not concerned with the social position of a person but with a person's virtue. I do not look at a master or a slave but a human person. It is for the human being that the heaven opened, the sun shines, the moon rises, the air fills everything, the springs well-up water, the sea stretches out immeasurably. It was for the human person that the only begotten son of God became human. My Lord shed his blood for the human being. Who am I to have contempt for any human being? How should I expect to be forgiven if I would do so?[46]

What kind of social conditions prevailed that motivated the church to conduct its rich philanthropic ministry in the fourth century and beyond? There exist a great number of poor, of course. We do not know the number of the poor in either urban centers or the countryside, nor do we know whether the church concentrated its philanthropic work among the poor of the cities or reached out to the poor of the provincial towns and villages. While there were prosperous peasants and wealthy landlords, craftsmen, merchants, traders, civic servants, and people of the professions who lived a comfortable life, the poverty of many peasants was chronic. Equally, the condition of the working class in urban centers was no better. Poor crops, famines, ruthless taxation, and unscrupulous landlords forced many peasants to leave behind their possessions and flee to towns seeking the basic means for survival. But life in the city was no improvement. All were heavily taxed. In Constantinople as in ancient Rome, city officials sometimes supplied the poor with cheap bread in times of shortages, but the poor in most cities depended on churches and individual philanthropy for such supplemental food.

How many poor were there in Constantinople, Alexandria, Antioch, Nicaea, Ephesus, and other cities of a similar size? We do not really know. That

---

46. *In Lazarum*, PG 48:1029.

Emperor Constantine instituted a free ration of bread to 80,000 in Constantinople[47] in a population of perhaps no more that 150,000 reveals the magnitude of the poor in the capital. Several years later John Chrysostom spoke of the poor constituting 10 percent of Constantinople's population. Was he realistic in his calculation? We are told that in a population of nearly 200,000 in Antioch, the church fed daily some 7,000 poor people. The Cappadocian fathers are very important sources for the study of social conditions in the fourth century. Gregory of Nazianzus, later patriarch of Constantinople, Basil of Caesarea, and John Chrysostom write of riches, luxury, and self-indulgence, but also of widespread poverty. The question is, where do we draw the line between rhetorical hyperbole and realistic assessment? Whatever the answer to this question, the church responded to the needs of the poor and indigent, and it continues into the present to serve as a haven for society's peripheral and needy.

Patristic thought on *philanthrōpia* is included in prayers and hymns that have been published in liturgical books. The heart of Christian Orthodox worship in the Byzantine era is the divine liturgy. The whole service is no less than a reminder of the spiritual and practical application of *diakonia* by the faithful. It is a springboard for the expression of love for God and fellow humans, and it seeks to satisfy mind, heart, senses, and the stomach!

The "liturgy of the word," the petitions for peace, the authorities, the sick and the needy, the Gospel and Epistle readings, and the homily intend to satisfy the needs of the mind. The "liturgy of the mystery," the veneration, glorification, and participation in the mystery of the Eucharist of the invisible and incomprehensible God, who became human to elevate the human to divinity, intend to satisfy the heart, the mystical aspirations, and the spiritual quest of the human. The third part of the liturgy is rightly called "*diakonia* of service." The collections, which are intended for philanthropic causes, and the breaking of bread are symbols of the community's unity. Simply put, the liturgy embraces and serves the aspirations and needs of the total person.

The philanthropic spirit of the liturgy is evident in a profound and moving prayer, in the liturgy of St. Basil, calling on God to remember all officials and authorities; to nurture the infants and educate the youth; to support the elderly and comfort the fainthearted:

> Liberate those who are troubled by illnesses; sail with those at sea; accompany the wayfarers; plead for the widow; defend the orphans; free the captives; heal the afflicted. O God, look after those who are on trial, or condemned to the mines, or to exile and bitter slavery, or in any way hard pressed, in want, in extremity and all who plead for your boundless compassion. Remember, O Lord, those who love us as well as those who hate us . . . for you, O Lord, are the help

47. Cf. Ramsay MacMullen, *Corruption and the Decline of Rome* (New Haven: Yale University Press, 1988), 32–35.

of the helpless, the hope of the hopeless, rescuer of the tempest-tossed, safe haven for sailors, healer of the sick. Be all things to all people, for you know each of us and what we would ask, our homes, our needs.[48]

The church in the Byzantine era, including its monastic communities, often provided the essentials of social security for a large segment of the population of the empire throughout its existence. It took under its aegis orphans, widows, the old, the disabled, the stranger, and the unemployed; it saw to the release of prisoners of war and of those unjustly detained. In times of pestilences, earthquakes, and other natural catastrophes, the church played a major role looking after the needs of all. I have explored the philanthropic ethics and activity of churchmen, emperors, and ordinary people of the Byzantine era extensively elsewhere.[49]

The church continued to be the supporter of the needy from the seventh century on. We see this in the examples of monasteries, like the Stoudios in Constantinople, and church fathers, such as the great ninth-century patriarch Photius, who advised:

Do not overlook the poor and let not his tattered rags incite you to contempt, but let them rather move you to pity your fellow-creatures. For he is also a man, a creature of God, clothed in flesh like yourself, and perchance in his spiritual virtue mirroring the common creator more than you do. Nature has not made him indigent in this way, but it is the tyranny of his neighbors that has reduced either him or his parents to indigence, while our lack of pity and compassion has maintained or even aggravated his poverty.[50]

Even in the most critical period in the history of the church in the Greek middle ages, the Greek Orthodox Church stood by these principles. Poverty, civil wars, constant attacks from the Ottoman Turks, and confusions that resulted from the council in Florence made life in Constantinople, Thessaloniki, and other Greek cities and towns precarious and uncertain. Nevertheless, Christians stood by the needs of the common folk. In a beautiful admonition to students and young people, Gennadios Scholarios urged them to seek what is best in life, "to do without hatred and to think of education as therapeutic. Think of education as more important than money. Offer hospitality to strangers in order that you may not become a stranger to God. Give gladly bread to those who are hungry."

Elsewhere the same patriarch advised: "To turn your back against even one poor person is to show contempt toward all humanity. To refuse assistance

48. The *Liturgy of St. Basil*, as found in *The Lenten Liturgies*, with an English translation by Leonidas C. Contos (Northridge, CA: Narthex Press, 1995), 201–2.

49. Constantelos, *Byzantine Philanthropy*, esp. 50–61; and idem, *Poverty, Society and Philanthropy*, esp. 69–101.

50. Photius, *Hom.* 2.4.

to one indigent person is to commit injustice to all humanity because man is a microcosm and the convergence of all humanity."[51] Philanthropy for Scholarios was more than assistance to the poor. It encompassed other aspects of life: to console those in sorrow; to give advice to the timid and undecided; to teach the ignorant; to guide the sinner; to forgive the fallen; to be patient with the unruly and insolent; and to pray for all.

Conclusion

Greek patristic sources on philanthropy from the fourth to the fifteenth century interpreted faith and life in terms of the teachings and life of Jesus the Christ. Basil established the first complex of philanthropic institutions and washed the feet of lepers, setting an example of altruistic philanthropy. John the Almsgiver, a seventh-century patriarch of Alexandria, received numerous refugees and founded seven hospitals, including a gynecological clinic. Athanasios the First, patriarch of Constantinople in the fourteenth century, organized food distributions and served common meals to his people when Constantinople was besieged by the enemy. Theoleptos, mystic and spiritual man, cooked for and served his people when they defended their city against the Ottoman Turks in the fourteenth century.[52] And Patriarch Gennadios, as we noted above, became the champion of the destitute and the oppressed, the patriarch of the poor and the enslaved.

Several sources of the Latin fathers confirm that the philanthropic *diakonia* of the church during the Byzantine era became a prototype for the Western church and influenced the Islamic world after the seventh century. The philanthropy of the church of Byzantium became an inspiration for the development of a social consciousness and philanthropic *diakonia* in the nations that were converted to Christianity by its missionaries.

The *Russian Primary Chronicle* relates that the first thing that Vladimir, the prince of the Rus, did when he converted to Christianity was to found philanthropic institutions for his people. The poor and the weak, the sick and people of whatever need received distributions and protection. These benevolent acts are attributed to Vladimir personally rather than to the church.[53] As in the case of Vladimir, whose life and policies after his baptism reminds us of Constantine and his reign, the early Russian church and the church

51. Gennadios Scholarios, *"Parainetikē pros tous neous"* in *Palaiologeia—Peloponnēsiaka*, vol. 2 (Athens: B. N. Gregoriades, 1972), p. 330; idem, *Peri tōn kat' aretēn ergōn*, in *Oeuvres complètes de Georges Scholarios*, ed. Louis Petit, Xénophon A. Sidéridès, and Martin Jugie, 8 vols., Orthodoxos Ekklēsia tēs Hellados (Paris: Maison de la bonne presse, 1928–1936), 3:419–20.

52. D. J. Constantelos, "Mysticism and Social Involvement in the Later Byzantine Church: Theoleptos of Philadelphia, a Case Study" *Byzantine Studies* 6 (1979): 83–94.

53. Samuel H. Cross and O. P. Sherbowitz-Wetzor, eds. and trans., *The Russian Primary Chronicle* (Cambridge, MA: Harvard University Press, 1953), 120–22.

in the Slavic nations used the church of Constantinople as the prototype in terms of theology, polity, and practice.

Whatever the background and the nature of patristic thought on philanthropy in the early Byzantine centuries, overwhelming evidence indicates that the church throughout the Byzantine millennium responded to the needs of the poor and served as a haven for society's indigent and neglected.

Four

WEALTH, TRADE, AND PROFIT IN EARLY BYZANTIUM

14

Gilding the Lily

A Patristic Defense of Liturgical Splendor

A. Edward Siecienski

The image strikes us as incongruous or even hypocritical—the great ascetic preachers of antiquity denouncing ostentatious displays of wealth while standing in the most extravagantly decorated buildings in the known world. As the crowds listened to these holy men extol the Christian virtues of poverty and simplicity, they mingled about in churches "floored with marble slabs of various colors" with roofs "overlaid throughout with the purest gold, causing the entire building to glitter as with rays of light."[1] Even the great John Chrysostom, whose denunciations of the rich sometimes strike the modern listener as abusive and harsh, paraded about the great city of Constantinople behind a series of beautifully tapered silver crosses given to him by the em-

---

1. Eusebius, *Life of Constantine*, book 3, chap. 36 (*NPNF*[2] 1:529). This is taken from Eusebius's description of the Church of the Holy Sepulchre in Jerusalem. He goes on to write: "This temple, then, the emperor erected as a conspicuous monument of the Savior's resurrection, and embellished it throughout on an imperial scale of magnificence. He further enriched it with numberless offerings of inexpressible beauty and various materials—gold, silver, and precious stones, the skillful and elaborate arrangement of which, in regard to their magnitude, number, and variety, we have not leisure at present to describe particularly." Ibid., book 3, chap. 40 (*NPNF*[2] 1:530).

press. As he did so, he led elaborate processions to the newly erected (and magnificently decorated) shrines built by his imperial patrons.

Was any justification ever given for this seeming inconsistency, or, for that matter, was an inconsistency even recognized? Why did the fathers never apply their denunciation of wealth to the church itself, where marble, gold, and silver were freely used to enhance the splendor and majesty of the liturgy? First, it must be admitted that these and similar questions spring from what Dominic Janes, in his book *God and Gold in Late Antiquity*, calls "modern preoccupations."[2] The fathers, by and large, simply presumed that there was nothing wrong in employing wealth for the worship of God.[3] As one reads through the patristic corpus, however, one discovers an underlying theology that goes a long way toward explaining the phenomenon: while jewels and precious metals were inappropriate ornamentations for sinful flesh, promoting the glorification of the self rather than love of neighbor, there was no problem with "gilding the lily" to demonstrate the inherent worth of Christian worship. Gold could show forth the inner beauty of the liturgy; it could never, regardless of its value, adequately cover or conceal the shame of a polluted soul.

Wealth, Charity, and Splendor

It is clear that the fathers never believed that gold and wealth were absolute evils to be avoided at all costs. John Chrysostom wrote that gold was "good for almsgiving, for the relief of the poor, unprofitable when it is hoarded up or buried in the earth. . . . It was discovered for this end: that with it we should loose the captives, not form it into a chain to enslave the children of God."[4] Because money could be used to assist the poor and the destitute, thus aiding the mission of the church, bishops often found themselves asking for, and receiving, huge sums of money from their wealthier congregants. Often bishops—for example, Basil of Caesarea—set up institutions and charities to facilitate distribution of these funds, while others opted for a more personal method, determining need on a case-by-case basis. Bishops also received gifts that were earmarked for the aggrandizement of the church and its liturgy. Although individual donors had their own motives, not all of which were particularly religious, these gifts nevertheless became an important part of the church's patrimony.

---

2. Dominic Janes, *God and Gold in Late Antiquity* (Cambridge: Cambridge University Press, 1998), 3.

3. Janes does believe that a few did protest the move away from Christian simplicity, and that "such people would have looked to the wilderness as the place to save them from the linked horrors of urbanity and sin. But the eloquence that has preserved so many early Christian voices was the product of urban classical culture. Eloquent opposition was heresy. The result, for the most part, was silence." Ibid., 156.

4. John Chrysostom, *Hom. 1 Tim.* 7 (*NPNF*[1] 13:432).

What is interesting is that there was rarely (if ever) any justification given by the church for accepting these generous, and often extravagant, donations. It was simply assumed to be appropriate.[5] If the wealth of ancient Rome had at one time been spent on gilding the idols of the pagans, should not the cross of Christ, which represented our victory over death, be adorned all the more splendidly? Should not the riches given to the gods now be given over to worship of the one true God? Most certainly Eusebius and Sozomen thought so. They described the elaborate building projects undertaken by Emperor Constantine in great detail, the implicit message being that the exorbitant cost and elaborate nature of these projects was a manifestation of the emperor's love for Christ and his church. In his *Life of Constantine*, Eusebius gives the emperor's instructions and his motivations for building the Church of the Resurrection. Constantine insisted not only that the church buildings themselves should "surpass all others in beauty, but that all the details of the building should be such that the fairest structures . . . of the empire may be surpassed by this, for it is only fitting that the most marvelous place in the world should be worthily decorated.[6]

Even Theodoret of Cyrus, an ascetic who had passed along his entire personal inheritance to the poor, lauded the piety of Constantine's mother, Helen, since she was responsible for erecting "the most spacious and most magnificent churches in the world. . . . I need not describe their beauty and grandeur; for all the pious hasten there and behold the magnificence of the buildings to this day."[7]

That tension remained between the money spent on church decoration and the money spent on the poor is apparent from several sources. However, there is something akin to a *consensus patrum* on the primacy of charity over ornamentation, even though the most cantankerous ascetics never called for an end to liturgical extravagance. Jerome, in some advice to his friend Demetrius, argued that such gifts have their place. He wrote:

Some may build churches, may adorn their walls when built with marbles, may procure massive columns, may deck the unconscious capitals with gold and precious ornaments, may cover church doors with silver and adorn the altars with gold and gems. I do not blame those who do these things; I do not repudiate them. Everyone must follow his own judgment. And it is better to spend one's money thus than to hoard it up and brood over it. However your duty is of a different kind. It is yours to clothe Christ in the poor, to visit Him in the sick, to feed Him in the hungry, and to shelter Him in the homeless.[8]

5. Janes believes that the attitude of Christians on the receiving end of this imperial largesse is easy to understand: "If this be the Lord's will then God be praised!" Janes, *God and Gold*, 52.

6. Eusebius, *Life of Constantine* 3.31 (*NPNF*² 1:528, alt.).

7. Theodoret of Cyrus, *Ecclesiastical History* 1.17 (*NPNF*² 3:55).

8. Jerome, *Letter 130 to Demetrius* 14 (*NPNF*² 6:268–69). In *Letter* 58 to Paulinus, Jerome again clearly stresses the priority of charity over liturgical ornamentation: "The true temple of Christ is

There are more than a few similar examples of this priority of charity over liturgical splendor, even when it meant diverting gifts given for the church's worship in order to assist the poor. According to Sozomen,

> [When] Jerusalem and the neighboring country [were] . . . visited with a famine, the poor appealed in great multitudes to Cyril, as their bishop, for necessary food. As he had no money to purchase the requisite provisions, he sold for this purpose the veil and sacred ornaments of the church. It is said that a man, having recognized an offering which he had presented at the altar as forming part of the costume of an actress, made it his business to inquire whence it was procured; and ascertained that a merchant had sold it to the actress, and that the bishop had sold it to the merchant. It was under this pretext that Acacius deposed Cyril.[9]

Among the charges leveled at Chrysostom at the Synod of the Oak was that he had sold a group of marble slabs for personal gain, when in fact they had been intended for the Church of Anastasia, once used by Gregory of Nazianzus.[10] While few scholars today would accept that John kept the money from this transaction, J. N. D. Kelly thinks it likely that John did sell the slabs and other donated items that he thought unsuitable for the church, "not . . . to enrich himself but to finance his charities."[11]

It was Ambrose of Milan, explaining his sale of the church's sacred vessels to ransom members of his congregation, who gave the most thoughtful and eloquent response as to why such actions were justified. Defending himself, Ambrose claimed:

> It was far better to preserve souls than gold for the Lord. For the Church has gold, not to store up, but to lay out, and to spend on those who need.
>
> Would not the Lord Himself say: Why did you allow so many needy to die of hunger? Surely you had gold? You should have given them sustenance. Why are so many captives brought on the slave market, and why are so many unredeemed left to be slain by the enemy? Is it not better to preserve living vessels than gold ones?
>
> What could we reply? That we feared that the temple of God would need its ornaments? He would answer: The sacraments need not gold, nor are they proper to gold only. Thus I preferred to hand over to you free men, rather

---

the believer's soul; adorn this, clothe it, offer gifts to it, welcome Christ in it. What use are walls blazing with jewels when Christ in His poor is in danger of perishing from hunger?" Jerome, *Letter 58 to Paulinus* 7 (*NPNF*[2] 6:122).

9. Sozomen, *HE* 4.25 (*NPNF*[2] 2:321).

10. For a full list of the charges, see J. N. D. Kelly, *Golden Mouth: The Story of John Chrysostom—Ascetic, Preacher, Bishop* (Ithaca, NY: Cornell University Press, 1995), 299–301.

11. Ibid., 222.

than to store up gold. This crowd of captives surely is more glorious than the sight of cups.[12]

Chrysostom adopted a similar approach, arguing that the altar decorations, no matter how splendid, meant little when compared to our treatment of the Lord's body found outside the church's precincts. He asked his congregation what value was there

if after we have stripped widows and orphans, we offer for this table a gold and jeweled cup. . . . Would you do honor to Christ's body? Do not neglect Him when naked; do not while here honor Him with silken garments, [while] neglecting Him perishing outside of cold and nakedness.[13]

Like Ambrose, Chrysostom does not reject gifts intended to increase the beauty of the church or its liturgy, although he elaborates the principles by which such gifts should be given:

For what is the profit, when His table indeed is full of golden cups, but He perishes with hunger? First fill Him, being hungered, and then abundantly deck out His table also. Do you make Him a cup of gold, while you refuse Him a cup of cold water? And what is the profit? Do you furnish His table with cloths bespangled with gold, while you refuse Him even the necessary covering? And what good comes of it? Do not therefore while adorning His house overlook your brother in distress, for he is more properly a temple than the other.

Honor Him with this honor, spending thy wealth on poor people, since God has no need at all of golden vessels, but of golden souls. I say this, not forbidding such offerings; but requiring you, together with them, and before them, to give alms.[14]

Gold and the Truly Beautiful

The unanswered question raised by all this is why Jerome, Chrysostom, Ambrose, and other fathers allowed *any* money to be spent on marble, gold, and silver church decorations when the problems associated with poverty in the ancient world were so pervasive. Given their frequent, harsh denunciations of both the rich and their ostentatious displays of wealth, how could the fathers credibly preach in increasingly opulent surroundings, in churches whose magnificence dwarfed even the most splendid private homes? Why was the call for liturgical simplicity never raised?

12. Ambrose of Milan, *On the Duties of the Clergy* 2.28.137–39 (*NPNF*[2] 10:64–65).
13. John Chrysostom, *Hom. Matt.* 50 on Matt. 14:23–24, chap. 4 (*NPNF*[1] 10:313).
14. Ibid.

There are some nontheological considerations that must be taken into account. In Antioch, for example, Chrysostom was in direct competition with the Jews and their festivals, and thus he offered his congregation magnificent feasts and processions to sway them away from such temptations.[15] In Constantinople he faced the additional lures offered by the Arians and by the imperial capital itself (e.g., the hippodrome and the theater) and introduced newer and grander spectacles aimed to stimulate both the physical and the spiritual senses. It was for this reason that the empress donated a series of beautifully tapered silver crosses, and why the feasts dedicated to the apostles and martyrs were celebrated with such pageantry and exuberance.[16]

Yet it would be a mistake to attribute the fathers' acceptance and use of liturgical splendor solely to their desire to keep the attention of their congregants, or, even more cynically, to their desire for increased imperial patronage. There was, in fact, theological justification for increasing the liturgy's magnificence, a principle that concurrently allowed them to denounce the wealthiest Christians who tried to enhance, by means of decoration and ornamentation, their own physical beauty: *physical realities must reflect, rather than distort or hide, spiritual truths.* Nothing ignoble could be made pure by being gilded, but gold and jewels could be used to communicate the inherent spiritual worth of objects or actions deemed glorious in God's sight. What was required was a harmony between the physical and spiritual senses that made it easier for one to see true beauty behind the realities of this world.

The idea of the spiritual senses finds its roots in Origen, who applied it to the Christian's understanding of the Scriptures. He wrote:

> We distinguish . . . between "substance," or that which is, and that which is to be, between things apprehended by reason, and things apprehended by sense; and we connect truth with the one, and avoid the errors arising out of the other.[17]

What was said of the Scripture was certainly applicable to the temple worship of the ancient Israelites, where Solomon, following the Lord's command, constructed one of history's most magnificent buildings. Yet in their inability to see beyond the physical sense, finding splendor only in the temple's

---

15. For a discussion of Chrysostom's relationship with the Jews of Antioch, see Robert Wilken, *John Chrysostom and the Jews: Rhetoric and Reality in Late Antiquity* (Los Angeles: University of California Press, 1983). This competition contextualizes John's more disparaging remarks about Judaism as found in his *Discourses on Judaizing Christians*, FC 68 (Washington, DC: Catholic University of America Press, 1979).

16. A collection of John's homilies on the saints and their relics can be found in *The Cult of the Saints*, trans. by Wendy Mayer and Bronwen Neil (Crestwood, NY: St. Vladimir's Seminary Press, 2006).

17. Origen, *Contra Celsum* 7.46 (*ANF* 4:630).

gold and jewels, the Jews became incapable of grasping its true beauty. They could not see with the eyes of faith, realizing that each golden and jeweled object was merely a "type" for the spiritual realities of the new covenant that was to be offered in Jesus Christ. Yes, the temple was beautiful, claimed Chrysostom,

> with the walls on every side resplendent with much gold, and where, in surpassing excellence, costliness of material and perfection of art met together, and demonstrated that there was no other temple like this upon earth! . . . Nevertheless, this Temple, thus beautiful and marvelous and sacred, when those who used it were corrupted, became dishonored, despised, and profaned, that even before the captivity it was called a den of robbers, a cave of hyenas.[18]

The temple's greatest treasure was not to be found in the radiance of the priests' robes or in its marble decorations. The true magnificence of the temple lay in the spiritual realities each of these things represented, and unless these were perceived under gold and silver they meant little. That is why Chrysostom and others urged their congregations to attune their senses to these deeper spiritual realities, lest they follow the Jews in their blindness, counting the pageantry and pomp more than the realities they signified. He wrote:

> Fearful, indeed, and of most awful import, were the things which were used in the temple before the dispensation of grace—the bells, the pomegranates, the stones on the breastplate, the girdle, the mitre, the long robe, and the plate of gold. . . . But if anyone should examine the things which belong to the dispensation of grace, he will find that, small as they are, yet are they fearful and full of awe. . . . For when you see the Lord sacrificed, and laid upon the altar . . . can you still think you are still among men, and standing upon the earth? Are not you, on the contrary, straightway translated to Heaven? Oh! what a marvel! What love of God to man![19]

Mystagogical catechesis became the chief way that the liturgy's deeper meaning was conveyed to the ordinary believer.[20] Depending on the particular approach followed, objects and actions of the liturgy could be seen either as representations of the mysteries of Christ's life and the fulfillment of Old Testament "types" (the Antiochene model favored by Chrysostom), or as an

---

18. John Chrysostom, *Homilies on the Statutes* 17:11 (*NPNF*[1] 9:456).

19. John Chrysostom, *On the Priesthood* 3.4 (*NPNF*[1] 9:46).

20. For an examination of mystagogy in the early church, see Enrico Mazza, *Mystagogy: A Theology of Liturgy in the Patristic Age* (New York: Pueblo, 1989). Edward Yarnold's *Awe Inspiring Rites of Initiation: The Origins of the RCIA* (Collegeville, MN: Liturgical Press, 1994), examines Theodore of Mopsuestia's and Chrysostom's catechetical homilies, and includes English translations of several of them. Critical editions of Chrysostom's mystagogical catechesis are found in John Chrysostom, *Huit catéchèses baptismales*, trans. Antoine Wenger, SC 50 (Paris: Cerf, 1957); idem, *Trois catéchèses baptismales*, trans. Auguste Piédagnel, SC 366 (Paris: Cerf, 1990).

allegory of the soul's progress from sin to divine communion (the Alexandrian school).[21] Regardless of the approach, to truly grasp the great mystery of the altar, the believer "must see one thing and believe another"—the realities of salvation must become concrete to the eyes of faith. The earthly liturgy must allow the believer to be transported to the heavenly liturgy, where Christ himself was both high priest and victim.

For this reason not only mystagogy but also the physical environment and objects used for worship were used as a way to communicate the spiritual worth of the liturgy and the inherent beauty of the sacrifice offered there. After all, as John of Damascus would make clear in the eighth century, "the divine Word, foreknowing our need for analogies and providing us every-where with something to help us ascend, applies certain forms to those things that are simple and formless."[22] Quite naturally, materials that were considered ennobling and beautiful (gold, silver, jewels) were the first to be employed for this purpose, not to "give" value to the sacrifice of the altar, but to assist those present to more easily see the value within. John writes, "Just as the purple dye and the silk worn by the emperor have by themselves no honor, but only share the honor of him who wears it, so material things on their own are not worthy of veneration."[23] Gold, silver, and jewels thus had only symbolic value, enabling the believer to see the majesty of the heavenly liturgy.

While none of the fathers ever established a *necessary* symbolic relation-ship between the use of precious metals and the celebration of the liturgy, on the level of praxis gold and silver were thought the best representation of heaven's majesty.[24] It was for this reason, among others, that gold later became the standard background for icon painting. As Leonid Ouspensky has noted:

> The radiance of gold symbolizes divine glory. . . . Indeed, gold radiates light but at the same time it is also opaque. These properties correspond to the spiritual

21. Robert Taft summed up the commonly accepted distinction between the Antiochene and Alexandrian approaches to mystagogy: "The Antiochenes, more attentive in exegesis to the literal sense of scripture, favored a mystagogy that saw the Church's mysteries chiefly as a portrayal of the historical mysteries of salvation. The Alexandrines, following the Origenist exegetical penchant for the allegorical, interpreted liturgy by a process of anagogy whereby one rises from the letter to spirit, from the visible rites of the liturgical mysteries to the one mystery that is God." Taft, "The Liturgy of the Great Church: An Initial Synthesis of Structure and Interpretation on the Eve of Iconoclasm," *DOP* 34–35 (1980–1981): 61.
22. John of Damascus, *Treatises on the Divine Images* 1.11, trans. Andrew Louth, Popular Patristics Series (Crestwood, NY: St. Vladimir's Seminary Press, 2003), 26.
23. Ibid., 43.
24. Janes, *God and Gold*, discusses this issue at some length, especially as it relates to Christian-ity's adaptation of Roman cultural values and the use of symbol.

domain gold is expected to express, to the meaning of what it should translate symbolically—the attributes of Divinity.[25]

However, gold and jewels could just as easily symbolize something other than the divine glory of heaven: human greed. It was on this level that fathers such as Chrysostom denounced members of their congregations who used (or overused) jewels and precious metals as decoration, foolishly emulating the rich man who gathered up wealth while Lazarus starved outside his gate.[26] Women were particular targets for Chrysostom's scorn in this regard, especially those who arrived at church covered head to toe in jewels, like harlots and concubines (Chrysostom's words). Regardless of how resplendent these women might seem on the physical level, no matter how stunning to the eye, the fathers realized that "the groundwork of this corporeal beauty is nothing else but phlegm, and blood, and humor, and bile, and the fluid of masticated food."[27] Not only were these women vainly trying to conceal their physical shortcomings, but through their greed and disregard for others such people had done something far worse: they had made their *souls* genuinely ugly in the sight of God. Chrysostom asked them:

> Why do you overlay these bits of gold as if about to put to rights God's creation? Would you appear comely? Clothe yourselves in alms; clothe yourself in benevolence; in modesty and humbleness. These are all more precious than gold; these make even the beautiful yet more comely; these make even the ill formed to be beautiful in the sight of the righteous.[28]

Should people choose this path to true beauty, the church itself will become even more majestic, for the church is not simply a building, but a "house built on the souls of us men."

> There we may see many who are in the place of the gold which adorns the ceiling. Others again we may see, who give the beauty and gracefulness produced by statues. Many we may see, standing like pillars, not only on account of their strength but also on account of their beauty, adding as they do, much grace, and having their heads overlaid with gold. . . . This Church, of which I speak, is not built of these stones, such as we see around us, but of gold and silver, and of precious stones, and there is abundance of gold dispersed everywhere throughout it.[29]

25. Leonid Ouspensky, *Theology of the Icon*, trans. Anthony Gythiel, vol. 2 (Crestwood, NY: St. Vladimir's Seminary Press, 1992), 496.

26. See, for example, the sermons contained in John Chrysostom, *On Wealth and Poverty*, trans. Catharine Roth (Crestwood, NY: St. Vladimir's Seminary Press, 1984).

27. John Chrysostom, *Two Letters to Theodore after His Fall*, letter 1.14 (*NPNF*[1] 9:103).

28. John Chrysostom, *Hom. Col.* 10 (*NPNF*[1] 13:308).

29. John Chrysostom, *Hom. Eph.*10 (*NPNF*[1] 13:101).

This was the church's true adornment and demonstrates quite vividly the relative value of liturgical splendor for the fathers. Yes, there was justification for the gold, silver, marble, and jewels used during the liturgy inasmuch as these material goods helped believers see the spiritual realities behind them. And yet, as we have seen, money spent on such items was always secondary to charity and, in the end, secondary to the church's true beauty, which lay in the pure and spotless souls of its members. Gold was not evil, but neither was it inherently valuable. While gold's chief value was found in the good it could do for the poor, the fathers also recognized its symbolic importance and its power to transport the believer to the celestial realm. On this level money spent on liturgical splendor was a good, even if it was universally recognized that it always remained a relative good.

15

WEALTH, STEWARDSHIP, AND CHARITABLE "BLESSINGS" IN EARLY BYZANTINE MONASTICISM

DANIEL CANER

A s the most extraordinary socioeconomic experiment to emerge from early Byzantium, Christian monasticism resists any easy description in conventional terms of wealth or poverty. Monks, after all, identified themselves neither as "the rich" nor as "the poor," but as "the poor in spirit." That designation had already had a long history in Judeo-Christian tradition, where it referred not so much to material conditions as to the righteous humility of those who considered themselves totally dependent on God for their existence, having chosen to abandon all worldly ambitions for God's sake.[1] The result was a rather flexible notion of voluntary poverty, one that found its complement in the Orthodox monastic ideal *aktēmosynē*, "freedom from possessions." This ideal derived from Stoic philosophy, where it referred to the austerities taken to liberate oneself from the unnecessary attachments and distractions that came with ownership, corresponding in effect to the modern notion of

1. Gildas Hamel, *Poverty and Charity in Roman Palestine, First Three Centuries C.E.* (Berkeley: University of California Press, 1990), 173–97; Peter Brown, *Poverty and Leadership in the Later Roman Empire* (Hanover, NH: University Press of New England), 22, 59–73.

"simple living."[2] In Christian monasticism of the fifth and sixth centuries, it primarily meant spiritual detachment and the avoidance not so much of material acquisitions as of excess, the touchstones being utility and sufficiency. Total divestment of property was expected only of "perfect" monks, that is, anchorites, who were often supported by the monastic communities in which they had trained. Otherwise rules could be fitted to circumstance, "to each as any had need" (cf. Acts 4:35).[3] Thus Barsanuphius, the famous recluse of sixth-century Gaza, assured one infirm novice that the renunciations claimed by Jesus's disciples in Matt. 19:27—"We have left everything and followed you"—concerned not money or material possessions but worldly thoughts and attitudes.[4] It was therefore permissible for him to retain a plot of land for his own upkeep on joining the monastery.

These points need to be made from the start, because scholars who encounter the impressive remains of certain early Byzantine monasteries still sometimes express surprise at what appears to be a departure from the strict ideology of ascetic poverty depicted in early monastic literature, like the *Life of Antony* or "Sayings of the Desert Fathers."[5] But as Roger Bagnall has observed, such literature was mainly about anchorites, and contemporaries drew a major distinction between the *aktēmosynē* of anchorites (or of individuals within a cenobium) and the corporate wealth of cenobitic

2. See James Francis, *Subversive Virtue: Asceticism and Authority in the Second Century Pagan World* (University Park: Pennsylvania State University Press, 1995), 19.

3. See esp. Nilus of Ancyra, *Magn.* 2–3 (PG 79:972d–973d); Richard Newhauser, *The Early History of Greed: The Sin of Avarice in Early Medieval Thought and Literature* (Cambridge: Cambridge University Press, 2000), 156–57; and Diana Wood, *Medieval Economic Thought* (Cambridge: Cambridge University Press 2002), 42–63. More radical stances toward property and poverty had been largely discredited by the mid-fifth century. See Daniel Caner, *Wandering, Begging Monks: Spiritual Authority and the Promotion of Monasticism in Late Antiquity*, Transformation of the Classical Heritage 33 (Berkeley: University of California Press, 2002).

4. Barsanuphius, *ep.* 254, in *Barsanuphe et Jean de Gaza, Correspondence*, vol. 2, *Aux cénobites; Tome I: Lettres 224–398*, ed. F. Neyt and P. de Angelis-Noah, SC 450 (Paris: Cerf, 2000), 212. Justinian's *Nov.* 5.5, issued in 535, marks a watershed in rulings on monastic property arrangements, in that it required novices to transfer ownership of all that they owned to whatever cenobium they were joining. See Richard Kay, "Benedict, Justinian, and Donations 'Mortis Causa' in the 'Regula Magistri,'" *RBén* 90 (1980): 169–93. However, we do not know whether it held force outside Chalcedonian communities. Illness and infirmity may have always constituted grounds for exemption. See Andrew Crislip, *From Monastery to Hospital: Christian Monasticism and the Transformation of Health Care in Late Antiquity* (Ann Arbor: University of Michigan Press, 2005), 68–99.

5. E.g., Beat Brenk, in his otherwise useful survey, "Monasteries as Rural Settlements: Patron-Dependence or Self-Sufficiency?" remarks that "the monks of Khirbet ed-Deir [an anchoretic lavra in the Judean Desert] were monastic fundamentalists and economic equilibrists whereas the monks of Deir Turmanin [a cenobitic complex in northern Syria] flaunted their wealth unself-consciously." In *Recent Research on the Late Antique Countryside*, ed. W. Bowden, L. Lavan, and C. Machado (Leiden: Brill, 2004), 447–75, at 464. Cf. Beat Brenk, *Die Christianisierung der spätrömischen Welt: Stadt, Land, Haus, Kirche und Kloster in frühchristlicher Zeit* (Wiesbaden: Reichert Verlag, 2003), 149–50.

communities.[6] According to the sixth-century *Rule of the Master*, the latter type of monastic wealth should cause no embarrassment, especially in view of the charitable obligations that accompanied it:

> Since the life of our body cannot be maintained without the food that sustains it, and especially in view of a possibly numerous community and the necessity of providing the needs of visiting strangers, and also because we do not want to be stingy to anyone asking alms, for these reasons we are seen not to renounce worldly possessions, but we openly and legitimately retain monastery property for the benefit of God's workmen.[7]

Hence Besa, John of Ephesus, Cyril of Scythopolis, and other hagiographers of the period do not hesitate to mention (although they may not dwell on) the material assets that saintly abbots secured for their monasteries.[8] Indeed, not to have any such affluence might be considered a sign of divine disfavor. When John Rufus asked about an abandoned monastery he saw under thickets and thorns outside Jerusalem, it sufficed to explain that it had once belonged to monks of the accursed Chalcedonian creed.[9]

This, of course, is not to say that the monastic "poor in spirit" were usually rich, or that early Byzantine monasteries tended to be wealthy.[10] Nor is it to

6. Roger Bagnall, "Monks and Property: Rhetoric, Law, and Patronage in the Apophthegmata Patrum and the Papyri," *GRBS* 42 (2001): 7–24; Wood, *Medieval Economic Thought*, 25–29. Moreover, it is now recognized that such literature did not reflect the full range of early anchoretic experience. See James E. Goehring, "The Word Engaged: The Social and Economic World of Early Egyptian Monasticism," and "Through a Glass Darkly: Ἀποτακτικοί (αἱ) in Early Egyptian Monasticism," both in idem, *Ascetics, Society, and the Desert: Studies in Early Egyptian Monasteries* (Harrisburg, PA: Trinity International Press), 39–52, 53–72; also Ewa Wipszycka, "Les aspects économiques de la vie de la communauté des Kellia," in *Études sur le christianisme dans l'Égypte de l'antiquité tardive*, SEAug 52 (Rome: Institutum Patristicum Augustinianum, 1996), 337–62.

7. *Reg. mag.* 86.18–22 (A. De Vogüé, ed., *La Règle du maître*, vol. 2, SC 106 [Paris: Cerf, 1964], 352–54). Translation by L. Eberle, *The Rule of the Master*, CS 6 (Kalamazoo, MI: Cistercian Publications, 1977), 252.

8. E.g., Besa, *V. Sinuthi* 30, 48, 140; John of Ephesus, "Life of Z'ura," *HBO* 2; "Life of Addai," *HBO* 8; and "Life of Caesaria," *HBO* 54; Cyril Scyth., *V. Euthymii* 18; Theodore of Petra's *Life of Theodosius* (H. Usener, ed., *Der heilige Theodosius, Schriften des Theodoros und Kyrillos* [Leipzig: Teubner, 1890]), 28–35); *V. Pachomii Bo.* 183; *V. Theodorii Syceonis* 42 and 140; *V. Marutae* 6.

9. John Rufus, *Plērophoria* 16 (PO 8:32–33). For the attitudes of Shenoute of Atripe, Paulinus of Nola, and other early fifth-century abbots, see Caroline T. Schroeder, "'A Suitable Abode for Christ': The Church Building as Symbol of Ascetic Renunciation in Early Monasticism," *CH* 73 (2004): 432–521 (my thanks to Betsy Bolman for this reference). Positive or unproblematic descriptions of monastic wealth come mainly after the Council of Chalcedon (451) and may reflect sectarian pride, showing which side was "blessed." Indeed, it seems to have become a prominent focus of "Nestorian," i.e., East-Syrian hagiography. See Cynthia Villagomez, "The Fields, Flocks and Finances of Monks: Economic Life at Nestorian Monasteries, 500–850" (PhD diss., University of California, Los Angeles, 1998).

10. The best general assessment to date is still Evelyne Patlagean, *Pauvreté économique et pauvreté sociale à Byzance, 4e–7e siècles*, Civilisations et sociétés 48 (Paris: Mouton, 1977), 320–40. A systematic study has been undertaken by Lukas Schachner of St. John's College, Oxford University.

deny that some pagan critics and ascetic Christian writers castigated their monastic contemporaries for amassing land or living too luxuriously (as such critics might be expected to do).[11] It is simply to note that the monastic notion of voluntary poverty was sufficiently flexible in early Byzantium to accommodate a broad spectrum of material circumstances, ranging from the harsh austerity of hermits at Egyptian Scetis—said to possess so little that they had to "eat each other," that is, scavenge what each one had left in his cell at death[12]—to the grander monasteries of Egypt, Syria, and Palestine, whose monumental archways and colorful floor mosaics can still be seen today, adorned with the flora and fauna of paradise.[13] Once that is recognized, we may examine more fully the other, largely neglected side of the matter: how were early Byzantine monks taught to conceptualize and manage whatever material abundance—that is, surplus material resources, or "wealth"—that they actually did have?

The question is one of monastic *oikonomia*, both in theory and in practice. The term *oikonomia* is usually translated as "stewardship" (cf. Luke 12:42), but to the monastic mind it was nearly synonymous with the idea of divine dispensation (*oikonomia*). Any study of early monastic economic ideals must begin with the patristic understanding that this was an area in which humans were expected to collaborate with the divine, so as to ensure that all of God's gifts might be distributed in proper fashion.[14] At the same time, however, the austerity of monks or monasteries, and their relative isolation from ordinary sources of largesse, sometimes put them in situations that required ascetic ingenuity just to survive—let alone to do so charitably. To study monastic stewardship is therefore to examine how early monks learned to reconcile two obligations that came with their extraordinary profession: the obligation to trust that God would sustain them with the necessary resources in both good times and bad, and the obligation to handle such resources in a

11. The pagan critic Eunapius of Sardis (d. ca. 415) charged monks with amassing land "under the pretext of sharing with beggars, thereby making beggars of us all": Eunapius of Sardis, *apud* Zosimus, *Hist. nov.* 5.23 (F. Paschoud, ed., *Zosime: Histoire nouvelle*, 3 vols. [Paris: Les belles lettres, 1986], 3:35 [translation mine]); cf. the Christian critic Nilus of Ancyra (d. ca. 430), *exerc.* 6–7, 12 (PG 79:725a–d, 732d) and below, n. 47.

12. Palladius, *Paradise of the Fathers* 2:413, in L. Regnault, *Sentences des Pères du désert: Nouveau recueil* (Sablé-sur-Sarthe: Abbaye de Solesmes, 1970), 244. This represents an unusually vivid example of the monastic practice of living off leftovers, described below.

13. E.g., Yitzhan Magen and R. Talgam, "The Monastery of Martyrius at Ma'ale Adummim (Khirbet el-Murassas) and Its Mosaics," in *Christian Archaeology in the Holy Land New Discoveries: Essays in Honour of Virgilio C. Corbo, OFM*, ed. G. C. Bottini, L. Di Segni, and E. Alliata (Jerusalem: Franciscan Printing Press, 1990), 91–152; and Georges Tchalenko, *Villages antiques de la Syrie du Nord: Le massif du Bélus a l'époque romaine*, 3 vols., Bibliothèque archéologique et historique 50 (Paris: Geuthner, 1953), 1:145–82.

14. See Charles Avila, *Ownership: Early Christian Teaching* (Maryknoll, NY: Orbis Books, 1983), 47–80; and Jacob Viner, *Religious Thought and Economic Society: Four Chapters of an Unfinished Work by Jacob Viner*, ed. J. Melitz and D. Winch (Durham, NC: Duke University Press, 1978), 1–45.

charitable fashion in both good times and bad. Fulfilling both obligations often required an ability to find wealth and generosity amid scarcity. Yet such challenges were also mitigated, at least to some extent, by the flexible way in which early Byzantine monks were taught to conceptualize God-given abundance itself. As we shall see, the key lay in their concept of a material "blessing," a concept that enabled monks to see the most paltry quantities as a charitable surplus.

Monastic Stewardship Ideals, Fourth-Century Cappadocia to Sixth-Century Palestine

Since no treatise or financial register survives to show in detail how early Byzantine monks were expected to practice stewardship, the best introduction may be Cyril of Scythopolis's story about how Abba Euthymius, founder of a famous community in the Judean desert, was rewarded for his generosity in a time of scarcity. One day, Cyril explains, four hundred Armenian pilgrims arrived at his monastery in need of food. Euthymius told the monastery's steward to give them all something to eat. But the steward, whose name was Domitian and who had been in this office for only a year, replied that the monastery did not have enough to feed its residents, let alone their unexpected guests. Euthymius nonetheless assured him, "They shall eat and have something left over" (2 Kings 4:44). And so it turned out:

> Going accordingly to the small cell called by some the pantry, where a few loaves were lying, Domitian was unable to open the door, for God's blessing [*eulogia*] had filled the cell right to the top. So calling some of the men, he took the door off its hinges, and out poured the loaves from the cell. The same blessing [*eulogia*] occurred likewise with the wine and the oil. All ate and were satisfied [cf. Matt. 15:37; Mark 8:8], and for three months they were unable to reattach the door of the cell. Just as God through the Prophet's voice made the jar of meal and cruse of oil well up for the hospitable widow, so in the same way He granted this godly elder a supply of blessings [*eulogia*] equal to his zeal for hospitality. (*V. Euthymii* 17)

The story ends with Domitian's throwing himself down and apologizing for having been so *anthrōpinon*—so human—in his initial response, and with Euthymius explaining that their monastery's future prosperity depended on giving all strangers their due, reminding Domitian that "he who sows in blessings will also reap in blessings."[15]

15. ὁ σπείρων ἐπ᾿ εὐλογίαις ἐπ᾿ εὐλογίαις καὶ θερίσει, 2 Cor. 9:6. Cyril of Scythopolis, *V. Euthymii* 17 (E. Schwartz, ed., *Kyrillos von Skythopolis* [Leipzig: J. C. Hinrichs, 1939], 27–28). *Cyril of Scythopolis: Lives of the Monks of Palestine*, trans. R. M. Price, CS 114 (Kalamazoo, MI: Cistercian Publications, 1991), 22–23.

Cyril wrote this story in late sixth-century Palestine. It presents a motif that became commonplace in monastic hagiography from the fifth century onward, namely, that of material resources that miraculously multiply in the storerooms of saintly abbots or monks.[16] At first such stories might not seem a promising basis for any serious study of monastic economy. They were patently modeled on scriptural stories, especially Elisha's multiplication of the twenty loaves (2 Kings 4:42–44) and Jesus's feeding of the multitudes (Matt. 14:13–21; Mark 6:30–44; 8:1–10; Luke 9:10–17; John 6:1–13). Yet, like other *topoi* in late antique hagiography, they are rarely formulaic.[17] The presence of dialogue, vocabulary, and other details not found in their scriptural antecedents indicates that they were carefully crafted to convey lessons appropriate to their own monastic experience and circumstances. Indeed, the early Byzantine multiplication stories reveal much about the terms in which contemporary monks were taught to think about wealth and its proper stewardship. It is notable that early Byzantine hagiographers, by treating scriptural stories of miraculous feeding as models to be understood literally, departed from the practice of most earlier Christian writers, who had usually interpreted scriptural accounts of divinely bestowed abundance as denoting spiritual rather than material bounty.[18] As we shall see, such stories provided them with a ready framework to conceptualize the material "blessings" that many monks began to enjoy from the fifth century onward, as well as to dramatize the charitable ideals that monastic authorities like Barsanuphius of Gaza or Isaiah of Scetis (cited below) held regarding the proper use of such blessings.

Cyril's story is unusually instructive in this regard.[19] It is, after all, about the education of a monastic steward. Note that when first confronted with a potential strain on the material resources of his monastery, the young steward made an economic calculation that anyone might have made, but that he eventually learned to repudiate as *anthrōpinon*. Cyril implies that, had Domitian continued in that "human" cast of mind, not only would the four hundred Armenians have gone hungry, but Domitian himself would have never realized the potential role of a *eulogia*—a "blessing"—in his monastery's economy. To emphasize the conceptual importance of that term, *eulogia*—a

---

16. E.g., *V. Sinuthi* 138–43; *v. Sym. Syr.* 11; *v. Nicolai Sionitae* 45; John Eph., *HBO* 35; Thdr. Pet., *V. Theodosii* (Usener, ed., *Der heilige Theodosius* 35–39); *v. Georgii Chozibaitae*, 37; *v. Theognii* 22; Jo. Mosch., *Prat.* 85; *Verb. sen.* 13.15.

17. Cf. Joel Thomas Walker, *The Legend of Mar Qardagh: Narrative and Christian Heroism in Late Antique Iraq*, Transformation of the Classical Heritage 40 (Berkeley: University of California Press, 2006), 207–8, 244.

18. See Robert M. Grant, "The Problem of Miraculous Feeding in the Graeco-Roman Period," in *Center for Hermeneutical Studies: Colloquy* 42 (Berkeley: Graduate Theological Union, 1982), 1–15.

19. Cf. Bernard Flusin, *Miracle et histoire dans l'oeuvre de Cyrille de Scythopolis* (Paris: Études augustiniennes, 1983), 125–26, 187.

term not found in any scriptural model—Cyril repeats it three times: twice to refer to the divine force that caused surplus material resources to appear in the monastery, and once to the material resources themselves. Lest we miss his point, Cyril concludes by directing our attention to Paul's dictum in 2 Cor. 9:6, "he who sows in blessings, will also reap in blessings."

Before considering the significance of that reference, we should give Euthymius's steward his due. To judge from contemporary literature, there could not have been a more thankless job in a late antique monastery than that of a steward.[20] In one hagiographical text after another, it is always the cellarer or steward who is cast in the role of "doubter" regarding his monastery's charitable capacities, ever to be proven unnecessarily cautious, stingy, or otherwise faithless in his outlook by some more saintly abbot or monk. Of course, this hagiographical role had already been scripted well in advance by gospel narratives of Jesus's feeding of the multitudes, in which Jesus disproves his disciples' doubts by blessing small bits of bread and fish, thereby making them multiply to feed the masses in the desert. Clearly Cyril had those narratives in mind when framing his story about Euthymius and his doubtful steward.

But hagiography is not the only literature of the period to give the impression that monastic stewardship required the virtues of a saint to be properly done. In various letters and rules, Basil of Caesarea (d. 379) and Barsanuphius of Gaza (d. ca. 540) both warn that the task of steward should be entrusted not to just anyone but to someone who had been carefully tested to ensure that he would show no favoritism, partiality, possessiveness, contentiousness, or pride—and that was just for deciding how the material resources of a monastery should be distributed within a monastery itself.[21] Such a person had to be all the more judicious when faced with the question of whether to give away such resources to outsiders. Indeed, we get a better sense of the challenges that question posed from Basil and Barsanuphius than we do from hagiography. Basil's fourth-century rules, for example, addressed such practical and ethical monastic concerns as, "Shall we send away those that come to the door and beg?" (*Reg. brev.* 100); "Must he who has been entrusted with stewardship . . . fulfill the command, 'Give to everyone that asks of you' (Matt. 5:42)?" (*Reg. brev.* 101); and, "Is it right to give out of the common store to non-Christians who are in need?" (*Reg. brev.* 302).[22]

20. On this monastic office in general, see Joseph Patrich, *Sabas, Leader of Palestinian Monasticism: A Comparative Study in Eastern Monasticism, Fourth to Seventh Centuries,* Dumbarton Oaks Studies 31 (Washington, DC: Dumbarton Oaks, 1995), 173–79.

21. Bas., *Reg. fus.* 9:34; *Reg. br.* 149; Barsanuphius, *Ep.* 618. On Basil's views, see Graham Gould, "Basil of Caesarea and the Problem of the Wealth of Monasteries," in *Church and Wealth: Papers Read at the 1986 Summer Meeting and the 1987 Winter Meeting of the Ecclesiastical History Society,* ed. W. J. Shields and D. Woods (Oxford: Blackwell, 1987), 15–27.

22. All translations are mine unless otherwise noted.

In light of Cyril's story, we might expect Basil to respond to such questions by advocating a similar policy of openhanded generosity. On the contrary, Basil replies to each query by citing Jesus's declaration regarding the Canaanite woman, "It is not fair to take the children's food and throw it to the dogs" (Matt. 15:26). Only after careful investigation, Basil says, should a steward give anything away to beggars.[23] As for those who were not Christian, Basil notes that "it is not necessary to give what was destined for those who are dedicated to God [i.e., monks] and spend it on those who are indifferent" (*Reg. brev.* 302). Nonetheless, he adds, a steward might consult with his elders to determine if their community had enough in abundance (*perisseuma*) to give it away so indiscriminately, thereby emulating the unconditional generosity of God, who makes his sun rise "on the evil and on the good" (Matt. 5:45).[24]

Basil thus leaves the impression that indiscriminate charity, though a lofty ideal, was to be the exception rather than the rule in monasteries of fourth-century Cappadocia. It was permissible only after careful calculation as to whether a monastery actually had enough to do so out of the abundance (*ek . . . perisseumatos*) of its stores. His recommendations clearly assume that most would have only limited resources, and reflect a pragmatic concern to protect what was "destined for those who were dedicated to God."

It is important to recognize that Basil's stance was not idiosyncratic for his day. Ambrose, Jerome, and other fourth-century fathers (John Chrysostom marks the major exception) similarly advised discrimination in almsgiving and proposed a sliding scale of eligibility. Topping nearly every list were "the poor in spirit," those "holy poor" whose neediness was voluntary and stemmed from love of God, such as those for whom the apostles Paul and Barnabas had made their Jerusalem collections (Rom. 15:25–29; 1 Cor. 16:1–3; 2 Cor. 8–9; Gal. 2:10).[25] Although privileging this type of poverty may seem self-serving to modern readers, it was quite logical for an aristocratic society and surely would have come as a relief to monks and clerics who already found themselves strapped for resources. As one such bishop reminded a deacon in the early sixth century:

> Holy Basil, that teacher of truth, said in his ascetic treatise that he who is entrusted with the duty of ministering to the needs of a monastery, even if he be an abbot, ought not use or spend any of the property of his brotherhood on any pious object such as the support of the poor and needy, or the ransoming of captives.[26]

23. Bas., *Reg. br.* 100 (PG 31:1152b): μετὰ δοκιμασίας τοῦτο ποιείτω. Cf. idem, *Ep.* 150.

24. Bas. *Reg. br.* 302 (PG 31:1296c).

25. Boniface Ramsey, "Almsgiving in the Latin Church: The Late Fourth and Early Fifth Centuries," *TS* 43 (1982): 232–33; Richard Finn, *Almsgiving in the Later Roman Empire: Christian Promotion and Practice (313–450)* (Oxford: Oxford University Press, 2006), 67–74; Wood, *Medieval Economic Thought*, 61–62. The idea is prominent in Clement of Alexandria, *Quis dives salvetur*, esp. sections 31–32.

26. Sev. Ant., *Ep.* 1.63, in *The Sixth Book of the Select Letters of Severus*, ed. and trans. E. W. Brooks, 2 vols. (London: Williams and Norgate, 1902–1904), 1:217 (Syriac) and 2:195 (English).

In light of this tradition and outlook, we must ask, was the openhanded charity idealized by Cyril and other hagiographers merely a hagiographical conceit, or was there another way of thinking about material resources that helped resolve some of the ethical and practical problems that Basil saw, so that all monks—even stewards—might emulate God, or give like saints?

I believe that there was, at least by the time that Cyril was writing in sixth-century Palestine. It is important to observe exactly how Barsanuphius, writing in Gaza in the early sixth century, differs from Basil, writing in Cappadocia more than a century before. Monks and laypeople in southern Palestine frequently consulted Barsanuphius and his colleague John on practical and ethical aspects of Christian stewardship, posing questions that were often quite similar to those that Basil had received: How, for example, should we practice hospitality and the commandment of love toward the poor? Must we receive each and every person who comes in off the road?

In many respects, the answers of Barsanuphius and John are similar to Basil's: hospitality must be provided only to the degree that a monastery was able; beggars were to be carefully examined as to why they had come; if one had to choose between giving to the destitute and giving to monks, preference was to go to latter, "since they are God's slaves: for it is written: 'to whom the honor, give honor' (Rom. 13:7), and the Lord honors them first" (Barsanuphius, *Ep.* 636).[27] Yet while Basil implies that questionable beggars should simply be turned away, Barsanuphius and John make a notable concession: even if the beggar were a thief, Barsanuphius says, he should be given a *eulogia*—a "blessing"—and be sent on his way (*Ep.* 587); likewise, if he were a vagabond monk, just "give him a *eulogia* and let him go" (*Ep.* 588).[28] As for a non-Christian beggar, John affirms that it was perfectly fine to give him a "*eulogia* of the fathers," since it might "turn him to truth" through the power of God's blessing that it held (*Ep.* 752).[29]

Note that in each response Barsanuphius and John use the same word, *eulogia*, as Cyril did in his Euthymius story, to denote a material resource that is to be given away in charity. How should we account for this use of the word by Barsanuphius, John, and Cyril, as well as in other church and monastic texts of their day?

27. Barsanuphius, *Ep.* 317, 587, 588 (to monks); 618–36 (to laypeople); quoted from *Barsanuphe et Jean de Gaza, Correspondence*, vol. 3: *Aux laïcs et aux évêques, lettres 617–848*, ed. F. Neyt and P. de Angelis-Noah, SC 468 (Paris: Cerf, 2002), 62–64.

28. Barsanuphius, *Ep.* 587: ἐὰν γὰρ ᾖ κλέπτης, καθὼς εἶπον οἱ Πατέρες, δότε εὐλογίαν καὶ ἀπολύσατε, *Ep.* 588: χρὴ εὐλογίαν διδόναι καὶ ἀπολύειν, in *Barsanuphe et Jean de Gaza, Correspondence*, vol. 2: *Aux cénobites*, tome 2: *Lettres 399–616*, ed. F. Neyt and P. de Angelis-Noah, SC 451 (Paris: Cerf, 2001), 784–86; translation mine. "The Fathers" may refer here to Isaiah of Scetis, who lived at Gaza in the mid-fifth century: see below, n. 51.

29. John of Gaza, *Ep.* 752, SC 468:194–96: συμβαίνει διὰ τῆς εὐλογίας τῆς ἐχούσης Θεοῦ δύναμιν, κἀκεῖνον εἰς ἐπιγνῶσιν ἀληθείας ἐλθεῖν, translation mine. John Moschus, *Prat.* spir. 125 (PG 87(3):2988b), uses the phrase εὐλογία Πατέρων to refer to loaves of bread sent to local anchorites.

A Monastic Economy of Charitable "Blessings"

Here Cyril, by ending his story with Paul's dictum, "the one who sows bountifully will also reap bountifully," provides the necessary clue. The saying comes from a passage where Paul is trying to urge readers at Corinth (2 Cor. 9:5–8) to donate their excess material resources in support of the Christian "holy poor" (here simply called "the holy ones") in Jerusalem. To this end Paul repeatedly uses the word *eulogia*, "blessing," to designate not only the donation he is urging them to make but also the essential spirit behind that gift and the material result of giving that gift. Since most English translations obscure his terminology, we should recall exactly what Paul wrote:

> I thought it necessary to ask the brothers to go on ahead to you and arrange in advance this *eulogia* that you have promised, so that it may be ready as a *eulogia* and not as an extortion. The point is this: he who sows sparingly will also reap sparingly, but he who sows in blessings [*ep' eulogiais*] will also reap in blessings [*ep' eulogiais*]. So let each give as he has decided in his heart, not with grief, or under compulsion, for God loves a cheerful giver. And God is able to make every grace abound [*charin perisseusai*] for you, that by always having enough of everything, you may have abundance [*perisseuēte*] for every good work. (2 Cor. 9:5–9, my translation)

In this way Paul established the word "blessing" (*eulogia* in Greek, *benedictio* in Latin, *burktha* in Syriac, and *smou* in Coptic) as a Christian term for a special kind of charitable gift. Elsewhere I have explored its role more generally in Christian communities of the fifth, sixth, and seventh centuries.[30] As hagiography and other late antique sources attest, the word "blessing" in this period came to designate a gift that was conceptually distinct from all others known to antiquity (including alms), in that it was believed to have come from God—having only been "passed on" by its human donor—and therefore required no reciprocation between human donor and receiver. This feature made it ideal for supporting early Byzantine "holy ones" (i.e., clerics and monks) and made it central to the church and monastic economic thought of the day. Most important for our purposes is Paul's assurance that giving such "blessings" would beget more "blessings," and his repeated use of the verb *perisseuō*—variously meaning "to be in abundance or excess," "to possess in abundance," or "to be leftover"—to describe the essential state of

---

30. Daniel Caner, "Towards a Miraculous Economy: Christian Gifts and Material 'Blessings' in Late Antiquity," *JECS* 14, no. 3 (2006): 329–77. Previous treatments of gifts called *eulogiai* have not recognized their origin in Paul and have mainly focused on one particular species, namely, those given out at pilgrimage sites or holy shrines: e.g., Gary Vikan, "Art, Medicine, and Magic in Early Byzantium," *DOP* 38 (1984): 65–86. For general overviews, including the Judaic background, see Alfred Stuiber, "Eulogia," *RAC* 6 (1966): 900–928; and Paul Drews, "Zur Geschichte der 'Eulogien' in der alten Kirche," *Zeitschrift für praktische Theologie* 20 (1898): 18–39.

both giver and gift. According to Paul, gifts called "blessings" were to derive from whatever excess, surplus resources (or superfluity, *perisseia*) that God had granted a person and therefore represented something extra or super-fluous (*perisseuma*) that could be easily given away in a manner beloved to God, that is, cheerfully and without grief.[31]

Although references to charitable gifts called "blessings" can be found in church and monastic literature written anywhere in this period, most come from the Holy Land, where, for example, Cyril and Barsanuphius lived. This localization is not surprising, considering the original intent of Paul's passage, as well as the fact that Christian congregations continued to heed its call to support Jerusalem "saints" from abroad throughout the early Byzantine peri-od.[32] Such *eulogiai* often amounted to no more than a few coins handed out at a single distribution. But the term *eulogia* was also used in this period to designate more substantial donations of gold that individual donors gave on an annual basis to support a favorite monastic community. Cyril, for example, repeatedly uses it to designate the gifts that wealthy admirers sent to various abbots in Palestine each year.[33] Nor was this term used only by hagiographers. Besides being attested in a sixth-century inscription describing the funds used to build a church at Gerasa,[34] the term is also prominent in seventh-century papyri records discovered in the ruins of the St. Sergius monastery at Nessana, located about forty miles from Gaza in southern Palestine. These records include a list of *eulogiai* that the monastery received one year from nine donors in various amounts of grain, as well as a list in which *eulogiai* donations marked "to the monastery" are carefully distinguished from other lay offerings (*prosphorai*).[35]

What needs to be emphasized is that such *eulogiai* donations were consid-ered to be something supplemental, providing a church or monastery with the extra superfluity necessary for them to provide charity on a generous

31. For Paul's use of the term *eulogia* and its relation to the idea of περίσσευμα and of inexhaustible resources, see Dieter Georgi, *Remembering the Poor: The History of Paul's Collection for Jerusalem* (Nashville: Abington Press, 1992), 93–99. Paul had stressed the notion and role of περισσεία and περίσσευμα in the preceding chapter (2 Cor. 8:2–14).

32. E. D. Hunt, *Holy Land Pilgrimage in the Later Roman Empire, A.D. 312–460* (Oxford: Clarendon Press, 146); cf. *Panegyrica Rabbulae* (J. J. Overbeck, ed., *S. Ephraemi Syri, Rabulae episcopi Edesseni, Balaei aliorumque opera selecta* [Oxford: Clarendon Press, 1865], 205, lines 22–27).

33. Cyril Scyth., *V. Euthymii* 47; *V. Iohannis* 15, 20; *V. Theodosii* 3; cf. Thdr. Pet., *V. Theodosii*, 27.10–21, 28.9; *V. Syncleticae* 7–8; and John Philip Thomas, *Private Religious Foundations in the Byzantine Empire*, Dumbarton Oaks Studies 24 (Washington, DC: Dumbarton Oaks, 1987), 48, 75.

34. C. B. Welles, *Gerasa, City of the Decapolis: The Inscriptions* (New Haven: Yale University Press, 1938), 479n304.

35. *P. Ness.* 79 ("Account of Church Offerings to the Church of St. Sergius," early seventh century); and *P. Ness.* 80 ("Account of Church Offerings," ca. 685), in *Excavations at Nessana 3: Nonliterary Papyri*, ed. and trans. Casper J. Kraemer Jr. (Princeton, NJ: Princeton University Press, 1958), 227–34.

scale of their own.[36] In other words, the notion of *perisseia* was always in the background. This is exemplified in part by the use of the word in church and monastic settings to designate the ration (or allowance) of extra bread that bishops gave to their clerics after a Eucharist service, or that abbots gave to their monks after a communal meal.[37] In each instance, a *eulogia* provided an extra supply of resources, above and beyond whatever else a cleric, monk, church, or monastery might receive in income, food, offerings, or alms. Ideally, it was a gift that gave them the extra material resources they needed to pass a "blessing" of their own on to others.

In this way "blessings" could come from "blessings," as Paul had foretold. Either alone or compounded with other sources of income, such *eulogiai* donations helped fuel a veritable economy of "blessings" in Palestine and elsewhere. To be sure, scholars have long surmised that donations left by pilgrims or sent by lay folk must account for much of the material prosperity evident in churches and monasteries of the early Byzantine Holy Land.[38] But there is more to it than that. This emergence of church and monastic prosperity also corresponds to, and should be linked to, the more general rise in economic prosperity that occurred in the Byzantine hinterlands of the fifth, sixth, and seventh centuries. This trend, caused by various factors, left its permanent mark in the proliferation of villages and large stone houses whose ruins still stand in remote agrarian and desert regions of Syria and Palestine.[39]

Archaeologists have recognized that such constructions reflect not only a general increase in prosperity on all levels but also the attendant problem, common to precapitalist, preindustrial economies, of how to dispose of surplus, agricultural wealth.[40] Such surplus could not be kept in a bank or

36. See esp. Cyril Scyth., *V. Theodosii* 3, and Besa, *V. Sinuthi* 138–43; cf. Jean Gascou, "Monasteries, Economic Activities of," in *The Coptic Encyclopedia*, ed. A. S. Atiya (New York: MacMillan, 1991), 5:1641–42.

37. For details, see Caner, "Towards a Miraculous Economy," 340–48.

38. I.e., based on donations brought by pilgrims or sent by pious lay folk: see M. Avi-Jonah, "The Economics of Byzantine Palestine," *Israel Exploration Journal* 1 (1950–1951): 39–51; Yizhar Hirschfeld, *Judean Desert Monasteries in the Byzantine Period* (New Haven: Yale University Press, 1992), 102–4, 236–37. As discussed below, there were other sources of monastic income, any of which could have produced surplus "blessings": besides labor or rents from monastic land, property bestowed by Byzantine officials who retired to monasteries was important, as were imperial subsidies of metropolitan churches and monasteries: see Caner, "Towards a Miraculous Economy," 375–76.

39. See esp. Jairus Banaji, *Agrarian Change in Late Antiquity: Gold, Labour, and Aristocratic Dominance* (Oxford: Oxford University Press, 2001); and J. H. W. G. Liebeschuetz, *Decline and Fall of the Roman City* (Oxford: Oxford University Press, 2001), 66–73; for Syria and Palestine, see the review surveys by Clive Foss, next note.

40. As observed by Clive Foss, "The Near Eastern Countryside in Late Antiquity: A Review Article," *The Roman and Byzantine Near East: Some Recent Archaeological Research, JRA* Supplement 14 (1995): 221–22; and idem, "Cities and Villages of Lycia in the Life of Saint Nicholas of Holy Zion," *GOTR* 36 (1991): 336.

invested in new technology. One alternative was to store it "in heaven" as Scripture (cf. Matt. 6:20) and preachers advised, through the construction and support of local Christian institutions.[41] Indeed, these religious investments were made in no small part with the hope that God would continue to bless the donors' families, fields, and flocks. That certainly seems to have motivated lay contributions to the building of Rabban Hormizd's seventh-century monastery outside Mosul:

> When the believing people of the country heard [that Hormizd was building a monastery], they rejoiced with an exceedingly great joy, and each one of them brought out whatsoever goods he had in his possession, and gave them unto Rabban as things appertaining unto blessing [*bagna burkthaya*] for the building of that holy monastery.[42]

In nonurban areas, such institutions provided lay donors not only with an outlet for pious offerings, but also with communal places of paradisal repose, as at Shenoute's White Monastery in Egypt, where a local duke might choose to "take his ease in the abundance of the monastery" for three days,[43] or at Ahudemmeh's monastery in central Iraq, where an "abundant table, laden with all kinds of goods, was prepared for those who arrived at its gates," making it seem "like a garden, filled with all the goods from the land where it was located, all of which the people of that land had provided."[44] Even monasteries in small villages were provided by lay donors with gold or silver plate, "creating a communal store of easily convertible wealth."[45]

41. "So shall thy land be filled with blessing": thus John Chrysostom, *Hom. Act.* 18.4 (PG 60:147; *NPNF*[1] 9:118), discussed by Thomas, *Private Religious Foundations*, 29–30; cf. *Const. Ap.* 2.34.5; and Patlagean, *Pauvreté*, 275. Invocations for blessings were made for Jewish donors at synagogues. See J. Naveh, *On Stone and Mosaic: The Aramaic and Hebrew Inscriptions from Ancient Synagogues* (Jerusalem: Israel Exploration Society, 1978), 19, 54, and 121–22 (my thanks to Stuart Millar for this reference). Donations of surplus wealth to Syrian monasteries are especially well discussed by Philippe Escolan, *Monachisme et Église: Le monachisme syrien du IVe au VIIe siècle; Un ministère charismatique* (Paris: Beauchesne, 1999), 199–200.

42. *Life of Rabban Hormizd* 15, in *The Histories of Rabban Hôrmîzd the Persian and Rabban Bar-'Idtâ*, ed. and trans. E. W. Brooks, 2 vols. (London: Luzac, 1902), 1:79 (Syriac) and 2:116 (English). For further examples, cf. sections 16–17.

43. Besa, *V. Sinuthi* 104, in *Besa: The Life of Shenoute*, trans. D. N. Bell, CS 73 (Kalamazoo, MI: Cistercian Studies, 1983), 73.

44. *V. Ahoudemmehi* 4, in *Histoires d'Ahoudemmeh et de Marouta*, ed. and trans. F. Nau (PO 3:28). Liebeschuetz, *Decline and Fall*, 73, notes that the new Syrian villages had no communal centers. This was true of all postclassical communities; monasteries helped fill the void, to an extent and with an effect that await future study.

45. Foss, "Near Eastern Countryside," 222, referring to the treasure from Nicholas's sixth-century Sion monastery in Lycia, on which there is more below.

One consequence of this religious use of newfound surplus was a new moral appreciation of such surplus wealth and its charitable possibilities.[46] This is signaled by the hagiographical motif of material "blessings" that multiply in monastic granaries and storerooms. As noted earlier, that motif only begins to proliferate in the fifth century. Its association of stored-up bread, grain, and other staples with God-given abundance and saintly generosity marked a significant departure from earlier Christian depictions of surplus wealth, as exemplified by the sermons and writings of the fourth-century Cappadocians (Basil, Gregory of Nyssa, and Gregory of Nazianzus), who usually portrayed material surplus in negative terms, as something hoarded, sold dear, or left to rot in caves or silos by the self-serving rich.[47] If, as Wendy Mayer has suggested in chapter 10 in this volume, fourth-century discourse on charity was guided by an underlying notion of a "limited good," it may be said that the discourse of the fifth, sixth, and seventh centuries focused instead on the notion of an "unlimited good" as formulated by Paul, developed by hagiographers, and inculcated in monastic culture.[48]

Of course, to be considered a channel of "unlimited good," monks and monasteries participating in this charitable economy had to live up to extraordinary expectations and be ready to convert whatever surplus they had, whenever it was needed. Nonhagiographical evidence shows that some of them did so in extraordinary fashion. For example, Shenoute gave a sermon on how his monastery managed to feed more than twenty thousand refugees for three months (a miracle he likens to Jesus's multiplication of the loaves and attributes to God's continual blessing).[49] Elsewhere, the door of a monastic granary in sixth-century Asia Minor was inscribed: "By the Prayer of Holy Seleukos, Ten Thousand"—referring, we are told, to the number of people fed by the monastery's founder during a famine.[50] Such examples should be

46. Accompanied, of course, by some ascetic grumbling about a betrayal of standards: see Escolan, *Monachisme et Église*, 216–17; also *V. Danielis Scetiotae* 8.2A; Jo. Mosch., *Prat.* 52; and Arthur Vööbus, *History of Asceticism in the Syrian Orient*, vol. 3, CSCO 500, Subsidia 81 (Louvain: Secrétariat du Corpus SCO, 1988), 87–91, on Isaac of Antioch.

47. Susan R. Holman, *The Hungry Are Dying: Beggars and Bishops in Roman Cappadocia* (New York: Oxford University Press, 2001), 77–79; Raymond Van Dam, *Kingdom of Snow: Roman Rule and Greek Culture in Cappadocia* (Philadelphia: University of Pennsylvania Press, 2002), 44–47; Peter Garnsey, *Famine and Food Supply in the Graeco-Roman World: Responses to Risk and Crisis* (Cambridge: Cambridge University Press, 1988), 177–78. Brown, *Poverty and Leadership*, 41, suggests such examples constituted a Christian "discourse on poverty" born out of crisis.

48. See Wendy Mayer, chapter 10 above; for "unlimited good," cf. Vincent Déroche's study of "miraculous economy" motifs in fifth-, sixth-, and seventh-century Byzantine hagiography, *Études sur Léontios de Néapolis*, Acta Universitatis Upsaliensis, Studia Byzantina Upsaliensia 3 (Uppsala: Uppsala University, 1995), 238–54.

49. Shenoute of Atripe, "De Aethioporum invasionibus III," trans. J. Leipoldt, *Sinuthii archimandritae vita et opera omnia*; CSCO 42/Script. Copt. 2 (Louvain: Durbecq, 1955), 3:38–40.

50. Eustratius, *V. Eutychii* 16 (PG 86:2293d): καὶ ἀπὸ τῆς προσευχῆς τοῦ ἁγίου Σελεύκου μυριάδες δέκα. Though reported in a hagiographical source, the fact that it is abbreviated and has to be

regarded not as propaganda but rather as an indication of how far the multiplication stories and the blessings concept were used to shape the way early Byzantine monks understood wealth and the charitable obligations that came with it. One point was clear: since all the surplus "blessings" they possessed were believed to have ultimately come from God, the blessings had to be handled with an equally selfless spirit of generosity. Proper stewardship meant passing them on to anyone in need. Thus Abba Isaiah, writing long before Barsanuphius in fifth-century Gaza, advised monks regarding questionable beggars, "Do not send him off empty-handed, but give him the *eulogia* you received from God, knowing that whatever you have is from God."[51]

Nevertheless we may doubt, as did Euthymius's steward, whether such resources would have always been so limitless in actual practice. God's "commandment of love" was incumbent on all, including "indigent monasteries." We hear about these only as recipients of charitable distributions by more affluent communities.[52] How could they live up to similar expectations? Moreover, such distributions made by affluent monasteries are usually presented as a response to a windfall. Indeed, it is clear that a material "blessing" was always unpredictable, inasmuch as its receipt was wholly premised on the voluntary generosity of lay donors: everything depended on whatever *eulogia* "God had put" in a layperson's heart to give in the first place.[53] Indeed, the Nessana papyri indicate that St. Sergius's monastery received "blessings" far less often than it did *prosphorai* offerings (probably earmarked to fund liturgical services for the donors).[54] At the same time we read about anchorites who tried to subsist entirely on the *eulogiai* rations they received.[55] And so we may ask, was there anything special about a "blessing" that helped monks not

---

explained by the hagiographer assures its authenticity. Cf. Frank Trombley, "Monastic Foundations in Sixth-Century Anatolia and Their Role in the Social and Economic Life of the Countryside," *GOTR* 30 (1985): 52–53.

51. Isaiah of Scetis, *Asceticon* 10.5, in *Les cinq recensions de l'Ascéticon syriaque d'Abba Isaïe, I: Introduction au problème isaïen; Version des logoi I–XIII avec des parallèles grecs et latins*, ed. R. Draguet, CSCO 293, Script. Syr. 122 (Louvain: Secrétariat du Corpus SCO, 1968), 141. Cf. Cyril of Scythopolis, *V. Euthymii* 50.

52. E.g., *V. Marcelli* 30, in "Vie ancienne de saint Marcel l'Acémète," ed. G. Dagron, AnBoll 86 (1968): 313; πτωχοῖς μοναστηρίοις ἐχορήγησεν; cf. *V. Matronae Pergensis* 46 and Basil, *Reg. brev.* 181 and 284.

53. John of Cyprus, *V. Jo. Eleem.* 9 (A. J. Festugière, ed., *Vie de Syméon le Fou et Vie de Jean de Chypre* [Paris: Paul Geuthner, 1974], 355:36–37: τὴν εὐλογίαν ἣν ἐνέβαλεν ὁ θεὸς ἐν τῇ καρδίᾳ . . . προσενέγκαι).

54. *P. Ness.* 79 does not preserve the quantities given for either *eulogiai* or *prosphorai*, but *P. Ness.* 80 shows that, in this instance, most were provided by a single donor; the amounts given by the remaining donors were quite modest (2–6 *medimnoi* of grain).

55. See John Moschus, *Prat.* 41, and Sophronius of Jerusalem, *V. Mariae Aegyptiae* 26–27 (PG 87:3716c), in which Mary's subsistence on three bread "blessings" for seventeen years by chewing them in pieces (κλάσματα) may be meant to recall the "abundance of pieces" (περισσεύματα κλασματῶν) of blessed bread consumed by the multitudes in Matt. 14:20 and Mark 8:8.

only stretch it out as a resource, but also give it away as charity, cheerfully, in both good times and bad?

A Monastic Economy of Charitable Leftovers

As already indicated, the key lies in the flexible way that monks conceptualized the God-given superfluity from which a "blessing" was supposed to derive. In one of his letters regarding charity to beggars, Barsanuphius rephrases his usual recommendation, *dote eulogian kai apolysate* ("Give him a *eulogia* and send him off"), with an alternative formulation, *mikron perisseuon dos kai apolyson*: "Give him a *mikron perisseuon* and send him off."[56] Here Barsanuphius effectively provides a gloss as to what he otherwise meant when referring to a "blessing." For him, a *eulogia* meant a *mikron perisseuon*, "a small superfluity."

At first that might seem a strange oxymoron, until we recall how Paul used the verb *perisseuō* to describe the surplus resources from which a *eulogia* was supposed to be made in 2 Cor. 9:8. Translations usually emphasize the verb's sense of abundance, that is to say,

> God is able to provide you with every grace in abundance [*charin perisseusai*], so that by always having enough of everything, you may share abundantly [*perisseuēte*] in every good work.

However, it is important to remember that *perisseuō* and its cognates can also mean "to be leftover," or "to have something leftover." Therefore Paul's passage can also be read:

> God is able to grant you every grace in excess [*charin perisseusai*], so that you have everything you need at all times and even have plenty leftover [*perisseuēte*] for much good praxis.[57]

Whether or not that is what Paul meant, his words allowed later readers to adopt a conveniently flexible notion of what constituted excess material resources, that is, the surplus wealth from which a charitable "blessing" might derive.[58] By insisting that monks give a *eulogia* to anyone who came by,

56. Barsanuphius, *Ep.* 589 (SC 451:786): ἐὰν ᾖ χρεία τοῦ δοῦναι αὐτῷ μικρὸν περισσόν, δὸς καὶ ἀπόλυσον; translation mine.

57. 2 Cor. 9:8: δυνατεῖ δὲ ὁ θεὸς πᾶσαν χάριν περισσεῦσαι εἰς ὑμᾶς, ἵνα ἐν παντὶ πάντοτε πᾶσαν αὐτάρκειαν ἔχοντες περισσεύητε εἰς πᾶν ἔργον ἀγαθόν. The first translation is from the NRSV, the second from Georgi, *Remembering the Poor*, 96.

58. Basil uses περίσσευμα as analogous to leftovers from a meal in *Hom. in divites* 1 (PG 31:304a). For other examples, see G. Lampe, *A Patristic Greek Lexicon* (Oxford: Clarendon Press, 1961), s.v. περισσεία, περίσσευμα, and περισσεύω.

Barsanuphius was merely insisting that they give such people a *mikron peris-seuma*: a "little leftover," anything that they did not need for themselves.

To some extent this was akin to what Barsanuphius recommended to lay readers. Asked whether beggars should be given the higher-quality bread or wine that one had set aside for oneself, or something out of a second-rate stock, Barsanuphius advised:

> Concerning beggars: whenever we cannot treat them on an equal footing, nor love our neighbor as ourselves, then we must act according to our ability, acknowledging our feebleness, and give them the second-rate.[59]

But his recommendation to monastic readers seems to have primarily addressed the problem of quantity and reflects certain early monastic practices regarding the prudent use of leftovers. Pachomian stewards, for instance, were required to take back what remained of their monks' rations after a three-day period and mix them up with the rest of the stores for later redistribution.[60] George of Choziba, like other hermits, was said to live on whatever scraps he found leftover on local monastery tables; these he would take home, roll into balls, and bake in the sun for later use.[61] Such practices were motivated in part by a pious concern not to waste anything that belonged to or had been provided by God.[62] Yet they also represented a strategy for making more out of less, whereby leftover scraps provided a cheap extra resource that a monk could utilize either to feed himself or to provide charity for others.

An outstanding example of this stewardship strategy is found in John of Ephesus's account of the monk Hala the Zealous. Hala received this name, we are told, because of the extreme measures he took to provide charity to the poor. This included collecting the "leavings" that remained after every meal in his monastery. These he would cook back up and give to beggars waiting outside the monastery's gate: "and so he would perfectly carry out all [his] ministration to the needy with superfluity."[63] Hala is said to have done this only after his community had become impoverished, and much to his steward's annoyance. Elsewhere, however, it seems to have been a regular practice. The sixth-century *Rule of the Master*, for example, anticipates that a monk might wish to leave some bread on his plate "to be added as a gift

---

59. Barsanuphius, *Ep.* 636 (SC 468:62–64): δὸς αὐτοὺς τὰ δευτερεῖα.

60. *Reg. pach.* 38; cf. *Reg. mag.* 23.33–37; 25.

61. *V. Georgii Chozibitae* 3.12; cf. ibid., 2.6, Cyril of Scythopolis, *V. Sabae* 44; *Apophth. Patr.* Benjamin 1; *V. Lupicini* (one of the Jura fathers) 72.

62. In a passage that explains how everything in a monastery belongs to God, John Cassian, *Inst.* 4.20 describes how penance was imposed on a bursar for wasting holy goods, after carelessly neglecting three lentils that had spilled on the ground. The scruple recalls those concerning Eucharist elements that had fallen from a church altar.

63. John Eph., "Life of Hala the Zealous," *HBO* 33, ed. and trans. E. W. Brooks, PO 18:600–601.

to the monastery's aims," so as to be "given by the cellarer into the hand of a poor beggar."[64] Indeed, leaving food on one's plate so as to provide something for others had already been recommended as a charitable policy in the third-century church manual, the *Apostolic Tradition*.[65]

Thus sixth-century monks perpetuated an old Christian strategy for generating charity out of leftovers. More to the point, however, is that such leftovers were now being identified as resources out of which charitable "blessings" could be derived: the *Rule of the Master*, for example, allows monks to sell "anything superfluous that might be leftover" from their handwork if it were useless for their monastery "or for sending out as *eulogiai*."[66] In other words, monastic gifts might come from leftovers that were useful as such, but were considered leftovers all the same. Not only that: such leftovers were also now being identified as charitable "blessings" themselves. We see this above all from an episode in the sixth-century *Life of Nicholas of Sion*. Nicholas was the abbot of a monastery called Sion, located in the highlands of Lycia (above the coast of southern Turkey). One year famine devastated the region. According to his hagiographer, Nicholas responded by taking grain, wine, and oxen from his monastery stores and heading off to visit one village martyr shrine after another. At each he would call the people together, make a sacrifice, and feast them on the remains. This he did at ten shrines for three weeks without receiving any additional supplies. He managed to do so because "many eulogiai were leftover from" each feast, leaving "a superfluity of eulogiai"—that is, leftover grain, wine, and oxen—from which he could draw for the next. In this way, we are told, "his provisions kept multiplying."[67]

Here, of course, we have another multiplication story, inspired by scriptural precedents. Yet this example, more than any other, illustrates how the early Byzantine concept of a "blessing" blurred any distinction between abundant material resources and leftover material resources. Therein lay its practical and spiritual importance: in monastic thought, the quality associated with either type of resource (or the gifts derived from them) was considered to be equal and ever the same: all were to be appreciated as God-given "blessings" and so valued to the highest degree, even if by ordinary "human" standards

64. *Reg. mag.* 27.47–51; trans. Eberle, *Rule of the Master*, 186–87.

65. *Trad. ap.* 28; *Hyppolyte de Rome: La tradition Apostolique d' après les anciennes versions*, ed. B. Botte, SC 11² (Paris: Cerf, 1968), 103: *Si . . . omnes gustent sufficienter, gustate ut et superet et quibuscumque voluerit qui vocavit vos mittat tamquam de reliquiis sanctorum*. See Charles Bobertz, "The Role of Patron in the *Cena Dominica* of Hippolytus' *Apostolic Tradition*," *JTS*, n.s., 44 (1993): 177–78, with further references.

66. *Reg. mag.* 85.1 (SC 106:346–47), translation mine. Cf. *reg. mag.* 87.73–74 (SC 106:362), where alms (*elemosyna*) are to be given by the abbot from *quidquid necessariae utilitati monasterii supervacuum abundare viderit*.

67. *V. Nicolai Sionitae* 56–57 (I. Sevcenko and N. Sevcenko, eds., *The Life of Saint Nicholas of Sion*, Archbishop Iakovos Library of Ecclesiastical and Historical Sources 10 [Brookline, MA: Hellenic College Press, 1984], 88–90). On this passage, see also Trombley, "Monastic Foundations," 57–58.

such charitable resources might sometimes seem to be second-rate. Thus the "blessings" concept helped monks cope with fluctuations in quantity while maintaining a high sense of quality and dignity. It provided a highly functional concept that could accommodate a wide spectrum of material circumstances and enable monks to find wealth amid scarcity in both theory and fact.

This religious and economic approach to leftover resources appears to have been conceptually akin to Jewish thought concerning "gleanings."[68] The practice of scavenging whatever remained after a harvest may have been a survival strategy familiar to people throughout the Near East; certainly it was known to early Byzantine Christians.[69] In Jewish tradition, however, it was identified as a means by which God would provide for those who could not possess or work any part of the promised land. Rabbinic teachings on the matter are preserved in the Mishnah's tractate *Pe'ah*. This prescribes how Jewish farmers at harvest time were to neglect a marginal part of a field or leave whatever fell from their tools or hands, so that Jewish priests and the poor could take the grain that was left behind and use it for themselves. Note that, according to this system, Jewish farmers were not supposed to actively allocate or provide charity from anything they had reaped for themselves. Rather, all was to come from whatever fell by chance: "precisely the random . . . 'accidental' nature of the discarded harvest made it into pe'ah."[70] In this way, "God claims that which is owed him and then gives it to those under his special care, the poor and the priests."[71]

As with any windfall, the sheer element of unpredictability must have helped make such "gleanings" seem divine. So too with material "blessings." These similarly represented superfluous resources that were dignified by their association with God, and through which God might ideally feed "those under his special care," in such a way as to not unduly tax what God had given to others. In other words, "gleanings" and "blessings" were both concepts meant to guarantee that charity would always be provided to those in need, despite variations in economic circumstance. It is apparent, however, that monastic thought regarding material "blessings" differed from rabbinic thought regarding "gleanings" in at least three respects: first, by explicitly identifying whatever

68. For biblical prescriptions on gleaning, see Lev. 19:9–10; 23:22; Deut. 24:19–21; 26:12. Here I follow Roger Brooks, *Support for the Poor in the Mishnaic Law of Agriculture: Tractate Peah*, Brown Judaic Studies 43 (Chico, CA: Scholars Press, 1983), 17–40. Hans Dieter Betz, *2 Corinthians 8 and 9: A Commentary on Two Administrative Letters of the Apostle Paul* (Philadelphia: Fortress Press, 1985), 116, relates Paul's notion of generosity in 2 Cor. 9:10 to that of gleaning in Lev. 19:9–10.

69. In fact, to my knowledge it is only in Christian sources (from late antique Syria and Egypt) that we find references to gleaning actually being practiced: see *Canons of Ps.- Athanasius* 69, *Apophth. patr.* Macarius 7, and *v. Sym. Styl. Syr.* 11. These references assume that contemporary readers needed no explanation of either gleaners or gleaning.

70. Holman, *Hungry Are Dying*, 44.

71. R. Brooks, *Support for the Poor*, 18.

God had given—even if a mere leftover—as a "blessing" itself;[72] second, by insisting that such "blessings" should be made available throughout the year, and not just at harvest time; and third, by emphasizing the active responsibility of humans to pass on whatever "blessing" God had given.

Much that was distinctive about monastic thought regarding *eulogia* derived from 2 Cor. 8–9, including the emphasis on human responsibility in providing such a gift.[73] Another reason for that particular emphasis was that willingness to give a *eulogia* indiscriminately and cheerfully to the anonymous poor at all times of the year, even if it were only a "little leftover," always required a conscientious benevolence toward others, and sometimes a deliberate self-denial. Symeon Stylites the Younger, for example, forbade his monks from taking offerings that laypeople brought to his column near Antioch, thereby forcing them to live entirely off their own manual labor, so that all such donations could pass directly to the poor.[74] As his monks grumbled, this was an unusual stewardship policy,[75] one that denied them the use of any free surplus for themselves. Not surprisingly, this policy is mainly attested among solitaries, for whom the "regifting" of lay gifts was considered an ideal way to provide charity while maintaining ascetic poverty and independence.[76] In cenobitic settings, the challenge more often seems to have been that of being willing to fast so as to provide any charity at all during a crisis. Thus in an unusual multiplication story John of Ephesus describes how the monks of a Syrian monastery at Amida (modern Diyarbakir, Turkey) denied themselves food during a famine in order to feed the poor at their gate. When all the bread had been served and only a "little remained over," the abbot addressed the monks in their refectory, saying, "Let each of us receive a little 'blessing' with thanksgiving, and continue without murmuring, for thus we will have recompense from God." Because the abbot and his monks so generously fasted on their "blessings"—that is, on leftover crumbs—"the tables were found to be full of bread in abundance."[77]

72. Stuiber, "Eulogia," 904–5; and A. Murtonen, "The Use and Meaning of the Words *Lebarak* and *Berakah* in the Old Testament," *VT* 9 (1959): 173. Note that the word is not used in a material sense of "gift" in rabbinic sources; certainly it does not seem to have become technically used as such as it did in Christian church and monastic settings.

73. Cf. Georgi, *Remembering the Poor*, 94–95. The role of *proairesis* is especially emphasized in *V. Dalmatii* 1.2, discussed in Caner, "Towards a Miraculous Economy," 361–63.

74. See Paul van den Ven, *La vie ancienne de S. Syméon Stylite le Jeune (521–592)*, 2 vols., Studia hagiographica 32 (Brussels: Société des Bollandistes, 1962), 1:212–13.

75. *V. Sym. Styl. Iunioris* 123, where Symeon's monks grumbled that his policy was unusual and unwarranted, since Paul had allowed those who served the altar to live on offerings (1 Cor. 9:13). Comparable policies (of refusing to use any gifts) are otherwise mainly attested for anchorites (see next note) or *anargyri*—saints who refused to charge any fee for healings (Symeon Jr. was primarily a healing saint).

76. See John Cassian, *Coll.* 24.12, *Apophth. Patr.* Zeno 1; and Caner, "Towards a Miraculous Economy," 360–64.

77. John Eph., "Of the Amidene Convents," *HBO* 35, ed. and trans. Brooks, PO 18:616.

In early Byzantine monasticism, one sure sign of holiness was the ability to see the world in transcendent terms, that is, in a manner not *anthrōpinon*. So too, as this story shows, one responsibility of an early Byzantine abbot was to teach his monks how to appreciate whatever leftovers they received as God-given "blessings," and to accept them thankfully, "without murmuring," like manna from heaven (Exod. 16:3–35; Num. 11:1–6). It was precisely this appreciative yet self-denying attitude toward surplus wealth that made monks and monasteries seem different from the ordinary poor, and attractive to lay donors—with the result that the monastery of a reputed holy person might abound with material "blessings" in actual fact.[78]

It is notable, however, that most of the multiplication stories discussed in this essay are set amid scarcity. This does not merely reflect a hagiographical need to place monastic life in a scriptural framework. In a later time, Coptic monks would perform a liturgy remembering Jesus's feeding of the multitudes every spring on Palm Sunday in their monastery's refectory and alms gate.[79] Early Byzantine monks also knew that the possibility of famine always loomed until the new year's harvest had been secured.[80] No doubt the communal labor and discipline of a monastery helped shelter its members from vicissitudes that kept most other people on the brink of starvation,[81] and certainly monastic ideology assured that God would eventually always save the truly "poor in spirit." Nevertheless, monks were also expected to share whatever "blessings" they received with anyone else in need, even though, to judge from the papyri, such "blessings" might amount to no more than token quantities of grain.[82]

The danger of actually depending on such charity is indicated by one final multiplication story, told by Gregory of Tours (d. 594) about the monks of the Theotokos Monastery in Jerusalem. Due to lay piety, he says, this monastery was accustomed to receiving many offerings, the biggest being sent by the emperor. At one point, however, for reasons unexplained (no famine is mentioned, nor the arrival of unexpected guests), the monastery ran out

78. John Chrysostom, *Hom. 1 Tim.* 14.3; Nilus of Ancyra, *Magn.* 4–18, *Epp.* 2.60, 136, and 3.58; Besa, *V. Sinuthi* 34; Cyril Scyth., *V. Euthymii* 39.

79. L. Villecourt, "Les observances liturgiques et la discipline de jeûne dans l'Église copte," *Le Muséon* 38 (1925): 261–320, at 271.

80. See Garnsey, *Famine and Food Supply*, 17–34, on general questions of frequency or perceptions thereof; cf. Peter Brown, "Response to Robert M. Grant, 'The Problem of Miraculous Feeding in the Graeco-Roman World,'" *Center for Hermeneutical Studies: Colloquy* 42 (Berkeley: Graduate Theological Union, 1982), 19–24.

81. Patlagean, *Pauvreté*, 338–40, considers this was one of the great contributions of early monastic organization.

82. See above, n. 54. Ewa Wipszycka, "Contribution à l'étude de l'économies de la congrégation pachômienne," *JJP* 26 (1996): 185, notes that land parcels donated to Egyptian monasteries appear to have been small and marginal, suggesting that few would have been able to subsist on such gifts alone.

of supplies. After two days of hunger, its monks told their abbot, "Give us food, or else allow us to go somewhere else where it is possible to support ourselves; otherwise, we are leaving without your permission so that we do not die of starvation."[83]

Eventually, of course, the Theotokos heard their prayers and filled their granary. Gregory's story makes clear, however, not only how this monastery depended on outside donations but also how perilously ephemeral such resources could be. It indicates that even a "wealthy," well-known monastery, despite being amply subsidized by lay gifts and imperial largesse, might run out of supplies and face grievous want, with or without the problem of feeding unexpected guests. For this reason it also vividly illustrates why a monastic economy of "blessings" in this period also sometimes had to be one of leftovers.

83. Greg. Tur., *Gloria mart.* 9, in *Monumenta Germaniae historica*, ed. B. Kusch, Scriptores rerum Merowingicarum, vol. 1, no. 2 (Berlin: Weidmannsche, 1969), 44, *in quo tam loco devotio populi saepe plurima confert, venum etiam ab imperatoris iussa ibi non minima largiuntur.* Translation by Raymond Van Dam, *Gregory of Tours: Glory of the Martyrs* (Liverpool: Liverpool University Press, 1988), 31.

16

TRADE, PROFIT, AND SALVATION IN THE LATE PATRISTIC AND THE BYZANTINE PERIOD

ANGELIKI E. LAIOU

C an the rich enter the kingdom of Heaven? With great difficulty, as we all know. The fearsome statement, "Again I tell you, it is easier for a camel to go through the eye of a needle than for someone who is rich to enter the kingdom of God" (Matt. 19:24), supplemented by the statement on charity, "If you wish to be perfect, go, sell your possessions, and give the money to the poor, and you will have treasure in heaven" (Matt. 19:21), encapsulates two of the most influential teachings of the church on wealth, its dangers, the way to avoid these dangers through almsgiving, and the reversal of fortunes in this world and in the next. Since salvation is the desired end of all Christian life, the good Christian will try to avoid the pitfalls inherent in the acquisition and the ownership of wealth. It has been argued that the church teachings of the formative centuries regarding wealth, profit, and specifically its acquisition through trade, changed both the economic ideology and the practice affecting the economy, as Christianity took a hold on both the

In the research for this topic I was helped considerably by the Dumbarton Oaks Hagiography Database.

minds and the behavior of the faithful. An eleemosynary culture has specific attitudes toward wealth accumulation, the redistribution of resources, the creation of wealth, and the pursuit of individual profit.[1] Whether or not one agrees with all the corollaries of such statements, and I do not,[2] there is no question that the early church had specific, although complex teachings in matters economic and sought to alter the behavior of economic actors. In this pursuit, the church incorporated, and thus gave new life to, some ideas of ancient Greek philosophers.

Nowhere is the economic teaching of the church more evident than in its approach to exchange, trade, profit from trade, and the profit that accrues to money, that is, the interest drawn on loans. In ancient and medieval European societies, agriculture had a privileged place. Not only was it the basis of the economy, the sector that engaged the activities of most humans, the largest creator of surplus; it was also the most acceptable economic pursuit. The appropriation of the surplus by rich landlords may have been considered problematic, especially by men of the church who saw in it two unacceptable or at least suspect elements: love and accumulation of wealth, and profiting from the labor of others. On the whole, however, agricultural activity was considered a good thing: productive and morally unobjectionable, both necessary and meritorious. Patristic teaching on agriculture seems primarily to reinforce ancient ideas about the desirability of autarky, and the same holds true for all but the most rigorist of saints' lives. However, trade, credit, banking, the work of the merchant and the moneylender, and the money that is derived from it have created problems for thinkers since antiquity. Christianity added its own ideological force to negative stereotypes about trade, exchange, and merchants. The economy of exchange continued to pose problems to those who create moral and social values even into the nineteenth century—in effect, from Aristotle to Karl Marx. The major questions that engaged Christian thinkers and writers are, Where does the merchant's profit derive from? What part of it is legitimate? Is the merchant allowed a specific profit, and if so, how much and on what grounds?

In this essay, I discuss the values established by the church on trade, profit, and the merchant, and how these values played out in Byzantine society. At the end, we will see how the perception of the merchant in Byzantine sources works with Byzantine ideas of the structure of society. I deal briefly with some of the most influential ideas of the fathers of the fourth century and later, and

1. See E. Patlagean, *Pauvreté économique et pauvreté sociale à Byzance, 4e–7e siècles* (Paris: Mouton, 1977), esp. 181–203; and A. Giardina, "Modi di scambio e valori sociali nel mondo bizantino (IV–XII secolo)," in *Mercati e mercanti nell'alto medioevo: L'area euroasiatica e l'area mediterranea* (Spoleto: Presso la sede del Centro, 1993), 523–83.

2. A. E. Laiou, "Economic Thought and Ideology," in *The Economic History of Byzantium from the Seventh through the Fifteenth Century*, ed. A. E. Laiou (Washington, DC: Dumbarton Oaks Research Library and Collection, 2002), 1123–44.

concentrate on the period down to the eleventh century, with a few references to later texts. This is a partial discussion because, apart from patristic teachings, the focus is primarily on hagiography. Thus the source base is specific, and the topics addressed are almost purely ideological. In the Byzantine Empire, hagiographic production is concentrated in the period between the sixth and tenth centuries, with a few important vitae written in the eleventh century and far fewer in the twelfth. A few general introductory points are important. First, saints' lives do not speak in a single voice any more than do other sources. Much depends on the time and the author, not to mention the saint herself or himself. Rigorist saints' lives can carry deep into the eleventh century ideas that had most of their force in earlier eras. Second, there is a problem that affects primarily the lives of early saints who lived in the first, second, third, or fourth centuries, but whose lives were written in the seventh century or after. What period is reflected in the ideology?

Early Teachings on Wealth

One must start in the beginning—not so much the New Testament, which seems to value poverty over wealth, for men interpreted this foundational text as they saw fit, but rather with the economic teachings of the fourth-century Greek fathers, especially St. Basil of Caesarea and St. John Chrysostom. Both knew their classics very well, but they were also sharp observers of contemporary reality and reacted to the great inequalities of their day. They, and their successors, were aiming to replace economic modes of behavior with noneconomic ones. They deplored wealth, for it makes entry into the kingdom of Heaven difficult. The accumulation of wealth on earth must be replaced by the accumulation of wealth in heaven. That can be achieved only by noneconomic behavior: charity, which involves the redistribution of wealth from rich to poor, is the cardinal virtue. The quest of profit on earth is condemned; the search for profit in heaven is praised.[3] The accumulation of goods beyond what is strictly necessary for survival is denounced in the strongest terms by St. Basil: "What goes beyond need has the appearance of avarice, and avarice is condemned as idolatry."[4] These ideas are applied to various economic activities. Writing about agriculture, St. John Chrysostom turns to discuss those who appear to be just. They are

> those who own land and gain their wealth from it. But who could be more unjust than they? For if one were to examine how they treat the poor and miserable

3. St. John Chrysostom, *Peri eleēmosynēs* (PG 64:433ff).
4. St. Basil, *The Letters*, trans. Roy J. Deferrari, LCL (London: W. Heinemann, 1926), 1:138–40: ὅτι ἡ περίσσεια ἡ ὑπὲρ τὴν χρείαν εἰκόνα πλεονεξίας ἐμφαίνει, ἡ δὲ πλεονεξία ἀπόφασιν ἔχει εἰδωλολατρείας (the translation is my own).

peasants, one would find them worse than the barbarians. . . . They demand unbearable rents and corvées from those who are [already] almost destroyed by famine, those who work ceaselessly all their lives. [The rich] use the bodies [of the peasants] as though they were donkeys or mules, or, really, stones, not allowing them to breathe at all; whether the land is productive or not is all the same to [the landlords], who exploit the peasants equally and grant them no respite. (*Hom. Matt.* 61 [PG 58:591])

Thus, there is general condemnation of the desire for wealth, especially if it entails the exploitation of others. The model presented is that of autarkic production, and the one thing that justifies economic activity is labor. The labor of the peasant is evident, as is that of the artisan: "Let us examine the race of creators, the manufacturers. They, more than anyone, seem to be living off their rightful labor and sweat" (*Hom. Matt.* 61 [PG 58:591]). Of great importance is the idea that the only input that may be rewarded is labor.

Exchange or trade is condemned, because the labor involved in it is not evident and because the profession itself is constructed on lies and deception. John Chrysostom warns the merchant of the dangers of his profession: the dangers of the journey, the hazards of the weather. But the dangers are also spiritual: one has to haggle, and haggling means lying, and lying is dangerous to the soul (PG 64:436). The two following passages make this point as well as a few related ones:

a. [on artisans]: But even they, if they are not careful, gather much evil from this. For they add to their rightful labor the injustice that comes from buying and selling, and often pile oaths and perjury and lies onto their greed [*pleonexia*], and they care only for earthly things. They do everything they can to gain money, while they do not try very hard to give to those in need, since what they want is constantly to increase their property. What can one say about the mocking, the insults, the loans, the interest, the exchanges that smell of trade, the shameless bargaining? (*Hom. Matt.* 61 [PG 58:591])

b. Great are the benefits of alms-giving. Nothing else is equal to almsgiving. No virtue is as powerful to expunge sin. . . . Give to the poor and God will repay the debt. He hastens to take care of the guarantees of the debts you have given to the poor, and he will not simply repay them, he will repay them with many blessings. . . . Great is the profit from almsgiving. If you desire to buy a cloak or an ox you go to the fair, and you suffer from heat, and sometimes from hunger and thirst. And after suffering all this you barely manage to meet your purpose. Even when you are successful, the seller will not give you [the merchandise] as you wish, but as he wishes. You swear, "I will not buy it at this price," and he swears, "I will not sell at such a price" and thus the first sin falls between you; for, as Solomon says, "between buying and selling sin is born." Necessarily, one or the other will lie, or even both of you, for quite frequently neither the buyer nor the seller is truthful. And, then, after you have bought [the item] with such pains, you are still not safe. Many times, before you reach home your purchase has died, or become lost, or is seen to be unsuitable, and your toil is doubled. None of this will happen to you if you pursue the Kingdom of Heaven. . . . As you sit in your house, the poor man comes to you and says, "give me bread and take Paradise; give me a rag of a dress and receive the Kingdom of Heaven." (*Homily on Almsgiving* [PG 64:434ff])

The points that emerge are that greed is a sin, that trade means haggling and lying, that it holds dangers both physical and spiritual, and that the dangers of trade are contrasted to charity, the free gift. The negative attitude to "haggling and lying" has good classical antecedents, which the fourth-century church fathers perpetuated.[5]

The same church fathers also condemn loans given at interest, although they do acknowledge that such loans exist. Their efforts seem to be not to prohibit lending at interest but rather to persuade people that it is much better to distribute their wealth and receive interest in heaven.[6]

The most highly rigorist text in this connection, as also in the condemnation of the profit of money, what is called usury in the western Middle Ages, is the *Opus imperfectum in Matthaeum*. Today it exists only in a Latin version, possibly a summary of an original text that, according to scholarly opinion, was Greek, composed in the fifth or sixth century.[7] Here are the most pertinent parts of the text:

"And He drove out [of the Temple] those who bought and those who sold." (Matt. 21.12)

This means that a merchant can never or almost never please God. Therefore, no Christian should be a merchant. Or, if he wishes to be a merchant, let him be thrown out of the church according to the saying of the prophet, "Because I have not known bargaining I will enter into the Kingdom of Heaven." . . . He who buys and sells cannot be free of lies and perjury: for it is necessary that one of the merchants swear that the thing he is buying is not worth its price, while the other swear that the thing he is selling is worth more than the sale price. Nor is the property of the merchants stable. It is either destroyed while the merchant

5. L. Soverini, "Parole, voce, gesti del commerciante nella Grecia classica," in *Annali della Scuola normale superiore di Pisa, Classe di lettere e filosofia*, series 3, vol. 22, no. 3 (Pisa: 1992), 811–83; see also the important work by Giardina, "Modi di scambio."

6. John Chrysostom, *Hom. Matt.* 66, PG 58:630ff.

7. Giardina, "Modi di scambio," 546, dates the text to 420 and makes considerable use of it. On the text and its date, see A. E. Laiou, "*Nummus parit nummos*: L'usurier, le juriste et le philosophe à Byzance," in *Académie des inscriptions et belles lettres, Comptes rendus* (Paris: De Boccard, 1999), 588; and O. Langholm, *The Aristotelian Analysis of Usury* (Bergen, Norway: Universitetsforlaget, 1984), 72; cf. O. Bardenweher, *Geschichte der altkirchlichen Litteratur*, 5 vols. (St. Louis: Herder, 1913–1932), 3:597.

is still alive, or it is dissipated by bad heirs or it is inherited by outsiders and enemies. Nothing that is collected evilly can come to any good.[8]

The dependence of the text from John Chrysostom is evident. The author then asks who may be considered a merchant. Since all people appear to be merchants, as, for example, the farmer who buys oxen and sells the produce of the land, he answers his own question by establishing who is not a merchant:

> He who buys a thing not so as to sell it in the same unchanged and complete form but rather in order to work with it, he is not a merchant, for he is selling not the thing itself but rather his own work: that is to say, if one sells a thing whose value lies not in the thing itself but rather in the work he has put in it, that is not commerce. But he who buys a thing so as to resell it complete and unchanged and thus realize a profit, he is a merchant who was thrown out of the Temple of the Lord. Of all merchants the most accursed is the usurer. For, if he who buys in order to resell is a merchant, and accursed, how much more accursed is he who gives at interest money that he has not bought but that has been given him by God? (*Opus imperf. in Matt.* [PG 56:840])

The tenor of this passage is that the value of a thing lies not in the thing itself but in the labor that has gone into it, which creates added value, in modern parlance. We note that labor, in this construction, is work that creates something tangible, whether in crops or in manufactured objects, so no labor is recognized for the merchant. The text, very influential in western Europe, may have been unknown or little known in Byzantium, but its rigorist principles, especially with regard to trade, may be found in other Byzantine sources as well—except, perhaps, for the frightening statement that "no Christian should be a merchant."[9]

Greatest Virtue: Charity

There can be no question that the burden of Christian teaching in the first centuries was to turn economic behavior—the pursuit of profit on earth—into noneconomic behavior: the pursuit of profit in heaven. This may be found in sermons as well as in pious *exempla*, that is, edifying stories, and in saints' lives, in the sixth century and later.

In hagiography, the first and greatest virtue is, of course, charity, which takes the transfer of resources and commodities completely outside the realm of economic activity and the marketplace. Gifts, donations, and alms

---

8. *Opus imperfectum in Matthaeum* (PG 56:839–840); *Hom.* 38 on chap. 21.

9. It is noteworthy that Karl Marx voiced very similar thoughts: *Capital: A Critique of Political Economy*, 3 vols. (London: Lawrence & Wishart, 1970), 3:609.

are the form of exchange that hagiographic sources are most interested in presenting. The highest virtue in that respect is giving to the poor everything, including what one needs for one's own survival—and a number of saints did so: St. Philaretos (late eighth century), St. Paul of Latros (tenth century), and St. Cyril Phileotes (late eleventh century), among others. An extreme example is St. Paul of Latros (d. 955) who, having distributed his entire property to the poor, approached a man he did not know, asking him to take him to a place where he himself would be unknown, and there to sell him as a slave and distribute the money to the poor.[10] Pious laypeople are also mentioned as performing acts of charity, without ever going nearly as far as St. Paul of Latros.

An important variation on the theme of charity may be found in a number of saints' lives or pious *exempla*. In these texts, we sometimes find the ultimate purpose served by a complex process: the hero engages in behavior that is, on the face of it, uneconomic and ostensibly goes against his interests; then he is rewarded by a miracle, and thus not only does he gain credit in heaven but his economic interests on earth are better served than if he had engaged in normal economic behavior.[11] Such a story appears in the *Life of David, Symeon, and George*. At a time of famine, George was sent to the mill to grind the monastery's wheat into flour. On his return, he met two poor men to whom he gave the flour, and, since they had trouble carrying it, the monastery's donkey as well. The abbot chastised him, but two hours later an unknown man arrived, bringing two donkeys carrying wheat, cheese, and other foods. Various forms of the verb *antameibo*, "to reward," are used to describe the event.[12] The basic traits of these stories may be summarized as follows. A saint or another pious person gives money or goods away in charity; his or her behavior is, and is considered to be, extreme. Yet the hero is right in all ways and in all realms, for what is given away is eventually returned, multiplied many times over. The point, however, is that this reward on earth is not expected, not predictable, perhaps not repeatable. It is a miracle, by definition an extraordinary event.

This is what has been called the "économie miraculeuse," the miraculous economy. Vincent Déroche uses this felicitous term to describe the idea,

10. H. Delehaye, ed., "Vita S. Pauli Iunioris," in *Milet* 3.1, ed. T. Wiegand (Berlin: G. Reimer, 1913), 129.

11. See the example of a man from Nisibis, narrated in the *Pratum Spirituale*, PG 87 ter, no. 185, discussed in A. E. Laiou, "The Church, Economic Thought and Economic Practice," in *The Christian East, Its Institutions and Its Thought: A Critical Reflection (= Orientalia Christiana Analecta 251)*, ed. R. F. Taft (Rome: Pontificio Istituto orientale, 1996), 13ff.

12. AnBoll 18 (1899): 240. Similar acts of charity occur in the vita of St. Cyril Phileotes, *La vie de Saint Cyrille le Philéote moine byzantin*, ed. E. Sargologos (Brussels: Société des Bollandistes, 1964), 235ff, and a number of other texts. The vita of St. Cyril also reports tension between the saint, who distributed much of the monastery's liquid assets, and the other monks, who wanted to use the money for their own needs.

common in ecclesiastical writings of the seventh century but also later, that God gives rewards *in this world* to those who perform their Christian duty of almsgiving. God provides much more than is spent on alms, perhaps a hundred times more. The more charity one performs, the more one receives earthly rewards.[13] The central point must be stressed, that what is rewarded by riches on this earth is noneconomic behavior. Furthermore, the reward is a gift from God: it is a miracle, attributable to God's freedom of action and not to any freedom of the market. The idea that behavior that is considered irrational from the economic viewpoint is more profitable *on this earth* than is rational behavior is in modern eyes more subversive to economic activity than any overall condemnation of profit-seeking. The hagiography of the Byzantine period is replete with such stories, but it is important to note that the benefits attributed to uneconomic behavior are attenuated by the reported debate or dispute with other ecclesiastics who urge economic rationality of sorts.

Charity and the Marketplace

Thus the church sought to turn economic behavior upside down. But the behavior of the merchant, if he is to remain a merchant, must be economic; to make a living, he must buy cheap and sell dear (or at least try to); he must take advantage of the vagaries of supply and demand; and he cannot base his profession on charity. How did men of the church, then, see the merchant? Specifically, how does the merchant appear in the hagiographic sources, which carry a moral lesson, to be sure, but which also present everyday situations in which people function? Market exchanges and merchants do find their way into saints' lives. The market exchanges found in hagiography can be subdivided into three categories: charity that uses the marketplace; the presence and participation of saints in the market; and the activities of professional merchants.

It is possible for saints to use the market as well as the money market to obtain funds to invest in charity. St. Mary the Younger, a saint of the early tenth century, paid off the debts of the poor, and she borrowed money for those who could not pay their taxes and were therefore imprisoned; on her deathbed, she ordered that the remainder of her goods be sold to pay off the debts of others.[14] St. Michael Maleinos, who lived in the tenth century, sold his patrimony to distribute part of the proceeds to the poor,[15] and so did

13. V. Déroche, *Études sur Léontios de Néapolis* (Uppsala: Uppsala Universitet, 1995), 240ff.

14. A. E. Laiou, trans., "Life of St. Mary the Younger," in *Holy Women of Byzantium*, ed. A.-M. Talbot (Washington, DC: Dumbarton Oaks Research Library and Collection, 1996), 258, 266.

15. "Vie de Saint Michel Maléinos," *Revue de l'Orient chrétien* 7 (1902): 557–58; on St. Michael Maleinos, see A. E. Laiou, "The General and the Saint: Michael Maleinos and Nikephoros Phokas," in *EYΨYXIA: Mélanges offerts à Hélène Ahrweiler* (Paris: Publications de la Sorbonne, 1998), 399–412.

St. Michael Synkellos (761–845).[16] Some vitae show that the saints were very aware of accountancy and used accounting methods in their works of charity. The patriarch of Constantinople Tarasios (784–806) not only bought in the marketplace woolen coats and blankets to distribute to the poor but also had an account book in which he registered the poor as well as the money he gave them each month in alms (*mēniaia argyriou dosis*), which they would then spend in the marketplace.[17] The same is true of St. Theophylact of Nicomedia (d. 840s), who was named bishop of Nicomedia by Tarasios. One version of his vita reports that he had a register of needy widows, including wellborn ones who were too ashamed to ask for alms, and each month he recorded the amount of money given them in cash (which they then presumably spent in the marketplace). Another version of his vita mentions the details of the register: widows were registered by name, family, place of origin, and appearance. According to this version, they were given gifts in kind once a month.[18] None of this posed any ideological problem: both the New Testament and patristic writings urge one to *sell* one's property and give the proceeds to the poor. Nor do the hagiographers find it in any way necessary to justify the use of the market.

What is interesting here is, first of all, the mention of accounting and accountability—the gifts of a good manager in a rationally organized, economic concern—and the fact that the market plays a positive role, even if only incidentally: a positive role that appears in hagiographic sources in other contexts as well. The hagiographic sources adduced above date mostly from the period of recovery after the difficulties of the time extending from the mid-seventh to late eighth centuries, when trade had been much reduced because of political, demographic, and economic problems. In sources of the sixth and the first half of the seventh centuries, when the late-antique economy was still burgeoning prior to the slump, the marketplace and even the market in money are ubiquitous: a prime witness is the vita of St. John the Almsgiver, patriarch of Alexandria, by Leontios of Neapolis.[19] The marketplace becomes highly visible again in the tenth and eleventh centuries, as the economy expands.

16. Mary B. Cunningham, ed. and trans., *The Life of Michael the Synkellos* (Belfast: Belfast Byzantine Enterprises, Queen's University of Belfast, 1991), 48–49.

17. *Ignatii diaconi Vita Tarasii archiepiscopi Constantinopolitani*, Acta societatis scientiarum Fennicae 17 (Helsinki, 1891), 402.

18. F. Halkin, *Hagiologie byzantine* (Brussels: Société des Bollandistes, 1986), 175; A. Vogt, ed., "St. Théophylacte de Nicomédie," AnBoll 50 (1932): 67ff.

19. English translation in E. Dawes and N. H. Baynes, *Three Byzantine Saints* (Crestwood, NY: St. Vladimir's Seminary Press, 1977), 199–270. The same may be said about the miracles of St. Artemios, which take place in seventh-century Constantinople: A. Papadopoulos-Kerameus, *Varia Graeca sacra* (1909; repr., Leipzig: Zentralantiquariat der Deutschen Demokratischen Republik, 1975), 5, 6, 10, 21, 45, 55.

Second, we have the relationship of saints with the marketplace. In the vitae of the ninth and tenth centuries, the saints go to market frequently, either to buy necessities (wood, food, lamps, and olive oil for their lamps) or to sell the fruits of their labor. There is also the land market, more or less everywhere. Here, ideological difficulties may indeed occur. Selling what one has produced or created or fashioned in order to provide for the necessities of life seems permitted by Christian morality as preached by the fourth-century fathers. But there are two potential problems. One is that the act of sale is an alternative to charity, which is always preferable. Such a case occurs in the twelfth-century vita of St. Cyril Phileotes. The saint had given to a pious (*philochristos*) man, who must have been a merchant, eleven woolen cloaks to sell in the city of Anchialos. With the proceeds, he would buy grain, following the injunction that one should earn one's bread by the sweat of one's brow. The merchant forgot to sell the cloaks, and St. Cyril interpreted that as the work of divine providence, since he should have distributed the clothes to the poor without recompense. Jesus Christ would look after the saint's need for food.[20] This is the vita of an especially ascetic saint.

A second problem is the danger that the very act of selling would give rise to the sin of greed, the desire to realize profits that would go beyond autarky. In the vita of St. Theodore of Edessa, a monk makes baskets and sells them in the marketplace. The hagiographer is careful to specify that some of the money was given to the abbot so that the monk and his teacher, Theodore, should not eat without working, while some was distributed to the poor. In a sermon to the monks, Theodore enjoined them to work for their food, but not to be avaricious (*philargyron*), and not to exceed the bounds of self-sufficiency.[21]

Thus for monks or saints and therefore by extension in the morality of hagiography, personal participation in the marketplace can pose problems, especially in the vitae written after the mid-seventh century. This follows the concerns expressed in the fourth century by St. John Chrysostom regarding the labor of artisans and the dangers inherent in the sale of their products. There is, however, an important difference. In the hagiographic sources, the dangers of the marketplace are stressed when the participant in market exchange is a monk or a clergyman, rather than a layperson, while St. John's injunction was a general one.

The third category is that of the professional merchant: the man who buys in order to resell. It is here that hagiography should, in principle, face the most important ideological problems. However, things are not quite what we might expect. One might start by posing the question whether the

20. Sargologos, *La Vie de Saint Cyrille*, chap. 25.

21. I. Pomialovskij, *Zhitie izhe vo sviatykh otsa nashego Feodora Arkhiepiskopa Edesskago* (St. Petersburg, 1892), 15, 34. Theodore was bishop in 836; the vita may have been written in the tenth century, according to Alexander Kazhdan's notes in the Dumbarton Oaks Hagiography Database.

hagiographic sources consider commerce to be essential to the well-being of society, thus a necessary activity for humans. While the question is not posed by the sources in exactly this way, we note that commercial activity sometimes appears in hagiographic texts that sing the praises of a city. In the tenth century, Nicaea, Nicomedia, and Amastris are celebrated as cities that are, among other things, centers of commerce. The vita of Constantine the Jew, who died after 886, extols Nicaea as a city "full of all good things, which attracts those who deal in money/merchandise [*epitēdeuontai to chrēma*], for it is well placed for commerce." Similar are the texts for Nicomedia and Amastris.[22] Trebizond is said to have been a glorious city of great renown: "for there were many important persons [*prouchontes*—the political elite], and valiant soldiers [*stratiōtai epilektoi*—the military elite], very numerous and wealthy merchants [*emporoi te pleistoi kai olvioi*—the economic elite], and a huge number of people, difficult to count."[23] Here we have a presentation of the constituent elements of a good polity: wise counselors, brave soldiers, wealthy merchants, and a large population. So commerce, implicitly or explicitly, and the presence of merchants contribute to the wealth of a city.

The distinguishing traits of commerce and merchants, as depicted in the hagiography, are risk and the pursuit of profit, which makes them even more risk-prone. This is a well-known and ever-present topos in all sorts of sources, from the fourth century to the twelfth and even later. In the writings of the fathers, the risks are economic, physical, and above all moral. In some vitae (for example, that of Germanos of Kosinitza) there is the simple statement that merchants suffer much in the pursuit of profit; no moral hazard is attached.[24]

Very interesting in this respect is the vita of St. George of Amastris (d. ca. 802–807). Some merchants of that city had been accused of an unspecified public crime by the authorities in Trebizond and condemned to death. The saint went from Amastris to Trebizond and took great pains to save the life of the merchants and ensure their freedom. They were probably important people, since they claim that their execution would shame their native city, and their salvation is presented as a gift. At the end of the narration, the hagiographer makes a number of moralizing comments, of which the most relevant are the following.

22. *AASS Nov.* 4, 642; for Nicomedia, see Halkin, *Hagiologie byzantine*, 175–76; for Amastris, *In laudem S. Hyacinthi Amastreni*, by Niketas of Paphlagonia (PG 105:421).

23. J. O. Rosenqvist, *The Hagiographic Dossier of St. Eugenios of Trebizond in Codex Athous Dionysiou 154* (Uppsala: Uppsala Universitet, 1996), 212. This was written during the reign of Alexios II Megas Komnenos of Trebizond (1297–1330), but it refers to the Byzantine period, and specifically to the reign of Basil II (976–1025).

24. *AASS Maii* 3, *7a.

From how many evils would men have been delivered, of how many benefits
would they have been worthy if they had entrusted to the Lord the fulfillment
[of their everyday needs]?

Men should not have invented trading by land and sea, the inopportune cares
and solicitudes, the long travails, the labor, the sleeplessness; for all of these
are the bitter offspring of the love of money [*philargyria*], which causes envy,
murder, shipwrecks, creates thieves and robbers and lies and oaths and perjury,
and a myriad other evils. Oh, if they had entrusted their cares to the Lord, who
feeds the birds that neither sow nor reap, from how many evils they would
have been delivered![25]

The hagiographer is in a long and venerable tradition of commonplaces,
going back to classical antiquity by way of the fourth-century fathers. But
there is a difference. Here the calumnies (the *sykophantiai* of St. Basil) and
murders are the result of avarice as well, but it is the avarice of others (the
functionaries of Trebizond), not of the merchants. Finally, at the end of the
passage, the hagiographer says that as a result of original sin men have to
earn their bread by the sweat of their brows. In context, this is an allusion to
the work of the merchant that would therefore be considered as legitimate
labor, in which case it would legitimately be worthy of a reward. We shall
return to this point of the labor of the merchant.

Another important question in the medieval context is whether the merchant can exercise his profession without sin. Professional merchants appear
with some frequency in our sources. They are not condemned for exercising
this trade. Some among them are exemplary and even saintly: they are pious,
religious, good people who are given to charity while at the same time being
very good at their profession. For example, there are merchants who become
monks, as did Demetrios (d. 897), a wood merchant. He is described as a
man adorned with wisdom (*phronēsei kekosmēmenos*) and piety (*eulabeia*),
who eventually became *hēgoumenos* of Exavoulion. His earlier profession
posed no problem whatsoever, and the presentation of the man is entirely
positive, even if he preferred to sell his shop rather than give it away.[26] Other
pious merchants appear in various hagiographic sources.[27] Thus the answer,
in this context, appears affirmative.

25. V. G. Vasilievskij, *Russo-Vizantijskiya izsljedovanija* (St. Petersburg, 1893), 52–53.

26. "La vie de S. Evariste higoumène à Constantinople," AnBoll 41 (1923): 317–18. Cf. the
vita of St. Lazaros Galesiotes, who died in 1053: *The Life of Lazaros of Mt. Galesion*, trans. R. P. H.
Greenfield (Washington, DC: Dumbarton Oaks Research Library and Collection, 2000), 163–64,
184–85. The reference is to sailors and boat-owners, but in the Middle Ages such people often
doubled as traders.

27. See, e.g., E. von Dobschütz, "Maria Romaia: Zwei unedierte Texte," *ByzZ* 12 (1903): 199–200;
Vita of Constantine the Jew, *AASS Nov.* 4, 29–30, 649.

Of Saints and Merchants and Seafarers

Sometimes saints intervene to help the merchant, and these stories too provide us with information about attitudes toward the merchant; they are connected to the question of the legitimacy of the merchant's profit, for rarely would a saint countenance a questionable activity, unless a more important moral is to be gained. In this twilight zone we must place a miracle affecting St. Spyridon of Tremithous in Cyprus (d. after 346). An early vita, of the seventh century, talks of a sea captain who, like most medieval sea captains, also engaged in trade, and to do so borrowed money from the saint. Then the sea captain tried several ruses to cheat the saint, but he was discovered and repented. Here we have a merchant engaging in lies and deception, and a saint who nevertheless lends him money to engage in his profession. This is the seventh-century version of the vita. In the tenth-century rewriting of the text, the merchant still tries to cheat. But his sin, or at least the occasion for the sin of lying, is that he had spent the money he had originally borrowed from the saint, not in investment that would bring him profit, but on other things. As a result, he became poor and had to lie to the saint to borrow again. When the saint has finished his role in the story and sends the merchant off, he says to him, "Do not covet the goods of others or pollute your conscience with ruses and lies. For the gain acquired by such actions is not profit but manifest damage."[28]

Therefore, the saint lends money to the merchant for him to put it to work. The hagiographer considers that it was given for profit-making investment, not for luxuries. The saint draws the distinction between bad acquisition of money and the merchant's legitimate profit. Indeed, whatever the church fathers might have said, here, in the tenth-century text, we have full acceptance of the profession of the merchant and full acceptance too of commercial profit. It must be added that by the tenth century a number of texts, both hagiographical and other, do accept the legitimacy of profit, as long as it is *just* profit.

In a number of other miracles, the saint intervenes to deliver sailors and merchants from enemies and pirates, especially Arab pirates. Such was the case with St. Gregory the Decapolite and some merchants of Ephesus who were traveling to Constantinople; with St. Blasios of Amorion and merchants who were captured, presumably by Arabs; and with a posthumous miracle of St. Nikon.[29] In all these stories there is no negative commentary on the merchant's profession; the emphasis is on the miracle.

28. P. van den Ven, ed., *La légende de S. Spyridion, évêque de Trimithonte* (Louvain: Publications universitaires, 1953), 92–95; *Symeonis logothetae Metaphrastae opera omnia* (PG 116:457–60).

29. F. Dvornik, *La vie de Saint Grégoire le Décapolite (d. 842?)* (Paris: Champion, 1926), 53; *AASS Nov.* 4, 666; D. Sullivan, *The Life of St. Nikon: Text, Translation, and Commentary* (Brookline, MA:

Marie-France Auzépy has written an interesting study on economic miracles in Byzantine hagiography of the sixth to ninth centuries.[30] In it, she distinguishes a category of miracles that make capital multiply. She notes that these miracles involve maritime commerce and large sums of money, and that they come to an end after the seventh century, whether because economic realities changed after that, as trade receded for a while, or because hagiographic models changed with iconoclasm. Two of these stories, possibly related to each other, are worth mentioning. One involves a ship, belonging to the church of Alexandria, that the patriarch entrusted, along with a load of grain, to a captain. The ship lost its bearings in a storm and ended up in Britain. There the sailors found that the island was suffering from a famine. They sold their grain, evidently at a high price, against a sum of coins and a load of what they were told was tin. The first miracle, then, involves the salvation of the ship and, perhaps, the favorable trading conditions. The second is pure miracle, for when the sea captain returned to Alexandria and tried to sell the tin, it had turned into silver. The miracle, says the hagiographer, is not strange, "for he who multiplied the five loaves and at one time converted the waters of the Nile into blood, transformed a rod into a serpent, and changed fire into dew, easily accomplished this miracle too in order to enrich His servant [the almsgiving Patriarch] and show mercy to the captain."[31]

The other story involves a private individual, trading in his own name. He was a pious man from Constantinople named Theodore, who was rich from his commercial activities but had fallen into hard times. He borrowed money (fifty pounds of gold, no mean sum) from Abraham, a Jew, naming as guarantor of the loan an icon of Christ Antiphonetes. The first venture failed; Theodore borrowed another fifty pounds of gold; there was, again, a tempest, and he and his mates found themselves in the Atlantic, in a land that was at the end of the earth, clearly Britain again. Here they traded their merchandise and with some of the proceeds they bought tin and lead, while for the rest they got gold coins—difficult to imagine in Britain. Theodore sent Abraham his fifty pounds of gold in a box, which he entrusted to the waves. The end result was the conversion of Abraham to Christianity.[32] The moral as far as Abraham is concerned is obvious. As far as the merchant and his work go, his risk and his trading activities are rewarded with enough cash for him

Hellenic College Press, 1987), 92–94, 250ff. The vita of St. Ioannikios mentions a man who went off trading, was captured, and then was liberated: *AASS Nov.* 2.1, 425.

30. M.-Fr. Auzépy, "Miracle et économie à Byzance (VIe–IXe siècles)," in *Miracle et karāma*, ed. D. Aigle, Hagiographies médiévales comparées, Bibliothèque de l'École des hautes études, vol. 109 (Turnhout: Brepols, 2000), 331–51.

31. Dawes and Baynes, *Three Byzantine Saints*, 216–18. This life of St. John the Almsgiver was written after 641.

32. M. Hoferer, *Ioannis Monachi Liber de Miraculis* (Würzburg: Theinsche Druckerei, 1884), 7–41.

to repay his debt and gain profit for himself and his mates. His activities are clearly not condemned; indeed, they are countenanced. Christ is just about made a partner in the venture. This is what Theodore wrote to Abraham, in a letter accompanying the wooden box:

> In the name of the lord God, the Savior and Lord of All, Jesus Christ, my guarantor. I, humble Theodore, salute and address, as if I were in his presence, Abraham who, with God's grace, is my benefactor and creditor. I wish you to know, sir Abraham, that God has protected us and we are all well. And since, *through divine providence*, we have carried out our trade well and profitably, I am sending you, *through my guarantor*, fifty pounds of gold. Receive it from Him and be well and remember us.

Then he put the letter on top of the gold in the box and sealed it securely all around. He stood on the seashore, and, looking up to the sky, he called on God and said,

> My Lord Jesus Christ, intercessor between God and man, who inhabits heaven and supervises the humble things below, you who trade in [*pragmateuomenos*] everything toward the salvation of mankind, heed the voice and the prayer of your unworthy servant. As you *were my guarantor for the loan*, so give this gold back to my benefactor and creditor Abraham through Your divine power and providence. Being emboldened by Your philanthropy, and secure in Your power, I place this box in the sea in unhesitating belief.[33]

In the matter of saints (or, in this last case, Christ) offering help to merchants, what emerges above all is the physical risks in the pursuit of the profession, especially when it involves maritime commerce. The story discussed earlier, of the merchants of Amastris, is a particular case, a remarkable one altogether. One of the more remarkable points about it is that the problems of the merchants are connected to their profession, to be sure, but only because of the risks inherent in traveling from place to place. The profession itself is not condemned.

Dirty versus Clean Money

What we have seen up to now is that, contrary to what one might have expected from the patristic teachings, there is no negative representation of merchants in the hagiographic sources when the reference is to individual merchants—that is, apart from general clichés and commonplaces. The examples given above also answer the question, can the merchant carry on his or her profession without sinning? The answer is manifestly yes. The question

33. Ibid., 30–31 (para. xxxix).

may be asked in other forms: Is the money earned by the merchant in some way dirty or contaminated? Can the saint touch this money? Is it possible to distribute it to the poor without first laundering it, as it were? The question was a vexed one in the medieval West, where it was much discussed with reference primarily to profits coming from moneylending, usury, but also from commerce. It seems that Western theologians were greatly influenced by the *Opus imperfectum in Matthaeum*, with its intransigent condemnation of commerce and merchants; the reference to the eviction of merchants from the temple of the Lord; the idea that "whoever buys and sells cannot be free of lying and perjury," the statement that "no Christian ought to be a merchant."[34] As a result, some Western thinkers argued that the merchant's profits consist of stolen money, and that it is not even permitted to accept them as alms.[35] In the Byzantine saints' lives, there is certainly dirty money. Such, for example, is the money left by the last iconoclast emperor, Theophilos, upon his death, to be distributed to the poor and the monks: St. Symeon of Lesbos did not want to touch it. St. Gregory the Decapolite, when he was in Reggio in Calabria, refused to accept some alms because the money came from a tax collector who had confiscated for the public treasury the goods of those dying intestate and without immediate heirs.[36] There are other cases where the money of fiscal agents and tax collectors is considered dirty.

So the hagiographic sources do indeed state that some money is so ill-gotten that it is condemned and may not be touched. But it does not consist of the profits of the merchant. It is the money made by people by virtue of their function, their membership in the ruling class, their place in the officialdom. They are the ones who oppress the poor, the weaker members of society, who seize the property of their neighbors, and whose greed and avarice grow along with their wealth.[37] Doubtless this is an accurate representation of Byzantine social realities: indeed, the greatest source of wealth and power was public office, and those with access to it were even formally recognized by the government as being in a position to oppress the bulk of the population, while the merchant's profits were, in this period, inconsiderable by comparison. But there seems to be something else at work as well. In a rudimentary and unsystematic way, as one might well expect from this

34. "Qui emit et vendit, sine mendacio et perjuria non posset esse. . . . nullus Christianus debet esse mercator"; PG 56:839–40. Cf. the statement of Roland of Cremona (1219–1259), that "nullus mercator posset fieri sine peccato": O. Langholm, *Economics in the Medieval Schools: Wealth, Exchange, Value, Money and Usury according to the Paris Theological Tradition, 1200–1350* (Leiden: Brill, 1992), 92.

35. Langholm, *Economics*, 9.

36. F. Dvornik, *La vie de St Grégoire*, 55. Gregory was born sometime between 780 and 790 and died in or before 842. The vita was written by Ignatios the Deacon soon thereafter. Cf., in a similar vein, Sargologos, *La vie de Saint Cyrille*, chaps. 16 and 35.

37. N. A. Bees, "Vie de Saint Théoclète évêque de Lacédémone," *Revue byzantine*, suppl. to vol. 2 (1916): 35ff.

literary genre, there seems to emerge the idea that the merchant's profit is legitimate, for two reasons: because of the risk merchants run, and for the much more important reason that merchants' work is conceived as true labor, which therefore is entitled to reward, as is the labor of anyone else.[38]

Admittedly, the indications that would support this last point are not very precise in the hagiographic sources. But the vita of St. Spyridon does speak of the *kamatos*, the work of the merchant. And there are two important texts that speak not precisely to the labor of the merchant as justifying his profits but rather to the legitimacy of mercantile activity. However, it seems clear that once the legitimacy of the activity is established, the idea that it should receive its just rewards becomes more probable.

One of these texts is an edifying story of the late ninth century concerning a peasant named Metrios, who was going to an annual fair to sell his produce. At a watering hole, he found a purse full of gold (fifteen hundred gold coins), which he did not open. In the following year, he went again to the fair, met a man who was weeping, and asked him what the matter was. The man explained that he was a successful trader (*pragmateutēs dokimos*); he had gone to the fair with his own capital (one thousand coins) and that of others, but on his return he lost his purse and was reduced to great poverty. The peasant returned the money, and everyone was happy.[39] This is a story in praise of Metrios. But another important point must be made: the property of the merchant, which included the profits from the trading of the previous year, is not considered illegitimate in any way, nor is it dirty money. The peasant gets the greatest reward for his honesty, but the merchant also behaves with perfect honesty, and the profile of the merchant has no negative traits, rather the opposite, in fact. Furthermore, the text does not differentiate in any moral fashion between the peasant who sells or barters his produce and the activities of the professional middleman, as the *Opus imperfectum* had done.

The second text is the *Life of St. Theophylact of Nicomedia*, the ninth-century saint who has already been mentioned as an almsgiver with accountability. His benefactions spread to the city generally. At a certain point, he observed that parents were encouraging their sons to become merchants. The saint saw what to him was an untenable situation: young people were learning how to enrich themselves and how to "commit injustices," but they acquired neither wisdom nor learning. As a remedy, he tried to persuade their parents to send them to school, arguing that in that way "they would keep their faith in Christ and, besides, your affairs will prosper more rapidly." When the parents claimed that they were too poor to afford teachers, the

38. In the West, Adhemar of Halles (d. 1245) interprets pseudo-Chrysostom to mean that the profit of the merchant is included among legitimate activities because of the risk involved, and also because of the change effected on the merchandise by travel: Langholm, *Economics*, 130–31.

39. *Propylaeum Acta Sanctorum Novembris: Synaxarium Ecclesiae Constantinopolitanae*, *AASS* 63, 722–24.

saint opened schools and paid the instructors so that all could attend. The young men of Nicomedia changed their barbarous language and behavior, speaking now an elegant Greek and behaving with all due propriety. The interesting point is that the saint did not aim to persuade the parents to turn their sons away from commerce. The only thing that concerned him was that the young merchants should be pious, speak good Greek, and behave properly.[40] His statement to the reluctant parents, that if their sons learned their letters they would prosper more as merchants, is fascinating for being perfectly true.

A third text deserves a brief mention. Michael Psellos, the polymath who flourished in the eleventh century (1018–ca. 1081), wrote a *Life of St. Auxentius*, a fifth-century saint. The life is thought to include autobiographical references to the author. One of the "miracles" recounted is pertinent to our topic. The shops and workshops of Constantinople are described as being in a poor state, because there had been an interruption in the import of raw materials and merchandise, perhaps due to the weather. Prices had increased, demand had plummeted, and the merchants and artisans were in dire straits. The situation was resolved by the intervention of the saint, who apparently managed to negotiate a price acceptable to all and thus restore the proper functioning of the market.[41] Truly a stunning miracle it is that consists of price negotiations!

Thus the activity of the merchant is presented as legitimate in many (not all, of course) hagiographic sources. The basis of the legitimacy is only hinted at, but it seems to me that saints' lives adopt a more general middle-Byzantine idea concerning trade and the profit of the merchant. That idea can be exemplified by two texts far removed from each other in terms of chronology, genre, and tenor. One is a normative text of a highly rigorist nature, attributed to the ninth-century patriarch of Constantinople Nikephoros (806–815):

> And as for the retail merchants, and those who buy and sell for vain profit, we order the following. Because of their work, labor and pains, if they are laymen and untutored they are allowed to have, of the whole number [= the capital], whether it is ten *nomismata* [gold coins] or whether it is more than ten, one *nomisma* for the instability of the times [the risk they run]. That is, for every ten *nomismata* one will be surplus [= profit]; so also for wine, animals, olive oil, and all other things that are bought and sold. But for excessive profit, the double or even more, for this they will have to suffer the

40. Halkin, *Hagiologie byzantine*, 175–76; emendations by I. D. Polemis, "Philologikēs paratērēseis se byzantina hagiographika kai rētorika keimena," *Hellēnika* 40, no. 2 (1989): 405–8.

41. Michaelis Pselli, *Orationes hagiographicae*, ed. E. A. Fisher (Stuttgart: Teubner, 1994), 19; A. P. Kazhdan, "Hagiographical Notes," *ByzZ* 53 (1983): 546ff, put forth the valuable theory that Psellos had engaged in "hagio-autobiography" but misunderstood the events described in this miracle.

same punishment as the usurers of whom we have spoken [i.e., they will be anathematized].[42]

The patriarch, then, accepts the *labor and risk* theory of merchants' profit, which is quite different from the modern liberal idea of profit that results from the free functioning of the market. He mandates a 10 percent rate of profit. The general idea of a mandated just profit was adopted and put into practice by the *Book of the Prefect*, an early tenth-century text that regulated the market of Constantinople. However, what interests us here is not the practice but the theory, which is quite different from that of the fourth-century fathers.

The second text is a remarkable sermon by the great mystic Symeon the New Theologian (late tenth to early eleventh centuries). He elaborates on Eph. 5:16 ("making the most of time, because the days are evil"), taking as an example five types of improvident merchants who are too lazy to do their job and do not even try to make a profit. He contrasts this with the good merchant who is provident, takes all necessary precautions, works hard, and turns a good profit.[43]

No other ecclesiastical text, to my knowledge, so clearly legitimizes the merchant's profit: the risks and the hard work are all undertaken in the search of profit, and profit is good. What is bad and condemned is to miss the opportunity to engage in trade properly and receive the rewards of one's labor. In capsule form, this is the middle Byzantine answer to the questions regarding trade, mercantile activity, profit, and salvation.

What do the hagiographic sources of the period from the seventh through the eleventh centuries teach us? First, they provide a nuanced view of the market. Exchanges outside the market—gifts and charity—obviously occupy an important place in hagiography. However, the market is also present, and it is accepted either without commentary or with a positive commentary in the praises of cities. There is no theoretical discourse on the role of markets— these are saints' lives, not treatises on commerce or the marketplace. But it is evident that the marketplace is an everyday reality that does not provoke anxieties except in the case of convinced and rigorous ascetics, such as St. Cyril Phileotes. Therefore, economic exchange is accepted implicitly, although gifts and charity, that is, noneconomic exchange, is lauded. Of relevance is a statement of Vincent Déroche: "The eastern concept [of the relations between sanctity and money] is more simplistic [than that of the

42. J. B. Pitra, *Iuris ecclesiastici Graecorum historia et monumenta*, 2 vols. (Rome: Typis Collegii urbani, 1868), 2:323.

43. J. Darrouzès, *Traités théologiques et éthiques, Syméon le nouveau Théologien*, 2 vols. (Paris: Cerf, 1967), 2:385ff.; on this, see A. E. Laiou, "Händler und Kaufleute auf dem Jahrmarkt," in *Fest und Alltag in Byzanz*, ed. G. Prinzing and D. Simon (Munich: C. H. Beck, 1990), 53–70.

West] but also larger and more generous in that it does not lose sight of the fact that everyone's needs must be satisfied."[44]

Second, the merchant's profit and profession are not considered illegitimate. There is certainly condemnation of avarice and excessive wealth, but that is another matter. The hagiographic sources do not describe or clearly define the basis of mercantile profit, although there are some allusions to it, and they do not state what the legitimate rate of profit is. That was the job of civil authorities.

Third, it is also important that the merchant, in exercising his or her profession, follows rules similar to those governing other professions. In the saints' lives there is a very powerful idea that is also a basic tenet of Byzantine legal and economic thought: the almost absolute respect of contracts. Debts must be paid and so they are, in one way or the other, whether it is the saint and other pious people, men and women, who pay the debts of indigent persons as an act of charity, or whether the debtors find the money themselves. Some saints go to extremes to pay off their contracts: in a couple of cases, the saint, incapable of paying artisans he has employed, asks them to bind him in chains and bring him to the nearest city where the faithful might take pity on him and give him alms with which to pay off his obligations.[45] Of course, respect for contracts has many important implications. For our purposes, it is sufficient to note that it is an absolutely essential prerequisite for any orderly economic activity, especially that of the merchant.

The most important element to retain is that the profession of the merchant is neither illegitimate nor despised. Merchants can be perfectly good and pious people, and no one considers that their money is too dirty to touch. They are not unjust, and they certainly are not the ones who oppress the poor. All this suggests that the place of the merchant in the Byzantine social value system, as reflected in these sources, is much less suspect than some scholars think. Furthermore, we have seen faint suggestions that the merchant's labor and the risks he runs are the basis for his profit, the rewards of labor. The idea that the merchant does a job for which he must be remunerated is a very important development in the history of economic thought. While this interpretation goes against the usual statements about merchants in Byzantine society, there is sufficient basis in the hagiographic sources to advance it, and their evidence is borne out by other, different texts.

Indeed, the interpretation offered here is quite consistent with the concepts and the reality of social organization that were prevalent for much of this period. Between the seventh and the tenth centuries, Byzantine society was rather flat. Even when a powerful aristocracy emerged, in the early tenth century, its power was circumscribed by that of the state, a situation that would

44. Déroche, *Études*, 238n30.
45. Sullivan, *Life of St. Nikon*, 128–30; St. Germanos of Kosinitza, *AASS Maii 3*, *9–*10.

not really change until the establishment of the Komnenian dynasty in the late eleventh century. The state was powerful, and the elite was composed, to a large extent, of state officials who owed their political and economic strength to the state. In official state ideology of the tenth century, society was divided in two parts: the powerful and the poor. The powerful were defined as those who held high office in the civil, ecclesiastical, or military administration, and could, by virtue of their position, oppress the poor. This latter category was composed not of the destitute but of those who had relatively little property, who did not hold office, and who had to be protected against the excesses of the powerful. In civil legislation, the "poor" are people of the countryside. The merchant was not included in these categories as they were elaborated and did not really fit in them in practice. As a group, the merchants of this period had nowhere near the same capacity to oppress as did the high officials. They did not present a menace to the poor, nor were they considered highly threatened by the powerful. They were accepted as a constituent part of society, and it is this acceptance that is reflected in the hagiographic sources. Disdain for the merchant is primarily an aristocratic affair, and thus it is most evident in periods when the aristocracy was powerful: down to the sixth century, and then again after the eleventh, when a self-conscious aristocracy was once again well established.

Conclusion

The fourth-century fathers tried to change human behavior on the basis of Christian beliefs informed by certain tenets and principles elaborated by ancient Greek philosophers. They taught Christians to eschew love of possessions and the pursuit of profit. They extolled the virtues of redistribution of wealth through alms and decried accumulation; indeed, these two positions are two sides of the same coin. For the fathers, economic activity was valid primarily as it provided for one's needs. In this ideological universe, the activities of merchants were suspect: their labor was not evident, they provided luxuries as well as necessities, they were too mobile, and they were permitted by law to try to circumscribe the buyer. Hagiographic works allow us to gauge both the success and the limitation of these teachings. The limitation is that not only was nonautarkic activity eliminated; it continued to be carried out, and it was valued. The merchant was really not relegated to the position of a liar and a cheat, and certainly the rigorist teachings of the *Opus imperfectum* were not followed.

The success of patristic ideas, however, was in many ways considerable. The idea that labor forms the basis of value had a long life. Charity, a profoundly uneconomic activity in intent, if not so much in effect, retained its force. Profit, while accepted, was broadly deemed to have limits in order

to be considered legitimate. Justice in exchange, an Aristotelian idea made
Christian by St. Basil,[46] was a basic tenet of Byzantine legislation and ideology through the tenth century. The hagiographic sources are wise: they allow
the merchant's position in the "city," a term that designated society in the
ancient world. They accept the merchant's labor and a reward for it; but in
order to gain salvation, a merchant was expected to exercise his profession
in the name of God and was always reminded that profit was earned at the
will of the Lord.

46. Through St. Basil, these concepts of justice were incorporated in Byzantine legislation: St. Basil,
PG 31:400–405; L. Burgmann, ed., *Ecloga* (Frankfurt am Main: Löwenklau-Gesellschaft, 1983), 164.
On these matters, see A. E. Laiou, "Koinonikē dikaiosynē: To synallatesthai kai to euēmerein sto
Vyzantio," *Praktika tēs Akadēmias Athēnon* 74 (1999): 103–30.

Part Five

PATRISTIC STUDIES FOR TODAY

17

St. Basil's Philanthropic Program and Modern Microlending Strategies for Economic Self-Actualization

Timothy Patitsas

We [modern economic policy makers and theorists] do not understand how to catalyze development in backward economies, and we do not understand how to prevent developed economies from sliding into backwardness themselves: two sides of the same mystery.

Jane Jacobs, in *Cities and the Wealth of Nations*[1]

What does St. Basil the Great's fourth-century philanthropic program teach us about poverty relief in our own day, at a time when vast resources have been and continue to be marshaled to tackle the problem of destitution, especially in the Third World? Could a premodern church father and bishop really have anything to teach contemporary analytic economic science?

This essay develops four distinct "snapshots" of some aspect of poverty or of poverty relief, in the hopes of crystallizing a clearer overall vision of what poverty is and of the further contribution that Christian doctrine and

---

1. Jane Jacobs, *Cities and the Wealth of Nations* (New York: Random House, 1983), 9.

practice might make in its transformation into prosperity. The first snapshot portrays the founding of St. Basil the Great's Basileias, his "new city" in late fourth-century Cappadocian Asia Minor. The second snapshot is a profile of the fifty-year-long effort to alleviate world poverty through international economic development aid. The third frames Vanderbilt-trained economist Muhammad Yunus's contribution to the invention of "microlending" and his success as a "banker to the poor." The fourth snapshot focuses on the practical "economic development" theory of Jane Jacobs, whose inquiry into the causes of prosperity and the organization of commerce is so accurate and far-ranging that she has supplanted Adam Smith, I argue, as the "founder" of economic science.[2]

Finally, with the aid of the additional clues visible in the three contemporary portraits, the essay returns to the Basileias to reflect again on what that city might or even must have been like, and on what it teaches us about helping the poor today. Basil's philanthropic program somehow succeeded in catalyzing lasting prosperity out of the ashes of deep poverty, whereas our international development efforts to do the same have failed. His program anticipated the microlending movement's discovery that usury was a major onus on the poor and a chief obstacle to development. And his program is understandable through the principles outlined in the very best theoretical approach to prosperity, that of Jane Jacobs. Moreover, Basil's program included additional innovations[3] that could be retrieved now to help aid workers and policy planners put the worst of global poverty to rest, in the most effective and humane ways possible.

Known Facts about the Basileias

One problem in attempting to enlist Basil in the service of modern practical charity is that we don't have a very detailed or precise account of his antipoverty program in Caesarea. What do we really know about the functioning of his new city, his Basileias? According to the information collected in Brian

---

2. This essay was originally delivered less than a year before Jane Jacobs passed away. Her death was for me an event of great sadness, as we had become friends through the course of my dissertation work on her intellectual accomplishments. For a short obituary, see "Jane Jacobs, anatomiser of cities, died on April 24th, aged 89," *The Economist*, May 11, 2006, www.economist.com/obituary/displaystory.cfm?story_id=6910989 (accessed August 29, 2006).

3. I am not here using the term "innovation" in its classical sense for Orthodox Christian theology, where it is almost invariably used to describe a doctrinal aberration that is recognizably heretical because it has no true organic or logical precedent in the theological tradition of the church. A doctrinal "innovation" is a cancerous devolution, not an authentic flowering of seeds latent within the church's life. This latter phenomenon is nevertheless what I have in mind in using the term: an authentic incarnation of the historical Christian *kerygma*, perfectly suited to its unique context.

Daley's 1998 North American Patristics Society address,[4] in Philip Rousseau's biography of Basil,[5] in William Ramsay's *The Church in the Roman Empire before A.D. 170*,[6] and in Susan Holman's *The Hungry Are Dying*,[7] there seem to be eight essential facts about his efforts that we can still discern from across the centuries. These are the points that I hope the modern "snapshots" will clarify and make practical.

First, Basil's new town was centered on a chapel[8] and was administered by *chorepiscopoi*. These dedicated clergy took the lead in organizing the day-to-day functioning of activities by the residents of the new town and perhaps in caring for the poor and the sick.[9] Second, the Basileias was established either on the site of Basil's family country estate[10] or on property that was deeded by the emperor.[11] In either case, it was built at a small remove from the city of Caesarea, on largely undeveloped land. Third, the new town contained institutions such as some kind of hospital; residences for travelers and the poor;[12] residences for clergy; the bishop's palace; a leper hospital; and small factories or workshops for teaching and practicing trades.[13] Some of these institutions were either entirely unprecedented, or at least relatively novel, for their day.[14] Fourth, in the Basileias the poor were put to work and apparently were even trained in trades of some kind.[15] Fifth, as the Basileias grew, it attracted poor immigrants from many other places, some quite distant, who upon their arrival were also enrolled in its program of charity and work.[16] Sixth, one of Basil's nemeses among the nonpoor were what we would term "loan sharks"—people who lend to the financially desperate at highly usuri-

4. Brian E. Daley, SJ, "1998 NAPS Presidential Address, Building a New City: The Cappadocian Fathers and the Rhetoric of Philanthropy," *JECS* 7, no. 3 (1999): 440. Daley says that the charitable settlement was known as *basileias* by at least the early fifth century.

5. Philip Rousseau, *Basil of Caesarea* (Berkeley: University of California Press, 1994). On 139, Rousseau refers to the Basileias as the *"Basileiados."* On 141, Rousseau dates the origins of the "new city" to sometime between 369 and 372.

6. I refer to the ninth edition (London: Hodder & Stoughton, 1907).

7. *The Hungry Are Dying: Beggars and Bishops in Roman Cappadocia* (New York: Oxford University Press, 2001).

8. Rousseau, *Basil of Caesarea*, 140 and 142.

9. Daley, "Building a New City," 440. Daley quotes Sozomen the historian, who refers to the monastics who at some point became more involved in the settlement as "ecclesiastical philosophers." Also according to Sozomen, by the 440s there was a *chorepiscopus* on the scene directing the monks; cf. *HE* 6.34.

10. Holman, *Hungry Are Dying*, 74.

11. Daley, "Building a New City," 440. The latter account of the land's origin is the one given by Theodoret of Cyrus in his *Ecclesiastical History.*

12. Rousseau, *Basil of Caesarea*, 140. These workshops dealt in carpentry, blacksmithing, etc.

13. Ramsay, *Church in the Roman Empire*, 461.

14. Cf. Rousseau, *Basil of Caesarea*, 143, for the existence of "poor houses" in other cities.

15. Holman, *Hungry Are Dying*, 74.

16. Ibid., 75–76.

ous rates.[17] Seventh, Basil repeatedly made the rhetorical point that wealth should come off the walls and up from the floors and out of the treasuries of rich men's houses, in order to find its way back into philanthropic and productive circulation.[18] And eighth, Basil's city endured, while its parent and neighbor, Caesarea, decayed and finally became an uninhabited ruin.[19]

Some two hundred years later, when Emperor Justinian ordered that the major cities of Asia Minor be walled in for their defense, walls were built around the Basileias and the new economy and settlement that had continued to emerge around it—and not around the original Caesarea.[20] In fact, according to Ramsay, the modern Turkish city of Kayseri is built atop Basil's foundations, not on those of old Caesarea.[21] In other words, whatever Basil did, it somehow succeeded in fostering the formation of a self-sustaining economy for the inhabitants of his see.

The Intellectual and Practical Failure of Development Economics

If we don't have more than a few points to go on when examining Basil's efforts, the same cannot be said of the fifty-year-plus First World program to spark economic development in the Third World. A 2001 monograph by Terry Easterly[22] lays out in careful detail the economic theory behind, the funding for, and the results of the first fifty years of development assistance.[23] The aid can be said on empirical grounds to have failed to develop a single country and even seems to have made some countries poorer.[24] Moreover, the aid has contributed to making many countries politically more depraved and economically more dependent.[25] Surprisingly, the 2000 study showed that the more aid a country had received, the more likely it was to have declined economically over the course of taking that aid.[26]

Since Easterly's first account, there has been some encouraging news in the Third World economic picture, but this has been led almost entirely by

---

17. Ibid., 120–24.

18. Daley, "Building a New City," 444.

19. Ramsay, *Church in the Roman Empire*, 464.

20. Daley, "Building a New City," 458–59.

21. Ramsay, *Church in the Roman Empire*, 464.

22. Terry Easterly, *The Elusive Quest for Growth: Economists' Adventures and Misadventures in the Tropics* (Cambridge, MA: MIT Press, 2001). Easterly, a World Bank economist, offers the results of an internal study he headed on the effectiveness of aid. He was subsequently fired.

23. Cf. also Easterly's follow-up volume, *The White Man's Burden: Why the West's Efforts to Aid the Rest Have Done So Much Ill and So Little Good* (New York: Penguin Press, 2006).

24. Easterly, *Elusive Quest for Growth*, 37–44.

25. For corroboration of Easterly's account, see Joseph E. Stiglitz, *Globalization and Its Discontents* (New York: W. W. Norton, 2002). Stiglitz was the chief economist and senior vice president at the World Bank from 1997 to 2000.

26. Easterly, *Elusive Quest for Growth*, xi.

growth in China,[27] a nation that refused to follow First World advice,[28] and by growth in India, where economists feel the country is succeeding in spite of that advice.[29] The lion's share of other recent progress made in the Third World in the twenty-first century has been the result of increased raw material prices owing to actual development in China and India.

The official, empirically ineffective, First World aid effort, meanwhile, has been expensive in absolute terms, costing more than $1 trillion, measured in 1985 U.S. dollars.[30] This expensive disaster didn't happen haphazardly. Easterly reports that from the early 1960s through his 2001 publication date, almost all development aid to the Third World had been planned and dispensed according to an economic formula—the Harrod-Domar model[31]—that was being abandoned by academic economists at the precise moment it was adopted by the development community as a practical guide for aid planning.[32] In fact, no scientific evidence supports the use of this formula as a meaningful approach to economic growth, Easterly says.[33] And yet we also know that IMF and World Bank economists advising formerly communist nations of the East Bloc on their transition to capitalism in the 1990s continued to rely heavily, almost exclusively, on this same failed model[34]—even though this very model had its earliest origins, it now turns out, not in the minds of the British economist Harrod or the U.S. economist Domar, but in the first five-year plans of the Soviet era![35] When we learn that the guardians of capitalism are employing warmed-over versions of the economic models underlying the five-year plans of the Soviet Union, in order to assist formerly communist nations seeking to escape the effects of those very plans, we may suspect that the intellectual confusion regarding the meaning of "economic development" and the method to achieve it runs quite deep among economists charged with its accomplishment.[36]

To be sure, expensive First World development aid achieved some good as a form of welfare for the hungry and the sick, as a political payoff to

27. Nathan Smith, "Don't Look Now, but the World Economy Is Booming," *TCS Daily*, August 3, 2006, www.tcsdaily.com/article.aspx?id=080306C—99k (accessed August 19, 2006).

28. Bret Swanson, "What's Behind the Chinese Boom?" *Gilder Technology Report*, March 26, 2004, http://www.discovery.org/scripts/viewDB/index.php?command=view&id=1953 (accessed August 19, 2006).

29. The World Bank and the International Monetary Fund admit their befuddlement. Cf. Paul Blustein, "IMF, World Bank Short on Global Solutions," *Washington Post*, September 30, 2002, A16.

30. Easterly, *Elusive Quest for Growth*, 33. In *White Man's Burden*, Easterly updates and revises his estimate of the cost to $2.3 trillion.

31. Easterly, *Elusive Quest for Growth*, 28.

32. Ibid., 35.

33. Ibid., 37–44.

34. Ibid., 36–37.

35. Ibid., 31.

36. See the section on Jane Jacobs below.

client states in the Western struggle with communism, and as a temporary subsidy to rich world bankers, farmers, and manufacturers. But not
one of these successes negates the fact that the aid never did what it was
actually conceived to do, which was to accomplish development overseas.
In all probability this failure was not intentional; in fact, when "development aid" was aimed at the poorer regions of rich countries, the results
were no better.[37] But intentional or not, the failure of development aid
has meant continued, and in some cases increased, misery for the world's
poorest citizens.

The debt incurred to finance development schemes is politically destabilizing and economically debilitating, not only for poor nations but also
for rich ones. The push in 2005 for "debt forgiveness" is proof that poor
nations have not benefited from their development loans enough even to
carry the capital costs involved. This debt is so vast, even relative to the
economies of the First World, that we are from time to time warned by no
less an authority than the *Wall Street Journal* that a default by Brazil, Paki-
stan, Indonesia—or even Argentina—could bring down the entire world
banking system.[38] In other words, it is the developed world, as much as
the developing world, that is endangered by the failure of development
aid. We can deduce, therefore, that periodic offers of "debt forgiveness"
to Third World countries are almost certainly aimed as much at rescuing
our own banks, and at protecting our own economies that would surely be
imperiled by the bankruptcies of lending institutions that have made the
guaranteed loans, as at helping the foreign destitute.[39] And the Christian
churches, through such debt-forgiveness movements as Jubilee 2000, have
somehow volunteered to provide the moral cover for the vast transfer of
wealth from taxpayers in general to an elite few bankers whose bad loans
would otherwise result in bankruptcy for their lending institutions. That is
the substance of debt forgiveness.

Finally, we know that such assistance has aided and abetted various resource extractions, depletions, and general environmental ruinations in the
Third World, and that Western aid, when it *is* generous, sometimes wipes
out farmers and manufacturers in the Third World by pricing them out of
business.[40]

37. Jane Jacobs, *Cities and the Wealth of Nations* (New York: Random House), 122.
38. Ibid., 9.
39. Cf. Stiglitz, *Globalization*, 41, where he writes of the 1998 IMF bailout of Indonesia, "In
the end, ironically, much of the [aid] money went not to help Indonesia but to bail out the 'colonial
power's' private sector creditors."
40. Abraham McLaughlin, "One Kenyan Man's Mission: Free Africa from Yoke of Aid," *Christian
Science Monitor*, December 2, 2005, www.csmonitor.com/2005/1202/p01s02–woaf.htm (accessed
August 29, 2006).

Microlending: Practical Success in Search of Theoretical Justification

Probably the brightest spot in the last thirty years of development work has been the banking innovation known as "microlending," which was pioneered by, among others, the Bangladeshi economist Muhammad Yunus,[41] the U.S. industrialist Al Whittaker, and the Australian businessman David Bussau.[42] It is Yunus whom I discuss here, since he is better known and I have studied his work in greater depth, but the other microlenders have hit on principles similar to his. All three pioneers eschewed established academic models of development relief, relying on trial and error to find a path that would help the poor in a lasting way.

Yunus came to the awareness that the greatest bane and chief obstacle to the self-betterment of the poor in his country was the absence of capital at affordable rates. What capital his country's poor did have access to came courtesy of loan sharks charging interest rates of between 50 and 200 percent. Yunus began lending to poor vendors in his native Bangladesh, one at a time, in amounts averaging $50 at 15 to 20 percent rates of interest. In other words, Yunus, like Basil, took on the loan sharks and redeployed capital to the poor in a way that was small scale, to the point, and repayable. This is not to say that Basil disbursed actual loans; at least, there is no record of his having done so. But in both cases, small amounts of working capital were married to the efforts of the poor on their own and others' behalf.

Four qualities make Yunus's style of banking to the poor significant for policy makers hoping to generate bona fide Third World development. First, his borrowers are among the poorest of the poor. Helping these people literally and immediately saves lives, while traditional aid programs are likely to touch economically marginal people last, if at all. Second, such microloans to the poor are repaid, with interest, 98 percent of the time, year after year, and in many different regions and nations.[43] This high rate of repayment is clear evidence that the capital being disbursed is finding productive and profitable uses. It is contributing to an economic development, in other words, that is self-sustaining at some level. We cannot say this of our traditional World Bank–style development policies, which is why we periodically face the need to forgive such failed loans entirely. Third, microlending methodologies have

41. Muhammad Yunus with Alan Jolis, *Banker to the Poor: Micro-lending and the Battle against World Poverty* (New York: PublicAffairs, 1999).

42. Philippa Tyndale, *Don't Look Back: The David Bussau Story; How an Abandoned Child Became a Champion of the Poor* (London: Allen & Unwin, 2004). This book covers Whittaker as well.

43. "98" is, coincidentally, the percentage of Third World countries helped by official aid programs who did *not* transition into lasting development, according to the World Bank study; Easterly, *Elusive Quest for Growth*, 39. Bussau and Whittaker also report a repayment rate of 98 percent on microloans made by their joint nonprofit organization; cf. Opportunity International, "Lending Hope to Africa," www.opportunity.org/site/pp.asp?c=7oIDLROyGqF&b=218102 (accessed August 29, 2006).

proven to be, with minor cultural modifications, repeatable in many national and geographical settings. As an innovation, microlending represents a genuine increase in our practical knowledge about how to tackle poverty universally, rather than being a misleading fluke, localized to the culture of Bangladesh. Fourth, in most cultures almost 90 percent of microborrowers are women, and as they better their lots the microlending innovation becomes a great force for women's liberation.

The most famous instance of microlending, the Grameen Bank founded by Muhammad Yunus, has more than fifteen thousand successful branches within Bangladesh. Its methods are straightforward. Banking officials travel to a poor village and at some public meeting announce that they are interested in making loans at fair interest rates to anyone able to find a productive use for the money. Next, interested applicants are formed or form themselves into "borrowers' circles" of ten people each. Bank officials meet with the circles to discuss what sorts of projects are likely to be repayable and how the loans are administered. Next, each borrowers' circle selects two candidates whose ideas for productive use of the money seem most likely to result in a rapid repayment of the principal, with interest. The loans are disbursed, and when the loans are repaid, the circle elects the next two most-promising candidates for loan money.

This process, iteratively repeated, means that soon many of the poor can find the funds to improve the work they are actually capable of doing[44]— often work they are already undertaking, though with less capital backing— to fulfill the needs of their families, friends, neighbors, or fellow citizens. To increase the circles' effectiveness, Grameen officials have the borrowers meet regularly to advise and support the businesses of the several members. When one borrower is short a payment due to lack of customers, another borrower will typically have some suggestion as to where to make sales or on how to cut costs. The circles may sometimes recite, in a brief ritual, a list of "dos and don'ts" regarding lending practices, hygiene, and women's rights. The stress of the circles is on practical improvements in the lot of the poor, mutual support, and diligence and thrift.

Although the Grameen Bank as a whole did rely on capital backing from its national government for many years, it has gradually become self-sustaining. In the meantime, microloans made by the Grameen Bank have made real and permanent improvements to the economic status of the poor, lifting hundreds of thousands of families out of the ranks of the very poorest by putting them on the road to relative self-sufficiency.

---

44. Jacobs makes the same point about city economies as a whole: they have to begin their climb to prosperity by exporting the work they already do, to other cities at a level of development similar to theirs ("Why Backward Cities Need One Another," in *Cities*, 135–55).

Like Basil the Great, and unlike the postwar efforts of the international community in the Third World, Muhammad Yunus has achieved lasting improvements in the economic status of his clients. Can a common principle be found at work in all three cases, one that would explain the successes and correct the failures? Is there a flaw in accepted economic development theory that would account for so much expensive and heartbreaking failure?

Jane Jacobs Is the New Adam Smith

The bitterly ironic image presented above—that of the official guardians of world capitalism, the highly paid specialists at the IMF and the World Bank, drawing on failed Soviet development theory as they advised former communist nations earnestly seeking a transition to capitalism—has convinced me that Christian social activists cannot rely solely on contemporary economic experts for advice about how to tackle poverty. On the one hand, this outrageous image has driven me to examine the successes of past Christian leaders, such as the archbishop of late fourth-century Caesarea. On the other hand, it has driven me off the path of conventional development theory to the practical successes of Muhammad Yunus and those like him.

But while these examples show that success in helping the poor is possible, they do not help us isolate the salient aspects of their methods in a way that would lead to the reform of economic theory. And thus they have had only a very marginal impact on the way the multibillions of development aid are annually disbursed. What is the theoretical error underlying all the failed efforts at international development, and how can this error be corrected? Until those questions are answered, even the most lasting practical successes will be explained away as anecdotal and thus irrelevant.

Jacobs is the only economist of whom I am aware who has located the precise flaw within the theory of economic development: its failure to hit on the correct definition of "economic development" itself. Moreover, Jacobs has corrected the error in this subbranch of economic theory while patiently digging up, examining, and modifying or discarding the unquestioned foundational assumptions of the entirety of modern economic science laid by Adam Smith. In the process, she has laid stronger and better foundations that are also, it turns out, more compatible with both complexity theory *and* a mature Christian humanism.[45] It is Jacobs, I believe, who can help us to

---

45. In *The Economy of Cities* (New York: Random House, 1969); *Cities*; *Systems of Survival: A Dialogue on the Moral Foundations of Commerce and Politics* (New York: Random House, 1987); and *The Nature of Economies* (New York: Random House, 2001). At her death, Jacobs was working on a summation of her theory, tentatively titled *A New Hypothesis*, based on and inspired by my review of her findings in my doctoral dissertation. Cf. Timothy G. Patitsas, "The Future of Macroeconomic Science: Liturgical and Complex," in "The King Returns to His City: An Interpretation of the Great

understand why the Christian bishop and the Muslim maverick succeeded, while the IMF and the World Bank have continued to fail.

Defining "economic development" properly

Jacobs's definition of "economic development" is precise, clear, and surprising, where the official science's definition of its own object is broad, vague, and misleadingly obvious. When economic development textbooks even bother to define "development" (and historically they often haven't), they suggest that it is nothing more than an increase in a nation's production or output, a mere rise in gross domestic product (GDP). The only improvement, such as it was, in the definition employed in Easterly's World Bank study was the use of four-year averages for GDP growth.[46] With definitions of the goal this insightful, it's no wonder that Third World economies remain so impervious to aid efforts. Nowhere in these definitions are terms that would seem to belong to the basic English meaning of "development" in any context; the words "new," "experimental," "research," and "innovation" do not appear regularly in the economists' descriptions of their salient object.

Jacobs cuts the Gordian knot choking the discipline by disentangling two ideas currently conflated by development economists.[47] She reserves the term "economic expansion" to indicate an increase in the production of *already existing* goods and services. Once so clearly defined, it becomes immediately obvious that almost the entire historic practice of and theory behind international development aid was concerned with "economic expansion," *not* economic development. Thus if a newly invented fertilizer factory designed and operating in Des Moines were to be replicated by Western planners and construction workers in Ghana, this would then be misinterpreted by development economists as a sign of African "economic development"—rather than as a clear sign of *American* "economic development" and of *African* "economic expansion."[48]

By first defining "economic expansion" so carefully, Jacobs is free to reserve the term "economic development" for a much more mysterious and inherently local and indigenous process: the bringing forth of *new* goods and services[49]

Week and Bright Week Cycle of the Orthodox Church" (PhD diss., Catholic University of America, 2003), 417–91.

46. Easterly, *Elusive Quest for Growth*, 39.

47. Jane Jacobs, "How New Work Begins," in *Economy*, 49–84.

48. Might not the expansion also involve development? The two are intimately related, certainly. If the foreign enterprise genuinely learned, on its own, how to design and build the novel factory, or even if certain locally conceived minor adjustments were involved in building and operating the factory, then the line would become blurred. But technology transfer in aid programs is intentionally designed to be of the turnkey variety.

49. Jacobs, *Economy*, 49.

on the basis of older ones,[50] typically in the context of many economic actors who are doing the same thing, both within one's own city[51] and within the cities in its trading network.[52] While certain conditions either promote or inhibit this process, in the end true development involves a mysterious artistic moment, in which an innovator senses previously unexamined possibilities in a material, a process, or a problem, and then somehow brings those possibilities into existence.[53] The innovation at the heart of development is, as described by Jacobs, a process that a Christian would recognize as "incarnational" and "eucharistic"—perhaps suggesting that there is an additional significance to Basil's placement of a church at the center of his Basileias.

The difference between a country that can invent its own new goods and services and a country that must always rely on others for the solutions to its problems is the difference between economic maturity and independence, on the one hand, and economic stagnation, weakness, and dependence, on the other. *Our current conflation of "economic development" and "economic expansion" is the major conceptual error damning all our aid efforts to frustrated failure.* By investing the entirety of our development aid in foreign economic expansion, we have neglected or even suppressed the native processes of true development already operating within recipient countries. And by ever insisting on doing for others that which, by definition, they can do only for themselves, we have blinded ourselves to the ways we might instead be truly of service *to* them and have furthermore grossly misled them as to how they could actually help themselves.

Dethroning "efficiency" from its perch atop modern economic science

This redefinition of "economic development" as a softer and largely unpredictable process, a volatile and collaborative interchange, is of revolutionary importance to the history of economic thought. It represents the end of the Cartesian Enlightenment paradigm of economic analysis, according to which economies had come to be seen as statistically predictable machines, their behavior reducible to graphs charting inputs and outputs. Economies, according to Jacobs, are more like living organisms than like machines, and their most important capacity is their ability to solve problems in novel ways, and thus to frustrate predictions about their future behavior.

Even more of a conceptual shock to the current discipline of economics, Jacobs's softer and more accurate definition of "development" firmly relativizes what is *the* central and indeed absolute value of all modern economic science: efficiency. Real development, Jacobs says, actually requires

---

50. Ibid., 55.
51. Ibid., 180–82.
52. *Cities*, 140–55.
53. Jane Jacobs, "The Logic of Adding New Work to Old," in *Economy*, 59–63.

a certain amount of inefficiency in order to occur.[54] The inefficiency of trial and error;[55] of hunches followed that don't pan out but lead to unsought discoveries;[56] of duplication of research;[57] of breakaway employees and firms who go on to pursue their parent firm's side work as their main enterprise;[58] of the unplanned and often pell-mell distribution of capital into the hands of many actors, most of whom will fail;[59] of people abandoning their main intentions in order to involve themselves with peripheral issues that suddenly interest them more[60]—all these inefficiencies are of irreplaceable value to a developing, as opposed to a merely expanding, economy. To be sure, Jacobs still allows for the value of efficiency, but she shows how it, like economic expansion, is dependent on a symbiotic relationship with the inefficiencies that are the soul of true development. Development is neither reducible to nor caused by efficiency; rather, innovation and efficiency, like development and expansion, are symbiotes within a healthy economic life.

Because "development" is a dynamic process rather than a superficial end state, there are no permanently developed nations.[61] What we call "developed nations" are really those nations where a large degree of inefficiency in the service of innovation has somehow become normal, where innovation is done well and routinely.[62] Development, in other words, relies preeminently on the entrepreneur—who to Jacobs resembles nothing so much as an artist, and to me resembles a priest—and development relies moreover on the entrepreneur in a functioning network of many entrepreneurs and their supporters.

54. Jane Jacobs, "The Valuable Inefficiencies and Impracticalities of Cities," in *Economy*, 85–121.

55. Ibid., 90.

56. Ibid., 51–55.

57. Ibid., 89–91.

58. Ibid., 97–98.

59. Ibid., 212.

60. "From the viewpoint of efficiency, a man or woman trained to specific work, and good at it, is best kept at that kind of work as long as needed. But from the point of view of economic development, a man or woman trained to specific work is most valuable if he adds something new to that work, if he changes what he does. Of course, he may fail." Ibid., 102.

61. "Earlier I defined economic development as a process of continually improvising in a context that makes injecting improvisations into everyday life feasible. We might amplify this by calling development an improvisational drift into unprecedented kinds of work that carry unprecedented problems, then drifting into improvised solutions, which carry further unprecedented work carrying unprecedented problems." Jacobs, *Cities*, 221–22.

62. And yet, due to our civilization's loss of an explicit dependence on liturgy, we express this so heartlessly and so inaccurately: let the free market weed out the losers, we cry. But the losers have, in a sense, "died for our salvation"; one could no more have a dynamic economy without losers than a sacrificial cult without sacrificial victims. And there is no way of distinguishing ahead of time the losers from the winners. Therefore both are integral to our economic life and deserve our respect.

The missing heart of economic science

To understand the profound significance of Jacobs's contribution to her discipline, and consequently her indispensable importance for a proper understanding of Basil's economic program, it helps to imagine economic theory as treating phenomena along a continuum. At one extreme, economic science since Adam Smith has developed a very good and well-developed "economic psychology" in the form of game theory and the in-depth study of incentives. Contemporary economists know a great deal, in fine detail, about what motivates people's economic decisions. At the other extreme, economic science, again since Smith but especially since the dawn of the twentieth century, has come to possess a highly sophisticated "economic mechanics," in the form of its vast and subtle knowledge of markets of every kind, of how they form and how they clear. This knowledge is presented with impressive statistical precision.

Students of complexity theory, however, will at once notice a gap between these accounts. By treating economies as exhaustively reducible either to (1) "problems in simplicity"—that is, cases where the behavior of a system can be reduced to a very few variables[63] (to wit, "incentives are everything"), or to (2) "problems in disorganized complexity"—that is, one where there are thousands or even many millions of seemingly random variables (to wit, "markets must be allowed to form and clear"), the discipline has bypassed the middle realm of organic order. Here, in the realm of organized complexity, we find those problems that describe the entire class of living order. In this class belong those systems of which we can empirically state that the whole is greater than the sum of its parts. In the case of economies, we would need this type of science if we were to understand a human economy as, at least in part, a kind of collective intelligence, rather than a dumb brute or a dead machine. Economics remains firmly tied to the modern understanding of order and development—an understanding undermined and outclassed by postmodern studies in complexity theory, or "emergence." Economic science has yet to outgrow its Cartesian past.

In practice, this means that what is almost entirely lacking in the current science is a proper attention to, or even awareness of, the great middle range of economic reality that lies between "economic psychology" and "economic physics"—the realm where economists must account for the generation of wealth, the rise of new cities, and the means for catalyzing wealth creation

---

63. Jacobs presents the three main scientific classes of order in "The Kind of Problem a City Is," in *The Death and Life of Great American Cities* (New York: Random House, 1961), 428–48. She, in turn, borrowed this account from Warren Weaver, "A Quarter Century in the Natural Sciences," in *The President's Review, including a Quarter Century in the Natural Sciences by Warren Weaver, from the Rockefeller Foundation Annual Report, 1958* (New York: The Rockefeller Foundation, 1958), 7–15.

in poor regions and countries. What is missing is the very realm that ought to be the heart of economics itself.

Given that people make decisions about goods and services, and that the collectivity of these decisions and their results can be studied usefully through statistical analysis, the question still remains: where do these goods and services come from in the first place? Current economic thinking takes the most central and interesting fact of economic life—that there is prosperity at all—and either intentionally or unintentionally reduces it to a given. But in the Third World, by definition, prosperity is *not* a given: that's why the Third World is poor in the first place. Thus it is no accident that our economists are so poor at catalyzing development in actual practice, because their entire expertise is exhausted in the study of how existing prosperity performs and how people behave within a context of relative prosperity. Moreover, to switch their focus to the middle realm would not be easy: the two peripheral regions of "economic psychology" and "economic physics" can be handled comfortably and competently with recourse to good, solid, Enlightenment scientific methods—thus the prevalence of logical game theory, statistics, and statistical methodologies. The middle region cannot, and so it tends to remain mysterious or even invisible to trained economists.

Worse, and more debilitating, the universal practice of economists is to formulate their best thought about the *central* questions of wealth creation in the languages appropriate to the *peripheral* issues of incentives or markets. We have, through a historical quirk, developed economic specialties without having yet discovered "economics" itself.[64]

Jacobs, partly because she *is* schooled in the methodological mindset of emergence, begins her economic theory at the very center—at the question of what development and prosperity are, how they can be encouraged, and how they can be promoted. She begins, in other words, with what is empirically prior in economic life: the process governing the creation of the new goods and services concerning which incentives can operate and around which markets can form. She begins, therefore, in the realm where "efficiency" is of subsidiary importance.

The mystery of order for free: The surprise beyond efficiency

In the analysis of a complex organic system in any field, the central question is always the way in which, in a world of increasing entropy, the second law of thermodynamics is sometimes violated. The moment that in some corner of the universe order has increased rather than decreased, or the moment that a particular whole is greater than the sum of its parts, we are dealing with a

---

64. For an older discussion of the intellectual crisis in contemporary economics, and its increased irrelevance to the real world, see John Cassidy's "Decline of Economics," *New Yorker*, December 2, 1996, 50–60.

new class of problems. Because economies are instances of complex organic order, the only possible foundation on which to build a truly scientific economic theory is the explanation of how prosperity itself arises. The current answer to the riddle of prosperity, which is "markets plus incentives," seems plausible until we remember that (a) it has for fifty years provided absolutely no traction for development practice, and (b) it glides superficially over the core issue: where do the new goods and services that define an economy as "developing" come from? As I said, conventional economists tend to take prosperity as a given; once "emergence" (another word for organic complexity) has produced prosperity, tried and true Enlightenment methodologies *do* come into play and have their very powerful and effective role—but not a moment sooner.

Complexity theorists have coined a term to describe the wonder of self-generating order in a world of entropy: order for free.[65] It is not that a true definition of development will negate the centrality of efficiency by replacing it with something wasteful or futile; rather, the reverse is the case. Development is more than "efficient"—it is, in some sense, "free"; this is the great mysterious miracle at the heart of economics, the one that classical science must ignore if it intends to keep its outmoded intellectual foundations intact, precisely because it is a miracle and a mystery.[66] To raise the question of "order for free" is also to recognize that our current economic science is insufficiently "eucharistic" in a scientific sense; it "takes for granted" the existence of wealth and asks absurd questions—such as "What causes poverty?"—rather than the more germane—"What causes wealth?"[67]

Jane Jacobs and the successful practice of development

Unless a currently underdeveloped country is always to be in the position of "catching up" to other economies, and is to halt its own development when advanced countries whose goods and services it imitates become stagnant, it follows that sooner or later the currently underdeveloped country must itself become a vigorous innovator of unprecedented goods and services. For this, the country must create new financial organizations, and must continue to create them. It would seem, from past experience in developing economies, that the way to create these organizations might be for the government to establish considerable numbers of small and decentralized lending agencies in the local economies of various cities—and to encourage them to specialize by seeking out promising new goods and services being added to older work in their cities. They would have failures, but they would also finance unprecedented

---

65. Stuart Kauffman is the author of this phrase, in his *At Home in the Universe: The Search for the Laws of Self-Organization and Complexity* (New York: Oxford University Press, 1995).

66. Perhaps so as not to appear too religious, we should characterize development using a safer term, such as "metaefficient."

67. Jacobs, *Economy*, 120–21.

industries. The new, creative financial organizations that became successful locally could then export their services too, and could become organizations working nationwide.[68]

Two of the "small and decentralized lending agencies in the local economies of various cities" that I have been discussing in this essay are the modern microlenders and Basil's Christian charitable program. They are the ground-breaking practical implementations corresponding to Jacobs's groundbreaking theoretical insights.

Return to the Basileias

Equipped with an improved account of what has and hasn't worked in the generation of lasting prosperity, let us now return to Basil's new town to find some things clarified and much that still remains mysterious. Specifically, let me return to the eight points of what I thought was known for sure about Basil's philanthropic program.

1. Supervised by *chorepiscopoi* and run along charitable lines, Basil's new city seems to have ensured that economic life there was kept "in motion." There was no hoarding of capital by the greedy rich, no wasting of capital on abstract projects, no hoarding of labor by the lazy poor, but rather a steady gambling of the present by all parties on a brighter future. Basil and the church's spirit of Christian philanthropy helped to ensure that the gains made by helping the poor were poured back into helping still others. This spirit also helped Basil to eschew the obsession of the rich with "efficiency" in favor of an ad hoc, messy, responsive process.

2. His location of the new town outside the city shows us that its success was genuinely the catalyzation of something new. The newness of the city, at least initially, meant that the saint's experiment presaged the microlenders in other way; the small scale of the early Basileias meant that people were helping other people they could see and get to know. Some spirit of mutuality could more easily arise under those conditions.

3. The program's focus on unprecedented or at least relatively novel insti-tutions is a reminder that, from the first, the Basileias had some connection with innovation[69]—innovation that drew new "customers" and workers from some distance.

4. Basil's provision of training for the poor fulfilled a basic requirement of Jacobs's economic vision, especially as that labor was employed to meet actual needs in the local economy. For Jacobs, all developing economies are "knowledge economies" in the sense that development revolves around in-

68. Ibid., 212.
69. See n. 2.

novation understood as the crystallization of a moment of insight, and Basil was marrying knowledge with labor through his training programs. Furthermore, his training was designed to put people to a use that was productive within their own setting, to give them work that was of benefit to the people around them in very concrete ways. This type of investment in training "pays off" because the services the poor learn to provide are desperately needed within the economy right around them, on a pay-as-you-go basis.

5. The pull of the Basileias, as we said, extended over some distance, evidence that it was economically vibrant.

6. Basil preached against, and inspired others to undercut, the loan sharks. Such usurers prey on people existing on the economic margins of society, rendering them still more marginal. By inviting the poor into an honor-system approach to investment, he made the usurious irrelevant and thus powerless.

7. His rhetorical attack on the sterile uses of wealth reminds us of the importance of working capital in a developing economy. Wealth is to be given away, whether literally as charity or figuratively as loan.

8. Taking all the above together, the long-term success of Basil's town means, somehow, that it was built around innovative services, that it deployed capital intelligently, and that it united the underemployed with innovation, training, and small-scale capital investment.

And yet there is no evidence that Basil "lent" money to anyone. Implicit in all the above is that contractual economic obligations can be made redundant by spiritual ties among people. My thesis for a specifically Christian economic science—a baptism of the real economic science founded by Jane Jacobs, that is—is this: charity can substitute for formal capital investment in the generation of empirically real development, as it establishes genuinely mutual interpersonal networks. People don't need to be legally obligated to give back to their donors/investors in the local economy when they have been sufficiently moved by the love shown them within that community. Rather, they do so willingly and with abundant generosity. Love repays love given, and it repays it with interest. This is the lesson that Basil's project offers to contribute to the contemporary fight against poverty.

In the medieval Russian period we have many such "Basil's towns"—whole cities that sprang up not just around a monastery, but even around a single worthy hermit. We find similar examples across history in Cyprus, Greece, Romania, and today in Arizona.[70] Outside the Orthodox Church, we find similar examples in Haiti and Peru, where mission monastic work by priests

70. For the Arizona example, see Kyriacos Markides, "Gift of the Desert," in *Gifts of the Desert: The Forgotten Path of Christian Spirituality* (New York: Doubleday, 2005), 17–38.

formed the kernel around which world-changing medical movements and new or healed cities could arise.[71]

We have here a very strong, if partial, explanation for the *avaton* as practiced in the Holy Mountain, in some other male monastic centers, and by the nuns at Ormylia, Greece. By excluding members of the other gender from close proximity to the monastery grounds, monastics enforcing *avaton* necessarily exclude also the settling of families with children, which would then be followed by businesses and services and the consequent inevitable transformation of monastic "deserts" into cities. That is, without the *avaton* monastic centers are altogether too apt to catalyze the formation of cities. Ramsay argues that the phenomenon of cities forming around vibrant cultic centers is so common a factor in the rise of urban centers that Christian historians ought to include it in their classifications of types of city genesis.[72] One thinks also of the U.S. Southwest and West, where so many major cities began as Spanish missions and still retain their ecclesiastical names.

The "entrepreneur elder" is a wonderful phenomenon I have seen most especially during the six months in 2004 I spent at the Monastery of the Archangel Michael in Tharri, Rhodes. There, on a typical day, nothing much beyond the buzzing of bees seemed to be happening once morning services had been completed, so pervasive was the seclusion and the atmosphere of calm. And yet, in less than fifteen years on that site, the abbot, Father Amphilochios (Tsoukos—recently elected the Greek Orthodox Metropolitan of New Zealand), had raised the funds to restore the formerly abandoned monastery's ninth-century church and see its iconography professionally cleaned and repaired, which in turn became a heavy draw for tourist buses all summer and helped to revitalize the two neighboring villages. He persuaded the local government to ensure that the roads to and from that village would be paved and improved, and he established a radio and a television station, whose profoundly beautiful local content was a needed antidote to globalized cultural uniformity. Funds he raised were used to build a petting zoo; dozens of monastic cells; guest quarters; workshops; kitchens; and a lovely church. He expanded the ruined monastery gardens and planted more

71. The Haitian and Peruvian examples are from the biography of Dr. Paul Farmer by Tracy Kidder, *Mountains beyond Mountains: A Man's Quest to Heal the World* (New York: Random House, 2003). Both Farmer's work in Haiti and his associate Jim Yong Kim's work in Peru followed in the footsteps of priests—in the first case an Anglican, in the second a Roman Catholic—who had left everything to serve the poor. Interestingly, not only is the economy around Farmer's hospital being healed, but the environment too; cf. p. 19. For another discussion of many of the problematic definitions discussed in this chapter, see Aaron Shakow and Alec Irwin, "Terms Reconsidered: Decoding Development Discourse," in *Dying For Growth: Global Inequality and the Health of the Poor*, ed. Jim Yong Kim, Joyce V. Millen, Alec Irwin, and John Gershman (Monroe, ME: Common Courage Press, 2000), 44–61.

72. Ramsay's footnote on 464 was apparently written with chap. 8 of George Adam Smith's *Historical Geography of the Holy Land* (London: Hodder & Stoughton, 1896) in mind.

than one thousand trees. And he tonsured and instructed more than thirty monastic fathers and has sent them off for permanent service to places as diverse as West Africa and Albuquerque, New Mexico. Just beginning as I left was construction on a hospital adjacent to the monastery, designed to be a resting station for people emotionally exhausted by modern life.

All this seemed to be happening, as I said, without much visible effort, other than the extremely intense vigilance at being prayerful and responsive to those in need that is normally exercised by a saintly abbot and his monastics. The monastery was a force in the declaration of the surrounding area as a national park, and, I am told, to the elder's prayers was attributed the sudden and abrupt halt of a forest fire that threatened to engulf both the monastery and the park.[73]

Conclusion

In such a short essay it has been impossible to do justice to all the phenomena touched on—St. Basil's program, the mess of modern aid, the mechanistic epistemology behind it, the difficulty of the postmodern world in envisioning a holistic science that would also be concrete and rigorous, the worth of microlending, and the way in which the late Jane Jacobs's accomplishments in the science of order, and especially of economic order,[74] tie so much of this together. This present essay has been a start.

The failure of our misnamed development aid may not have been entirely unintentional. A realist would surely ask whether it was or is in the interests of the Western powers to raise up economic, and thus eventually also military, equals to themselves in every corner of the globe. Given the weakness of human nature, could these equals not one day become rivals, then enemies, and later perhaps mortal enemies? Wouldn't it be better to reserve true development for ourselves and supply only enough charity—however labeled—to ameliorate the worst suffering of others?

It would take too much space to answer in detail this argument for planned failure. Suffice it to say that the persistence of abject poverty has left the

73. Anyone visiting Tharri today can see the massive devastation from the fire, stretching across hundreds of acres. The damage abruptly stops on the last ridgeline overlooking the monastery. A young monastic father present during the fire described to me an apparently miraculous sudden shift in the winds as the fire reached that ridge and the abbott gathered the monks in prayer. Like Paul Farmer, Metropolitan (then Archimandrite) Amphilochios was a guardian of his ecosystem.

74. After Jane Jacobs, economic science will no longer be the "study of the allocation of scarce resources," but rather (a) the scientific study of past resource-generating processes; (b) the experimental effort to catalyze future resource-generating processes; and only then, (c) the study of the allocation of those resources that are, at the present moment, scarce. This would be a "eucharistic economics," or an economics of gratitude, perhaps at least in principle not unlike what Daniel Caner discusses in chap. 15.

populations of the Third World vulnerable to virulent anti-Western ideologies whose adoption has made and will continue to make our position on this
earth mortally perilous. A halt to the bad loans of the World Bank and IMF
variety, the recognition that access to fairly priced capital is a basic human
right, followed by the provision of microlending and then of mesolending (to
coin a term) to every segment of the world's population,[75] the encouragement of property reform in the Third World,[76] long-term commitments by
thousands of Westerners to love and care for the world by emigrating to its
farthest reaches and remaining there—all this would be much less expensive
than our tried and failed approaches to development, and are likely to win
us many more friends than enemies among the currently humiliated nations
of this earth. We shall likely as not always have enemies, just as the poor we
shall always have with us, but why should increasing, rather than decreasing,
the numbers of both be the aim of so much effort, expense, and planning?

Christian social activists, meanwhile, have an additional offering to make—
the vision of a community where life begets life, and love begets love. "Development economics" in its current formulation aims to deliver a materialist
eschaton, a nirvana of universal consumerist bliss. But it claims, like the
Marxist economists whom it unknowingly and slavishly imitates, that it will
deliver this eschaton without recourse to God, to miracles, or even to the
scientific method. Christian economists have a moral obligation to expose and
ridicule this kind of sham religion for what it is: an unscientific science and a
depraved creed, standing as a barrier between the least of Christ's brethren
and the spiritual and material consolation they richly deserve.

75. If microloans have such high rates of repayment at fair-market prices, and the market for
such loans is potentially so vast, why haven't for-profit investors taken note? The answer is, they
are beginning to. See the work of Unitus Inc., a venture capital fund based in Redmond, Washington, that specializes in capitalizing microfinance institutions around the world (www.unitus.com
[accessed August 29, 2006]). The appearance in the First World of investment vehicles backing
finance to the poor is as significant a development in the fight against poverty as the invention of
microlending itself.

76. Hernando de Soto, a Peruvian activist, has cut another of the Gordian knots of twentieth-
century development, in his work *The Mystery of Capital: Why Capitalism Triumphs in the West and
Fails Everywhere Else* (New York: Basic Books, 2000). The issue of "land reform," for and against which
so much blood was spilled in recent history, he adroitly transforms into the question of "property
law reform." What the poor need in today's world of agrarian surplus is not the carving up of vast
landed estates, but a clear and transferable legal title to the property underneath the shack in the
hills of Rio de Janeiro, or wherever, that they have been living on and improving for many years. De
Soto proposes that the same squatter's rights that applied in the American West, and that led to the
vitality of its pioneer culture, now be applied to the urban slums, where the overwhelming majority
of the world's poorest live. Applying developed-world standards of squatter's rights in these settings,
de Soto argues, at once converts the poor residents there into property owners, manageable credit
risks, and stakeholders in their local economies. Like Yunus, Whittaker, Bussau, and Jacobs, de Soto
sees the poor as entrepreneurs, not as inert statistical objects.

18

THE USE OF PATRISTIC SOCIOETHICAL TEXTS IN CATHOLIC SOCIAL THOUGHT

Brian Matz

Starting in 2005 and continuing through 2009, the Centre for Catholic Social Thought at the Katholieke Universiteit Leuven (Louvain) is directing a research project that asks the following question: whither the influence of patristic texts in Catholic Social Teaching of the past, the present, and the future? In this essay I outline the center's activities related to this question and then offer a few insights into where we think the research will take us.[1] Despite the Catholic focus of the question, this research program targets an audience that includes scholars both Catholic and secular, both of patristics and of social ethics. We anticipate that the research tools we are developing will have wide application and interest.

Catholic Social Teaching (CST)[2] refers to a broad collection of documents that have emerged either from the Vatican or from regional bishops'

---

1. This essay reflects the status of our research program as of mid-2006.
2. This phrase is used in a technical sense, with the definition provided above, and is in contrast with "Catholic Social Thought." This latter phrase refers to the official texts *plus* the unofficial activities that take place in parishes, lay institutes, and Catholic worker movements, among other places. These unofficial activities not only involve in the work of alleviating injustice and caring for the marginalized; they also exhort the hierarchy to rethink continually its commitment to those people groups.

288   Patristic Studies for Today

conferences.[3] These documents have a wide readership in Catholic and even non-Catholic circles, addressed, as the documents often are, to "all persons of good will." They are a Christian voice amid a world that perhaps would otherwise seek only a political solution to the social problems facing us today. Although popes had written on matters of social concern prior to the late nineteenth century,[4] it is generally accepted that CST began in earnest with the publication of Pope Leo XIII's encyclical *Rerum novarum* in 1891. These official documents address social issues, such as transnational justice, health care, poverty relief, living wages, farmer and farmworker relief, antinuclear proliferation, and economic inequities in the world. The documents regularly buttress their arguments with citations of biblical writings, particularly from the Hebrew prophets and the Gospels, and with natural law theories articulated in various forms since the scholastic period. The documents of CST claim that Christ himself had given the mission of social justice to the apostles, and thus, by extension, to the church, through his teachings about ushering in the kingdom of God.

Having rooted the church's social justice message in this historical context, one expects to find a continuity of this teaching in the church's own history, including especially writers of the patristic period. As well, perhaps the CST documents draw on this patristic heritage in furtherance of their desire to demonstrate a historical continuity to their teaching. This essay demonstrates that the relative influence of that heritage on CST is inadequate; furthermore, a greater openness to patristic social teachings might lead to even stronger exhortations in future CST documents. We now turn to a summary of the research work completed thus far and to a preview of the work to come.

The Research Agenda

Our project is based, in part, on the identification of a gap in the scholarly literature concerned with whether CST documents have strayed from the social teaching of the church fathers. We are filling that gap in three ways and, in the process, creating a research tool that we expect will be of service to a variety of scholars. First, we demonstrate to what extent the CST

3. Our study examined twenty-one such documents, which are identified in table 18.1. While some followers of CST may disagree on the inclusion or exclusion of one or two documents, this list reflects a consensus in the scholarship reflected by two major books: David J. O'Brien and Thomas A. Shannon, eds., *Catholic Social Thought: The Documentary Heritage* (Maryknoll, NY: Orbis, 1992); and Kenneth Himes, ed., *Modern Catholic Social Teaching: Commentaries and Interpretations* (Washington, DC: Georgetown University Press, 2005).

4. Cf. Michael Schuck, *That They Be One: The Social Teaching of the Papal Encyclicals, 1740–1989* (Washington, DC: Georgetown University Press, 1991).

documents rely on patristic writings.[5] We have read carefully twenty-one documents that are generally considered to comprise CST. Seventeen of the documents incorporate patristic source citations into either their main text or footnotes, with 110 such citations in all. Our detailed study of these citations (summarized in table 18.1) has determined several points. One is that the CST documents owe a substantial debt to the theological formulations of the patristic period. Consider, for example, this statement in the encyclical *Centesimus annus* (1991): "The guiding principle of . . . all of the church's social doctrine, is a correct view of the human person and of his unique value."[6] What is more, *Centesimus annus* goes on to point out that a person's unique value may be traced directly back to the *imago Dei* given to people at the creation of the world, and that God gave to people this *imago Dei* as a consequence of foreknowing that the Son of God would one day incarnate himself as a human. In other words, human dignity is rooted in the gift of God to each person, and that gift itself is rooted in the mutual love existing among the persons of the Trinity. Christ would eventually redeem what had always been and will continue to be creatures in his own image. To the extent that the patristic world had correctly articulated the doctrine of the Trinity, of Christ and his two natures, of humans and their need for redemption, and the church's responsibility to pass along these truths to every new generation, then, the CST documents owe an incalculable debt to its theological acumen. Another point is that when the CST documents do cite patristic sources, they do so in nearly every case with little regard to the historical, literary, or theological context into which those documents were originally given voice.[7] We have found in the CST documents, among

5. The full version of this study is Brian Matz, *Patristic Sources and Catholic Social Teaching, A Forgotten Dimension: A Textual, Historical, and Rhetorical Analysis of Patristic Source Citations in the Church's Social Documents*, Annua Nuntia Lovaniensia 63 (Leuven: Peeters, 2008).

6. *Centesimus annus* 11; cf. O'Brien and Shannon, *Catholic Social Thought*, 447.

7. Our study confirms on a much broader scale the findings of two earlier essays that evaluate the patristic citations in Pope Leo XIII's *Rerum novarum*: Jean-Marie Salamito, "*Rerum novarum*, une encyclique néo-scolastique? La question sociale ou le déclin de la communauté," in *Rerum Novarum: Écriture, contenu et reception d'une encyclique; Actes du colloque international organisé par l'École française de Rome et le Greco n 2 du CNRS (Rome, 18–20 avril 1991)* (Rome: École française de Rome, 1997), 187–206; and Françoise Monfrin, "Pauvreté et richesse: Le lexique latin de l'encyclique: inspiration classique ou inspiration patristique?" in *Rerum Novarum: Écriture, contenu et reception d'une encyclique*, 133–86.

Salamito, see esp. 196, concludes that patristic ideas were more influential than any particular patristic text or author. He argues the drafters were hardly aware of particular patristic texts, relying instead, most likely, on a qualitatively poor sourcebook. Monfrin evaluates the linguistic choices made by the drafters of this CST document. He concludes that the document's drafters were favorably disposed to classical Latin and that they took it upon themselves to reword quotations of biblical and historical sources to fit their particular disposition. Our own study has confirmed Salamito's and Monfrin's findings and has extended the findings to include the CST documents that have followed *Rerum novarum*.

other things, word changes when quoting the original patristic texts and changes to the original meaning of the patristic texts once they are inserted into the CST text. Still another point is that the patristic citations in the CST documents are rarely citations of patristic socioethical texts.[8] Instead, the CST documents most often cite patristic passages that are theological in nature or are interpretations of a specific biblical text. The social ideas of the church fathers are still absent from the social ideas of the encyclicals. Finally, and to speak more positively, a sizable number of the footnote references to patristic sources provide invaluable elaboration on particular theological points, upon which the main body of the CST text has not taken the time to elaborate.

Table 18.1. Patristic Sources in the CST Documents—Summary

CST Text	Total	Quotations	References	Footnotes
Rerum novarum (1891)	2	2	0	0
Quadragesimo anno (1931)	2	1	1	0
Mater et magistra (1961)	3	2	1	0
Pacem in terris (1963)	3	3	0	0
Dignitatis humanae (1965)	8	0	8	0
Gaudium et spes (1965)	18	1	6	11
Populorum progressio (1967)	2	1	1	0
Medellin Documents (1969)	0	0	0	0
Octogesima adveniens (1971)	0	0	0	0
Iustitia in mundo (1971)	0	0	0	0
Evangelii nuntiandi (1975)	15	6	3	6
Puebla Documents (1979)	2	0	2	0
Laborem exercens (1981)	0	0	0	0
Familiaris consortio (1981)	4	3	1	0
The Challenge of Peace (1983)	5	3	1	1
Economic Justice for All (1986)	2	1	1	0
Sollicitudo rei socialis (1987)	6	0	6	0
Centesimus annus (1991)	1	1	0	0
Santo Domingo Documents (1992)	2	0	1	1
Compendium of CST (2004)	19	5	5	9
Deus caritas est (2005)	16	6	9	1
TOTAL	**110**	**35**	**46**	**29**

8. The only exception here is the citation of Tertullian's *Apology* 39, although our study has demonstrated the encyclical *Rerum novarum* changed the context in which its quotation of this patristic passage is to be read.

Second, we are cataloging what the patristic authors taught vis-à-vis social ethics. Specifically, we will focus on what is available in the Greek fathers.[9] This research will culminate in the publication of a compendium of Greek patristic socioethical texts.[10] We have gradually been compiling a database of such texts since 2005 and, as of mid-2006, have added more than 230 texts from thirty Greek patristic authors. We anticipate a complete database nearly double its current size. The compendium will be subdivided into several large socioethical themes, including private property, common good, land rights, slavery, the poor, and usury. Within each theme will be an English translation of several representative patristic texts. We intend to publish in the compendium only those texts that are invaluable for understanding Greek patristic social ethics and those texts that are either difficult to acquire elsewhere or for which the present English translation is dated. Accompanying the text will be a short bibliography and a brief introduction that provide historical context and guide the reader to see the main thrust of the text vis-à-vis contemporary social ethics.

The third and final element of our research agenda is the publication of a monograph treating several of the hermeneutical issues at stake in reading patristic socioethical texts. In furtherance of this study, we have invited scholars of patristics and of social ethics to Leuven for a seminar to identify the issues that ought to be considered in this regard. At a minimum, it is important to ask basic questions, such as to whom are the fathers referring when they speak of the "poor" in their homilies? In the first chapter of this volume, Steve Friesen has suggested there were at least three such levels of "poor" in the second century. Perhaps those classifications held for the third, fourth, and fifth centuries. Another question is, what are the various models for alleviating economic injustice operative in the minds of the Greek fathers? Moreover, how do those models influence the way the fathers spoke to the economic haves and have-nots? For instance, Gregory of Nyssa's text on usury

9. We limit the study to Greek texts for two reasons. First, we do so to keep the project manageable with respect to the time allotted for the work. Second, we believe the focus on Greek texts affords an opportunity for intra-Christian dialogue between Catholics and Orthodox, particularly valuable in our center's European context, where such dialogue contributes to the continued integration of former Eastern Bloc countries, with large populations of Orthodox Christians, into the European Union. If an evaluation of patristic texts in Latin or other eastern languages is made at a later date, it can benefit from a certain amount of hindsight. The organization and methodologies developed for this study, along with the helpful critiques from scholars who review its findings, will greatly improve the learning curve for future studies.

10. R. Sierra Bravo and Florentino Del Valle, eds., *Doctrina social y economica de los padres de la Iglesia: Coleccion general de documentos y textos* (Madrid: Biblioteca Fomento Social, 1967), is an indexed collection of Greek and Latin patristic documents, ranging in length from one-sentence excerpts to full texts. However, it is not accessible to a broad range of readers and has certain problems. Our search of the major library catalog databases have identified fewer than twenty-five copies in all of continental Europe and across the United States. The volume also contains a number of bibliographic errors.

reveals that he believed economic injustices are alleviated by an appeal for charity to the self-serving motives of the rich. What is more, his appeal was almost entirely secular, for he nowhere addresses the wealthy based on their connection with Christ. Yet, is that how Gregory of Nyssa writes in other socioethical texts? Does he have other models for alleviating economic injustice? And, if so, what contextual factors surrounding the homily suggest to him one model over another? These are the types of questions we intend to address in the project's closing phase.

Our Research and the Future of Catholic Social Teaching

Having just described the three aspects of our project, it is appropriate at this point to turn a corner and discuss some preliminary reflections on the import of this research for the future of CST. First, as was made clear above, there is a need for future CST documents to nuance more carefully their use of patristic texts. For example, there is room for improvement either in the documents' faithfulness to the original wording and to the original contexts of the patristic sources, or in their willingness to provide an explanation when such changes have been made. To a certain extent, this will restrict the freedom of CST documents to use patristic texts in a merely ornamental or proof-text fashion. However, the theological and pastoral proclivities of the patristic texts may reinvigorate CST and give it a powerful, newfound voice.

Second, and related to this last point, many of the Greek patristic, socioethical texts rely on a consistent set of biblical themes and passages that exhort the rich to give their excess to the poor. Regularly, one discovers the claim in the Greek patristic texts that the poor are the ones truly rich before God. It is rare for a Greek patristic text to denounce the rich for being such. Similarly, it is rare to find a Greek patristic author calling for the abolition of poverty; most seem to accept it as part of the necessary balance between people that exists in the world. These are examples of narrative ethics at work that may be summarized as follows: the Christian story of God's compassion for the poor and marginalized as expressed in various biblical pericopes (i.e., the historical narrative) demands to be told and retold in every generation. That story, when read in light of one's present situation (the present narrative), requires a response: either engage in social action or consciously decide not to do so. The Greek patristic authors often recalled the same biblical pericopes in expositing their vision for Christian social justice, and this served to preserve the historical narrative for action in the present narrative of their hearers. The same must be done in Catholic social thought today.[11] The

11. For a more in-depth description of this vision, see Johan Verstraeten, "Re-Thinking Catholic Social Thought as Tradition," in *Catholic Social Thought: Twilight or Renaissance?* ed. J. S. Boswell, F. P. McHugh, and J. Verstraeten (Leuven: Peeters Press, 2000), 59–77.

CST documents over the past century reflect a paucity of these particular biblical themes. We believe that using narrative ethics may help revitalize CST's arguments. There might be greater willingness, for example, to speak unequivocally of sin and greed in calling economic power players to account for their treatment of the disenfranchised. At the same time, we recognize that this may result in a reduction of the intended audience for CST documents (e.g., a shift away from "all persons of good will" to "all Christians of good will"). The publication of a compendium of Greek patristic source texts will aid CST in better utilizing this narrative ethic.

Third and finally, there is room to improve the theological underpinnings that support the vision for solidarity that is often expressed in official documents of the past few decades (relying instead, as they do, on a natural law framework).[12] The Greek patristic authors envisioned humanity sharing in the life of the poor Christ, an image that is currently missing from the official documents. If that image were more fully expressed, it might help to close the long-standing gap that some social activists claim exists between their own incarnational work of social action and the official vision of solidarity put forward by the CST documents.[13]

Conclusion

The research project at our center invites scholars to consider at least two related questions. They are ongoing questions for anyone interested in a link between the past and the present for Catholic social thought. First, what might be some of the sociocultural or theological forces that led various patristic authors to think as they did regarding social ethics? Second, what impact ought patristic socioethical texts have on contemporary Christian reflection about ethics in twenty-first century society? The answers to both coincide with the life work of students and laity who refuse to surrender a vision for a better future to the pressing demands of daily work.

12. Cf. Charles Curran, *Catholic Social Teaching, 1891–Present: A Historical, Theological, and Ethical Analysis* (Washington, DC: Georgetown University Press, 2002). Curran points out that, beginning with Vatican II, CST shifted from a "natural law" approach to an *attempt at* an integrated theological approach. However, he does not believe the approach has succeeded, in part because of the two distinct audiences (church and "persons of good will") the documents address. In fact, the one document that is addressed to a church audience *only* (*Evangelii nuntiandi*) is, in Curran's opinion, the most theologically integrated.

13. Cf. Staf Hellemans, "Is There a Future for Catholic Social Teaching after the Waning of Ultramontane Mass Catholicism?" in O'Brien and Shannon, *Catholic Social Thought*, 13–32.

ABBREVIATIONS

For the abbreviations used for papyrological materials, especially in chapter 7, see J. F. Oates et al., *Checklist of Greek, Latin, Demotic, and Coptic Papyri, Ostraca, and Tablets*, 5th ed., BASPSup 9 (Oakville, CT: American Society of Papyrologists, 2001), now regularly updated at http://scriptorium .lib.duke.edu/papyrus/texts/clist.html.

AASS	*Acta sanctorum quotquot toto orbe coluntur* (Antwerp, 1643–)
AB	Anchor Bible
ACO	*Acta conciliorum oecumenicorum*, ed. E. Schwartz (Berlin, 1914–)
ACW	Ancient Christian Writers
AnBoll	Analecta Bollandiana
ANF	*Ante-Nicene Fathers*
APF	*Archiv für Papyrusforschung*
ASP	*American Studies in Papyrology*
BHG	*Bibliotheca hagiographica graeca* (Brussels: 1957)
BibS(F)	Biblische Studien (Freiburg, 1895–)
BSAC	*Bulletin de la Société d'archéologie copte*
ByzZ	*Byzantinische Zeitschrift*
BZNW	Beihefte zur Zeitschrift für die Neutestamentliche Wissenschaft
CBQ	*Catholic Biblical Quarterly*
CBQMS	Catholic Biblical Quarterly Monograph Series
CBR	*Currents in Biblical Research*
CCSL	Corpus Christianorum: Series latina (Turnhout: 1953–)
CE	*Chronique d'Égypte*
CÉFAR	Collection de l'École française de Rome
CH	*Church History*
CJ	*Codex Justinianus*
CNT	Commentaire du Nouveau Testament
CS	Cistercian Studies Series
CSCO	Corpus scriptorum christianorum orientalium, ed. I. B. Chabot (Paris: 1903–)
CSEL	Corpus scriptorum ecclesiasticorum latinorum
DOP	*Dumbarton Oaks Papers*
FC	Fathers of the Church (Washington, DC, 1947–)
FRLANT	Forschungen zur Religion und Literatur des Alten und Neuen Testaments
GCS	Die griechischen christlichen Schriftsteller der ersten drei Jahrhunderte
GOTR	*Greek Orthodox Theological Review*
GRBS	*Greek, Roman, and Byzantine Studies*
HBO	*Historiae beatorum orientalium*

HNT	Handbuch zum Neuen Testament
HTR	*Harvard Theological Review*
JECS	*Journal of Early Christian Studies*
JJP	*Journal of Juristic Papyrology*
JRA	*Journal of Roman Archaeology*
JRS	*Journal of Roman Studies*
JSNT	*Journal for the Study of the New Testament*
JSNTSup	Journal for the Study of the New Testament: Supplement Series
JTS	*Journal of Theological Studies*
LCL	Loeb Classical Library
LSJ	Liddell, H. G., R. Scott, H. S. Jones, *A Greek-English Lexicon*, 9th ed. with revised supplement (Oxford, 1996)
Mansi	Giovan Domenico Mansi, *Sacrorum conciliorum, nova et amplissima collectio* (originally printed 1759–1798; reprinted Paris: H. Welter, 1901–1927; reprinted by Graz, Akademische Druck- u. Verlagsanstalt, 1960–61)
NBA	*Nuova Biblioteca Agostiniana* (Rome: Città Nuova Editrice)
NHC	Nag Hammadi Codices
Nov.	*Novellae (=the Novels of Justinian)*
NPNF	*Nicene and Post-Nicene Fathers*, 2 series (*NPNF*[1], *NPNF*[2])
OCD	*Oxford Classical Dictionary*, ed. S. Hornblower and A. Spawforth, 3rd ed. (Oxford, 1996)
OrChrAn	Orientalia christiana analecta
PCPhS	Proceedings of the Cambridge Philological Society
PG	Patrologia Graeca, J. P. Migne, 162 vols. (Paris: 1857–1886)
PO	Patrologia orientalis
RAC	*Reallexikon für Antike und Christentum*, ed. T. Kluser et al. (Stuttgart: 1950–)
RBén	*Revue bénédictine*
RE	*Realencyklopädie für protestantische Theologie und Kirche*
RÉAug	*Revue des Études Augustiniennes*
RechAug	*Recherches Augustiniennes*
RIDA	*Revue internationale des droits de l'antiquité*
RSR	*Recherches de science religieuse*
SAC	Studies in Antiquity and Christianity
SB	*Sammelbuch griechischer Urkunden aus Ägypten*, ed. F. Preisigke et al. (1915–)
SBT	Studies in Biblical Theology
SC	Sources chrétiennes (Paris: Cerf, 1943–)
SEAug	Studia ephemeridis Augustinianum
SPap	*Studia papyrologica*
StPatr	Studia patristica
StudMon	*Studia monastica*
Stud. Pal.	*Studien zur Palaeographie und Papyruskunde*
SUNT	Studien zur Umwelt des Neuen Testaments
TS	*Theological Studies*
TU	Texte und Untersuchungen zur Geschichte der altchristlichen Literatur
VT	*Vetus Testamentum*
ZPE	*Zeitschrift für Papyrologie und Epigraphik*

Select Bibliography

The list given below includes select relevant secondary sources that contributors cite frequently, including common English translations of several primary sources. Also listed are relevant publications by contributors that are not otherwise cited in this volume, as well as a selection of contributors' suggested additional readings on this topic.

Atkins, Margaret, and Robin Osborne, eds. *Poverty in the Roman World.* Cambridge: Cambridge University Press, 2006.

Avila, Charles. *Ownership: Early Christian Teaching.* Maryknoll, NY: Orbis Books, 1983.

Becker, Adam H. "Anti-Judaism and Care for the Poor in Aphrahat's *Demonstration* 20," *Journal of Early Christian Studies* 10 (2002): 305–27.

Brändle, Rudolf. *John Chrysostom: Bishop, Reformer, Martyr.* Translated by John Cawte and Silke Trzcionka with revised notes by Wendy Mayer. Early Christian Studies 8. Strathfield, NSW, Australia: St. Pauls, 2004.

———. *Matt. 25,31–46 im Werk des Johannes Chrysostomus.* Beiträge zur Geschichte der biblischen Exegese 22. Tübingen: Mohr Siebeck, 1979.

Brown, Peter. *Poverty and Leadership in the Later Roman Empire.* The Menahem Stern Jerusalem Lectures. Hanover, NH: University Press of New England, 2002.

Buell, Denise Kimber. "'Sell What You Have and Give to the Poor': A Feminist Analysis of Clement of Alexandria's *Who Is the Rich Person Who Is Saved?*" In *Walk in the Ways of Wisdom: Essays in Honor of Elisabeth Schüssler Fiorenza,* edited by Shelly Matthews, Cynthia Kittredge, and Melanie Johnson-DeBaufre, 194–213. Philadelphia: Trinity Press International, 2003.

Caner, Daniel. "Towards a Miraculous Economy: Christian Gifts and Material 'Blessings' in Late Antiquity." *Journal of Early Christian Studies* 14 (2006): 329–77.

———. *Wandering, Begging Monks: Spiritual Authority and the Promotion of Monasticism in Late Antiquity.* Transformation of the Classical Heritage 33. Berkeley: University of California Press, 2002.

Clement of Alexandria. *Quis dives salvetur?* English translation by G. W. Butterworth, "The Rich Man's Salvation." In *Clement of Alexandria,* Loeb Classical Library, 265–367. Cambridge, MA: Harvard University Press, 1919.

Constantelos, D. J. *Byzantine Philanthropy and Social Welfare.* 2nd ed. New Rochelle, NY: A. D. Caratzas, 1991.

———. *Poverty, Society and Philanthropy.* New Rochelle, NY: A. D. Caratzas, 1992.

Coulie, Bernard. *Les richesses dans l'oeuvre de Saint Grégoire de Nazianze: Étude littéraire et historique.* Publications de l'Institut orientaliste de Louvain 32. Louvain-la-Neuve: Université Catholique de Louvain, 1985.

Countryman, L. William. *The Rich Christian in the Church of the Early Empire: Contradictions and Accommodations.* Texts and

Studies in Religion. New York: E. Mellen Press, 1980.

Daley, Brian E., SJ. "Building a New City: The Cappadocian Fathers and the Rhetoric of Philanthropy." *Journal of Early Christian Studies* 7 (1999): 431–61.

Doran, Robert, trans. *Stewards of the Poor: The Man of God, Rabbula, and Hiba in Fifth-Century Edessa.* Cistercian Studies Series 208. Kalamazoo, MI: Cistercian Publications, 2006.

Dunn, Geoffrey, "The White Crown of Works: Cyprian's Early Pastoral Ministry of Almsgiving in Carthage," *Church History* 73 (2004): 715–40.

Finley, Moses Immanuel, ed. *Studies in Roman Property.* Cambridge Classical Studies. Cambridge: Cambridge University Press, 1976.

Finn, Richard. *Almsgiving in the Later Roman Empire: Christian Promotion and Practice (313–450).* Oxford: Oxford University Press, 2006.

Friesen, Steven J. "Poverty in Pauline Studies: Beyond the So-called New Consensus." *Journal for the Study of the New Testament* 26 (2004): 323–61.

Fustel de Coulanges, Numa Denis. *Recherches sur le droit de propriété chez les Grecs et recherches sur le tirage au sort appliqué à la nomination des archontes Athéniens.* Morals and Law in Ancient Greece. New York: Arno Press, 1979.

Georgi, Dieter. *Remembering the Poor: The History of Paul's Collection for Jerusalem.* Nashville: Abington Press, 1992.

Glancy, Jennifer. *Slavery in Early Christianity.* Oxford: Oxford University Press, 2002.

Gordon, Barry. *The Economic Problem in Biblical and Patristic Thought.* Supplements to Vigiliae Christianae 9. Leiden: Brill, 1989.

———. "The Problem of Scarcity and the Christian Fathers: John Chrysostom and Some Contemporaries." *Studia papyrologica* 22 (1989): 108–20.

Hamel, Gildas. *Poverty and Charity in Roman Palestine, First Three Centuries C.E.* Berkeley: University of California Press, 1990.

Hamman, Adalbert Gauthier, ed., and France Quéré-Jaulmes, trans. *Riches et pauvres dans l'église ancienne.* Lettres Chrétiennes 6. Paris: Grasset, 1962.

Hanawalt, Emily Albu, and Carter Lindberg, eds. *Through the Eye of a Needle: Judeo-Christian Roots of Social Welfare.* Kirksville, MO: Thomas Jefferson University Press, 1994.

Hands, A. R. *Charity and Social Aid in Greece and Rome.* Ithaca, NY: Cornell University Press, 1968.

Harrison, Verna E. F. "Poverty, Social Involvement, and Life in Christ according to Saint Gregory the Theologian." *Greek Orthodox Theological Review* 39 (1994): 151–64.

Hengel, Martin. *Property and Riches in the Early Church: Aspects of a Social History of Early Christianity.* Philadelphia: Fortress, 1974.

Herrin, Judith. "Ideals of Charity, Realities of Welfare: The Philanthropic Activities of the Byzantine Church." In *Church and People in Byzantium,* edited by Rosemary Morris, 151–64. Birmingham, UK: Centre for Byzantine, Ottoman and Modern Greek Studies, 1990.

Holman, Susan R. "Constructed and Consumed: Everyday Life of the Poor in 4th Century Cappadocia." In *Social and Political Life in Late Antiquity,* edited by William Bowden, Adam Gutteridge, and Carlos Machado, 441–64. Late Antique Archaeology 3.1. Leiden: Brill, 2006.

———. "The Entitled Poor: Human Rights Language in the Cappadocians." *Pro Ecclesia* 9 (2000): 476–89.

———. "God in the Poor: Christology, Heterodoxy, and the Last Judgment in Early Christian Philanthropy Narrative." In *God in Early Christian Thought,* edited by Andrew McGowan and Brian Daley. Boston: Brill, forthcoming.

———. *The Hungry Are Dying: Beggars and Bishops in Roman Cappadocia.* Oxford Studies in Historical Theology. New York: Oxford University Press, 2001.

John Chrysostom. Sermons on Lazarus and the Rich Man. English translation in *On*

Wealth and Poverty, trans. Catharine P. Roth. Crestwood, NY: St. Vladimir's Seminary Press, 1984.

Klein, Richard. *Die Haltung der kappadokischen Bischöfe Basilius von Caesarea, Gregor von Nazianz und Gregor von Nyssa zur Sklaverei*. Forschungen zur antiken Sklaverei 32. Stuttgart: Steiner, 2000.

Leemans, Johan, Brian Matz, and Johan Verstraeten, eds. *Reading Patristic Texts on Social Ethics: Issues and Challenges for a 21st Century Christian Social Thought*. Washington, DC: Catholic University of America Press, forthcoming.

Liaou, Angeliki E. "The Church, Economic Thought and Economic Practice." In *The Christian East, Its Institutions & Its Thought: A Critical Reflection*, edited by Robert F. Taft, 435–64. Orientalia christiana analecta 251, Rome: Pontificio Instituto Orientale, 1996.

———. ed. *The Economic History of Byzantium: From the Seventh through the Fifteenth Century*. 3 vols. Washington, DC: Dumbarton Oaks Press, 2002.

Lowry, S. Todd, and Barry Gordon, eds. *Ancient and Medieval Economic Ideas and Concepts of Social Justice*. Leiden: Brill, 1998.

Maloney, Richard P. "The Teaching of the Fathers on Usury: An Historical Study on the Development of Christian Thinking." *Vigiliae Christianiae* 27 (1973): 241–65.

Mayer, Wendy. "Poverty and Society in the World of John Chrysostom." In *Social and Political Life in Late Antiquity*, edited by William Bowden, Adam Gutteridge, and Carlos Machado, 465–84. Late Antique Archaeology 3.1. Leiden: Brill, 2006.

Miller, Timothy S. *The Birth of the Hospital in the Byzantine Empire*. Baltimore: Johns Hopkins University Press, 1985. Revised 1997.

———. *The Orphans of Byzantum: Child Welfare in the Christian Empire*. Washington, DC: Catholic University of America Press, 2003.

O'Brien, David. "Rich Clients and Poor Patrons: Functions of Friendship in Clement of Alexandria's *Quis Dives Salvetur?*" PhD diss., University of Oxford, 2004.

Osiek, Carolyn. "The Ransom of Captives: Evolution of a Tradition." *Harvard Theological Review* 74 (1981): 365–86.

———. *Rich and Poor in the Shepherd of Hermas: An Exegetical-Social Investigation*. Catholic Biblical Quarterly Monograph Series 15. Washington, DC: Catholic Biblical Association of America, 1983.

———. *Shepherd of Hermas*. Hermeneia Commentaries. Minneapolis: Fortress, 1999.

Patlagean, Evelyne. *Pauvreté économique et pauvreté sociale à Byzance, 4e–7e siècles*. Civilisations et sociétés 48. Paris: Mouton, 1977.

Ramsey, Boniface. "Almsgiving in the Latin Church: The Late Fourth and Early Fifth Centuries." In *Acts of Piety in the Early Church*, edited by Everett Ferguson, 226–59. Studies in Early Christianity 17, New York: Garland, 1993.

Schroeder, Paul. "Getting Our Robes Dirty," In *Communion*, spring 2004, online at http://incommunion.org/articles/issue-33/getting-our-robes-dirty, accessed 2/28/06.

———. trans. *St. Basil the Great: On Social Justice*. Popular Patristics Series. Crestwood, NY: St. Vladimir's Seminary Press, forthcoming.

Scullard, Howard Hays. *Early Christian Ethics in the West: From Clement to Ambrose*. London: Williams & Norgate, 1907.

Sheather, Mary. "Pronouncements of the Cappadocians on Poverty and Wealth." In *Prayer and Spirituality in the Early Church*, vol. 1, edited by Pauline Allen, Raymond Canning, and L. Cross, 375–93. Melbourne: ACU Press, 1998.

Vasey, M. "The Social Ideas of Asterius of Amaseia." *Augustinianum* 26 (1986): 413–36.

LIST OF CONTRIBUTORS

David Brakke is chair and professor of religious studies at Indiana University in Bloomington. His most recent book is *Demons and the Making of the Monk: Spiritual Combat in Early Christianity* (Harvard University Press, 2006).

Rudolf Brändle is professor emeritus of New Testament and ancient church history at the University of Basel, Switzerland. He is the author of several monographs on John Chrysostom, including *John Chrysostom: Bishop, Reformer, Martyr* (St. Pauls, 2004).

Denise Kimber Buell is chair and professor of religion at Williams College. She is the author of *Making Christians: Clement of Alexandria and the Rhetoric of Legitimacy* (Princeton, 1999) and *"Why This New Race": Ethnic Reasoning in Early Christianity* (Columbia University Press, 2005).

Daniel Caner is associate professor of history and classics at the University of Connecticut at Storrs. He is the author of *Wandering, Begging Monks: Spiritual Authority and the Promotion of Monasticism in Late Antiquity* (Berkeley: University of California Press, 2002). His current project explores ideals of wealth and charity in early monasticism.

Francine Cardman is associate professor of historical theology and church history

at Weston Jesuit School of Theology, where she teaches early church history and theology, early Christian ethics, the history of Christian spirituality, and feminist theology. She is writing a book on the development of early Christian ethics.

Demetrios J. Constantelos is the Charles Cooper Townsend Sr. Distinguished Professor Emeritus of History and Religion at the Richard Stockton College of New Jersey, where he is also a Distinguished Scholar in Residence. His most recent book is *Renewing the Church: The Significance of the Council in Trullo* (Holy Cross Orthodox Press, 2006).

Steven J. Friesen is the Louise Farmer Boyer Chair in Biblical Studies at the University of Texas at Austin. His most recent book is *Imperial Cults and the Apocalypse of John: Reading Revelation in the Ruins* (Oxford, 2001).

Görge K. Hasselhoff is a fellow of the Center for Religious Studies at the Ruhr-Universität in Bochum, Germany. He is the author of *Dicit Rabbi Moyses: Studien zum Bild von Moses Maimonides im lateinischen Westen vom 13. bis 15. Jahrhundert* (Würzburg, 2004, 2nd extended edition 2005), as well as several other volumes, articles, and reviews.

Annewies van den Hoek is lecturer on Greek and Latin at Harvard Divinity

School. She is an international scholar on Clement of Alexandria and also publishes, with her husband, John Herrmann, on Greek, Roman, and early Christian archaeology. In cooperation with Alain Le Boulluec, she is preparing a revised edition of Clement's *Stromateis*.

Susan R. Holman is an independent scholar who holds advanced degrees in religious studies from Harvard Divinity School and Brown University. She is author of *The Hungry Are Dying: Beggars and Bishops in Roman Cappadocia* (Oxford, 2001).

Angeliki E. Laiou is the Dumbarton Oaks Professor of Byzantine History at Harvard University and a member of the Academy of Athens. She is an eminent scholar in Byzantine and medieval history and has published on social and economic history, the Byzantine family, the history of the Mediterranean in the later middle ages, and the history of modern Greece.

Brian Matz is assistant professor of historical theology at Carroll College in Helena, Montana. His areas of research interest include Greek patrology, social ethics, and the *filioque* debate in the ninth century.

Wendy Mayer is a research associate of the Centre for Early Christian Studies at Australian Catholic University. She is the author of several monographs on John Chrysostom, of which the most recent is *John Chrysostom: The Cult of the Saints* (St. Vladimir's Seminary Press, 2006).

Edward Moore is chair of the philosophy department at St. Elias School of Orthodox Theology (Pennsylvania), and executive editor of *Theandros*. He is author of *Origen of Alexandria and St. Maximus the Confessor* (Universal Publishers, 2005) and *Philosophy Insights: Plato* (Humanities E-books, UK, 2008).

Timothy Patitsas is assistant professor of ethics at Holy Cross Greek Orthodox School of Theology, where he specializes in issues of urban life and development economics. His doctoral dissertation (Catholic University of America) explored the work of Jane Jacobs in light of the Great Week and Bright Week cycle of the Orthodox church.

Adam Serfass is assistant professor of classics at Kenyon College in Gambier, Ohio. His research focuses on the diffusion of Christianity in late antiquity, especially in Italy and Egypt.

A. Edward Siecienski is assistant professor of religious studies at Misericordia University in Pennsylvania. In addition to a concentration in patristic and Byzantine studies, he has an abiding interest in the history and theology of East-West ecumenical encounters.

Efthalia Makris Walsh is an independent scholar and writer who lives in Bethesda, Maryland. Her dissertation at the Catholic University of America was on virgins, widows, and barren women in the writings of St. John Chrysostom, and her primary focus has been on women and women saints in the early church.

SUBJECT INDEX

Abraham (Byzantine moneylender), 256–57
abuse, 119
Acacius of Berea, 143
Acts of the Apostles: charity model in, 26–31; different perspective than in Paul's letters, 30–31
Aeschylus, 191
aging: care for the aged, 205; *gerokomeia*, 96, 100–101, 106n13, 202; monastic anxiety about old age, 83–84
Agrippa II, 30
Ahudemmeh (monastery), 233
aktēmosynē, 221–22
Alexander the Great, 195
Alexandrian "school," 55
alms: benefits for the trader, 246–47; monk as recipient and donor, 83–84, 86; from poor donors, 37–47; widows' almsgiving better than virginity, 181. *See also* collection; property distribution; redemptive alms
altar: poor as, 181; widow as, 181
Ambrose of Milan, 214
Amphilochius (abbot), 284–85
Amphilochius of Iconium, 143
anargyroi, 118, 123, 240n75
Anastasius: companion of Maximus the Confessor, 106; *Life*, 107n21
anger, 79, 80
Anician (Roman family). *See* Demetrias; Juliana: of the Anician family; Proba
Anthony, 67, 82
Antioch, splendor of, 128
apatheia as a philosophic ideal, 71

Aphrodito, 90, 94
aphthartodocetism, 109, 120, 124
Apiones (family), 91–92, 98
Apocalypse. See *Hermas, Shephard of*: as an apocalypse; Revelation, book of
Apollinarius, 53n19, 114–15
applause in church, 136, 173
Aquila. *See* Priscilla and Aquila
Arab invasions, 106–7
archiatroi. See under physicians
Arete (mother of Nausicaa), 194–95
Aristides, 193
Aristotle, 191–92, 202, 244, 264
Arsacius (priest), 187
Arsinoe (city), 90, 93; hospital in, 102
Artemis, wife of Platonianus, 196
Artemius, *Miracles*, 118, 251n19
ascetic poverty. *See* poverty: voluntary
Asclepius, 104–5, 123–24
Atalanta, 196
Athanasia, 108, 113
Athanasios I (patriarch), 207
Athanasius, 50; pseudo–, 54, 82
Augustine, 45–46, 50; commentary on the Letter of James, 51–54, 67–69, 145, 147, 154
autarkeia, 33
Auxentius (Byzantine saint), 260
avarice. *See* love of money

baker, 94; bakery, 94; grain for a baker's bride, 99
barber, 122

302

Modern Authors Index

ANCIENT SOURCES INDEX

Scripture

Old Testament

New Testament

9:8, 236, 236n57; **9:10**, 239n68; **9:13**, 28;
  11:1–21, 29; **12:2–4**, 61; **12:9**, 61
Galatians **2:10**, 42, 228; **3:28**, 40n9, 198, 199
Ephesians **5:16**, 261
Philippians **2:9**, 51; **2:25–30**, 29; **4:12–13**, 29
Colossians **2:8**, 60; **3:11**, 198
1 Thessalonians **2:1–12**, 29; **2:9**, 82; **4**, 182;
  4:11, 29
2 Thessalonians **3:8**, 82
1 Timothy **5**, 177; **5:9**, 177; **5:10**, 185; **6:7–8**,
  85; **6:10**, 85

Titus **3:4**, 191
Philemon **4–22**, 29; **10–19**, 29
James **1:10–11**, 51; **2:1–7**, 24; **2:1–8**, 57;
  2:1–6, 25, 52; **2:1**, 50; **2:2–7**, 10, 48–55;
  2:10, 51, 52, 52n13, 53; **2:12**, 49n2; **2:13**,
  54; **2:26**, 54; **4:14–16**, 25; **5:1–6**, 25; **5:4–6**,
  25
1 John **4:7–8**, 199; **4:11**, 199
Revelation **13**, 22, **13:16–17**, 22; **18**, 22; **18:3**,
  23; **18:4**, 23; **18:9**, 23; **18:16–19**, 23; **18:23**,
  23

Other Ancient Sources

Acts of Thomas, 57. See also *Hymn of the Pearl*
Aeschylus, *Prometheus Bound* **123**, 191
Ambrose of Milan, *On the Duties of the Clergy*
  2.28.137–39, 215
Apophthegmata patrum
  Benjamin **1**, 237
  Macarius **7**, 239
  Zeno **1**, 240
Apostolic Constitutions **4**, 200; **2.34.5**, 233;
  5.1.3, 43
Aristotle
  Nicomachean Ethics **5**, 192; **7.3.14–4.6**, 193;
    8.9.5–14.4, 193
  Politics **3.1–10**, 192
Athanasius. See also *Canons of (Ps.-)Athana-
  sius of Alexandria*
  Historia Arianorum **13.3**, 95; **61.2**, 95
  Vita Antonii **50.4–6**, 82
Augustine
  Confessions **2.3.5**, 68; **8.6.14**, 67
  De bono viduitatis **21.26**, 145
  Enarrationes in Psalmos **102.12**, 46
  Epistulae **130**, 147; **167**, 51–54
  Retractationes **2.32**, 51

Barsanuphius, *Epistulae* **254**, 222; **317**, 229;
  587, 229; **588**, 229; **589**, 236; **618–36**, 229;
  618, 227; **636**, 229, 237; **752**, 229
Basil
  Epistulae **150**, 228
  Homilia dicta tempore famis et siccitatis **8**,
    197
  Homilia in divites **1**, 236
  Regulae brevius tractatae, 227–228, 235
  Regulae fusius tractatae, 227
Bede, *In epistulam Iacobi expositio*, 50–51

Besa, *Vita Sinuthi* **30**, 223; **34**, 241; **48**, 223;
  104, 233; **140**, 223; **138–43**, 226, 232
Book of the Prefect, 261

Canons of (Ps.-)Athanasius of Alexandria **6**,
  95; **16**, 92, 95; **34**, 94; **61**, 91, 95; **69**, 239;
  70, 95
Canons of Hippolytus, 95
Chrysostom. *See* John Chrysostom
1 Clement, 42–44; **55.2**, 44. *See also* Ps.-Clem-
  ent, *Homilia*
Clement of Alexandria
  Paedagogus, 74
  Quis dives salvetur, 37–38, 40, 62, 67–75,
    79, 228
  Stromateis **2.23**, 200; **2.145.3**, 72; **2.82.3**, 74;
    2.86.3, 74; **3.54.1–56.3**, 40
Cyril of Alexandria, *Homiliae diversae* **18**, 108
Cyril of Scythopolis
  Vita Euthymii **17**, 225; **18**, 223; **39**, 241; **47**,
    231
  Vita Iohannis **15**, 231; **20**, 231
  Vita Lupicini **72**, 237
  Vita Sabae **44**, 237
  Vita Theodosii **3**, 231, 232

Demosthenes, *Against Timocrates* **24.1**, 190
Didache, 42, 44–46; **1.5–6**, 45; **4.5–8**, 44; **4.89**,
  42; **10.7–11.12**, 46; **12.3–5**, 46; **13.4**, 46;
  13.1–7, 45
Didascalia Apostolorum **19**, 43
Diogenes Laertius **6.2.63**, 197
Diognetus, Epistle to, 200

Evagrius
  Antirrhetikos (Talking Back), 79–86
  Chapters on Prayer **17**, 78